The Grotesque Æsthetic
in Spanish Literature

Juan de la Cuesta
Hispanic Monographs

FOUNDING EDITOR
Tom Lathrop
University of Delaware, Emeritus

EDITOR
Michael J. McGrath
Georgia Southern University

EDITORIAL BOARD

Samuel G. Armistead
University of California, Davis

Annette G. Cash
Georgia State University

Alan Deyermond
Queen Mary, University of London

Juan F. Egea
University of Wisconsin-Madison

Steven D. Kirby
Eastern Michigan University

Vincent Martin
University of Delaware

Mariselle Meléndez
University of Illinois at Urbana-Champaign

Eyda Merediz
University of Maryland

Enrico Santí
University of Kentucky

Dayle Seidenspinner-Núñez
University of Notre Dame

Noël Valis
Yale University

Amy Williamsen
University of Arizona

The Grotesque Æsthetic in Spanish Literature, From the Golden Age to Modernism

by

Paul Ilie

Juan de la Cuesta
Newark, Delaware

Cover image: *Saturn Devouring His Son*, Francisco Goya, circa 1819–1823.
Cover design by Michael Bolan

Copyright © 2009 by Juan de la Cuesta—Hispanic Monographs
An imprint of LinguaText, Ltd.
270 Indian Road
Newark, Delaware 19711-5204 USA

(302) 453-8695
Fax: (302) 453-8601

www.JuandelaCuesta.com

MANUFACTURED IN THE UNITED STATES OF AMERICA

ISBN: 978-1-58871-151-9

Table of Contents

Purpose and Overview 7
1. Grotesque Elements in the Pastoral Novel 11
2. Gracián and the Moral Grotesque 23
3. Grotesque Portraits in Torres Villarroel 43
4. The Grotesque Before Goya 71
5. "Capricho" / "Caprichoso":
   A Glossary of Eighteenth-Century Usages 87
6. Larra's Nightmare 107
7. Espronceda and the Romantic Grotesque 129
8. Bécquer and the Romantic Grotesque 151
9. Antonio Machado and the Grotesque 193
10. Paranoid Grotesquerie in Solana 207
11. The Grotesque in Valle-Inclán 217
12. Synthesis 265
Bibliography 287
Thematic Index 295
Name Index 297

Purpose and Overview

THE PATHFINDING STUDENT OF the grotesque, Wolfgang Kayser, said that in regard to creating grotesque art, the Spanish genius is unrivaled.[1] The chapters in this book attest to the fact that the grotesque aesthetic is a prominent feature in Spanish literature, from the Renaissance to the Modern period. To the question, What is the grotesque? there is no simple definition. It is identifiable by stylistic and thematic incongruities that create a distorted or uncanny vision of reality. The nuances of this vision are what this book intends to emphasize. The literary grotesque can be found in scenic descriptions, in characterization, and in subjective discourse. These features vary in Spain from the Renaissance to the Baroque, and from Neoclassicism and Romanticism to Modernism. Each period is represented in this book by one or several authors who are the central focus of the individual chapters.

These studies first appeared in scholarly journals as random articles with no connection other than the fact that the authors under study favor grotesque elements in their works. This common factor has become the organizing principle for a book whose purpose is to demonstrate the coherence of the Spanish grotesque. The chapters, viewed collectively, reveal an evolution of grotesque styles and motifs. They also reveal a shifting grotesque sensibility. The combination of style, motif, and sensibility is what I have called an "aesthetic." This intricate concept became visible to me many years after the articles were written, and has justified their union in book form. It also made necessary the inclusion of a new, synthesizing chapter at the end of the book. Here the narrow applications of the grotesque by particular writers enter the comparative framework of larger contextual trends and typologies.

The studies did not appear in chronological order when they were first published. But as a book, they have been arranged by successive

---

[1] Wolfgang Kayser, *Das Groteske in Malerei und Dichtung* (München, 1960), p. 12.

literary periods, beginning with the Golden Age pastoral novelists and ending with Valle-Inclán. This progression allows the grotesque's conceptual development to appear under two distinct categories, literary history and aesthetic practice.

In this framework it becomes clear that the traits of a literary period color the grotesque, just as the grotesque submits to the author's personal treatment. The Renaissance preference for Classical beauty and mimesis is challenged by the pastoral novel of that epoch. The Baroque crisis of appearances and reality is reflected in Gracián's moralistic distortion of human behavior. In the Neoclassical period, the distortive portraits of Torres Villarroel reflect and revalue 18th-century social and linguistic conditions. Both early and late Romanticisms find their freedom and fantasy exploited by the less controlled imaginations of Larra, Espronceda and Bécquer, whose different stylistic and psychological mechanisms advance the art of deforming reality. Throughout these centuries, the Classical notion of art as a transfiguring mirror evolves into a disfiguring subjective aesthetic. Finally, in 20th-century Modernism, Machado's grotesque irruptions prefigure lyrically the more radical and objective concave mirror of Valle-Inclán and the later Surrealists.

The second category of the grotesque's evolution—its aesthetic practice—reveals the grotesque to be a psychostructural phenomenon whose formal devices are often contingent upon authorial mind-sets. In this view, the grotesque retains an essential core regardless of the historical moment or the literary genre that concretizes it. Thus, the grotesque is definable as the expression of absurdity or incongruity, whether through impersonal depictions or subjective assertiveness. This point will be elaborated in the final chapter.

The very word "grotesque" has its own semantic development in Spain, and one that is complicated by the related terms *capricho* and *esperpento*. The lexical history of the Spanish *grotesco* begins with the dictionary listing by Covarrubias in the 16th century. This entry registers the spelling *grutesco* and defines it in terms of painting in the style of "follajes, figuras de medio sierpes, medio hombres, syrenas, sphinges" that evoke the painter Bosch. The definition gradually fell into disuse, and by 1705 Sobrino's dictionary gave only the French meaning of "bizarre," "ridículo," and "extravagante." However the *Diccionario de Autoridades* (1734) restored Covarrubias' evocation of the visual arts imitating Nature's "cosas toscas, e incultas: como breñas y grutas." Later dictionaries made further elaborations, such as ornamental monsters, while Neoclassical preceptists like Luzán and Mengs began to evaluate the use of grotesquerie as a device invented by caprice and fantasy. The details of this history appear in Chapter 4. In the 19th century, Bécquer expanded the term beyond its architectural nuances to include disharmonious emotional experiences.

Furthermore, the specifically Spanish literary history and aesthetic of the grotesque must be related to their European counterparts. The history begins not as a genre but rather as a style. Its Classical form is architectural, serving an ornamental purpose with its arabesques and sculptured monsters drawn from mythology. This spatial decoration has a textual counterpart and can be found transferred in the pre-Renaissance chivalric novels that allude to giants and other bestial beings. At the same time, two different traditions arise that inspire the grotesque in later centuries. Dante's Medieval infernal vision (itself an elaboration of Virgilian motifs) emerges to serve Quevedo's grotesque scenes in the *Sueños*, while the *commedia dell'arte* inspires caricature in Golden Age theater, followed much later by harlequin types and carnival scenes during the Romantic period. As for Renaissance authors like Rabelais who practice the grotesque, Bakhtin sees an indulgence in "festive madness" in order to deny terror through laughable monsters. The style of Gracián's moral grotesque echoes this satire, and also shows a clear affinity with the Baroque verbal exuberance of his period, as Chapter 2 reveals. This style grows excessive in the 18th century in Torres Villarroel's grotesque portraits (Chapter 3), but other Spanish authors reflect a Neoclassical awareness of preceptist issues similar to European writers, in this case concerning an aesthetic evaluation of the grotesque and the caprice (Chapters 4-5).

The variations throughout these centuries justify naming the grotesque phenomenon a "mode" because its essential discomforting incongruities remain at the core. In the 19th century, the widespread journalistic vogue of caricatures and hyperbolic illustrations is paralleled by Larra's satirical articles, which additionally border on the nightmarish and are fraught with subjective disorder (Chapter 6). In a different vein, Espronceda creates a Dantesque fantasy world that poses an epistemological problem rather than a social one. Again in regard to the carnivalesque, Bakhtin observes its use of atmosphere in the Romantic grotesque as a mask that conceals an underlying ominous reality. This is certainly true of Espronceda's sinister perception of events (Chapter 7). In contrast, the historical consciousness that pervades Romanticism also permeates Bécquer's musings on the grotesque (Chapter 8).

Finally, the European worldview that emerges from post-Romanticism and Symbolism to embrace all forms of Modernist irrationality has its Spanish representatives in Machado, Solana, and Valle-Inclán (Chapters 9-10-11). Here the grotesque reaches its plenitude by its disfiguring perceptions of self, objective reality, and narrative art colored with quasi-Surrealist elements.

When the above-mentioned authors are placed in the sequence of their literary history, the study deepens the meaning of the grotesque precisely because they display unequal degrees of stylistic, thematic, and psychological effort. The final chapter, however, will attempt to integrate their variations into a reasonably coherent mosaic.

I
Grotesque Elements in the Pastoral Novel

THE MANY GROTESQUE ELEMENTS scattered throughout Golden Age literature still need to be classified in an orderly fashion. The way to approach this task is to separate each genre and treat it individually. The pastoral novel is a good place to begin because the incidence of grotesque episodes in an idealized setting provides the sharpest possible contrast for viewing the real nature of the grotesque. These episodes may be of limited interest for the aesthetics of the pastoral mode alone, but as another source of the grotesque tradition in Spanish literature they are of great value.[1]

One of the first principles of the pastoral aesthetic is harmonious composition: an environment having a calmly disposed landscape, a

---

1 Relying on Juan Bautista Avalle-Arce's *La novela pastoril española* (Madrid, 1959), I have examined the following novels, all but the last three of which were useful for this study: Jorge de Montemayor, *La Diana*, ed. F. López Estrada (Madrid. 1946), 1st ed. 1559; Alonso Pérez, *Segunda parte de La Diana* (Venice. 1585), 1st ed. 1564; Jerónimo de Tejeda, *La Diana de Monte-Mayor* (Paris. 1627); Juan Arce Solórzano, *Tragedias de amor* (Madrid, 1607), 1st ed. 1604; Cristóbal Suárez de Figueroa, *La constante Amarilis* (Madrid, 1781), 1st ed. 1609; Lope de Vega, *La Arcadia*, ed. C. Rosell, *B.A.E.:* XXXVIII (Madrid, 1950), 1st ed. 1599; Bernardo de Balbuena, *Siglo de oro en las selvas de Erifile* (Madrid, 1821), 1st ed. 1608; Gabriel de Corral, *La Cintia de Aranjuez*, ed. J. de Entrambasaguas (Madrid, 1945), 1st ed. 1629; Antonio de Lofrasso, *La fortuna de amor* (London. 1740), 1st ed. 1573; Bernardo González de Bobadilla, *Ninfas y pastores de Henares* (Alcalá de Henares, 1587); Gil Polo, *La Diana enamorada*. Ed. R. Ferreres (Madrid, 1953), 1st ed. 1564: Gaspar Mercader, *El prado de Valencia* (Valencia, 1600); Miguel de Cervantes, *La Galatea*, ed. Schevill y Bonilla (Madrid, 1914), 1st ed. 1585.

symmetrical architecture that imitates this landscape, and an underlying philosophy of rapport between Nature and Art. The grotesque operates within this framework of natural harmony and artistic verisimilitude. Basically, the "natural" elements in Nature (woods, meadows, grottoes) remain undistorted, while the artificial elements that are closely related to her, such as fountains, temples, and patios, are subject to a certain artistic mutation. When ugly naturalistic details (insects, dung) are included in a rustic setting, the reason is the author's sympathy for everything in Nature rather than a desire to use any of her features for aesthetically unidealistic ends (Pérez, 157v-158r).

This inviolability of Nature's perfection, coupled with a comparable admiration for Art, together produce a special perception of beauty. Nature's proportions remain intact, no trace of monstrous growth is visible, and if a rare storm disturbs her tranquility, it is usually a conventional tempest at sea. On the other hand, man-made precepts based on the laws of harmony observed in Nature can lead to grotesque consequences.[2] There is a tendency to broaden the literary precepts that too narrowly interpret the notion of Art as being in competition with Nature. In the natural world, the rules must be respected. But in holding up the mirror of Art to that world, the novelist may alter some of the symmetries. Not that the pastoral novelist goes too far in this direction. But he does regard cultivated Nature, especially the garden artifacts and architectural designs that imitate her, to be suitable material for aesthetic license. If the novelist must not distort the natural world, he may at least devise grotesque variations for his representation of fountains, garden sculpture, and landscape painting. Thus, he takes the first step in the eventual repudiation of the idea that Art is a reflection of reality.

The result of this relationship between the strict laws of Nature and the unlimited possibilities of Art is a paradox of dissimilar qualities. Natural horror can be reflected faithfully. but it cannot be considered to be grotesque. Conversely, whatever is grotesque is anathema to Nature. These axioms are demonstrated remarkably by a description of a paint-

---

[2] One anecdote tells of a man who blindly applies the rule that smallness is a quality of beauty: he loves a girl because her face is small, but it is so small that it appears deformed in proportion to the rest of her well-shaped body. The story is followed by a lengthy preceptual critique of beauty based on Nature's laws of harmony (Arce Solórzano. fols. 67-71).

ing which

> ... ofrecía un cielo enojado, y trasladado tan al natural, que casi obligaba a que quien le miraba, se escondiesse por el horror de su ceño, y el temor que infundían sus imaginadas flechas. Estaba en medio un pequeño arbol, cuyas cortas raíces sujetaban las inmensas fuerzas de uno, que por la parte de la gran cabeza que tenía fuera, prometía ser ferocíssimo Gigante. (Suárez de Figueroa, 83)

The novelist seems to accept the mirror-of-Art concept. since he is impressed with how convincingly the sky is rendered in the painting. At the same time, he places a grotesque element in antithesis to the natural world. The giant, unlike the tree, cannot be represented as being in accord with Nature, nor can he be portrayed by any observable rules of measure. He is a grotesque figment of the imaginary realm, unnatural, fantastic, and inimical to the realm of Nature. The struggle between the tree and the giant dramatizes this contrast, with the stronger power of the tree-roots a reminder that Nature is superior to whatever opposes her. Another aspect of this opposition is the difference between the terrible aspect of the sky and the horrible giant. The two forms of terribleness are distinct in kind and substance. The contrast is precisely what separates Nature's awesomeness, even horror, from the category of monstrosity, which is beyond the natural realm. In the terminology of a later age, it is the distinction between the sublime and the grotesque.

These, then, are the norms of aesthetic idealism that serve as the point of departure for grotesque deviation. The pastoral novelist can describe a landscape and evoke two kinds of emotions: those commonly elicited when Art reproduces Nature, and those additional nuances arising from the presence of a grotesque element. As in the painting. other descriptions of the natural setting reveal the same attention to Classical rules occasionally deflected by a grotesque note. Elaborate garden scenes· with fountain motifs show a symmetrical composition that also admits certain grotesque variations.[3] These occur mainly in the use of animal statuary and painted or relief figures, where the incongruity

---

3 E.g., four fountains with statues in Tejeda, II, 219-220, and the whimsical design of "diuersos animalexos figurados de diferentes guijas" (*ibid.*, II. 108).

of wild and domesticated elements is aesthetically removed from the Aristotelian and Horatian precepts of the day.

Dominating the fountain motif is the statuesque figure of the giant, whose proportions make him both absolutely grotesque and a monument of enormous grace. This ambiguity stands out in one scene in

> ... un ameno bosque, en medio del qual estaua vna cristalina fuente que por quatro figuras de poderosos Gigantes arroxaua cantidad de agua en vna marmorea taza. de tantas y tan diuersas colores matiçada que ofuscaua las vistas de los que la mirauan... (Tejeda, II, 212)

On the one hand, the conventions are still observed: the setting in a gentle Nature, the architectural symmetry of the number four, and the textural plasticity of the fountain. On the other hand, the chromatic confusion violates the principle of compositional harmony, resulting in perceptual difficulties and weakened aesthetic concepts such as linear clarity. In the midst of these dissonances rise the giants, pure grotesque figures by virtue of size and character, and essentially paradoxical in their hugely conceived proportions. They differ from other fountain statuaries in that the power they represent is not commensurate with the mild atmosphere of the "ameno bosque." Although sculpted animals are also used for the contrasting effect of captive wildness, the giants create a special grotesque effect, as we shall see.[4]

Both statuesque giants and their live counterparts constitute one of the central features of the pastoral grotesque. They are by their very nature the adversaries of everything normal in pastoral idealism: beauty, peace, love, virtue. The giant is often quite similar to the *salvaje*, a fact easily corroborated by the latter's uncommon size in the novels. As alter egos, they are virtually indistinguishable paradigms of human deforma-

---

4 Cf. ".... vna fuente de marauilloso alabastro, que por las bocas de quatro fieros leones de transparente cristal, brotaua cantidad de agua... " (Arce Solórzano, 87v). More traditionally, "... las vasas y capiteles, de alabastro con muchos foliages a la Romana... las columnas estavan assentadas sobre Leones, Onçs, Tigres de arambre y tan al vivo que parecían arremeter a los que allí entravan" (Polo, 173).

tion.[5] Their architectural role requires that formal qualities dominate, with moral ones remaining secondary or irrelevant. In their role as personages, their evil and destructive traits are uppermost, while their ugliness is exploited for aesthetic as well as moral reasons. To illustrate the complexity of the giant motif, the following description of a fountain serves very well. In the center of its large basin

> ...estava un grande salvage de bronze, que con sus manos y cabeça tenía otro vaso de alabastro mas pequeña, dando agua al debaxo, por veinte y quatro bocas de delfines de plata. Tenía el salvage un collar de oro, con estas letras diziendo.
> De tormentos y enojos,
> Muy mas agua dan mis ojos. (Lofrasso, I, 192)

The metallic colossus stands boldly between the vessels whose pillar he is, a contrast by virtue of material as well as size. The effect of this savage presence in a pastoral atmosphere is hardly tranquilizing (the setting itself is a wooded "laberinto" frequented by a sorceress). And the use of Classical marine animals without the familiar Neptune, Triton, or other accompanying deity breaks with long-followed patterns of mythological sculpture. As a final incongruity, the usurping savage bears a sentimental message, a curious humanizing feature that we will encounter again later.

The prominence of the savage in a Classical framework of statuesque design fulfills the grotesque purpose of the composition while continuing to retain the desired evocations of mythology. The author still associates "salvàge" with classical myth, a detail confirmed by another description of a patio with "veinte y quatro Faunos salvàges, en guarda" (I, 174). Yet it is the bestial quality that is suggested—regardless of whether "salvàge" is an adjective or a noun—the element that deforms humanity and reduces human gracefulness to a lesser beauty of hybrid proportions.

In emphasizing the function of the savage as a grotesque foil to the condition of men and gods, it is important to remember that he is an

---

5 On the *salvaje*. see further: Oleh Mazur, "Various Folkloric Impacts upon the *Salvaje* in the Spanish *Comedia*," *HR*. XXXVI (1968), 207-235; and Avalle-Arce, *op. cit.*, for bibliography.

anonymous giant. Unqualified to be ranked among the Polyphemuses of antiquity, he is nameless and nondescript. He becomes, consequently, a marginal figure, a commoner in the ranks of wild men with only his distorted semblance of humanity to distinguish him. Even so, his ultimate kinship with the multifarious species of Classical deformations is never lost sight of. The intricate chain of associations called up by this family of grotesques is revealed by the following passage:

> Todas las cornisas y molduras gruesas estaban adornadas de brutescos á este mesmo propósito, en que se vian sátiros, faunos, silvanos, ninfas, oréadas, dríadas y amadríadas, napeas y otras figuras de semidioses… se vian varias fuentes en formas de ninfas desnudas, que de los pechos y boca arrojaban agua; los medios cuerpos de peces, sierpes ó cabras, que sobre tazas de jaspes se sostenian… (Lope, 67b)

A thick web of relationships is spun around the word "brutescos," the alternate form of "grutescos," which here identifies architectural adornment in the grotesque style with satyrs, fauns, and nymphs. Brought together are bestial and shapely forms in an all-embracing category of grotesquerie that exceeds the dictionary definition of "imitación de cosas toscas, e incultas: como breñas y grutas" given by Covarrubias. Also described are other nymphs in half-animal shapes, not all of them mermaids. In other words, from giant to savage to satyr to faun, and so on down the line, a common grotesque feature is implied in the magnification, brutalization, and hybridization of pure forms. The use of the variant term "brutescos" instead of "grutescos" is revealing in this context because it evokes "bruto." This contrasts with the use of the original word when the intent is exclusively architectural: "Estauan cubiertas las cornisas, frisos, basas, y chapiteles de diuersidad de follages, y grutescos" (Arce Solórzano, 5v). Far beyond the amusing coils of half-floral, half-animal decoration that is usually called "grotesque" in this period, we find here the pastoral grotesque and its implication of sylvan creatures removed from Classical mythology and enlisted to provide a deformed contrast to the idealized formal beauty of the novels' setting.

There is nothing pejorative about this contrasting deformity. It must be understood as a counterpoint integral to the idealized pastoralism in the novels. The real issue is that the grotesque is extended beyond the strange decorative carvings of cornices and friezes. The coincidence of grotesque stonework and the man-beast metamorphoses means that giants and savages are not isolated eruptions in the pastoral novel. They appear in related architectural frameworks as part of a mythological disfiguration which operates in the novels for its own purposes. Abstracted from their woodland kindred, the satyrs and fauns are focused upon and magnified until they stand apart from their background. The savage is especially unrecognizable in this regard. His metamorphosis from the breed of "Faunas salvages" to the fraternity of giants places him at the center of the grotesque mode. If the savage motif can also be traced to other sources, these are inconsequential with respect to the novels' pastoral idealism. Confirming this is the linkage to architectural design through *brutesco-grutesco* as well as the vestiges of Classical myth. Additional proof can be found in another elaborate description that progresses from unadulterated myth to the grotesque. The passage begins in classic fashion with the columns of a palace where "encima de sus chapiteles estavan al natural dos figuras de hermosas nimphas de alabastro" (Lofrasso, I, 172). The account then proceeds to its grotesque counterpart:

> Las puèrtas con que se cerràva èran tambien de fino bronze, buidas con mil manèras de animàles sutilmente relevàdos, con sus aldàvas, que de bòcas de fièros Dragònes salian, estàvan a parte de dentro doze sàtiros de guàrda, con dos Gigantes con sus escùdos y màças, que no dexàvan entràr a hombre ninguno… (I, 173)[6]

And finally,

> …la segunda puerta, la quàl era de diferente labor en la qual dos gràndes salvàges de màrmol havia que el arca y buèlta del portal con sus cabèças sostenìan, que muy feròzes se mostràvan, tenian en sus

---

6 Compare with the less dynamic: "…y entrando por la puerta de la màr, vido que estàva muy labràdo al Romano, el qual tenìa por la parte de afuera que mira al màr, quatro figùras grandes de Gigantes, de muy buena piedra fina, dos a càda lado de la puerta, hombres y mugeres, que con sus cabèças sostenìan el àrco del portàl…" (II, 123).

mànos ùnas pesàdas màças con sus puntas azeràdas… (I, 114)

The progression moves in three stages: from a pair of life-size nymphs standing alone to a pair of savages, also standing alone, with the middle stag being the two giants accompanied by dragons and other animals. In previous instances, the savage figured amidst wild creatures, whereas the situation is reversed in this scene. The change confirms the reversibility of the giant-savage roles, although this is complicated by the presence of a chivalric note in the grouping of dragons and giants.

To turn from inanimate giants to live ones is to move from decorative formalism to philosophical idea. The well-known intrusion of three "salvages de estraña grandeza y fealdad" in *La Diana* illustrates this difference.[7] The episode shatters the idyllic mood of the novel with the reminder that Nature's harmony can be challenged by the principle of monstrosity. The event marks the high point of an artistic sensibility dominated by the idea of universal harmony. When the Baroque concept of discordant concord gains ascendency, it will be the sentimental giant that is poeticized, in the person of Góngora's Polifemo. Between these two pastoral monsters, the grotesque reveals a wide range of practices, from a cold, inhuman treatment of the savages by Montemayor to the cultivation of pathetic lyricism by Góngora.

The description of the three wild men in *La Diana* makes a fine tapestry, one which relies less on color than on rough textures and angular spatial relationships for its vivid impact. The type of distortion leading to the scene's grotesque character is based on associations rather than on the lines themselves. Instead of misshapen forms there are incongruous evocations: associations built around chivalric literature and its stereotypes. The primitive condition of the savages' weapons suggests a barbarism alien to the traditional battle scenes of such romances. The knightly armor and headdress—even of evil knights and giants—are

---

7 "Venían armados de coseletes y celadas de cuero de tigre. Eran de tan fea catadura que ponían espanto; los coseletes trayan por brocales unas bocas de serpientes, por donde sacavan los braços que gruessos y vellosos parecían, y las celadas venían a hazer encima de la frente unas espantables cabeças de leones; lo demás trayan desnudo, cubierto despesso y largo vello, unos bastones herrados de muy agudas púas de azero. Al cuello trayan sus arcos y flechas; los escudos eran de unas conchas de pescado muy fuerte" (87-88).

transformed into the hideous remnants of fierce animals. Clearly, these hairy creatures must be extirpated from any idealistic setting, whether pastoral or chivalric, and indeed they are quickly destroyed.

Directly opposed to the inhuman savage but no less grotesque in his setting is the love-stricken "monstruoso Alasto," enamoured of a nymph,

> ... que con unos roncos albogues de mal juntadas cañas, como otro Polifemo por Galatea, cantaba y tañía, prometiéndole los recien nacidos osos, los tiernos leones. los nidos de las tigres y las silvestres frutas de solitarios árboles. (Lope, 71a)

This subhuman giant with all-too-human feelings is surrounded by incongruities, from his clumsy music-making to his notion of what gifts are suitable for the nymph. In truth. these grotesque details are tempered by the familiar set of emotions that comprise pastoral sentimentalism, and to which we respond more readily. For this reason we must guard against pathos weakening our sense of distortion, since nothing can be more grotesque than a giant suffering like a shepherd in love. Not surprisingly, therefore, such giants are treated harshly by the novelists, and their lives end violently. In the case of another tearful monster, Gorphorosto, the "fiero Saluage" comes to the aid of the shepherds and even hides from some maidens "por no las espantar con su feroz vista," but to no avail: he is coldly slain by Diana after he disobeys her (Tejeda, II,183, 191).

The onesided emotional relationship between giants and maidens is an age-old motif, but it also can be seen as a prototype for the Beauty and the Beast theme of a later age. Its folkloric roots in the primitive fears of man can sometimes be detected, as in the case of one shepherd's dream that his beloved has been carried off "en los brazos de vn feroz Saluage" (Tejeda, I. 301). In the same psychological vein is an animalistic version of this fear, a shepherd's dream of a girl attacked while gathering flowers: "... repentinamente vna ossa grande y terrible salia de entre los arboles, y arrebatãdola en braços se emboscaua con ella a largo passo" (Arce Solórzano, 159v). These fantasies are the same as those which fascinated the Romantics, who viewed fairy tales as a source of aesthetic distortion as well as anthropological truth. Other glimpses of a future Romantic grotesque may be seen in the proximity of male barbarism and feminine beauty. Whereas the sentimental giant enacts the pathetic drama of abject strength, the cruel giant towers over a fierce pageantry of unrelenting primitivism. Thus, we find an "hombre bestial" embodied in the hugely proportioned Gorphorosto, in another prototype of the Beauty and the Beast scene:

> ...Era tan uelloso, que a penas dexarle uian las carnes de su cuerpo... estaua el vello derecho a manera de cerdas de puerco montes. Los ojos espãtosos y encarniçados. De uestidos le seruian pieles de fieras.... Sobre la cabeça traya vna gruessa concha de pescado marino que morrion parescia... Casi vn entero pino bastante para gouernalle d'una gruessa naue, de cayado le seruia, el remate del qual estaua guarnescido de azero con unas grandes y agudas puas. (Pérez, 74v-75r.)

The richly detailed portrait is followed by still another of an elegantly clad nymph. whose aura of classical mythology clashes sharply with the wild man. In an effort to overcome this conflict, Gorphorosto is introduced as "un fierissimo pastor," but he remains an integrated anomaly in the pastoral setting. His ugly and horrific counterpoint to the scene's tranquil beauty makes him easily recognizable as a member of the grotesque family seen before. He also leans toward the embryonic theme of Beauty and the Beast in that it is a giant, not a satyr, who is engaged in the sport of pursuing nymphs. This shift from classical moods and motifs does not alter the novel's sylvan atmosphere, but it does cause the woodland background of mythology to recede still further.

A final characteristic of the giant's role involves the influence of grotesque elements from other literary contexts. Just as the pastoral novelist can ignore Classical grotesque forms. so too does he enter the crosscurrents of different genre traditions. His creations are likely to be composites from several nonpastoral sources, especially if he tries to conceive of increasingly more fantastic monsters. The result is that his imagination breeds hybrid stereotypes based on incompatible strains that have been intermingled. For example, the admixture of chivalric legend and Classical tradition produces the following:

> ...abrio el monte vna horrenda boca, que dio lugar a vn monstruoso

jayan; si bien muchos crecieron el numero, viendo q[ue] reboluia a todas partes tres cabeças, que jugaua diuersas armas, con seis manos; y en cada passo assimismo senalaua seis huellas. Todos conocieron que era Gerion aquel monstruo Español; ficcion gallarda de los antiguos... (Corral, 387-388.)

Borrowed from chivalric fiction's repertoire of grotesque allusions are the word *jayán*, the weapons, and the combat scene (not quoted here). The reference to Geryon, however, is a literary note appended to a variation on a theme of Virgil or Dante. The monster begins as a giant and ends as a beast, both forms being morphologically sufficient for the grotesque. The touch of erudition at the end, and the bizarre nature of the description, suggest an erosion of the pastoral sensibility, and an attempt to devise new combinations of grotesque elements.[8]

Beyond the giants and savages, the pastoral grotesque contains other kinds of ugliness and monstrosity. Repugnant images, scenes of violence, and dreams of a sinister nature all join to make the grotesque the dark underside of pastoral idealism. At times, the jarring recurrence of unsavory realism cannot be reconciled with the atmosphere of bucolic calm (Arce Solórzano, 5v, 9r, v, 148r), while at other times a benign grotesque combining magic with gruesome detail is harmonized with the generally fantastic air of the novel (Tejeda, II. 338-339). One portrait of a witch is especially revealing for its exposure of the infrastructure of ugliness, superstition, and occasional violence which, together, are antithetical to the "real world" of Classical beauty depicted in the pastoral novel (Bobadilla, 61r. v). Still other sequences involve dreams and even nightmares, a realm quite different from the cluster of aberrations and discords reviewed here.[9] These latter categories of the grotesque have implications which extend beyond the scope of pastoral fiction, and are studied elsewhere in this book. Nevertheless, they are lapses into incongruity of the same order as those already examined.[9]

---

8 Another pastiche of monstrous parts: a statue of Apollo, "Puesto el vn pie sobre vn horrible monstro de tres cabeças, de lobo, leon, y perro, cuya cola era de vn enroscado dragõ" (Arce Solórzano, 6v).

9 This study was first published in *Homenaje a W. L. Fichter*. Eds. A. D. Kossoff and J. Amor y Vázquez. Valencia: Castalia, 1971, 319-28.

2
Gracián and the Moral Grotesque

IT HAS LONG BEEN evident to scholars that the presence of distortion and monstrosity in *El Criticón* makes these elements prime factors for consideration when dealing with the work's aesthetic and philosophical disposition. Karl Vossler characterized the satire as "eine Harmonie von aufgelösten Dissonanzen,"[1] while Romera Navarro found in it a "fantasía caricaturista y grotescamente burlón."[2] The Bosch-like world glimpsed by Correa Calderón, "compuesto de gentes atrabiliarias y grotescas,"[3] is also commented on by Xavier de Salas and Werner Krauss, while Camón Aznar thought he saw in Gracián's monstrous creatures a Goyesque quality.[4]

However, it was not until Gerhart Schröder published *Baltasar Graciáns "Criticón"* (Munchen, 1966) that any serious attention was given to the details of Gracián's grotesque. This study not only provided much needed information about the literary background of the "allegorical grotesque," but it also established the validity of such categories as the "Bildgroteske" and the "Sprachgroteske." Schröder's orientation is ethical and philosophical, with emphasis on the roles of contradiction, antithesis, disillusion, and the implications of the thesis that Gracián's grotesque becomes "die Bildstruktur, die Ausdruck des 'Verkehrten,' d.h. des dem Geist Entgegengesetzten ist" (p. 207). With this sort of approach articulated at last, it is now possible for critics to look more

---

   1 *Einführung in die Spanische Dichtung des Goldenen Zeitalters* (Hamburg, 1929), p.103.
   2 *Estudios sobre Gracián* (Austin: Univ. Texas Press, 1950), pp. 54-55.
   3 *Baltasar Gracián: Su vida y su obra.* (Madrid, 1961), p. 191.
   4 In, respectively, *El Bosco en la literatura española* (Barcelona, 1943); *Graciáns Lebenslehre* (Frankfurt, 1947); and "El monstruo en Gracián y en Goya" in *Homenaje a Gracián* (Zaragoza, 1958), pp. 57-63

carefully at the nature and workings of the grotesque in *El Criticón* from the standpoint of aesthetic analysis and exegetical meaning.

At the very least, it is demonstrable that many of the aforementioned antagonistic forces make up a counterpoint of dissonances, a fairly coherent subaesthetic of grotesque motifs and effects. Much can also be done along two other lines of thought: evaluating Schröder's survey of the origin and typological development of the more bizarre images used by Gracián, and, perhaps more useful at this point, locating the position of these images in the evolution of grotesque literature in Spain. It is this second area which I intend to explore here, conscious of the vast preparation brought to this field by scholars of the Spanish Renaissance and Baroque. Nevertheless, there is a need for the type of approach that is undertaken from another perspective. While Gracián's work is the product of a complex tradition before him, his aesthetic does not end there. It also represents one phase in the creation of forms and concepts that, over the centuries, has come to be known as the grotesque mode.[5] And conversely, the history of aesthetic ideas in Spain does not begin with the twentieth century, and it is necessary, in order to speak intelligently about the Valle-Incláns and the Solanas, to understand earlier literary periods: first the Romantic grotesque, then the epochs of Goya and Torres Villarroel, then the Baroque of Gracián and Quevedo, and so on in a receding process that has been the traditional direction of scholarly investigation. Thus, there are several reasons for hoping that a study of this kind will be useful. It may be that Quevedo is the more obvious cultivator of the grotesque in the last-mentioned period. But Gracián is the more manageable artist for a chapter in this book, and to a scholar whose specialization is not the Golden Age, he is the more natural choice.

The grotesque in *El Criticón* does not stand out as an independent phenomenon against a background of undistorted elements. Neither does it appear in easily isolated passages that can be separated from the general prose fabric, as in the case of the grotesque portraits in Torres'

---

5 By "grotesque" I mean the deliberate use of plastic deformation for aesthetic effect. This definition excludes some of the vaguer psychological categories proposed by Wolfgang Kayser, not because they are untenable, but because a restricted definition here will help us to focus squarely on the problem of Gracián's "moral grotesque."

Visiones y visitas. Nor is it, finally, a part of the self-contained episodes that frequently occur in Romantic works, where scenes of fantasy and supernaturalism alternate with other moods and episodes. In *El Criticón*, the grotesque is a function of context. Its deformations have a functional role requiring an explanation set in terms of the work's basic themes, which themselves do not suffer any deformation. These themes include, above all, Gracián's ideas about Nature, a concept which must be posited explicitly by the work if its grotesque violations of the natural order are to be understood. There is also the problem of what role is cast for artistic forms—especially architecture—and, finally, what patterns are imposed upon the conventions of allegorical symbolism.

This kind of thematic approach must, of course, deal with both form and idea. Philosophically speaking, Gracián makes use of a "moral grotesque," a technique of distortion that upholds the moralistic idealism of the Golden Age while rejecting many of the aesthetic ideals of that Age. Gracián prepares a metaphysical groundwork that slopes away from theology toward the ethics of Nature and society. But at the same time, his formal expression depends upon allegories that break away from Classical restraint and proliferate their animal motifs until the entire structure becomes swollen and deformed. This revision of allegorical convention is one aspect of Gracián's grotesque, and others, like the use of metamorphosis and carnivalesque grotesquerie, have new implications that will all be discussed later in this chapter.

First, however, we must be clear as to what notions of natural order and cosmic harmony were posited by Gracián and held as a contrasting background for the grotesque reliefs of his more fantastic scenes. His representation of reality is more than simply abstract and unreal, for he makes very concrete statements about the structure of social reality and the inherent traits of Nature. Gracián's representation is often antinatural, so to speak, conceived in opposition to the natural workings of the universe. The narrative situation itself comes about because Critilo is "un náufrago, monstruo de la naturaleza y de la suerte,"[6] a phrase which suggests the violation of an underlying principle, the belief in the existence of predictable laws and equilibrium both in Nature and in the course of human events. Even Fortune's wheel is a circle, although the

---

6 *El Criticón*, ed. M. Homera-Navarro (Philadelphia, 1938-40), I, 104. All references are to this edition.

direction of its spin is beyond human divination. Gracián also refers to "la sabia naturaleza" (I, 109), to "el concierto, la firmeza y la variedad desta gran maquina criada" (I, 119), and to the fact that Nature and Fortune are two counterbalancing forces (II, 217).

Everything, then, indicates that the concept of Nature involves a structural order that is harmonious but free to produce variants, and that due to the peculiar tension arising from Nature's role in the universal concert of discords, such variants can sometimes become monstrous. This structure within Nature is further detailed by Gracián in two similar areas. The first of these points to generic order, a hierarchy in which "los inferiores sirven a los superiores" in three categories: "la sensible sobre la vejetante" and a "tercer grado de vivientes mucho más perfectos" (I, 135). These groups refer to plant, animal, and human life, and when the grotesque emerges it is from the disruption of the hierarchy, with results conveyed by such words as "monstrimuger" (II, 186) and "serpihombre" (II, 128). Thus, deformation becomes synonymous with deviant variation, with whatever deviates from the fixed order of life. Then, too, there is a second aspect to Gracián's idea of Nature. This concerns the structural support for the vital order just described, a framework that provides the means whereby life can take on a physical dimension. Such an arrangement is classical in structure, with emphasis on symmetry, proportion, stability, and beauty. In a long passage describing these physical properties of Nature, the key phrase is "prolixa anatomía de su artificiosa composición" (I, 131-132). That is, Nature's beauty is conceived of both analytically, in terms of its structural composition, and universally, as a total phenomenon that responds to the laws of growth and harmony. Once again, the breakdown of this arrangement has grotesque consequences, but even without them, the wondrous and gigantic vision described in the passage ("tan agradable laberinto de prodigios") pushes the frontiers of reality to their farthest limit.

In all of this, it goes without saying that the natural world is the work of a Divine Creator. But whatever the relationship between God and Nature may be, it is also clear that the conditions leading up to the grotesque stem from the deterioration of an "armonía tan plausible de todo el universo, compuesta de una tan estraña contrariedad que, según es grande, no parece avía de poder mantenerse el mundo un solo día" (I, 137). Just as the notion of a prodigious universe makes it possible for immensity to overflow into gigantism and monstrosity, so too does the tension of contrasts make it easier for exaggerated and distorted elements to rush forward in the event of a temporary disruption. Although this seldom happens in *El Criticón*'s realm of natural phenomena, there are cases, as in one violent storm (I, 117), where Nature seems to be on the verge of a cataclysm. Thus, Critilo's observation that "todo este Universo se compone de contrarios y se concierta de desconciertos" (I, 137) can be interpreted in either direction, toward concord or toward discord. Gracián did, therefore, as an artist, become aware that individual elements are in themselves disproportionate, even though they find their just equilibrium in the larger concert of harmonies.

These ideas are not very new from the standpoint of intellectual history.[7] But their aesthetic implications are far from being commonplace, at least as far as literary practice is concerned. They have little to do with Aristotelian poetics or, for that matter, with the theories of Plato, Horace,[8] or the Renaissance theorists. It is true that evidence exists to show that among the latter several thinkers were aware of the artistic potential of discord. However, there is no study indicating that the literary practice of using discords on the grotesque scale devised by Gracián had been realized before *El Criticón*.[9] In terms of actual aesthetic procedure, therefore, Gracián's notion of a harmony of disharmonies offers a new alternative to the literary depiction of reality, whether the latter be idealistic or realistic, allegorical or picaresque. It opens the way to the use of conflict, violence, and, ultimately, destruction, all of which increase the probability of distortion in the presence of any of these elements.

This potential for distortion is stressed less in the world of natural

---

7 On the topos "Concord in Discord" see Otis H. Green's discussion of the diptych "Cosmic strife-Cosmic harmony" in *Spain and the Western Tradition* (Madison, 1963-66), II, 54-63.

8 As Schröder points out, "Man erinnere sich an den Vers, mit dem Horaz in der *ars poetica* die Beschreibung des Monstrewesens abschliesst: das Lachen, das dort dem Unvermögen des Künstlers gilt, ist im *Criticón* ein eingeplanter Effekt" (p. 208).

9 Green cites Pico della Mirandola's "'true definition of Beauty, namely, that it is nothing else than an amicable enmity and a concordant discord'" (loc. cit., 59). But this quotation gives weight to a discussion of cosmology, not aesthetic practices.

phenomenon than in the moral realm. However, the point of departure for most ethical statements made by grotesque means is, as Critilo's philosopher-guide explains, cosmic strife:

> No ay cosa que no tenga su contrario con quien pelee, ya con vitoria ya con rendimiento; todo es hazer y padecer: si ay acción, ay repassión. Los elementos, que llevan la vanguardia, comiençan a batallar entre sí; síguenles los mistos, destruyéndose alternativamente; los males assechan a los bienes, hasta la desdicha a la suerte. Unos tiempos son contrarios a otros, los mismos astros guerrean y se vencen, Y aunque entre sí no se dañan a fuer de príncipes, viene a parar su contienda en daño de los sublunares vassallos: de lo natural passa la oposición a lo moral... (I, 137).

Although the transition is vague, a bridge exists between natural order and moral order, and once it is crossed we are led directly to the Christian landscape of ethics and aphorisms that is so typical of the itinerary followed by Critilo and Andrenio. And the grotesque enters each time a perversion of Christian morality is depicted in terms of the violation of the norms that I have been describing thus far. Here, then, is the link to the moral aspect of the grotesque in *El Criticón*. Having defined the norms of reality as consisting of order, structure, and the conflict of opposites, Gracián projects them into the ethical realm. What happens in the natural world has its counterpart in the world of value judgments.

This is not to say that evil and vice are not portrayed by other techniques as well. Nor are these norms the only ones that guide Gracián's philosophy in this work. As I suggested at the beginning, the grotesque is a function of the narrative as a whole, and it is only one aesthetic mode in the author's total allegory. But, granted all of this, there can be no doubt that his grotesquerie goes beyond the animal symbolism and bestial representations of the Dantesque tradition. Gracián consciously links moral aberration to a corresponding deformation of the natural and human orders. In a sweeping transvaluation, "todo anda al rebés, y todo trocado de alto abaxo... las bestias hazen del hombre y los hombres hazen la bestia" (III, 90). What methods are actually used in this animalization will be discussed in another context; at this point it is enough to note that the origin of the moral grotesque is the transformation just described, influenced as it is by the intention to deform Nature and human life.

There is one final aspect to be considered with regard to the norms of symmetry, order, and beauty in the natural realm. This is the problem of their deterioration. An analogy with architecture is developed in this connection, a fact which should not surprise us given Gracián's concept of a "structure" in Nature. Architectural parallels are also appropriate for conventional reasons as well, since they evoke the work of Roman and Italian antecedents like Vitruvius, Raphael, and Luca Signorelli. Then too, there is the etymological link between *grotta* and *grottesco*, a link which brings Nature and architecture closer together under the two auspices of aesthetic experience and philosophical discourse. A good example is the description of "la cueva de la nada," a scene where abstract elements are combined with natural ones in an architectonic manner:

> …una tenebrosa gruta, boquerón funesto de una horrible cueva que yacía al pie de aquella sobervia montaña, en lo más humilde de su falda, antípoda del empinado alcáçar de la estimación honrosa, opuesta a él de todas maneras… Avía la distancia de uno a otra que va de un estremo de altivez a otro de abatimiento y vileza. Campeava más la entrada quanto más obscura y tenebrosa, que su mismo deslucimiento lo hazía más notable. Era muy espaciosa, nada suntuosa, sin género alguno de sinmetría, basta y bruta; y con ser tan fea y tan horrible, embocava por ella un mundo de cosas… (III, 261).

This passage is, first of all, in the mainstream of the early grotesque tradition because of its setting. Moreover, the adjective *bruta* is reminiscent of the linguistic identification of *brutesco* and *grutesco* in the seventeenth century.[10] Beyond this, what makes the cave so horrible and ugly is its physical isolation from the grandeur of Nature, and its moral kinship with the vileness of materialism. Neither cause by itself is particularly conducive to the grotesque, but together with the deliberate

---

10 In the *Diccionario de la lengua castellana (Autoridades)* (Madrid, 1734), "brutesco" is defined as "Term. de pintura y arquitectura, que vale lo mismo que imitación de cosas toscas, e incultas: como breñas y grutas, de donde se deriva este término, que más propiamente se dice Grutesco." Examples from Cervantes and Quevedo are also given.

exclusion of architectural beauty, their result at least in Gracián's mind is a grotto of horrors antithetical to everything shapely and noble in the universe.[11]

On the other hand, *El Criticón* shifts away from Renaissance grotesque associations with arabesque design and other bizarre architectural decorations. Although this type of ornamentalism was called *grottesco* because styles similar to it were discovered after certain late fifteenth century excavations, its fantastic scrollwork had little to do with the ominous mood that subsequently grew out of the grotto-like scenes of later periods. The word *grottesco*, and the grotesque adornments associated with architecture, traditionally evoked an air of whim, caprice, and, above all, relative calm. Thus, the wild *gruta* motif so prominent in Part One of *El Criticón* represents a violence and upheaval far removed from the architectural tranquility of the Renaissance. This fact is consistent with Gracián's dialectic of Nature's opposites, and, in addition, it brings new implications to the entire idea of natural and artificial distortion. For example, one mountain-grotto setting becomes a study in space and sound, without reference to Renaissance grotesque motifs:

> ...conmovióse todo el [el monte], temblando aquellas firmes paredes, bramava el furioso viento vomitando en tempestades por la boca de la gruta, començaron a desgajarse con horrible fragor aquellos duros peñascos y a caer con tan espantoso estruendo que parecía quererse venir a la nada toda aquella gran máquina de peñas (I, 117).

What is grotesque in this scene is not so much the deformation of a particular architectural design, but the imminent breakdown of a

---

[11] The lack of symmetry is particularly decisive since Gracián rates visual perception as "el mas noble de los sentidos" (I, 132). The best example of architectural beauty in *El Criticón* is this description of an abstract, ethereal Baroque structure: "En vez de firmes Atlantes en columnas, coronavan el atrio hermosas ninfas, por la materia y por el arte raras, assegurando sobre sus delicados ombros firmeza a un cielo, alternado de serafines, pero sin estrella. Señoreava el centro una agradable fuente, equívoca de aguas y fuegos, pues un Cupidillo que cortejado de las Gracias, ministrándole arpones todas ellas, estava flechando cristales abrasadores, ya llamas, y ya linfas; íbanse despeñando por aquellos nevados tazones de alabastro, deslizándose siempre y huyendo de los que las seguían... " (I, 3.52).

universal concept: Gracián's law of balanced opposites. The landscape is rent asunder, and the laws of harmony are opposed by forces of disintegration within Nature. Thus, the episode depicts more than just a menacing storm. It is the author's way of conveying grotesque horror by depicting an elementary stage of naturistic evil in the world.

This naturistic or "natural" evil, arising without human cause in a realm beyond human control, constitutes the physical base of the world's moral evil, which is the author's real subject. With it, Gracián can represent any perversion of Christian morality against the background of a horrible or threatening Nature. The importance of this technique should not be underestimated, for by identifying it in this way, we can understand how the monstrous storms and supernatural backdrops of the Romantic period came to be different from those of the Baroque, especially in their detachment from the ethical concerns of the Christian world. In Gracián, we have the primitive prototypes of the violent landscapes and Gothic terror of Romanticism. Once again, we may cite the grotto motif as a factor in the development of these prototypes:

> Era noche, y muy oscura, con propiedad lóbrega. En medio desta horrible profundidad... començaron a salir de entre aquellas breñas y por las bocas de las grutas exércitos de fieras, leones, tigres, osos, lobos, serpientes y dragones, que arremetiendo de improviso dieron en aquella tierna manada de flacos y desarmados corderillos, haziendo un horrible estrago y sangrienta carnicería... (I, 170).

This scene depicts the moment just prior to a shift in distortion from a natural to an ethical level of meaning. However, what is monstrous for Gracián is the enormity of the violence and evil, not the supposition that this is an unnatural act, since the beasts are in fact behaving naturally. Therefore, the distortion in this picture of Nature's creatures stems from the awesome magnitude of the incident, which can be described best by a phrase used in another context: "esta no es la octava maravilla, el octavo monstruo sí" (I, 201).

What we have, then, is the kind of grotesque that developed in Europe from Dante to the Baroque, in which horrible forms function not autonomously but as part of a larger Christian cosmology, and where deformation usually serves an ulterior didactic purpose. This is the tradition inherited by Gracián and modified by him through the *concordia discors topos* discussed earlier. Inherent in this grotesque, and absent in its subsequent Romantic forms, is the shifting of a convulsive order from the physical plane to the moral one. Also, the wilder aspects of Nature grow uncontrolled, forming an appropriate background for the human vices depicted by the narrative. On the other hand, the means used to describe these upheavals is the conventional technique of animal symbolism. But in contrast to the Dantesque tradition, Gracián's allegory turns into grotesquerie because of the inordinate presence of corporal as well as moral correspondences between animals and men. Thus, we find strained physical parallels mixed with excessive conceits, all built upon a moral foundation whose lesson is made graphic by a familiar, yet fantastic, realism:

> Tenían otros cabeças de camellos, gente de cargo y de carga; muchos, de bueyes en lo pesado, que no en lo seguro; no pocos de lobos, siempre en la fábula del pueblo; pero los más, de estólidos jumentos, mui a lo simple malicioso... Todos eran hombres a remiendos, y assí, quál tenía garra de león y qual de osso e[l] pie; hablava uno por boca de ganso, y otro murmurava con ozico de puerco; éste tenía pies de cabra, y aquél orejas de Midas; algunos tenían ojos de lechuza y los más de topo; risa de perro... (II, 169).

This lack of economy in animal representations certainly helps to make the entire scene bizarre. But *El Criticón* is a work with various kinds of bestial presences, ranging from Classical monsters to straightforward animal allegories (I, 151-152, 190, 229; II, 195-196; III, 80). Thus, the piling up of bestialized men and humanized beasts in this particular case tends to broaden the traditional category of animalizations while it also distorts the normal configuration of the work's allegorical form. From an aesthetic standpoint, this nominalistic catalog of physical correspondences is less conventional than the "Tiersymbolik" emphasized by Schröder, just as the purely imagistic qualities of style are more dramatic than the conventions of a "Psychologie der Körperdefekte."

This modification of descriptive techniques in the area of animalization is best summed up by an allusion to the works of Hieronymus Bosch. The well-known reference is made in connection with an episode concerning people whose "acciones las hazían al rebés [de la

Naturaleza]": "Hazed cuenta—dixo el Quirón—que soñáis despiertos. ¡O qué bien pintava el Bosco!; aora entiendo su capricho. Cosas veréis increíbles… No hallaréis cosa con cosa. Y a un mundo que no tiene pies ni cabeça, de merced se le da el descabeçado" (1,192-193). The idea here of Nature's values being reversed harks back to what what we have just seen: moral perversion taking the external guise of a physical transvaluation. There is also the suggestion that the element of *capricho*—whim, fantasy, chimera, grotesque humor—had entered Gracián's awareness, although the extent to which he approached Bosch's methods is an uncertain matter. We cannot know whether he intended to emulate the painter or not, but the fact that he was conscious of the *capricho* as an aesthetic possibility, drawing an analogy between it and his own work, should be sufficient even for cautious critics.[12] We should also remember that Bosch's paintings can also be interpreted in allegorical terms, which is to say that their deformations, like those of *El Criticón*, conform to definite iconographical patterns. Similarly, both Gracián and Bosch reflect the grotesque in its early stages, as it had developed from the Middle Ages to the Baroque. Therefore, the notion of *capricho* enters as a new factor in the deformation of medieval allegorical motifs, gaining significance both as a technique and as an attitude in the light of what was to come in the decades after Goya.[13]

Beyond the interrelationship between moral transvaluation, physical inversion, and Gracián's ironic self-awareness, there is one further point. That is the concept of monstrosity. The theory and practice of monstrous creation is not new in Gracián, although no one has studied his debt to the aesthetic forms popularized by such models as *La Divina Commedia*, the chivalric novels, emblem literature, and other compendia

---

12 Gracián's age was well aware of the affinities between Bosch and grotesque art. Under Covarrubias' listing for *grutesco* we read in part: "Se dixo de gruta, y es cierto modo de pintura… Este género de pintura se haze con unos compartimientos, listones y follajes, figuras de medio sierpes, medio hombres, syrenas, sphinges, minotauros, al modo de la pintura del famoso pintor Gerónimo Bosco."

13 Another factor in Quirón's allusion to *capricho* is the concept of *soñar despierto*, whose implications go beyond the present discussion. Aside from the religious and secular evolution of this concept, there is also a grotesque evolution to be studied: Christian demonology, the transformation of Classical myths, the phantasia of reality.

of monsters and fiends.[14] But what makes Gracián interesting in this respect is that he marks the high point in one particular stage of grotesque development: Baroque moralism. This means that along with the Christian lesson to be learned from the presence of these monstrosities, there is also a good deal of attention paid to their physical anatomies. And here, the accumulation of formalistic details produces an elaborate texture of words and images in keeping with the best examples of Gracián's stylistic excesses:

> Veo un monstruo, el más horrible que vi en mi vida, porque no tiene pies ni cabeza; ¡qué cosa tan desproporcionada, no corresponde parte a parte, ni dize uno con otro en todo él! ¡qué fieras manos tiene, y cada una de su fiera, ni bien carne ni pescado, y todo lo parece! ¡qué boca tan de lobo, donde jamás se vió verdad! Es niñería la quimera en su cortejo: ¡qué agregado de monstruosidades! ¡Quita, quítamele de delante, que moriré de espanto!
> Pero el prudente compañero le dezía:
> —Cúmpleme la palabra, nota aquel rostro, que a la primera vista parece verdadero, y no es de hombre, sino de vulpeja; de medio arriba es serpiente; tan torcido tiene el cuerpo y sus entrañas tan rebueltas, que basta a rebolverlas. El espinaço tiene de camello, y hasta en la nariz tiene corcoba; el remate es de sirena, y aun peor, tales son sus dexos. No puede ir derecho; ¿no ves como tuerce el cuello? anda acorbado... (I, 258-259).

What should be evident at once is that Gracián's moral grotesque breaks the form of the conventional animal allegory. The author is clearly on the verge of a formal exercise here, juxtaposing animalistic parts at will without concern for an immediate one-to-one relationship between

---

14 Krauss has this to say on the subject of monstrosity: "Alle Torheit hat daher das Gesicht des Monströsen, das Odium einer verfehlten Harmonie. Wenn man unausgeglichene Gegensätze zusammenlegt, so ergeben sie eine Monstrosität. Im Monströsen erleidet die geistige Schönheit ihre heillose Niederlage" (op. cit., p. 150). And Camón Aznar remarks: "... en Gracián el monstruo es como la irradiación e incongruencia de cada conculcación moral..." (loc. cit., 58). He also believes that a "planteamiento del mundo como contradicción y perpetua negación de las apariencias, convierte a éstas en máscaras y surge así el monstruo. Cada ser es la negación de sí mismo... " (59).

those parts and their possible symbolic meaning. His ultimate purpose, true, remains as ethical as Schröder's exposition shows it to be, and the total picture of distortion conveys the feeling of moral revulsion which is so central to Gracián's didactic position. But in its details—not all quoted above—the picture is irrational. It lacks the logic of an inner vocabulary of images that might be translated into a comprehensive moral symbolism. In fact, the details are gratuitous from a didactic point of view, and their justification lies mainly in the design of their Baroque surface. In this stylistic excess, then, we have the significance of the moral grotesque: it goes beyond normal allegory by piling up an ornate superstructure of motifs that have intrinsic formal value without enriching the essence of the moral structure beneath it. And this, needless to say, is a Baroque phenomenon.

It is worth our while to pause and examine the plastic qualities of the grotesque aesthetic here. First of all, there is the type of deformation employed. One element is the lack of proportion, which we have already seen undermining the symmetrical harmony of Nature. Then too, there is the quality of the disfigurement, which is violent. We find a preoccupation with acts of wrenching and twisting out of shape, in contrast with other alternatives to distortion that might be considered less energetic or abrupt, such as elongation, foreshortening, or inflation. In addition, the synthetic quality of the monster is important, for while it is neither bird, beast, nor fish, it looks like everything and anything because of its combination of animal parts. And yet this is no true integration, but rather a grafting of members affixed to one another in a random conglomeration of limbs and organs. This condition of resembling anything and nothing at the same time takes still another form as well, that of a deformed variation of the theme "el engaño a los ojos." That is, the monster seems to be one thing at first sight, but something entirely different after a closer look. Once again, the emphasis is on the external quality rather than on any metaphysical problem, thus making the aesthetic element a dominant factor in the concept of monstrosity.

The moralistic force, however, is always in the background, and can be described by such statements as: "...siendo el hombre persona de razón, lo primero que executa es hazerla a ella esclava del apetito bestial. Deste principio se originan todas las demás monstruosidades, todo va al rebés en consecuencia de aquel desorden capital... " (I, 211). And yet what is truly the novel element in *El Criticón* is not this medieval account of moral failure, but the Baroque amalgamation of endless forms into an overgrown mass of impossible identity:

> Desta suerte iban discurriendo, quando interrumpió su filosofar otro monstruo, aunque no 1lo estrañaron, porque en este mundo no se topa sino una monstruosidad tras otra.... Venía dentro un monstruo: digo, muchos en uno, porque ya era blanco, ya negro; ya moço, ya viejo; ya pequeño, ya grande; ya hombre, ya mujer; ya persona, y ya fiera: tanto que dixo Critilo si sería éste el celebrado Proteo (I, 218).

The reference to Proteus should not mislead us into thinking that Gracián's grotesque is classical even in this limited area of mythological creatures. Although their roots have a classical origin, many of the figures are almost as far removed from conventional monsters as those of Bosch, whose creations we found Gracián to be impressed by. On the other hand, there is an important element in common with classical tradition, and this is the area of metamorphosis. Here, Gracián makes it clear that the physiological changes he is attempting to describe go beyond the conventions of antiquity. As we read in one episode, "- Aquí—dixo Andrenio—alguna Circe habita que assí transforma las gentes. ¡Qué tienen que ver con estas todas las metamorfosis que celebra Ovidio?" (II, 30). The answer, supplied by the thoughtful reader, is that aesthetically they have little to do with each other, for many reasons.[15]

One reason is that Ovid did not seek to draw a strong moral lesson, while Gracián does. Another is that the changes in form suffered by the figures of mythology were often the logical consequences of the events and personalities involved, whereas Gracián's figures are irrational. But

---

15   The literary antecedent here is Dante's Inferno, XXV, 97-102, although the differences are too complex to be discussed in this context:
> Taccia de Cadmo e d'Aretusa Ovidio;
> chè se quello in serpente e quella in fonte
> converte poetando, io non lo 'nvidio;
> che due nature mai a fronte a fronten
> on trasmutò si ch'amendue le forme
> a cambiar lor matera fosser pronte.

the most important differences are aesthetic in character. There is no purity of form in Gracián's grotesque figures: at best they are hybrids and more often they are mongrel, or else they sprawl unrecognizably, with their individual parts identifiable but their general appearance remaining beyond recognition. The concept of metamorphosis, therefore, is realistic for Ovid and just the opposite for Gracián. Of course, both writers created comparable fantasies in that their myths and fictions do not represent situations in reality. But only in Ovid do the transformed shapes correspond to plausible forms—and sometimes even whole entities—in reality. The monstrous mutations in *El Criticón*, on the other hand, are not intended to have formal verisimilitude. Their overall structures may have symbolic meaning, but they are grotesque insofar as they fail to conform to the proportions of real or imaginary animals.[16]

Be this as it may, what places Gracián's metamorphosis in a more modern context in comparison to Ovid's is its dehumanization of existence. As we know, twentieth century portraits of dehumanized man range from the loss of self and the acquisition of masks or mannequin shapes, to the physiological transformation of human figures into lesser forms of organic existence.[17] The scale on which this occurs in Gracián is obviously much more reduced, but once again it is the quality rather than the extent which is significant. What is essential in any grotesque dehumanization is the replacement of human factors by nonhuman ones. In a contemporary framework, this involves the substitution of mineral and vegetal states for higher forms of life. In *El Criticón*, the vocabulary alluding to these conditions is similar, and the philosophy which is implied has an unmistakable ring of modernity. This is best seen in the episode describing the evil effects of a "licor pestilencial" on its luckless drinkers:

---

16 In still another category, there is the benevolent power of metamorphosis held by the sorceress Artemia, who, contrary to her counterparts in Homer and Ovid, changes beasts into men, wild animals into tame ones, and "... hazía todo género de figuras y figurillas, personas de sustancia. Los mismos títeres convertía en hombres substanciales... los hombrecillos de paja convertía en hombres de veras... " (I, 244-245).

17 There are many examples of this, as in the paintings of De Chirico and Dalí. See too my study, *The Surrealist Mode in Spanish Literature* (Ann Arbor, 1968).

> ...todo el interior se les rebolvió y mudó de suerte que no les quedó aquella substancia verdadera que antes tenían, sino que quedaron llenos de ayre, rebutidos de borra: hombres de burla, todo mentira y embeleco. Los coraçones se les bolvieron de corcho, sin jugo de humanidad ni valor de personas, las entrañas se les endurecieron más que de pedernales, los senos de algodón, sin fondo de juizio, la sangre agua, sin color ni calor, el pecho de cera, no ya de azero, los nervios de estopa, sin bríos, los pies de plomo para lo bueno y de pluma para lo malo, las manos de pez, que todo se les pega, las lenguas de borra, los ojos de papel: y todos ellos, engaño de los engaños y todo vanidad (I, 226-227).

We find here a mixture of advanced and conventional images that aptly demonstrate the direction in which the grotesque was later to develop. Against such familiar comparisons as "entrañas... pedernales," "sangre agua," "pecho de cera," and "pies de plomo," we find more original images: "coraçones... de corcho," "senos de algodón," "nervios de estopa," "ojos de papel." The materials are the first inkling of things to come: the use of stuffed dolls, cardboard or wooden figures, and papier-maché representations. Moreover, whereas the moral note is still audible ("vanidad"), it is notably reduced in volume, with both the analysis of reality and the concept of what is human assuming the center of philosophical inquiry.

It is in this symbolic representation of the lack of human substance that Gracián's grotesque draws closest to the modern age.[18] In particular, there are two areas where this is true: the use of puppets and pastiche figurines to ridicule human dignity, and the use of masks to disguise personality or the lack of it. Men with wax torsos stuffed with cloth or cotton are the seventeenth century counterparts of contemporary figures symbolizing the demise of the hero. And the masked carnival at which they sport is the scene of psychological evasion as well as moral deceit. Thus, part of *El Criticón* makes a fairly modern statement about personality and values by means of images that are still being used by cultivators of the grotesque mode.

---

18 A lesser parallel of spiritual bankruptcy has been drawn by C. B. Morris in "Parallel Imagery in Quevedo and Alberti," BHS, XXXVI (1959), 135-145. I wish to thank Professor Florence Yudin for calling my attention to this article.

For example, during the "juegos bacanales" celebrated with disguises, people and animals alike change their identities by assuming the appearance of their opposites. Thus, the serpent dresses as a dove, and the usurer as an alms-giver. The result is a didactic description that covers the aesthetic framework with so heavy a tapestry of dissembling that the original carnival form is overshadowed. At the same time, Gracián attempts to relate the incident to his reader's experience by alluding to the Spanish practice of masquerading ("Andavan las máscaras más válidas que en la misma Barcelona" [I, 254]). In this way, he provides an instance of Baroque carnivalesque behavior, another subject which in subsequent literary periods becomes a favorite motif for Romantics and Surrealists. The difference, however, is that Gracián's norms are "de todos modos, no sólo de diablura, pero de santidad y de virtud." His deformation is achieved not only through what we now consider to be the conventional carnival mask, but also through nondeformed, realistic masks. That is, his carnival can be created without deformation. Whereas traditional celebrations—Bacchanalia, witches' Sabbaths, pre-Lenten carnivals—produce only distorted faces, Gracián's scene produces undistorted types as well. This is because reality in one case is assumed to be normal, and hence victimized by perverse disguises, whereas in the other case reality is already perverse. Therefore, in the latter, it would be inappropriate to conceal one deformation by masking it with another. Thus, the most eligible carnival masks for whores, adulterers, and rapacious beasts are those that represent austere penitents, faithful friends, and domestic animals. Since the figures are already morally misshapen, their participation in the general grotesquerie can only become possible through the guise of normal, undistorted shapes.

This throws us back again to the fact that we are dealing with a grotesque mode based on moral precepts. But what of the problem of personality and human substance? Here, Gracián's condemnation of immorality extends to a grotesque representation of people psychologically corrupted by vice. Physically dehumanized because they have forfeited human dignity, and mentally stunted by Gracián's refusal to invest them with human personality, they parade before the reader like marionettes of a later age: "…aquellos pequeños, y por otro nombre ruincillos (que por maravilla escapan de aí), aquellos que hazen del hombre porque no lo son, siquiera por parecerlo, semilla de títeres, moviéndose todos, que ni paran ni dejan parar, amassados con azogue, que todos se mueven, hechos de goznes, gente de polvorín, picantes granos… " (III, 129). What is remarkable about this passage is less its philosophical view of the human condition than the anatomical spectacle of dehumanized physiques. The diminution of man's social and moral status is a conventional theme in *El Criticón*, but the reduction of his vital movements to a mechanical analogy is far from being commonplace in the Golden Age.[19] If Gracián's outlook causes him to regard human beings as the "semilla de títeres," his own sensibility itself bears the seed of a new flowering of the grotesque in later periods. References to sawdust and hinges instead of to blood and muscle cause the description to turn upon a formally grotesque axis rather than a philosophical one. Thus, the animation of characters, rather than their analysis, makes the most impressive statement about life in a post-heroic age. On the other hand, despite his anticipation of Romantic motifs, Gracián's grotesque remains a Baroque phenomenon for several reasons. Its technique runs away with itself, impatiently jumping from figure to figure instead of elaborating an episode built around one grotesque subject. This lack of economy, plus the cumulative effect of many self-sufficient metaphors, creates a typically Baroque edifice of image upon image that exhausts the reader with its ponderous size.

Fundamentally, however, the grotesque in *El Criticón* is subordinated, while the concept of man as marionette is developed with prosaic ethical directness. But it is significant that the puppet image was not abandoned by Gracián, since the relationship between mannequins and the fall from heroism has, from his time to our own, come to be axiomatic. Thus, we find Andrenio saying that

> … assí como dizen que van degenerando los hombres y siendo más pequeños quanto más va (de suerte que cada siglo merman un dedo, y a este passo vendrán a parar en títeres y figurillas, que ya poco les falta a algunos), sospecho que también los coraçones se les van achicando; y assí, se halla tanta falta de aquellos grandes sugetos que

---

19 Klaus Heger echoes Krauss' oft-repeated concept of *persona*, pointing out that so-called *no-personas* are designated by the diminutives *personilla, personeta, figura*. The aesthetic implications, however, are not acknowledged. *Baltasar Gracián: Estilo lingüístico y doctrina de valores* (Zaragoza, 1960), pp. 170-171.

conquistavan mundos, que fundavan ciudades, dándoles sus nombres, que era su real *faciebat*.—¿Ya no ai Rómulos, ni Alexandros, ni Constantinos? (II, 57).

I will not go into the meaning of this statement, since so much has already been written about pessimism in Counter-Reformational Spain. I would suggest, however, that perhaps for the first time a Baroque writer has found a fairly original image through which he might express his vision of the fall from heroism. All of the famous conceits of the early Baroque—Quevedo's crumbling walls, Lope's shipwrecked beach, Cervantes' wooden horse—have a traditional basis for their inventiveness, and in any case, would later be exchanged for new metaphors in subsequent generations. In contrast, Gracián's marionettes reflect a different sensibility, and one whose ramifications would be exploited by Europeans everywhere after the eighteenth century.

This is not to make false comparisons about the quality of images in the early and late Spanish Baroque. Nor should we forget the place that puppets had on the non-grotesque popular stage. But the point is that a deep-seated preoccupation with decadence in the mid-seventeenth century found an unusual, if not unique, metaphor for its expression. What is more, this metaphor is grotesque, detached from Classical tradition, and conceived at the early dawn of a new sensibility rather than in the twilight of an old one. In other words, just as we found changes in the concept of metamorphosis from Ovid to Gracián, so now we find an image that opens up new possibilities for the future of grotesque aesthetics. In the last two quotations, we witness a deliberate attempt to reduce the human dimension to a stilted, mechanical framework. This may be in keeping with the general bent of seventeenth century moralism, and even with Gracián's own philosophy. But its formal expression does not reflect the techniques of literary convention. As we have seen, traditional allegories are like realistic statues: both groups rely on representationalism rather than deformation. The episodes discussed in this article have been no less moralistic, but they are unmistakably deformed renditions of men and events. And here again we are faced with the central issue. At certain moments, the balanced harmonies of Renaissance philosophy and art, and of Counter-Reformational cosmology, are upset by the distorted forms of Gracián's moral grotesque.[20]

---

20 This study was written during a leave of absence supported by the John Simon Guggenheim and the Horace H. Rackham Foundations. It was first published in *Hispanic Review*, 39 (1971), 30-48. Reprinted by permission of the University of Pennsylvania Press.

3
Grotesque Portraits in Torres Villarroel

SPANISH LETTERS IN THE first half of the eighteenth century are so barren that, Feijoo excepted, Torres Villarroel is the only author whose writings have some claim to literary validity. His *Visiones y visitas* (1727-28), make this claim persuasively because of their elaboration of the satirical technique which was used by Quevedo a century earlier.[1] His contribution to the history of aesthetic ideas differs in his more elaborate cultivation of the grotesque. The affinity between Torres and Quevedo has been discussed on several occasions by Russell Sebold, the only scholar who has taken an imaginative and synthetic view of Torres' complete works.[2] Sebold has mentioned the pictorial terminology of the *Visiones y visitas*, their expressionistic rendition of reality, and the interplay of moralistic and descriptive tendencies in Torres' formal technique. These ideas open the door to further analysis, especially into the implications of Torres' exaggerated use of the grotesque. The *Visiones y visitas* are unique in this respect, and we should, therefore, be as attentive as possible to what the intensification of grotesque forms means, in terms of aesthetics and also with regard to the intellectual temper of the eighteenth century.

Torres' visions were written for a moralistic purpose. I will try to

---

[1] Guy Mercadier has cast a wider net over Torres' complete works as well as his biography. I will quote from Sebold's edition in the "Clásicos Castellanos" (Madrid, 1966), which uses the full original title: *Visiones y visitas de Torres con Don Francisco de Quevedo, por la corte. Trasladólas desde el sueño al papel el mismo Don Diego de Torres Villarroel.*

[2] See the following two articles: "T.V., Quevedo y el Bosco," *Insula*, XV, clix (1960), 3, 12; "T. V. y las vanidades del mundo." *Archivum* (Oviedo), VII, i-ii-iii (1957-58), 115-146. Some of this material appears in modified form in the edition cited above.

show, however, that from the standpoint of literary history, their enduring quality lies in another area altogether. There are several reasons for not emphasizing their ethical content. First is the fact that the *Visiones y visitas* are a latter-day imitation of Quevedo's masterpiece, with the result that they have a derivative and even banal ethical message. Then, too, if we allow for intellectual differences between Torres and Quevedo, the work represents nothing new in moral thought because its premises were founded on the same orthodox values that prevailed in the Counter-Reformation. Indeed, it seems almost as if the two satirists had been contemporaries, for the difference between seventeenth- and eighteenth-century Spanish ethical theory is negligible when measured against the enormous contrast between Spain and France in the eighteenth century. In other words, if we compare the development of moral thought in Spain over two centuries with that of France during a comparable period, the rate of change for Catholic Spain is hardly perceptible. Thus, we find a greater distance between Torres and the French moralists of his own day than between Torres and the Spaniards writing over a century before. Hence, if we are to justify the literary value of the *Visiones y visitas*, it must be on grounds other than the moralistic ones usually associated with this work.

What is new and interesting in Torres' sketches is the presence of grotesque portraits. These long, graphic descriptions of people are more numerous than anything of their kind written earlier, and, more important, they are drawn more consciously and in greater detail. For this reason, the portraits call attention to the development of Spanish aesthetics in the seventeenth and eighteenth centuries. They remind us, first of all, that what we now call the Goyesque tradition in art had literary antecedents as well as pictorial ones, some of which are traceable to Golden Age satire.[3] Secondly, the portraits reveal a transformation in prose fiction whereby the aesthetic forms once held so firmly in the grip of intellectual and moral aims during the eras of Quevedo and Gracián, now begin to break away. This results in a gradual weakening in the relationship between content and form, so that aesthetic value comes to be released from the instrumentalism that had subordinated it earlier. Consequently, the interest which the *Visiones y visitas* hold for

---

[3] For a detailed treatment of this subject, see Edith Helman, *Trasmundo de Goya* (Madrid, 1963), 49 *et passim*.

us lies in the fact that their portraits face in two directions: toward the origins of grotesque representation in Spanish moral literature, and toward the subsequent evolution of the grotesque mode in the nineteenth and twentieth centuries.[4]

Even to the indifferent eye, the *Visiones y visitas* show themselves to be ruled by the basic norms of all grotesque art. That is, they have the usual constant of animalism, dehumanization, the metamorphosis of plant and animal physiology, a cruel or 'black' sense of humour, and a propensity for the absurd. These aberrations make sense in relation to the period in which Torres was writing, for the dominant tone of the first half of the eighteenth century was not Feijoo's rationalism but popular superstition and fear, not triumph and stability but uncertainty and violence, in short, not the glorious ruin of Quevedo's generation but the long-term, institutionalized decadence that led up to and engulfed the Bourbon accession. These are the historical determinants which affected a grotesque mode that was much more intense than anything Quevedo might have wished to cultivate.[5]

---

[4] By "grotesque" I mean an aesthetic mode, a psychostructural condition in art whose technique or form can be expressed in any age and through any medium or genre. Basically, the grotesque can be defined as the presence or use of a deformation which results in an incongruous or absurd situation. Not much more can be said by way of definition without becoming entangled in a nest of problems, See further, Wolfgang Kayser, *Das Groteske in Maierei und Dichtung* (München, 1960), and Arthur Clayborough, *The Grotesque in English Literature* (Oxford, 1965).

[5] This and several other generalizations about Quevedo are made in order to provide a basis for comparison, and are not intended to describe his own modest grotesquerie. In addition to the famous descriptions of the Licenciado Cabra and "La casada que se afeita," the kind of grotesque usage that I have in mind can be seen by the following samples from the *Sueños*. I quote from Luis Astrana Marín's edition of the *Obras completas* (Madrid 1932): "Con una cara hecha de un orejón, los ojos en dos cuévanos de vendimiar, la frente con tantas rayas y de tal color y hechura, que parecía planta de pie; la nariz en conversación con la barbilla, que casi juntándose hacían garra, y una cara de la impresión del grifo; la boca a la sombra de la nariz, de hechura de lamprea, sin diente ni muela, con sus pliegues de bolsa a lo jimio..." (p. 188); "... un diablo de marca mayor, corcovado y cojo; saca muchas culebras por lías, junto los sastres en dos haces, y arrojándolos en una hondura muy grande, dijo: —¡Allá va leña!... En esto hizo otro vómito dellos el mundo, y hube de entrarme, porque no había

As for the aesthetic determinants of the grotesque, they bear out what we will find to be Torres" evasion of responsibility for his "expressionism." That is, the distortions which he found in society might indeed have been real, but when depicted by his enflamed imagery, they were marked by the personal disfigurations of his imagination. Torres "projects" upon reality the irrational constructs of his mind. For example, his basic impulse is to find the animal character of people, in physical appearance as well as in ethical make-up. The scene in which he spies "[un] hombre con raza de mico" (p. 66) is typical of this effort to establish the animal roots of a sub-human genealogy. And yet one of Torres" earliest descriptions is of himself in an animal position: "la cabeza en la almohada. Y al caer, se enterraron la mitad de las facciones, hasta medias narices; y como el dibujo de las ancas, muslo y suras se distinguía sobre la manta, quedé un medio perfil, metamorfosis entre galgo y astrológo" (p. 15). So that even before he turns to the people around him, Torres is found to be viewing himself in terms of a baser and higher self that has nothing to do with religion.

This propensity to think in dualistic terms has its counterpart in literary technique as well. Torres sometimes adopts a double perspective in executing his portraits, viewing the subjects from the front and from the side at the same time. Unlike portrait-painting, however, these renditions give a composite picture taken from two different angles, full-face and profile. It is the simultaneity, just as much as the juxtaposition of the two faces, that is interesting. In the description of one subject, for example, "mirado de perfil, parecía su cara el lomo de un lechón magro y cerdudo; visto frente a frente, tenía cara de mula descarnada y caudalosa; y por todos lados era la más mala bestia de los brutos" (pp. 158-59). The two vantage points are taken in order to determine fully what the person's traits are, presumably because, like Torres "entre galgo y astrologo," there will be more than one generic feature. The point is, however, that even a dual perspective reveals Torres' specimens to be thoroughly bestial. Nor is this animalism linked in any way to the higher qualities of humanity, such as moral character or signs of personality. Indeed, it

---

donde estar ya allí, y el monstro infernal empezó a traspalar. Y diz que es la mejor leña que se quema en el infierno remendones de todo oficio, gente que sólo tiene bueno ser enemiga de novedades" (p. 150). See further, Sebold, loc. cit. and pp. lviii, lxxi-lxxxiii of his edition.

would be far-fetched to relate the animal references here with the ethical and religious symbolism of traditional allegory. On the contrary, the beast-like components of the portrait are selected for their physical—that is, visual—impact, and they are arranged so that the configuration stays on the same material plane of meaning.

The virtual lack of intellectual appeal in these portraits is interesting in comparison to the descriptive techniques that were available to Torres among the various forms of narrative fiction already in existence. He chose to ignore the kind of characterization that might have resulted from the multiple perspective of dialogue and description carried over a period of time, or through a series of different events and settings. As a result, there is seldom any life-history written on the lines of his creatures' faces. They are without a past and without a capacity to change with the passage of time. Their countenances are rendered graphically, but they are frozen, as it were, within the moment that they are observed by the writer. Consequently, the pictorial aspects of Torres' descriptions are more prominent than the characterological ones. A good example of this is the following: "un hombrecillo ostra, tacaño de estatura y chivo de fisonomía; tan saltarín y bullicioso, que más parecía engendrado con azogue que con materia prima;... Era una tortuga en zancos, cucaracha con chinelas y escarabajo con chapines" (p. 154). The main thrust of this passage comes from the constant assault of names from the impersonal sector of the animal world. Its purpose is to negate the subject's human appearance by overlaying the latter with as many references to insects and animals as the subject will bear. There is no logic or plan to this barrage, except for the demeaning associations and complete absence of unique identifying traits. The result, however, is to render the individual quality of the portrait ineffective.

We may draw several conclusions from this technique of animalization. Most important is the consequence of reducing man to the level of beast: such a reduction is the crucial first step in the gradual process of dehumanizing man altogether. Looking ahead to modern art, we can see how important this step was, and looking back to mediaeval and Golden Age animal symbolism, we can also see how different Torres' methods were from those of his predecessors. Let us note the following passage, where traces of this new dehumanization are already visible: "un hombrecillo entre persona y títere, mona con golilla, ratón con capa y renacuajo con bigotes; figura en que se dejaba ver la humanidad como en un mapa, escarabajo de nuestra especie; animal de retoño, como melón; hombre de falda, como perro; personilla de faltriquera, como pistola ..." (p. 68). There are other examples of dehumanization which we will examine in a different context, but even here, where the intention is to reclassify homo sapiens under a different genus as well as species, the encroachment of inanimate elements into the animal frame of reference is quite plain. The ambiguity of *persona-títere* will be, of course, one of Romanticism's stock-in-trade grotesque devices at the end of the century.

The second conclusion to be drawn involves the concept of Nature, and how it was understood to mean something other than the idealism of either the Golden Age or the Romantic period. In Torres' grotesque, the only explanation for man's sub-human and animalistic atavisms is that Nature, by some error or wayward bent, has missed the mark. This demonstration of Nature's inherent defectiveness meant, therefore, that Nature was neither the physical manifestation of God's wisdom and perfection, nor the material embodiment of a universal, spiritual beauty. Instead, it was often abortive, disordered, and monstrous. As Torres wrote succinctly of one personage, "juzgué que cuando le formó su Artífice, estaba a oscuras, o que al tiempo de su fábrica estuvo borracha la naturaleza" (p. 121). Needless to say, the Romantic elements of iconoclasm and Dionysian impulse are present here only in seminal form. Even so, Nature is far from being idealized, and this realistic view, as we will see, conforms to the overall approach which the Enlightenment was to adopt toward the natural world.

This approach assumed that the essential structure of reality adhered to a natural law, and that the universe functioned according to a series of laws which operated in harmony and which were awaiting man's discovery. Torres shared these ideas, although his belief took a reverse form.[6] That is, instead of affirming the principles of law and order, he pointed to them negatively by citing their malfunction. Nature's mistakes were the misapplications of natural law. One of Torres' grotesque portraits illustrates this very well:

---

6 Sebold has demonstrated that T. V.'s knowledge of modern science was negligible, thereby excluding him from the Enlightenment. My argument about law and order is based on the implications of T. V.'s aesthetic practices, and I see no real contradiction. See further, "T.V. y las vanidades del mundo."

Parece que la naturaleza se equivocó en el repartimiento de las facciones, y que le había trocado los lugares a los miembros; los ojos, cada uno tiraba por su camino, porque al uno se lo sorbía el entrecejo, y el otro se le entraba en el cogote; nariz a pino como campana, con los bordes hacia la frente y los labios colaterales a la oreja como degolladura de marrano. Era su cara el juego de los despropósitos; pues si la vista preguntaba por la colocación de los sentidos, respondían las facciones con un disparate. (212)

In this passage, most of the regulations controlling man's immediate world are implied in one way or another: order, symmetry, sense perception, verisimilitude, causality, and so forth. Had Torres been writing with any other concept of Nature in mind, the description would have turned out quite differently. We need only to turn to the grotesque counterparts in Dante and Gracián to see this point.[7] In Torres, Nature is not bound to a divine spirit or to morality. Its conduct is self-contained, and remains independent of the precepts governing non-scientific matters. In short, Nature behaves—or here, misbehaves—in the image of rationalistic ideals, and its defects are portrayed in terms of the latter.

The third conclusion to be drawn from these animalizations is the fact that Torres' cultural analysis does not suppose a humanistic orientation. His social criticism is zoomorphic, so to speak, negating man's human traits in favour of those common to most animal species. In particular, great pains are taken to stress the absence of rational faculties, a gesture that is significant in a century that was soon to value reason above all else. The best evidence for this can be found in Torres' remark concerning his own dreams. In one passage, he refers to the "mecanismo de mi animalidad," a phrase which we will return to later on. In another passage, he describes the physiological process just prior to having a dream, and there too we see the animal element, although it is balanced somewhat by his creative powers:

... se derribaron las pestañas, se tumbó el juicio, se remató el sentimiento, huyó la razón, y yo quedé como un bruto en los brazos del

---

7 As a point of reference in *El criticón*, compare Andrenio's eulogy of Nature in Part One, *crisi* 3, with the description of "la cueva de la nada" in Part Three, *crisi* 8.

> sueño. La fantasía, como vive a espera de estos descansos para desarrebujar sus locuras, luego que sintió al entendimiento divertido, a la voluntad durmiendo, y a la memoria roncando, empezó a formar en las calles de mi caletre una procesión de figuras tan proprias, tan vivas y tan ordenadas, que más parecieron obra de un discreto cuidado que pintura de una loca aprehensión... (p. 108)

Here, then, is the highest criterion: order. If order is lacking in man's rational processes, this makes him no better than a dumb beast. Hence Torres' delighted surprise when he finds the procession of deformed figures approaching in an organized formation. He had expected a chaotic dispersion instead. He implies, therefore, not only that all men are prone to falling into an animal state, but that even the creative act can have a sub-human basis. In Torres' case, his imagination is especially susceptible to the aberrations of imagery which arise when reason and will are neutralized. Exactly what this means in terms of the grotesque dream process will be discussed later. The point here, however, is that the animal factor takes over when the specifically human element of mental activity lies dormant. The orderly procession is the product of a later conscious artistry, although Torres credits his "fantasía" with this power of organization. What remains, in fact, is "un bruto en los brazos del sueño," his rational apparatus nullified, and a "loca aprehensión" in the ascendency until its material is later reorganized by "un discreto cuidado."

The loss of reason dramatized by Torres' animalistic imagery has several repercussions that estrange him from the ethical concerns of the previous centuries. One such repercussion is the gratuitous emphasis on various forms of physiological activity. This includes drunkenness, sexuality, and an obsessive interest in the body, organic decay, and the sensations common to both. Torres' portraits record these details without reference to any deeply-felt moralistic position. In fact, there is an orgiastic quality to the portraits that is very much like the indulgence in slang vocabulary that Torres so often permits himself: in spectacles as well as in words, the author seems to revel in the enormities around him. Several drunken scenes, for example, make allusions to Spain's besotted condition primarily for the purpose of furnishing a setting for a host of physical associations. Of one scheming fellow, we read that "derramábansele por los ojos malvasías, vinos del Rin y cuanta especie de licores ha arrastrado a España la viciosa sed de nuestros paladares; regoldando pollas, ventoseando perdices, todo cacoquimio de manjares y apopléctico de bebidas' (p. 41). Thus, the "rational republic" suffers from the same decline that besets its individual members. And the fact that this decline is couched in medical terms indicates Torres' morbid interest in spectacle rather than in any clinical analysis. There is even one description of the moments prior to sleep which shows the same pattern of thinking: "No podían mis pobres sentidos emborracharse en las tabernas de Morfeo, aunque lo solicitaban a punto el postre; porque bebiendo las potencias azumbres de sueño aguado con revoltosas inquietudes, sólo se suspendían a trasquilones y dormitaban a salpicaduras. No eran capaces las conchas de mi paciencia ni los callos de mi animalidad, de resistir..." (pp.107-08).

Torres' revealing use of the same vocabulary of drunkenness in relation to his own mental processes implicates him thoroughly. His tendency to see society as the drunken parody of a once-rational body cannot be accepted even as metaphorically accurate. What is does reflect is an artistic involvement with words, scenes, and subjective fantasies. Torres' portraits do not provide socially useful insights into people. Instead, they are aesthetic pieces sketched from the inner tableau of his overheated imagination. And, like a botanical hothouse, this literary one is luxuriant but dank, overredolent with the kind of growths that produce a sweetness unto putrefaction. Torres' vignette of one character might very well be symbolic of this feverish activity:..." las palabras hechas una sopa de vino; muy almagrados de cachetes, ardiendo las mejillas en rescoldo de tonel, abochornados los ojos en estíos de villa, encendidas las orejas en canículas de bodegón, y delirando los caletres con tabardillos de taberna" (p.98).

Our approach, then, must be that of an aesthete, staking out not the ethical surface but the aesthetic subsoil, and seeking not the flowers of evil but the roots of decay. For example, in the following bouquet of moral epithets we read that

> el contagio de lo codicioso, la lepra de falsos, la sarna de impíos y todas las malas costumbres" are all said to be adhesively sticky "a manera de moscas, buscando las llagas de la república en homicidas (p.171).

What is striking about these lines is not the ethical content but the terminology borrowed from medicine, and the insistent dwelling upon disease. These lend a certain fascination to the passage, and they reveal more of the author's sensibility than they do of his social philosophy. Torres is alert to the phenomenology of degeneration, and his perceptions eagerly seize upon details that turn his portraits into grotesques instead of critiques: "vientres podridos como ollas; cuasi se escuchaba el mormullo en los estómagos, en que se percibía los mendrugos y las tajadas andar a mojicones sobre tomar asiento empujándose unos a otros" (p.98). The fact that Torres' senses tend to record data which would normally be ignored or shunned is, of course, what makes their activity a grotesque enterprise. This, however, is only one reason for our judging aesthetics, rather than ethics, to be the stronger foundation in the *Visiones y visitas*.

A second reason is that Torres' fascination for degeneracy is matched by his fondness for physiological observation. Part of this is an attempt to be humorous, as in the episode where one man, "con el vendaval de un regüeldo, apagó las luces," and the other "disparó mucha artillería de estornudos occidentales' (p.99). But part of that interest in physiology goes much deeper, and, paradoxically, this is because it bears little resemblance to clinical pathology. Torres' affinity for the functions of the body is linked to his zoomorphic vision of humanity. That is, just as the animalization of mankind is a safeguard against dignifying the human race with personality, so too does Torres' physiological observation carry him away from a humanistic analysis. The reduction of man to a vocabulary of deformed physical parts assures that his likeness will not be represented in terms that transcend the organic world. For example, there is the following portrait: "tan gotoso de cachetes que las facciones las tenía embolsadas en los morrillos; y la carne repartida en bandos de burujones, corcovas, mendrugos y zoquetes, y tan hidrópicos que el más hético era como una breva de pino... un padre vejiguero, despertador de las carcajadas' (pp.140-41). And there is also an appalling description of Spanish midwives, which I shall not quote here, that makes equal capital of the mechanics and mistreatment of the body (p.59). The point is, therefore, that a concern with physiology does not necessarily indicate a "scientific" or even an objective critique of either the body politic or the human body, nor does it have to imply a metaphor of moral decay.

Quite the contrary, physiology can very well be exploited with a half-ribald, half-repugnant pleasure in the phenomenon of flesh, along with the latter's potential for aesthetic disfiguration.

Torres' use of things tumescent and rotten, let us repeat, establishes a link with the technique of animalism. At the same time, it forms another link with a typical grotesque feature: plant morphology. Not that Torres developed this to the full extent that is visible in the paintings of Bosch or Dalí, where the metamorphoses of vegetable, animal, and human orders are intertwined in defiance of the evolutionary scale. But Torres does mix plant references into his portraits to an extent greater than either Quevedo before him or Goya later on. One of the best portraits in the entire work depends in part on this technique: "un hombre magro, cecial y seco como raíz de árbol, con la cara tan sucia, que parecía el suelo de un queso; la cabeza oprimida entre dos corcovas mayores que dos escriños de vendimiar" (p.185). Admittedly, these analogies are crude and latent forms of what in grotesque art is normally a subtle morphological blend of men and plants. And yet the very novelty of such references in Spanish literature requires that we note them. A related portrait is interesting for the network of associations that cluster around the basic image of ripe fruit: "el rostro entre mascarón de navío, sumidero de taberna o escotillón de mosto... bostezando bodegas, resllando toneles, con los ojos pasados por vino, un tomate maduro por nariz, un par de nalgas disciplinadas por carrillos, barba bruñida a chorreones de zumo de marrano; un puerco espín de estopa por peluca..." (p.39), and so forth. Once more the author's compulsive prolixity carries him away from a homogeneous image. On the other hand, the very looseness of the association adds to the grotesquerie of the face, so that a phrase like "zumo de marrano" acquires overtones that an ordinary reference to either plant or animal would lack.

These hybrid images, with their intensely physical details, are supplemented by an odd strain of sexual insinuation. The erotic element is more revealing for the mental atmosphere in which Torres worked than for the vividness of the portraits themselves. As we will see in our discussion of style, a reference to a character's "diarrea en los sesos" describes the author's own excessive flow of words much more than it does the character's mind. So too in the case of sex: what is important is not so much that eroticism is used to illuminate a few portraits, but that Torres' phrasing should reflect a particular attitude of mind. This erotic groundswell involves the author personally on still another count: its relationship to the origin of the vision itself. Torres explains his dreams by saying that an incubus has mated with his imagination and sired the monstrous visions. What this means will be clarified later; the immediate point is the frame of reference: the literary work itself is engendered by the primary sexual act. Torre's creative act is tainted with abnormality under an aura of hidden subjectivity.

Consequently, when we find one portrait containing elements that purport to be objective but which in fact are closely linked to Torres' own creative processes, there is reason to look more carefully at all of his erotic references. One such portrait is, in part, the following:..." un mamarracho tan feo como no lo pudiera parir la imaginación, aunque se dejara fornicar de todos los diablos en sus figuras" (p. 200). If Torres had wished to convey the quality of ugliness to his reader, this comparison could hardly have been the most effective. On the other hand, it was indeed the most meaningful image in terms of his literary problems and private awareness. The sexual allusion is intended to supplement the other representations of a deformed and deforming Nature. But its real impact is to underscore the aesthetic process of the grotesque as the author experiences it. Torres portrays his mind as being possessed by an evil master who is suspiciously like an indwelling force, an incubus. The sex factor, then, takes the form of an unholy assignation, during whose intimacy Torres' ideas are conceived. When these notions are to be verbalized, the image goes on to describe the act as a state of physical gestation: "tuve preñada la lengua y cuasi con la barriga a la boca, de mil razones" (p.120). The concept grows as if feeding upon an internal system, and Torres acts in fact as his own midwife in the birth of his ideas. However, since he repeatedly insists on his lack of complicity in these deliveries, the evil nature of this aspect of sex attracts the most attention.

Thus, by extension, the erotic conceit throws an unpleasant shadow on everyone whom Torres wishes to ridicule, and this is extended to non-living subjects as well ('[un sonido] pareció maullo concebido en caniculares de lujuria gatesca' [p.25). There is, of course, a traditional element in the technique of moral condemnation ("burdel de Calvino... lupanar de Lutero... zahurdas de otros protestantes" [p.148]), but what is most prominent is another kind of allusion. This is the picture of a neutralized sexuality. People and situations are deprived of their gender and vital force by a reference designed to cast ambiguity on their essential qualities. For example, there is "un mozuelo semimacho... más relamido que plato de dulce en poder de pajes" (p.25). Then, too, there is "un mozo puta, amolado en hembra, lambido de gambas, muy bruñidas las enaguas de las manos" (p.72). And finally, we have fops who "gastan tocador y aceite de sucino porque padecen males de madre; gastan polvos, lazos, lunares y brazaletes, y todos los disimulados afeites de una dama. Son machos, desnudos y hembras, vestidos" (p.74). In all of these portraits, the same desexualization is visible. It is not simply a matter of ridiculing effeminate people and customs, although some of this is certainly involved. More critically, it is the attempt to liquidate the sexual element from a society which the author wishes to present in as unnatural a way as possible. How else is one to explain the excesses of obscenity throughout the book? Given Torres' view of Spain as being deformed, he uses every means to confirm that view, including the ambiguous description of sex. This crucial area of human productivity and life cannot be accepted in a sound form without undermining the grotesque vision as a whole. Fundamentally, therefore, Torres is incapable of providing a healthy account of sexuality because to do so would mean confessing that the social scene was in fact more normal than he cared to acknowledge.

The results of this ambiguity even affect the language used in connexion with things. A book, for instance, is "hermafrodita de cartera y bolsón" (p.53), and of the profession of midwifery we read: "esta facultad en la Corte es hermafrodita, porque tiene ya macho y hembra" (p.59). Thus, the world is depicted with the imagery of confusion. If this concept were developed in the visual arts, the deformation would, naturally, have stronger grotesque overtones. In Torres' visions, on the other hand, the effect is not so much dramatic as it is verbally interesting. More important, however, is the way in which the *visiones* define any defect in terms of confusion. The critique of a blind and blundering Nature, which we have already noted, finds its most basic example in the eradication of sexual distinctions. The most telling scenes, therefore, are drawn with the grey pigments of hermaphrodism, which symbolizes not only the bland neutralization of life, but the irrationalism inherent in man and in Nature. With this binomial standard of confusion-order, Torres takes one more step away from the seventeenth-century religious ethos, and approaches the threshold of the Enlightenment, however tentatively.

The grotesque portraits and allusions in the *Visiones y visitas* represent the practical side of Torres' technique, but behind them stands a vast new scaffolding of grotesque theory. This structure consists of the dream genre itself, the generic form that makes the grotesquerie possible. With respect to its literary antecedents, the *Visiones y visitas* is a pivotal work because it is not governed by the theological norms that influenced Golden Age literature. Its satirical apparatus derives from Quevedo's, but what is different and therefore significant about it is that the visionary quality of its dreams does not show a marked religio-moral orientation. Moreover, in contrast to tradition, its didactic features do not conspire to hold the purely aesthetic aspects of the composition in check. Torres' grotesque visions dramatize one factor above all others: that the aesthetic autonomy of the dream remains undisturbed by the aims of the *fantasía moral* as Quevedo had conceived it. Whether this was Torres' intention is another matter, but such is the effect. The point is debatable, naturally, and Sebold takes an entirely different position both in his edition and his article in *Archivum*, where he relates the *Visiones y visitas* to the mystic tradition.

If we compare the traditional religious vision with its grotesque counterpart in Torres, we find that only the former contains a prophetic and apocalyptic series of images. The prophet describes, as in Ezekiel and Revelations, a future situation, often violent, that will arise in order to remedy the present defective reality. In contrast, the grotesque form of vision presented by Torres is an inverted Apocalypse. Instead of predicting a future reality, it depicts an absurd and distorted situation that seems to proceed from the defects of the present. In Torres' *visiones*, the present is deformed by having its imperfections carried to an extreme, but the resulting deformation neither remedies nor revaluates the situation. Whereas the religious vision provides some alternative for the future, the grotesque dream converts defect into an irremediable absurdity.

Another factor that separates Torres' moral vision from tradition is the kind of emotion that characterizes the visionary scene. Normally, the prophet succumbs to an ecstasy which transports him to a level of reality outside of himself. He is uplifted from his subjectivity and is placed in contact with an Absolute that is external to his psychic life. Torres, on the other hand, undergoes an inverted ecstasy. His is a delirium rather than a communion, an internal frenzy based on personal associations and even obsessions, as we will see. The excesses that stem from Torres' private explorations are closer in their distortion to human madness than to the irrationalism of mystic rapture or religious prophecy. Moreover, in the latter, the condition is inspired with the help of an outside source, whereas in Torres' case the fantasy depends upon how he stimulates his own imagination. What is revelation in the one is creative revelry in the other, as Torres turns away from the Divine in order to exercise his private sensibility.

Although Torres never used the word "grotesque" to describe his dreams, their bizarre character was not only apparent to him but was deliberately cultivated. He freely acknowledges the impure or hybrid nature of his genre, along with the odd deviations that such hybridization spawns. Most revealing in this respect is his attempt to classify his dreams within the categories of oneiric theory as it then existed. For example, in *La barca de Aqueronte*, a work related to the *Visiones y visitas*, he notes that

> a los insomnios (que vulgarmente llaman sueños) dividen los filósofos en naturales y animales. Asientan que el sueño animal se cría de aquellos cuidados y pensamientos que son regularmente amables tareas en el desvelo, siendo fantasmas nocturnas las repetidas operaciones y discursos del día...[8]

Thus, explains Torres, the student will dream about intellectual debates, and the soldier about warfare. On the other hand, "el sueño natural dicen que lo forma la cualidad del temperamento," so that "sanguine" people will have gay dreams and phlegmatic or melancholy people dreams appropriate to their personalities. Quite apart from this classification, however, Torres cites a third grouping, the theological view of dreams. Here, too, there is a pair of opposites—those dreams inspired by the "Angel de Luz," and those which "escribe el demonio en el cerebro para asustar y burlarse de las criaturas" (p.267).

Nevertheless, despite these different categories and interpretations, Torres does not assess his own dream content with any of their criteria in mind. He explains that "pues en mí ni son naturales ni animales estos

---

8 In *Sueños morales* (Madrid, 1960), pp. 265-66.

sueños, porque en mis venas jamás he sentido a la melancolía, que es la madre de estos horrores... Despierto busco la lisonja a mis ojos en los buenos semblantes, y soñando solamente se me representan infernales visiones" (p. 266). As for the religious explanation, it is dismissed even more summarily. The grotesque dream, with its perversions, is the product of everything that Torres consciously repudiates. And yet its material is mined from an inner source which the author confesses to be his own. While there is a certain unwillingness to accept responsibility for being the creator of such unpleasantness, Torres confirms the responsibility as being his by the very analysis of his dream process. As he remarks,

> viene el sueño y, ¿que hace?, da un soplo a la luz de la razón... Acostada el alma, y ligados los sentidos a escondidas de las potencias, se incorporó la fantasía, y con ella madrugaron también otro millón de duendes que se acuestan en los desvanes de mi calvaria... (p.16).

What, then, are we to make of this ambiguity? When a human's soul, senses, and other faculties are dormant, the imagination leaps to do mischief. But imagination does not sport alone; its companions are mischievous goblins that are hosted in the crevices of the person's mind. The question, then, is, who is the instigator, the imagination or its devilish cohorts? And how diabolical can the latter be if Torres does not give them a theological explanation? This is one of the basic ambiguities of the grotesque mode. And, as we will see, it results from the failure to authorize a single overseer to direct the literary material, so that we often have a divided and contradictory set of aesthetic forces. In all dreams, however, there is a discordant interaction between the human source of creativity and the agents of subversion, whatever the latter's origin. Working with the raw materials of a common external reality, dreamer and dervishes alike twist the uneven strands of a problematic world into a web of deformed images.

The grotesque, then, has a reality and a psychology all its own. It follows its own logic and feelings, and it builds upon a defect, carrying the latter to a logical conclusion by means of images inspired from within. The result is necessarily a deformed configuration, and the language brought to play in verbalizing it acquires a grotesque quality as well. Indeed, in a unique sense, the style of the *Visiones y visitas* is unparalleled in the complexity, range, and obscurity of its lexicon. Here, too, a process of inversion is apparent. The convolutions and rarities of the work's popular speech may remind us of the grammatical structures of *conceptismo*, but they are just the opposite of the latter's remote Latinate vocabulary. If both poles share a common axis, it consists of the richness and inaccessibility of the words and images. Torres' style can, in fact, be described as the esoterica of slang. However, its vulgarity is concentrated in a kind of opposition to cultivated prose. Just as *conceptismo* embodies an idealism by virtue of its metaphysical abstractions, so too does Torres' infratranscendent argot convey the banality of proletarian culture. Rooted in the seamy materialism of common speech, Torres' language descends beneath the anti-Latin idiom of the street, and reaches underground into the hidden roots of a cultist slang.

I have not quoted any examples because what I have said about style will be readily admitted by anyone who has read the *Visiones y visita*s. The book is permeated with words rarely seen in literature, and the effect is just as grotesque as some of the language used by Valle-Inclán. And this is precisely the point. Even though Torres had literary antecedents for his prose, just as he had them for the *visión* as a genre, the uniqueness of his work is due to a process of inversion. The picaresque form, for instance, also produced some passages that were frank, fetid, and overgrown with vulgarisms. But Torres conserves none of the raciness and colour of that popular diction. Instead, he creates a peculiar conceptismo all his own, along the lines of a reverse Gothicism.[9] Like the oratorical excesses of the period, the same self-conscious pomposity is the stylistic rule of the *Visiones y visitas*, except that Torres descends to the lowest level of language. His metaphors are monstrosities of ugliness, his general imagery becomes cancerous in its complex growth, and his scatological references exceed the bounds of good taste, despite their being couched in conceit. In fact, although the visions do manifest humor, this humor is countered by a sense of repugnance in the areas

---

9 The term *goticismo* was used by eighteenth-century writers to designate the florid and mannered conceits so typical of the prose satirized by Padre Isla. See Sebold's edition of *Fray Gerundio de Campazas* (Madrid, Artes Gráficas Ibarra, 1960), III, 35-36, note.

just mentioned, while a vague psychological ambiguity hovers over the work as a whole.

There is one consequence of these inversions in both language and in the generic form of the vision which is directly responsible for the psychological atmosphere. That consequence is the fact that the descriptions are dissociated from their ethical context. There are many reasons for this, the main one being the author's unfeeling stance toward whatever he is describing. In contrast to the traditional moralist, who registers some note of emotional engagement regardless of whether this was positive or negative, Torres' reaction hardly goes beyond derision. He seems to regard his subjects as spectacles and as means of diversion, not as individuals worthy of humane feelings. Torres turns people into objects of laughter and scorn, more to be contemplated for their value as phenomena than recruited for their moral example. Thus, he lacks the affirmative attitude which is implied in any traditional desire to reform. Torres is in fact not so much a moralist, whose position would be one of commitment, as he is a disinterested painter of portraits. Even such reactions as repugnance and condemnation are missing, because he never progresses beyond the stage of a contemplative spectator. In short, Torres never achieves the kind of psychological rapport that would enable him to evaluate a situation in humanistic, and hence ethical, terms.

The result of this detachment shows up in the nature of Torres' distortions. His starting point is generally moralistic in that he selects a particular shortcoming—the ignorance of pharmacists, for example—as the object of his disapproval. Armed with this critical attitude, he invents an individual to personify the defect, conceiving a portrait which is deformed in proportion to the flaw that it embodies. It will be argued, and justifiably, that Torres' characters are drawn from real life, and that in no sense does he invent allegorical figureheads to represent his moral abstractions. My point, however, is not the degree of realism but the intention to distort the latter. The actual rendition of Torres' portrait involves an additional deformation, one which, admittedly, incorporates the author's judgement. Nevertheless, the severity of that judgement is expressed by further exaggeration. And since this involves compounding distortion with distortion, the literary product that emerges simply calls attention to the excesses of technique. The ethical content is overshadowed and goes unnoticed. We are struck, therefore, by the enormities of the portrait over and above the deformed original, and not by the moral judgement which motivated the portrait's execution.

Here, then, is the relationship between Torres' grotesque genre and his prose style. The visionary form and the language used to express it both defeat the ethical purpose which ostensibly motivates them. Sometimes the reason seems to be the author's desire to indulge in verbal play, as in the scene where he is stretched out one night "espoleando al meollo y arreando a la fantasía a fin de poner las mentiras solemnes de mis pataratas astrológicas en la solfa de alguna metáfora apacible" (p. 195). But even this good humoured confession smacks of self-consciousness. Not only is the author's irony directed toward himself, but it affects the content and meaning of his subject matter as well. There is more than mere word play in the progression *meollo-fantasía*. The "solfa de alguna metáfora apacible" bears the promise of a mixture worthy of being confected for its own sake. And in the process, a number of ingredients are introduced which have little to do with moralizing but which add weight and texture to the compound.

Thus, in addition to the details of the grotesque portraits themselves, we find that their verbal medium poses several problems. If it is a writer that is being described, we learn that he is "cara bandujo, con sus tizonazos de cagalar," and "tan pegajoso de humores, que estaba sudando albondiguillas (p. 141). Or else, if the person is a *petimetre*, we are told of his "camisa con sus pinceladas de chanfaina descomida," which makes him "más sucio y más hediondo que cocina frailesca en tiempo de capítulo" (p. 76). The words pile up offensively, like the heaps of cow-dung mentioned so frequently throughout the work. Indeed, there is a huge flow of words that covers each personage with a film of repugnant conceits set in an obscure jargon. What is more, Torres reserves his foulest epithets for the person who is closest to him—the writer: "un rostro-plasta a manera de boñiga picada de escarabajos… nos pareció figura de castillo cagada de moscas" (p. 134).

None of this scatology is either gratuitous or haphazard. It is no accident that the area of scatological references blends into the general imagery, for Torres himself is hopelessly involved in the conditions he describes. It is a part of his sensibility, and while we cannot discuss the biographical implications here, we can at least recognize that his language is more than a reflection of something outside of him. Torres goes beyond the customary picaresque use of scatology as a device for naturalistic detail and humour. His own *meollo-fantasía*, his own preference for prolixity and inverted Gothicism, are the determining factors in his style, rather than the social conditions around him. Undeniably, the environment is often physically distasteful, but the author consistently singles out the "hombre despreciable y casi de los excrementos de la república" (p. 122). This is what he finds to make the best material for his metaphorical mixtures, the *solfa* that takes precedence over the "mentiras solemnes" of the moral container. Torres' awareness is filled with the stench of the decay around him. And it seems that he cannot control the torrent of words which strains to be released from his own mind. Like one of his characters, Torres "padecía diarrea en los sesos" (p. 134).

There is one final factor in this idea that Torres, more than his society, is responsible for the unusual concentration of grotesque images. This is his notion of what the *visión moral* is in terms of imagination and subject matter. Although we must not forget that Torres and his contemporaries were quite aware of the decadent aspects of Spanish life, this does not mean that they were able to translate that awareness into an aesthetic of objective realism. At the same time, the sensibility of the age could not permit Torres the kind of lyrical subjectivism that Jovellanos was to manifest at the end of the century. What did happen, then, was that Torres produced what Sebold has called an "expressionism" in which the social reality is recast in accordance with the author's fleeting subjective impressions. As Sebold puts it in his article on "Torres Villarroel, Quevedo y el Bosco," Torres describes his world "justamente en ese breve momento en que su visión subjetiva descorre la cortina exterior de la realidad y le representa corroídos los cuerpos y las facciones de los transgresores por esa su podre moral."

Although the term "expressionism" in this context raises a number of problems, Sebold's observation is not only accurate, but may be carried still further. It is not just the immoral world which is suddenly glimpsed in all of its deformity, but reality as a whole which impinges its monstrous and decaying self upon Torres' inner faculties. As the product of his society, and as a writer whose understanding of the social order is exhibited in his autobiography, Torres has digested the vast complex of processes and problems within his environment. But since that complex is basically unwholesome to him, it is regurgitated in literary form, and accompanied by images aptly chosen for their power to nauseate the reader with their symbolic stench. We have seen evidence of this in the scatological references, but the fact was not easily recognized by the author himself. Torres' own view of the vision, therefore, gave as much credence to the traditional theory of "inspiration" as it did to the role played by his own faculties.

This view is stated in an extraordinary passage of *La barca de Aqueronte:*

> ¡Algún demonio íncubo empreña a la diabla de mi fantasía, pues la hace parir tamañas monstruosidades! ¡Jesús mil veces sea conmigo y me libre de sueños tan endemoniados! Si es el sueño para todo animal blanda quietud de los sentidos y sabrosa cárcel de los movimientos, ¿cómo para mi es potro de crue!es imaginaciones y quebranto terrible de mis miembros? Si todo hombre vive regalado en las dulces tiranías de esta suspensi6n, ¿cómo yo ni descanso durmiendo, ni gozo serenidades soñando? Sin salir del mecanismo de mi animalidad, conozco cuán vanas son las persuasiones de la filosofía. Yo estudié en ella que los sueños nacen de la revoltosa agitación de los humores y espíritus animales que residen en el cerebro; y que por esta conmoción se obstruyen los tránsitos y conductos comunes a los sentidos externos, y que mezcladas confusamente las especies, salen a danzar a la fantasía los objetos, sobrevestidos de la confusión y el desorden; pero mi cerebro no puede contener tan desagradables especies ni su cabida es habitación de tan monstruosos materiales. (p. 265)

What is immediately noticeable in this statement is the author's tendency to avoid responsibility for the content of his visions. At the beginning, he stresses the notion of impingement: he is victimized by an outside force which takes possession of the mind's creative centre and "activates" it. The image of an impregnating incubus, of course, has sexual overtones of a more serious nature, as we have seen. What is important here is Torres' passive stance, and his receptivity to an external agent. This submissiveness is a metaphorical way of indicating the superior strength of the social world over the individual. Since the inspiration springs from a diabolical source rather than a divine one, we know that the message must be secular, that is, dealing with social reality. Had

Torres intended a moral theme dealing with either heaven or hell, he would have used the traditional prophetic visitation.

In contrast to Torres' evasion of responsibility for the excesses of his dreams, we find an unusual insight into the psychology of imagination. This occurs in the allusion to the "espíritus animales que residen en el cerebro," an idea which he credits to the vanities of philosophy. Torres really accepts this idea, however, despite his disavowal, since he apparently distinguishes between the "mecanismo de mi animalidad" and the higher activities of the mind. But even if he rejects the commonplace theory of humours, his denial of his own capacity for bestial thoughts is unconvincing, especially when the seeds of these thoughts wax fertile within the matrix of his imagination. The fact is that the theory of "humores y espíritus animales" is the best explanation of Torres' appalling imagery. Having assimilated the elements of his decaying world, his literary reconstruction of it obeys a similar pattern of abnormality. At critical moments, "se obstruyen los tránsitos y conductos comunes a los sentidos externos," and his impressions of those social elements seethe in his mind and grow disfigured. When at last they find an outlet, they are conveniently represented as the feverish images of an alien incubus.

Now that we have discussed the details of the grotesque portraits and the theory behind them, let us conclude by considering the portraits as literary paintings in the grotesque manner. Most prominent of the features in this vein is the dehumanization, a fact which ought to cause us some surprise, especially if we define the term in its strictest sense. That is, to dehumanize means, or should mean, the reduction of life to mechanics, men to automatons, and human traits to their analogues in the inanimate world. Thus, the term means something above and beyond the animalizing techniques of earlier centuries. The most important examples of this kind of grotesque are found, of course, in German Romanticism. What is remarkable about Torres' portraits is that they prefigure the stilted personages of that movement without actually having any mechanical models as an influence. In other words, Torres dehumanizes his subjects to the extent that it was possible to do, given his cultural milieu. There is no real mechanization, but there is a full parade of warped and wooden figures: "un hombrecillo entre persona y títere" (p. 168); "un viejo enjuto como hueso de dátil" (p. 158);

'un perillán... con dos dientes paralelos a la nariz, algo mayores que dos ajos lígrimos' p. (77); 'un estantigua tan ordeñado de mofletes, que los carrillos eran dos tetas de diablo' (p. 144). There are many other figures of this type, and while they do not resemble mechanical dolls in any way, they do belong to the same class of puppets, scarecrows, and other stilted reductions of human life so frequent in modern art. In this light, it is interesting to observe how closely Torres relates the notion of dehumanization to his own creative faculties:

> ... el borracho de Morfeo me dejó tullido el espíritu, bozal el alma, atollado el entendimiento, en vacaciones a la memoria y en sábado a la voluntad. Luego que la imaginativa se vió sin pedagogo, empezó a travesear con una tropa de títeres, cucarachas y monicacos que se esconden en la covachuela de mi celebro; y pasando esta desordenada escaramuza a sacar otras figurillas a sus tablas, con orden, concierto y disposición admirable, representaron en el corral de mi chola la comedia que verán los que quisieren atender al sueño que se sigue. (p. 198)

From this statement, several things are apparent. First, Torres' claim that demons inhabit the crevices of his mind is contradicted. As we saw, such a claim suggests an unwillingness to be held responsible for the work's grotesquerie. The above quotation, however, repeats the image of "la covachuela de mi cerebro" without mentioning any outside fomenter in collusion with the imagination. Second, Torres links the grotesque with the theatre, and especially with the *retablos* of puppeteers. There is also a hint that he had the *figurones* and other decadent burlesque types in mind. In other words, the stated origins of the grotesque have more in common with the *comedia* than with the plastic arts. The drama has its visual aspects too, of course, but its literary features make it more directly related to the *visiones* than painting might be. And the third conclusion to be drawn from the passage is that Torres values reason and order much more than he does the disorder of the irrational grotesque. We have already noted a similar attitude in our discussion of animalizations. Now too, he is pleasantly surprised at finding his dehumanized types grouping themselves in an organized manner within his fantasy. Thus, is spite of the lack of harmony in Nature and an equal lack of logic in society, the norm which continues to impress Torres most is the secular one that later was to characterize the Age of Reason.

None of this is to deny the traditionalist mentality which was Torres', and here I would again cite Sebold's article on "las vanidades del mundo" for the proper perspective, especially with regard to Torres' antiquated scientific ideas. At the same time, the portraits are utterly devoid of any Counter-Reformational didacticism which, even by antithesis or negative example, might seek to convey a transcendental truth. Two examples in the dehumanized mode will serve to support this view. The first is the sketch of a "scarecrow" whose face is "todo embadurnado de grietas, verrugas y bigotes; hendido a chirlos, tajaduras y agujeros; y tan horadado de las viruelas, que su cara nos pareció la rejilla de un confesionario" (p. 144). Here, our attention is drawn away from the possibility that this creature might have any emotional or spiritual life. We see instead the correspondence of metallic object and face, and, ironically, the religious allusion fulfills a very uninspiring role. The second portrait is that of a *figurón*, and is perhaps the most effective in the dehumanized group:

> Los brazos eran dos tornillos de lagar, y por las bocamangas del vestido se le venían derritiendo dos muestras de guantero en lugar de manos;... tan hendido de horcajaduras que de medio cuerpo abajo parecía compás de carretero o tijera de aserrador. Su fisonomía era lánguida y sobada como pergamino de entremés; tan magro y descolorido de semblante que a lo lejos parecía tarjeta sin dorar... (p. 205)

The foregoing description is typical not only of Torres' dehumanization, but of his grotesque technique in general. The points of analogy with the inanimate world may often be strained and sometimes far-fetched, but they never fail to remove the scene from its human context. The language, consequently, is bizarre not only because of the Gothicism, but because objects are alluded to that are likely to produce a grotesque effect. Indeed, language supersedes painterly details, and we look in vain for traces of colour in these portraits, as distinguished from the examples cited by Sebold. Quite the contrary, what predominates is the word *descolorido*, a limitation on the eye's experience as severe as the conventional references to spatial relationships—"tablas," "retablo," "circunferencia," and, in one instance, the phrase "cuello cuadrado... vara torcida" (p. 185).

Thus we find that dehumanization means, in addition to mechanical reduction, a loss of realistic dimensions. The *visiones* take place on a level of abstraction that carries the grotesque out of the area of physical deformation and into a realm all its own: "muy pleonasmo de cabeza" (p. 120), "pordiosero de frente" (p. 120), "prólogos de calvo" (pp. 35-36), "flaco como propósito de puta" (p. 158), "conciso de cuerpo, muy lacónico de estatura, súmula de hombre"(p. 66). All of these examples, from the elimination of plastic appeal to the emphasis on abstract description, tend to isolate the formal qualities of the portraits and cause them to stand out. We concentrate less on the forehead, facial angle, and posture of the people in these portraits, and worry more about the images and adjectives that describe them. In short, our reading energy is directed away from the human phenomenon and toward the linguistic apparatus set up to stylize it. In contrast to his method of animalization, Torres has managed to dehumanize by substituting abstract correspondences for the human parts that he is supposed to be describing. It is not simply that these parts lack a human configuration, but that they are denied access to the norms of color and space which define the human dimension.

In conclusion, we may say that the *Visiones y visitas* is a unique work, coming as it does in early eighteenth-century Spain. It is true, of course, that we enjoy the hindsight of historical perspective. But it is equally clear that Torres created neither a wholly moralistic grotesque of the type perfected by Quevedo a century earlier, nor a fantastic grotesque of the kind developed by the Romantics at the end of the century. His literary mode was a type of distortion based on the criteria of human reason and natural order. Because these principles were, at least in this work, central to his thinking, he was able to conceive of a grotesquerie that grew out of the violation of their authority. Thus, while it may be hindsight to note that reason and order were later to become the foundations of secular thinking in the time of Carlos III, it is a plain matter of observation that Torres' grotesque derives its force from the perversion of those future norms in the age of Felipe V. The best evidence of this is found in the author's high esteem of the disciplined harmony to which his creatures submit as they emerge from the caverns of his imagination.

At the same time, there is no reason for denying the moral core of Torres' visions, since it is beyond dispute. I would submit, however, that the *Visiones y visitas* were symptoms of the growing strain that was eventually to divide Spain into two ideological camps. We can recognize this by studying the secularization of the grotesque aesthetic, and this is the point of this chapter.[10] The ends toward which the grotesque was used by Torres no longer had any meaningful relationship to the religious aims of his mentor, Quevedo. None, at least, that can add to the work's literary merit. Instead, the *Visiones y visitas* foreshadowed the attention which certain writers would later give to non-religious matters. In this, Torres approached the position of Feijoo, although there were many differences in outlook, as Sebold has indicated. That is, Feijoo's treatises on miracles, Spanish church history, and para-theological errors had also been secular in their ultimate intention. Torres, while not indifferent to faith or theology, dwelt more on the worldly impact of religious thought than he did on solving religious problems as such. Living in an age of transition, Torres used the framework of tradition for a new kind of social analysis, one which reflected values by means of aesthetic implication. He was a religious moralist in appearance, but the essence of his work prefigured the contradictions and conflicts of the coming Enlightenment. And the grotesque was the best vehicle for the prefiguration of conflict.

In terms of literary history, it would be foolish to seek to uncover traces of an early Romantic grotesque in Torres' remarks about dreams. On the other hand, we must come to grips with the uncontrolled and often tumescent style by which his portraits are outlined. No longer Baroque, this style is cancerous in its growth, and so vulgar that it can-

---

10 It may well be that this grotesque aesthetic is not typical of Torres' works as a whole, and that in fact it does not represent his total personality or general literary style either. As Torres once wrote of himself, he was like a "centauro mixto de pata galana y religioso, ya moral, ya desenfadado, ya místico y ya burlón" (Sebold, ed. cit., ix). However, my purpose is not to characterize the essential Torres nor to generalize on the basis of one work. I have, rather, tried to follow the methods of intellectual and aesthetic history: to identify change and to point out what is new or anticipatory. The fact that Torres' other works (excepting his autobiography) have not survived the test of time is perhaps the best confirmation of this approach.

not be deemed Rococo either. In effect, the language has gotten out of hand, and the author seems in these instances to be ranting in an access of distemper. The symptom—and gigantic symbol—of this malady is his logorrhoea. What is noteworthy about it in terms of the grotesque is how it enhances the latter with its own bizarre character. More fundamentally, however, it suggests the inability which Torres suffered in restraining his bulky material and allowing it to come forth with a normal consistency and proportion.

From the standpoint of the history of aesthetic ideas, this linguistic phenomenon is an early stylistic counterpart of the emotional excess suffered by the Romantics. On the other hand, in terms of intellectual history, it appears to indicate an irrationalism that was incompatible with the growing dependence on secular reason in the eighteenth century. But if we remember that Torres disclaimed responsibility for his grotesque, then the principle of rationalism can still be considered to form part of his avowed value system. His analysis of Spanish society, then, was identical to that of Feijoo, who judged the nation's thinking to be obscured by misconstrued ideas. His method, however, was different, although his irrational aesthetic led to the same conclusion that Feijoo reached through reasoning. And it is here that the *Visiones y visitas* is redeemed as a literary work. Its grotesque portraits reflect the absurdities of the body politic before 1730, but its aesthetic critique upholds the value of reason that was to become the cornerstone of the Enlightenment.[11]

---

11   This study was first published in the *Bulletin of Hispanic Studies*, 45 (1968), 16-37. Reprinted by permission of Liverpool University Press.

4
The Grotesque Before Goya

THE CRUEL, DARK FANTASIES of Goyesque satire, said Baudelaire, were modern in spirit, no longer jovial or gay as in Cervantes' time, but violent, full of the blank horrors of nature, and in love with the ungraspable.[1] We might add that the grotesque in Goya is more a point of departure for Romantic deformations of reality than the culmination of an eighteenth-century grotesque. It is simple enough to recognize the similarities between the Goyesque nightmare and an earlier Spanish tradition. But this relationship was not what a Romantic like Gautier had in mind when he compared the fury and gloom of the *caprichos* with Hoffmann's tales and Delacroix's illustrations for *Faust*. For us to regard Goya in this way as primarily a precursor of Romanticism does not require us to ignore the aspects of moral satire bearing kinship to the satirical sketches of Cadalso, Isla, and Villarroel; and from the grotesque portraits in Villarroel to their antecedents in Gracián and Quevedo is but one short step. However, my assumption for this paper, and I think it is easily proven, is that what attracted Baudelaire and Gautier was the irrational and private vision in Goya. The major aesthetic values of the eighteenth century may have been at work in Goya,

---

[1] "Les Espagnols sont très-bien doués en fait de comique. Ils arrivent vite au cruel, et leurs fantaisies les plus grotesques contiennent souvent quelque chose de sombre" ("De l'essence du rire," *Œuvres complètes*, ed. Y-G Le Dantec et Claude Pichois [Tours: Bibliothèque de la Pleiade, 1961], p. 988). On Goya: "Il unit à la gaieté, à la jovialité, à la satire espagnole du bon temps de Cervantes, un esprit beaucoup plus moderne, ou du moins qui a été beaucoup plus cherché dans le temps moderne, l'amour de l'insaissable, le sentiment des contrastes violents, des épouvantements de la nature et des physionomies humaines étrangement animalisées par les circonstances" ("Quelques caricaturistes étrangers," ibid., p. 1018).

but it was his fantastic cosmology, a world based on subjective symbols, which prompted Baudelaire to speak of "quelque chose de sombre." What enabled French Romantics to distinguish the Goyesque from the Cervantesque, was this deeply irrational factor, rather than any of the subjective components of neo-Aristotelian and eighteenth-century artistic theory.

Nevertheless, Baudelaire did not address himself to the century and a half that separated Goya from Cervantes, nor did he ask what had happened to the grotesque aesthetic during the Enlightenment and earlier. Yet in order to pose the question realistically, without overcomplicating a difficult problem, it is useful to exclude Goya's aesthetics. Therefore I propose that we think of grotesque manifestations independently of Goya, as the function of earlier traditions, and as a mode involving techniques partly governed by taste and partly dictated by the themes themselves. My purpose is to identify the concepts behind that mode, concepts of the grotesque prior to Goya as they appear on the interface between literary practice and the theory of artistic expression in general.

This means dealing with material of a certain kind, while passing over other sorts of material, and since I have gathered a large amount of information on the grotesque in eighteenth-century Spain, I shall outline below what will be omitted. But first let me define what I mean by "grotesque." I use the term in the narrow sense to indicate a particular modality, an expressive manner whose techniques of deliberate distortion are employed for the purpose of creating incongruous configurations. This definition excludes but does not reject the additional implications of the grotesque arising from non-textual considerations. For instance, the psychological ramifications of viewer perception are interesting to reflect upon, and eventually we must join with scholars like Kayser and Clayborough, and ask such questions as whether distorted phenomena arouse a sense of the uncanny or the absurd or the ridiculous. But for the purpose of this essay I wish to present a limited approach that focuses on the imagistic phenomenology of deformation, and especially on those ideas that seem to encourage such deformation. Now here, two kinds of material are available in the eighteenth century. On the one hand we have theoretical discussions of beauty and ugliness, of verisimilitude and inverisimilitude, of the roles of imagination, caprice, and dream. On the other hand we have literary examples of the grotesque. In this second area the instances are too many to digest in an essay of this length. But it is useful to sketch in the range of existing grotesque phenomena in order to have a point of comparison with the concepts that either led to an awareness of distortion or else helped to create a climate of creative freedom.

There are four categories of activity which deviate from Neoclassical norms by exhibiting pure deformation; and if they do not deform reality in the modern sense they constitute exaggerated elements that provoked commentators of the period to censure them with responses like "monstruoso," "extravagante," "delirante," "quimérico," "disparate," "demencia," "disonancia," and similar epithets of varying intensity. One category of grotesque contains the semi-folkloric creations of mass entertainment: the *gigantones* and *máscaras* of street parades whose literary counterpart in low comedy and burlesque ballads include *figurones*, harlequins, and satirical figures or phrases in such works as Luis Salazar y Castro's *Palacio de Momo*,[2] or Francisco Botello's *Historia de las cuevas de Salamanca*, or even some of the poems of Gerardo Lobo. This popular substratum eventually merged with more refined artistic levels, as occurred in Goya's case where he made use of masked figures. A good literary example is *La Serafina*, where the motif of the carnival retains the purity of its popular origins. The scene in this novel creates an at-

---

2 Momus as the god of mockery is referred at this time by Jonathan Swift: "What *Momus* was of old to *Jove*, / The same a Harlequin is *now;* / The former was *buffoon* above / The latter is a *Punch* below" ("The Puppet-Show," *Works* [London, 1766], XIV, 239). The context of Salazar y Castro includes a moralist background: "… se llama monstruo cualquier cosa en la naturaleza deforme, que exceda o falte a lo natural… desviándose de la ley de la naturaleza el hombre en el entender, y obrar, despreciando la razón que la misma naturaleza inspira, es *monstruo*. La naturaleza es arte de Dios en las cosas criadas: (eso en lo físico) es orden de Dios, que ilumina comunicado a la razón, que produce la luz natural: (esto en lo moral) quien se aparta de este orden es monstruo; porque es la ley de la naturaleza, ordenada de su Autor. Esta manda, que del conocimiento del hombre nazca la adoración a sólo Dios, y el amor, el culto, y la obediencia que se le debe; siempre que a esto falta, contraviene a la ley de la naturaleza, y es monstruo moral de sí proprio: desconforma la apariencia con la verdad, parece que forma otra especie de animal sin razón, o su locura… " *(Palacio de Momo* [León de Francia (Madrid) 1714], p. 117).

mosphere that exudes carefree gaiety. The motif contrasts with its counterpart in the Romantic grotesque, where the carnival is exploited for its epistemological delusion, as happens in Espronceda, while in Bécquer the motif appears in the context of spiritual malaise and disillusion.

The second category of grotesque practices, more deformed than the first, concerns moralistic caricature, which also uses popular types for satirical purposes. The grotesque portraits of Torres Villarroel's *Visiones y visitas*, discussed in the preceding chapter, feature character analyses that are meant to be ethical in content but in fact invite attention due to their representational aberrations. Similar effects can be seen in Isla's vignettes, such as the one of Fray Gerundio's mother:

> Como la buena de la Catania abría tanto la boca para pronunciar su *a*, y naturaleza liberal la había proveído de este órgano abundantemente, siendo mujer de un bocado se engullía una pera de donguindo hasta el pezón, quiso su desgracia que se la desencajó la mandíbula inferior tan descompasadamente, que se quedó hecha un mascarón de retablo, viéndosela toda la entrada del esófago y de la traquiarteria, con los conductos salivales, tan clara y distintamente, que el barbero dijo descubría hasta los vasos linfáticos, donde excretaba la respiración.[3]

Isla's extreme caricatures of the archpriest and the flagellant[4] illustrate what Fielding called the "burlesque" in his preface to Joseph Andrews: "an exhibition of what is monstrous and unnatural." Grotesque portraits even appear in moralist literature, where Calderón Altamirano condemns drunkenness by using the composite techniques of Arcimboldo.[5] In all of these caricatures the authors manipulate the

---

3 José Francisco de Isla, *Fray Gerundio de Campazas*, ed. Russell P. Sebold (Madrid: Espasa-Calpe, 1960), I, 117.

4 Ibid., IV, 121-22; I, 82-83.

5 The portrait begins: "Satirizar al ebrioso: La cabellera es de pámpanos: la frente una calabaza: las cejas dos corbillos: los ojos dos uvas gruesas coloradas: las narices espitas, las mejillas adormideras, la boca de tinaja, la barba de azadón, el cuello de cauce, el talle de cuba, las manos como cardos, los pies de pardal, el movimiento de un navío un poco lastre, el cuerpo de botejón, el alma de bota... Tiene la cabeza de pámpanos porque sus pensamientos son racimos. Es la frente una calabaza porque sólo para especies de vino se sirve esta vasija.

plastic surface properties of their subjects while placing ethical or religious defects in a sociological dimension.[6]

Now for the third and fourth groupings of literary examples. In the third category are instances that concentrate within a word or a phrase the entire impact of the distortive process. This is done by the placement of strategic qualifications like "frenético," "monstruo horrendo," "hospital de locos," "mico," "enano," "bufón," "sombras, visiones, fantasmas"—these are some of the references appearing in the *Cartas marruecas*. By the deployment of these lexical devices the author achieves his inframimetic goal. The fourth and final category includes material which in itself is not grotesque but which manifests a sensibility running counter to the Neoclassical values of moderation and order. Later I will have occasion to contrast the rational norms of Luzán's poetics with the grotesque implications of irrational creativity. The point to be made about the fourth category and its sensibility is that both show features of violence and antinatural phenomena. These features not only highlight their own exaggerated contours, but they rupture the unity of the work and become structural dissonances within the harmonic totality. The best illustrations are narrative epic poems like *El Alphonso* and *El Pelayo*, where both Botello and Solís utilize Virgilian episodes in combination with grotto elements, horrible beasts, and sinister magic. These fantastic components have their counterpart in prose fiction—the cave scene in Estrada Nava's *Vida del gran Thebandro español*—and in the pre-Romantic sensibility of Meléndez Valdés, especially in his second *elegía moral* to Jovino, where the atmosphere of macabre, funereal horror culminates in the poet's escape from the ghosts that menace him.

The four categories of literary examples comprise a wide spectrum extending from pure grotesquerie to a mild Romantic phantasmagoria. This range is one of the two major areas which I began by distinguishing in regard to grotesque material in the eighteenth century. The second

---

Ser las cejas corbillos es porque así se llaman los instrumentos que usan los viñaderos," etc. *Opúsculos de oro, virtudes morales cristianas* (Madrid, 1707), pp. 502-03.

6 Add to these the portraits of men and women in *discursos* 49 and 119 of *El Censor* (1781-1787), ed. E. García Pandavenes (Barcelona: Labor, 1972), pp. 99-100, 217; those by Juan Pablo Forner in *Los gramáticos*, ed. J. Jurado (Madrid, 1970), pp. 73-74, 113-14; and to some extent the sketch of the *proyectista* in José Cadalso's *Cartas marruecas*, carta 34.

major area is theoretical: the treatises that fix the rules and standards to be followed in composing literature or creating works in the visual arts. The examples of literary practice form a backdrop against which to place the treatises on literature and painting, a metaphorical horizon making visible whatever protrusions emerge from the artistic norms and ideals of the theorists. These norms of beauty, proportion, and verisimilitude are known and require little comment. They do place restraints on a capricious artist with a strong imagination. Let us recall Luzán's maxim that the basis of poetic beauty is truth, and that truth is beautiful because it is always uniform, regular, and proportioned. In contrast, said Luzán, "la falsedad ostenta siempre la fealdad y la descompostura de las partes que la componen, en las cuales todo es desunión, irregularidad y desproporción."[7] It follows therefore that "lo irregular, lo desordenado y desproporcionado no puede jamás ser agradable ni hermoso en el estado natural de las cosas... consistiendo su belleza en lo vario y uniforme, en lo regular, en lo bien ordenado y proporcionado de sus partes" (I, 118).

Another aspect of this rationalist formulation is its perfectionism, the degree to which it puts the artist under the obligation to press his invention into the service of idealization. As late as 1780 we find Antonio Mengs beginning his treatise with two assertions: first, that we apprehend the beautiful through an intellective act involving our understanding of perfection; and second, that an object is beautiful when it corresponds to the idea we have of its perfect state: "La belleza consiste en la perfección de la materia según nuestras ideas.[8] To aspire to and correspond with perfection is to fulfill the concept of conformity. And conversely, to disconform is to abandon the pursuit of perfection. But when all the parts of an object conform to our idea of a perfect whole, that object appears to be beautiful. Therefore to disconform is to fall from beauty to ugliness, from perfection to imperfection. The question is, what kind of imperfection? If beauty is perfection, it has the quality of proportion. And if an object is ugly, if it is imperfect, then it is disproportioned. But if proportion is congruity, a disproportioned object must be incongruous. Incongruity is that feature of ugliness which proceeds

---

7 *La poética*, ed. L. de Filippo (Barcelona: Selecciones bibliófilas, 1956), I, 120.

8 *Obras de Don Antonio Rafael Mengs*, ed. J. N. de Azara (Madrid, 1780), p.8.

from disproportion. On this point Mengs bears us out by an unusual illustration: "Un niño será feo, si tiene cara de viejo: lo mismo sucederá al hombre que tenga cara de mujer; y la mujer con facciones de hombre no será ciertamente hermosa" (p. 8). The statement addresses itself not simply to ugliness or imperfection, but to the incongruous mixture of qualities. It is the Neoclassical counterpart to the famous warning by Horace in the *Epistle to Pisos*, a warning against hybridization which in Mengs is more subdued because the incongruities are confined to the human species. Nevertheless, the transexual examples are striking, not to say Goyesque.

All of this is to say that while deformation kept appearing erratically in literary practice, the theorists legitimized its existence by recognizing it to be a subject of discussion. They did not sanction ugliness or incongruity, but they called attention to these errors with a consistency that will become apparent. Had they ignored the ugly or reduced its visibility, public awareness of deviant forms might have been weak. But theorists gave negative examples of the ideal by citing the defective. It is true that when Luzán praised Virgil's perfect description of the grotesque Polifemo, his applause was not for the creature itself. Even so, in effect the appearance of Polifemo as a deformed subject was tolerated. From there it was a short step to Arteaga's assertion of the aesthetic pleasure to be found in "esta metamorfosis admirable de feo en hermoso."[9]

Linked to the mythical giant was another horrendous myth from antiquity: Laocoon and the writhing contortions of the serpent. Arteaga was joined in his enthusiasm by Mengs and by Rejón de Silva, who advised young painters to study the sculpted group. Nevertheless, even Arteaga was detained from embracing the full implications of a universal grotesque for all media. Again citing the Polifemo, he noted that while the subject suited poetry, no one could stomach a painting or statue of the giant crushing the bones of Ulysses' companions between his teeth, "ni dejaría de horrorizarse viendo la hedionda y descomunal boca de aquel gigante con un hombre atravesado en medio de ella, y la

---

9 *La belleza ideal*, ed. M. Batllori (Madrid: Espasa-Calpe, 1955), p. 50. At one moment, Arteaga exclaims with relish: "¡Qué cosa, por ejemplo, más asquerosa que la imagen de Polifemo... cuando, después de haberse atracado de trozos de carne humana y vaciado en su vientre dos o tres zaques de vino, se tumba boca arriba en medio de la cueva?" (pp. 35-36).

sanguaza que le ensuciaba" (p. 43). This statement was made prior to Goya's painting of Saturn devouring his child.

The retentive strength of Neoclassical values held these grotesque impulses in check. Where such impulses broke free they produced cracks in the stronghold of ideal beauty, the fortress built upon the foundations of geometrical proportion, rational order, good taste, and the sublime. Compared to the full range of grotesque examples I outlined earlier, preceptual statements like Luzán's and Arteaga's can hardly be said to represent invitations to distort and deform. On the other hand, there is no treatise or manifesto before the twentieth century which invites artists to cultivate incongruity. The fact that a grotesque current runs more strongly through eighteenth-century literature than seventeenth can be ascribed in good measure to the erosion of theoretical authority among the Neoclassical treatise writers. Their very legislation of values such as symmetry and proportion, or the balance of imitation and invention, led to increasing space devoted to the sublimation of ugly qualities by means of the aesthetic process. Even while Spaniards thus defended ideal beauty, they increased their awareness of distortive elements which might subvert that ideal.

One of the best indicators of this progressively wider consciousness is the semantic evolution of the word "grotesco" in Spanish usage. At the beginning of the century, lexicographers barely recognized that "grotesco" had currency. In 1705 Francisco Sobrino defined it in his *Diccionario nuevo de las lenguas española y francesa*, but he gave only the French usage. Under the listing "grotesque" are the synonyms "ridicule," "bizarre," and "extravagant" ("extravagante," "ridículo"). Yet under the Spanish counterpart we find a reference to look elsewhere: "grutesco, ve redículo," and under "redículo" the word "grutesco" does not appear. Even this cross-reference disappears in 1734, when the *Diccionario de Autoridades* reverts to the old Covarrubias definitions involving painting and architecture. These areas now draw more attention than before, and both adjective and noun are listed separately, with related meanings: "imitación de cosas toscas, e incultas, como breñas y grutas... especie de adorno... compuesto de varias hojas, peñascos y otras cosas, como caracoles y otros insectos." Note that value judgments are not implied in these terms, nor any suggestion of the kind of creative activity underlying "imitación." The word "grotesco" is not a concept but a strictly limited category of visual elements compounded artificially but patterned on the natural world.

By the middle of the eighteenth century, "grutesco" becomes associated with the creative act. In 1753 Miravel translates Moreri's *Gran diccionario histórico*, which modifies the information known to Spaniards from Covarrubias by adding a new note: "pequeñas figuras de hombres y animales, que se representan mezcladas de ornatos chiméricos y ridículos." This restores the lost valuation of "ridiculous," while the previous suggestion of imitation is now supplemented by the fantastic quality—chimerical—which is addressed antithetically to the idea of representation. Implicitly the Moreri definition recognizes inverisimilitude to be an acceptable norm of ornamentation for a genre of this kind. The outlines of a concept begin to emerge, but we must not forget that the historical dictionary translated by Miravel is destined for an elite readership, and in any event does not reflect the linguistic reality of the Spanish vocabulary. We may conclude from this that the awareness of the grotesque in the late eighteenth century alternates with a certain indifference to it. In 1780 the abridged one-volume Academy dictionary assumes a conservative role by perpetuating the 1734 definition; that is, it merely repeats the details of insects and snails in painting and architecture. In 1782, however, Forner uses the term "literatura grotesca" without regard to specific ornamentation when he attacks bombastic and ridiculous writing in his *Exequias de la lengua castellana*. Forner's valuative usage combines with the generic meaning in a listing by Terreros y Pando in the 1787 *Diccionario castellano... de ciencias y artes*: "lo que pertenece a gruta, y en la Pintura, Talladura, y Escultura se llama grutesco aquello que trae consigo una especie de fantasía y capricho... También... lo que es extravagante y ridículo." One year later Rejón de Silva places an entry in his *Diccionario de las nobles artes*: "grutesco o brutesco: Véase Follage."[10] And under "Follage" Rejón writes: "Adorno de cogollos, hojas harapadas, sátiros, bichas y otras sabandijas. Llámanse Grutescos, por haberse hallado esta moda en las grutas y subterráneas de Roma; como también Brutescos, por los animales brutos que en él se introducen." The preoccupation with zoomorphic elements, which increases here with the mention of satyrs, finds full expression in 1790 when Isidro Bosarte

---

10 The same cross-listing occurs in Palomino's *Indice de los términos privativos del arte de la pintura, y sus definiciones* of 1724.

quotes Horace's *Epistle to Pisos* condemning "los monstruos biformes, de dos naturalezas incompatibles, en las figuras de los adornos."[11] It was an impossible artistic hypothesis, said Bosarte: "semejante grutesco ni lo habia en Roma, ni en Grecia" (p. 15).

And so we have a philological diachrony in which the ornamentational constant unifies grotesque motifs in the public mind throughout the century. But as semantic changes lead to shifts in emphasis, the grotesque achieves immediacy by its increased repertoire of animalesque forms—even satyrs. And the same philological evolution amplifies the merely descriptive "imitacion" into a more conceptual framework of creative processes: "una especie de fantasía y capricho"—whatever these activities may be.

This brings us logically to a discussion of the terms *capricho* and *fantasía*, two topics broad enough to inspire separate chapters. The issues they raise—problems related to the creative process and the perception of reality—are complicated by still another faculty: the dream. I've already dealt to some degree with the *sueño* in Villarroel (chapter 3), and this need not be repeated. If space allowed me to present all the evidence related to dream, *capricho*, and imagination or *fantasía*, the conclusions that could be drawn might be summarized as follows. All three concepts refer to the phenomenology of irrational expression. They gain prominence in eighteenth-century treatises, after a century of casual references, because their psychological mechanisms pose difficulties for mimetic or Neoclassical rationalism. For example, the hostility to *capricho* can be found as late as 1792, when Valzania deplores the lack of planning in modern buildings, and attacks construction "cuando así la colocación como la expresión depende de un capricho sin fundamento."[12] Even Jovellanos can be shown to be ambivalent about *capricho*, for he makes statements both in support of and against the anti-mimetic quality of caprice in architecture.[13] This ambivalence is shown in the glossary

---

11 *Observaciones sobre las bellas artes* (Madrid, 1790), I, 15-16.

12 *Instituciones de arquitectura* (Madrid, 1792), pp. 118-19.

13 During the same period (1801-8), Jovellanos opposes *capricho* in painting while approving it in architecture: "Porque no debiendo haber en el arte lo que no pueda haber en la naturaleza, los volantes y colgantes de los paños, hechos a capricho, son defectuosos, y siéndolo, no se pueden autorizar con el ejemplo de otros pintores, y menos los movimientos y ondulaciones del dibujo

of usages of the words *capricho / caprichoso* in the next chapter. Examples aside, what arises is a conflict between preceptual respectability and aesthetic modality. Capricious and grotesque practices may not have been respectable according to seventeenth- and eighteenth-century rules, but practiced it was, and in fact esteemed, if the continued popularity of Bosch and Quevedo is any proof.[14] The use of distortion

---

en las figuras, cuya simplicidad es siempre preferible, no tanto porque la buscaron los griegos, cuanto por ser más conforme con la razón del arte, y con la naturaleza, que es su tipo" *(Obras* [Madrid, 1952], II, 158b). "Así es como el artista quiso representar estas bóvedas péndulas en el aire, y es fácil concebir cuán extraña y graciosa será su apariencia, y cuánto gusto y pericia supone la simétrica degradación de estos arcos, que enlazándose por todas partes y en todos sentidos entre tan desiguales muros, producen la más elegante y caprichosa forma" *(Obras,* I [Madrid, 1963], 394a). Jovellanos here changes his mind from the statement of 1785 about the Moorish style in twelfth- and thirteen century architecture: "hasta qué punto puede extraviarse el genio, abandonado a las inspiraciones del capricho" (I, 371b).

14 Bosch is praised by Palomino for "el dibujo intencional, o quimérico... *cuyo ser objetivo sólo está en el entendimiento;* esto es, que no tiene existencia física, y real... tales son los grutescos... cuya semejanza no hay *in rerum Natura,* sino solamente en la idea del artífice, que hace un conjunto de varias naturalezas, para formar un compuesto, cuya existencia repugna; en que fue extremadísimo el Bosco, en sus exquisitos y extravagantes sueños" *(El museo pictórico y escala óptica* [Madrid: Aguilar, 1947], p. 72).

A description of festivities during the War of the Spanish Succession tells of Philip V's return to Madrid after victories at Brihuega and Villaviciosa in 1710: "una célebre, hermosa, y vistosa máscara, con tanta variedad de invenciones que pudiera el Bosco tomar modelos para sus imaginarias ideas, pues era tan raro lo extraño de las orejas que se vieron." Pablo de Montestruich Fernández de Ronderos, *Viaje real del rey... Phelipe Quinto* (Madrid, 1712), p. 227.

Francisco de los Santos is impressed with Bosch's moral, not esthetic, value, and describes the Capilla del Colegio in the Escorial: "Encima de la cornija, sobre la del Entierro de Cristo, esta una original de Gerónimo Bosco, el que fundando en aquel lugar de Isaías, que dice: toda carne es heno, y toda su gloria, como flor del campo; pinta un carro de heno, y sobre el heno, los deleites de la carne, y la Fama y ostentación de su gloria y alteza figurado en unas mujercillas tañendo y la Fama de demonio, con alas y trompeta, que publica su grandeza y regalos. Tiran este carro siete bestias fieras, símbolos de los vicios capitales, y alrededor van siguiéndole los hombres... y al fin todo el anhelo es por alcanzar del heno. Yo confieso que se lee más en esta tabla en un instante para la ense-

is an aesthetic countermode, the undercurrent which gains prestige as concepts of imagination liberate the artist and his subjective impulse to create without regard to rational precepts. Hence the *capricho*, the *disparate*, and the *sueño* which, for example, is sanctioned at the end of Forner's *Exequias*. All these are phenomena in the world of art, although in the world of ordinary discourse they remain just words with a pejorative connotation.

We witness, then, degrees of rational disintegration. Neoclassical beauty is the norm, and deviation is described by value judgments: *extravagancia, monstruo*. These terms may not themselves represent anything grotesque, but they identify the forbidden area of creativity. As Eximeno pointed out in regard to music, "las circunstancias que pueden en nuestra imaginativa alterar la naturaleza de un objeto, son infinitas."[15] For Eximeno it was bad taste which encouraged the imagination to indulge in the infinite capacity for distortion: "el mal gusto consiste en la extravagancia o en la desconformidad de los objetos inventados con los naturales." Disconformity varied, of course: there were degrees of extravagance. For Luzán, as we have seen, the range was limited, whereas for Iriarte the game consisted of irrationalizing the rational to the extent that symmetry itself could begin in burlesque and end in caprice.[16]

Nor does the disintegration of rational values follow a comprehensible chronology. Cracks in the fortress of ideal beauty appear in 1702 in the *entremeses* of Francisco de Castro.[17] In 1717 Palomino dedicates one chapter of *El museo pictórico y escala óptica* to the freakish and marvel-

---

ñanza y desengaño que en otros libros en muchos días" (Antonio Palomino y Francisco de los Santos, *Las ciudades, iglesias y conventos en España* [Londres, 1746] , pp. 104-5).

The same painting is described in detail among others by Gregorio Mayans in the *Arte de pintar* of 1774 (Valencia, 1854), pp. 71-73, in a chapter titled "De la invención" which deals primarily with Bosch. See further footnote 26 and the next to last paragraph of this chapter.

15 *Del origen y reglas de la música* (Madrid, 1796), p. 193

16 "Los juguetes festivos y graciosos, / Compuestos de pasages caprichosos / En el estilo cómico, parlante, / Con un compás simétrico y saltante, / Propio de la burlesca pantomima, /Que al buen humor, y aun a la risa anima" *(La música* [Madrid 1779], p. 37).

17 cf. *Alegría cómica*, 3 vols. (Zaragoza, 1702), especially *Los gigantones, Los burlados de carnestolendas, La fantasma*. The collection *Cómico festejo*, 2

lous aspects of nature and calls it "Prodigios de naturaleza en abono de la pintura" (I, 12). In 1789 Preciado de la Vega publishes a treatise on painting in a format whose central metaphor is stated in the title: *Arcadia pictórica en sueño: Alegoría o poema prosaico*. Yet these same periods produce important formulations on behalf of artistic orthodoxy. Mengs treats the grotesque mode in terms of bad taste while ignoring its historical origins: "se hacían cosas necias, inverosímiles y falsas; y así nació el gusto que llamamos grotesco."[18] Yet even Mengs recognized the aesthetic beauty of mythological creatures: satyrs, fauns, centaurs, tritons (ibid., p. 386). True, he did not classify them among grotesques, but Palomino did just that by grouping them historically as one stylistic occurence among many rather than considering them in terms of good taste: "los grutescos de varios cogollos, hojas, tallos, y cartelas, artificiosa y galanamente compuestas, y otros diferentes adornos, con grifos, sátiros, faunos, silvanos, centauros, bichas y otras varias y exquisitas sabandijas, cuya semejanza no hay in rerum Natura, sino solamente en la idea del artiífice."[19]

The relationship between good taste and imagination presents itself as one key issue, and I will conclude by dealing briefly with the question of whether artists felt obliged to rule their private fancy with the yoke of collective good taste. Was it true, as Capmany suggested, that the abuse of imagination made the artist unable to "distinguir lo miserable de lo suntuoso, lo disforme de lo bello, lo monstruoso de lo regular"?[20] If so, then a paradox seems to have passed unnoticed, for when good taste was neglected, the work "se inunda de extravagancias *ingeniosamente* monstruosas" (p. 12, italics mine). Capmany's complaint was not against imaginative activity altogether, only against the failure to distinguish between "la bella imaginación siempre natural" and "la falsa, la que amontona cosas incompatibles" (p. 20). So-called false imagination

---

vols. (Madrid, 1742) contains the aforementioned plus *Las brujas, Los locos* and *Hombre mujer*.

18 "Reflexiones... sobre la belleza y gusto en la pintura," *Obras* (Madrid, 1780), p. 23; see too pp. 253-54. Mengs's disdain is attributed by his biographer Azara to his noble character. Highmindedness made Mengs averse to plebeian art forms: "No podía sufrir la música bufa, ni las bambochadas, y mucho menos los ridículos grotescos o arabescos" of such depraved standards (p. xxvii).

19 *el museo pictórico...* , p. 72.
20 *Filosofía de la elocuencia* (Madrid, 1777), p. 10.

was termed "la fantástica, la que pinta objetos que no tienen analogía ni verosimilitud" (p. 20).[21]

Capmany's position recognized the grotesque mode and rejected it, and he was joined by theoreticians in other media: music, architecture, painting. In tracts like the 1780 *Reglas generales para que una composición de música sea perfecta* by Pedro Aranaz y Vives,[22] and the 1783 *Arquitectura civil* by Benito Bails, the instinctive quality of individual taste was understood. Bails wrote of modern building design that "ni el capricho ni el acaso deben influir en este gusto" (p.625). As for music, Aranaz allowed for innovation provided that no incongruity entered to create "ridiculez y extravagancia." Bails argued that mixture was monstrosity, and that it caused "disparidad, y quita(r) la unidad tan esencial en la decoración de los edificios. Mucho mayor monstruosidad será todavía, si, conforme se ve en algunas obras modernas, se juntaren el orden dórico y jónico con el toscano" (p. 748). Unless the architect avoided "todos los atavíos que fuesen obras del capricho," unless he followed "la debida proporción" and the principle of unity, he would undermine "el buen gusto" whose "principal guía es la razón" (pp. 614, 625). But what about taste itself? Was it not already and inherently subjective? Bails understood the instinctive character of taste without dismissing it. Because individual taste had irrational origins, it could disfigure art. To imitate was one matter, to imitate capriciously was quite another. Yet if the steady hand of reasoned intelligence controlled private taste, then the true and difficult beauty of nature could be captured: "cuánto es difícil imitar la bella naturaleza, tan fácil es desfigurarla; es más fácil pintar ballenas gigantes, que no héroes" (p. 625).

The regulation of taste, therefore, was not isolated. It participated in the activities of imitation, and to imitate was to hold certain models of reality above patterns of taste. In other words, mimesis preceded individual preference and sometimes the mimetic impulse even aspired to universal representationalism. A particular manifestation of reality

---

21 Capmany's attack was aimed at rhetorical as well as pictorial grotesque ornamentation: "¡Que profusión! i que prodigalidad de... hipérboles colosales, de alegorías monstruosas... de frases afiligranadas... y de otros mil rasgos y follajes que no tienen nombre ni número" (pp. 12-13).

22 First published by Mariano Soriano Fuertes in *Historia de la música española* (Madrid: Martin y Salazar, 1856), III, 237, 238, 241.

could be improved and raised to a higher and universal or ideal level. For example, Mayans insisted that the artist's duty was to correct the defects found in the model chosen from nature: "si hay hombres tuertos, como el Rey Antígono, la pintura hermosamente ideal los representa con ojos vivos y sanos."[23] Horrible elements were of no interest; in fact, duty required their elimination. Yet Mayans viewed the spectacle of a horrible object in art within the context of aesthetic pleasure. That is, at least sometimes he conceded aesthetic experience to be more positive than the contemplation of a horrible object in its uncorrected form. Did this mean that Mayans was attracted by the grotesque in an ambiguous way? At the least, his chapter on "invención" deals kindly with Bosch's paintings. The prestige of Bosch had been established early in the century when Palomino praised his "exquisitos y extravagantes sueños."[24] Mayans subscribed to that position while adding the qualification that "si en algo mereció ser culpado, fue en ser demasiadamente ingenioso, y fecundo en amontonar representaciones simbólicas y de raras figuras." These excesses appear beyond reproach, perhaps because Bosch is welcomed for the religious content of his paintings. Whatever the reason, he is defended as a unique if bizarre painter. Among the nonrational categories of invention, only his finds acceptance, and it contrasts with the inferior work of another painter, Eustrapio, whose "invención" is "ridiculamente caprichosa." That is, Bosch's invention is "extravagantemente ingeniosa y maravillosa." His "disparate" "se compone de partes en sí perfectas al parecer, amontonadas disparatadamente, pero en realidad inventadas, y con relación al intento de la pintura seriamente ingeniosa." Even so, the grotesque representation and the idiosyncratic taste are exceptions for Mayans, not examples to be followed. Elsewhere his treatise places the subject of imitation and "imaginación interior" under a strong rationalistic idealization. Orthodoxy still dominates, yet an outstanding proponent of grotesque vision survives.

The following conclusions may be derived from my discussion: that the forms of distorted invention could be seen as alternatives to rational art; that these distortions arose from an extravagant use of imagination in the absence of rational controls; and that such practices were unde-

---

23 Mayans, *Arte de pintar*, p. 17.
24 See above, note 16. The next quotations are from Mengs, *Obras*, pp. 73 and 69.

sirable because they sprang from individual capriciousness rather than from collectively approved rules of taste and imitation. Those grotesque practices did exist nevertheless; they were widespread throughout the century; and on occasion they were combatted ambiguously by the very treatises that aimed at purging them. The grotesque before Goya not only existed in spite of its antagonists, but it survived in part by virtue of the attention paid to it.[25]

---

25 This study was first published in *Eighteenth-Century Culture*. Vol. 5. Ed. R. Rosbottom. Madison: Univ. Wisconsin Press, 1976, 185-201. Reprinted by permission of the American Society for Eighteenth-Century Studies.

5
"Capricho" / "Caprichoso": A Glossary of Eighteenth-Century Usages

IN THE CHAPTER ON Gracián's "moral grotesque," I cited the author's awareness of Bosch's paintings ("aora entiendo su capricho"). The fact that Gracián felt an affinity with an aesthetic category, the *capricho*, related to the grotesque highlights the kinship and difference between the two sub-genres.[1] During the sixteenth and seventeenth centuries, the word *capricho* carried nuances of both whim and distortion. However, usage of the word did not gain wide currency until the eighteenth century. For example, here is a late seventeenth-century usage in the context of artistic creativity: "Símbolo de los Sueños fue el capricho de Pintor célebre en un quadro, que por un lado se descubría un León, por otro una Aguila, y mirándole de medio a medio se veía un Hombre."[2] The overtones of bizarre creative choice outweigh the strange juxtapositions, making the term "caprice" more appropriate than "grotesque." These nuances largely disappeared when the word entered the vocabulary of general discourse at the beginning of the eighteenth century.

Nevertheless, the convergence of *capricho* and *grotesco* as aesthetic categories warrants a Glossary that constructs a spectrum of meanings attached to *capricho* during the eighteenth century, when the term reached its apogee in Spain. As a word and an aesthetic concept, *capricho* occurred in the written language with a frequency matched only by its numerous associations. Locutions which used the word varied in their connotation and in their implied value judgment. Yet we find modern scholars tending to construe *capricho* narrowly by linking it regularly

---

1 See Covarrubias' definition in the chapter on Gracián, note 12.
2 Félix de Lucio Espinosa, *Ocios morales* [1691], 2ª ed. [Zaragoza 1693], p. 18.

to Goya. At the end of the century, however, the Academy offered this definition in the third edition of the *Diccionario de la lengua castellana* (Madrid, 1791):

> [1] El concepto, ó idea que alguno forma fuera de las reglas ordinarias y comunes, y las mas veces sin fundamento, ni razón. *Judicium, sententia a communi rerum ordine aliena, dissona.* 2. En las obras de poesía, música y pintura es lo que se executa por la fuerza del ingenio más que por la observancia de las reglas del arte. HOMBRE DE CAPRICHO. El que tiene ideas singulares, y las dice con novedad y agudeza. Algunas veces se toma por lo mismo que CAPRICHUDO. *Ingenio praestans, summa vi mentis pollens, vel difficilis, tenax.*

The most common usages of *capricho* and *caprichoso* were pejorative in denoting the idea of whim or passing fancy. But writers also employed these words approvingly to describe imaginative elements in painting and architecture. By the time Goya used *capricho* to designate his series of engravings, the term had a history of semantic diversity. It is important to chart this philological synchrony in the eighteenth century for several reasons. Because of Goya's generic usage of *capricho*, the word has come to bear the limited nuances of caricature and extravagance. Yet his contemporaries distinguished between the engravings' content and the meaning of *capricho* as a classification.[3] Antecedents like the *capricci* of Callot and Tiepolo almost certainly provided Goya with a generic term. And earlier contexts cited by Edith Helman should also be considered:

> "Parece compuesta de caput y hecho, como si dixera hecho de propia cabeza." *[Diccionario de Autoridades]*... el pensamiento nuevo de los pintores originales a quienes comparaba [Carducci] con cabras,

---

3 A good example occurs in the *Diario de Madrid* of April 17, 1795, announcing a "Colección de cuatro estampas de caprichos, bien iluminadas y grabadas al aguafuerte" and containing the following: "el buen humor andaluz, la petimetra en el prado, la castañera madrilena y la naranjera murciana. Consta que estos caprichos que recuerdan los cartones para tapices tienen poco que ver con las estampas caprichosas que preparaba Goya al mismo tiempo" (E. Helman, *Trasmundo de Goya* [Madrid, 1963J, p. 39).

"porque van por los caminos de las dificultades inventando nuevos conceptos y pensando altamente, fuera de los usados y comunes; por sendas nuevas buscan por montes y valles, a costa de mucho trabajo nuevo pasto para alimentarse, lo que no hacen las ovejas, que siempre siguen al manso, a quienes son comparados los copiadores."[4]

Furthermore, there is no evidence here or later in this glossary that either *capricho* or *caprichoso* signified madness, delusion, or grotesque distortion in any degree.

These implications had disappeared as the eighteenth century unfolded and the word entered the vocabulary of general discourse. This Glossary will demonstrate the word's varied usage by selecting texts dealing with different subject matter: poetry, fiction, moralist tracts, philosophical and historical prose, treatises on painting, architecture, and poetics. In the light of these contexts, the "charged" implications of Goya's use of *capricho* become defused. It is particularly difficult to concur with Edith Helman's interpretation of Goya's meaning in his well-known letter to Bernardo de Iriarte (see item 1.9).

Professor Helman identifies *capricho* with *libre fantasía* and calls them both the creative faculty which produces monsters, citing Goya's nervous depression and the supernatural horror of his work as her justification.[5] She then refers to the advertisement of the *Caprichos* in the *Diario de Madrid* (see item IV, 11) which describes the human mind as "obscurecida y confusa por la falta de ilustración o acalorada por el desenfreno de las pasiones." Professor Helman then adds gratuitously, "esto es, en *caprichos.*" Assuming this to be true, the term seems to refer to a *product* of mind rather than a faculty creating such a product. Yet further on she concludes that "la libre fantasia o *capricho* es, pues, la fuente de la originalidad del artista, así como causa de aberraciones mentales." Now she is again speaking of a faculty, which in any event

---

4 Helman, *Trasmundo*, pp. 168-69.

5 *Jovellanos y Goya* (Madrid, 1970). All quotations are from pp. 146-47. This repeats Professor Helman's earlier interpretation of the announcement in the *Diario de Madrid:* "Por 'asuntos caprichosos,' Goya quería decir asuntos inventados por la fantasía, o sea, por el capricho, y no copiados ni de la naturaleza ni de otras obras… " *(Trasmundo*, p. 46).

is not identifiable with the imagination.[6] The confused dual meaning of *capricho* as creative power and the act or result of creativity is confirmed by this Glossary. But there is no evidence for identifying *capricho* with *fantasía*, nor for asserting that either one causes mental aberrations. Professor Helman insists on the point, however, by a reference to the *Noches lúgubres*, where the hero disinters his dead mistress:

> "Cadalso emplea *capricho* en este último sentido [como causa de aberraciones mentales]." Despite her inference, the word *capricho* does not appear in the passage cited,[7] and to the contrary, the Glossary shows Cadalso to employ the word elsewhere in a quite ordinary sense (see item V, 4-6).

If we turn to aesthetic sources of the period to find support for a strictly facultative interpretation, we are frustrated. The only aesthetician cited is Arteaga, who uses *capricho* in both senses, as faculty and product, but never in the context of uncontrolled passion or demented imagination (see items I,6, V,15). He speaks of love's power to dominate *fantasía*, "hasta formarse un ídolo mental que la provoque al delirio. Todo es exagerado, todo es más alla de lo natural, todo es ilusión."[8] *Capricho* would seem to be a likely word in this context, but it is absent here and in other highly irrational situations mentioned by Arteaga: one case observed to be "extravagante" (p. 109), and two others where creations are either "disparates" (p. 123) or "extrañezas inventadas por los poetas" (p. 124).

A contextual glossary therefore becomes the only method of dispelling misconceptions while restoring the semantic ramifications to their

---

[6] Elsewhere, Professor Helman negates her position by citing *El Censor*, which "ensalza la sátira porque habla a la imaginación, pintando al vicioso con tanta expresión que consigue efectos no dados a la simple persuasión, por lo cual incita a los filósofos a que 'empleen su pincel en trazar el retrato de tantas costumbres apoyadas sobre la moda, sobre el capricho...'" (*Trasmundo*, pp. 72-73). Similarly, *Capricho* 77 is explained this way by the Prado manuscript: "La fortuna dirige la fiesta y distribuye los papeles, según la inconstancia de sus caprichos" (*Trasmundo*, p. 240).

[7] I use Edith Helman's edition of *Noches lúgubres* (Madrid, 1968), p. 115, which is cited by her.

[8] *La belleza ideal*, ed. A. Batllori (Madrid, 1955), p. 108.

proper perspective. Broadly speaking *capricho / caprichoso* had meanings which fell into six discernible categories:

I. AN ASPECT OF THE PSYCHOLOGY OF CREATIVE ACTIVITY: that factor in the inventive mechanism which complements the will and imagination or else which works independently of them. An irrational psychological force, unsystematic and not bound by rules of art. Consequently, a detrimental impulse producing a defective result. *Capricho* refers also to the defective product itself: a mental form created by illusion. Neither an idea nor all image, it arises independently of intellect and sense perception.

II. A CONCEPT GOVERNING DESIGN: one of several motivating concepts referring to artistic principles that fix the standards of design. A haphazard agent or impulse in the post-psychological phase of the creative process. Denoting excessive freedom. Without method or prior plan. *Capricho* stimulates corresponding erraticisms in the work of art.

III. AN AESTHETIC QUALITY OF ART: a feature of composition exhibiting oddness in its *invención*. Antic without being ridiculous or absurd. Causing wonder through peculiar or fantastic effects. In music, disorder and agitation. In architecture, a haphazard and multiform spatial arrangement; a pleasing and irregular mixture of conventional and unexpected forms. A design graceful in its exception to rules.

IV. A SYNONYM FOR GENERAL IRRATIONALITY AND EXTRAVAGANCE: foolish, absurd, without basis in experiential reality. Fantastic in origin and opposed to system. Playful but patternless, lacking substance or weight; aimless divergence in the midst of intricate movement. Resulting from private impulse, an unpredictable force void of purpose or significance.

V. WHIM, FANCY, QUIRK: a fickle and faddish desire, especially among women. A sudden, unmotivated change of mind, a momentary wish. A strange or odd event. Luck or chance. A quirk in fortune.

VI. EMOTIONAL TONALITY: lighthearted, lively, festive, gay. Having an improbable, illusory quality.

These clusters of meaning are actually macrodefinitions, each one a synthesis of all the connotations pertaining to the category defined. No single example in the Glossary can illustrate the macrodefinition. Rather, the total meaning of a category constitutes a composite of individual meanings. In other words, the synthesized definition unifies all examples of a category, but only part of that unified statement will fit a given example.

Chronology appears to be a minor factor in the development of meaning, although the Glossary is arranged chronologically. Similarly, no significant pattern of distribution can be found in the pejorative usages of *capricho*, either by date of usage or relative to a particular subject or context. Consequently the most useful method of organizing the Glossary seems to me to be through a system of connotative categories. Study of usages in their full context reveals that significant meaning, both denotative and implied by context, can be differentiated into the six categories described above. The Glossary follows this arrangement. Each category bears a general semantic heading. Examples are listed with italicized English definitions preceding the Spanish text. Where appropriate, each example is accompanied by a paraphrase and gloss. For the sake of convenience the bibliographical sources follow in the text, instead of in footnotes.

It may not be amiss to conclude with a statistical observation. The examples listed by no means comprise an exhaustive lexicon of usages. But I am satisfied that they differentiate the semantic connotations of *capricho* sufficiently. If this chapter digresses from the purely grotesque, it both illuminates an aesthetic distinction and offers a provisional compilation until such time as a lexicographer assembles a numerically greater list of locutions. Such a registry may not soon be produced. But it will provide a useful measure for testing the quantitative implications of this Glossary. For instance, the number of entries dealing with the plastic arts is higher than the total for literature. Does this mean that *capricho* was more visual than verbal as a concept? How did architecture compare with painting? Music with poetry? What rates of incidence obtained for contexts involving women or clothing in comparison to the arts? In short, just how specialized or commonplace was this word? While the Glossary is more than just a sampling of a century, it cannot provide the basis for conclusions that could be reached more soundly by means of statistical information. The Glossary's conceptual evidence, however, will gain little from further quantification.[9]

---

9 The research for much of this chapter was supported by a grant from the Rackham Foundation.

Glossary

I. An Aspect of the Psychology of Creative Activity

1.1 1715. *A form arising independently of sensory perception and intellect. Neither an idea nor an image, but a shape created by illusion.* "...en una de las telas, o túnicas, de que se organizan los ojos, que llaman la retina, se imprimen las imágenes de los objetos, para que el sentido forme el acto de visión: sin omitir las ideas, y caprichos, que en las ilusiones del sueño representa en la fantasía, tan artificiosa; y (a el parecer) realmente, que parece verdad; como cada uno lo experimenta." (Antonio Palomino, *El museo pictórico y escala óptica* [Madrid:Aguilar, 1947], p. 303. The passage is paraphrased by P. Bartolomé Alcázar in his *censura*, p. 15.)

1.2 1742. *A strange conception or unusual foreplan.* Praise for the execution and theme of a religious painting about the resurrection done by Francisco Collantes: "cosa maravillosa; donde se ven muchos cadáveres salir de los sepulcros; otros a medio vestir los huesos de carne; otros ya enteramente resucitados, que es cierto es un cuadro de extremado capricho y habilidad." (Antonio Palomino, *Las vidas de los pintores*, in *El museo pictórico y escala óptica* [Madrid: Aguilar, 1947], pp. 882-83.)

1.3 1783. *A factor in the creative mechanism which contrasts with and complements the will.* As distinct from uniform rules for exterior architectural design, the individual wishes of each owner may be accommodated. The architect will take "particular cuidado en la forma exterior de sus edificios, dejando al arbitrio y capricho de los particulares las fachadas de sus casas." He may abandon the area of conscious decision for the free play of caprice, here a psychological impulse not subject to acts of will. (Benito Bails, *Arquitectura civil* [Madrid, 1783], p. 738.)

1.4 1785. *A detrimental creative impulse.* Arabic influence on architectural styles of the 12th and 13th centuries merit criticism: "... hasta qué punto puede extraviarse el genio, abandonado a las inspiraciones del capricho... " (Gaspar Melchor de Jovellanos, *Obras*, I, BAE, Vol. 46 [Madrid, 1963], 371b.)

1.5 1785. *An irrational creative force.* Apropos of the emergence of the "estilo gótico" from the Moorish style: "Pero criado una vez el arte, la razón no hizo más que perfeccionarle, sin perder de vista su modelo, y cuando el capricho le usurpó este oficio, ya no volvió a consultar con la naturaleza ni con la razón, sino que huyó de entrambas para seguir libremente sus ilusiones." (Gaspar Melchor de Jovellanos *Obras*, I BAE, Vol. 46 [Madrid, 1963], 383a.)

1.6 1789. *A defective product of the imagination; the faculty producing that defect.* Nowhere in Arteaga's aesthetics is *capricho* used in the sense of ridiculous or extravagant, a frequent meaning for his contemporaries. Given his numerous rebukes of the ridiculous in art, his vocabulary is remarkably restricted and consistent: "hace reír con lo extravagante de su descripción" *(La belleza ideal* [Madrid: Espasa-Calpe, 1955], p. 140); "caer en afectación y en extravagancias" (p. 46); "Todo es exagerado, todo es mas allá de lo natural, todo es ilusión... Lo más extravagante de todo es que... " (pp. 108-09); "si viésemos al viento convertido en un hombre a caballo que pasea por el mar, la imagen nos parecería no sólo extravagante, sino ridícula" (p. 38). Even where the work of wild fancy and imagination is the subject, *capricho* is not mentioned: "otras mil extrañezas inventadas por los poetas... lo mas portentoso y extravagante que puede concebir la imaginación" (p. 124); la desreglada fantasía del falso profeta Mahoma, y de otras invenciones semejantes" (p. 123).

These examples serve as points of reference to contrast with Arteaga's two distinct usages of *capricho*. The everyday meaning of a "passing whim" is given below (V.15). The aesthetic meaning relates to the imagination and its activities, which stimulate the production of artistically and morally faithful representations of nature. Disconformity with the principles of imitation and good taste is a fall from ideal beauty to personal vision. To heed those impulses of imagination which are insubordinate to the dictates of imitative good taste is to encourage imperfection in form and value. Imagination is a faculty which artists may enlist into the service of ideal beauty, but Arteaga recognizes its darker, individual mechanisms:

(a) "los artífices de mal gusto, que prefieren los caprichos de su imaginación a las perfecciones físicas y morales que hallarían en la naturaleza si las buscasen" (pp. 52-53). The precise relationship of *capricho* to imagination is unclear, since the term appears once again in the context of coefficient creative faculties. Apropos of the word *ideal*, Arteaga explains how it is wrongly understood:

(b) "no como una deducción del entendimiento, sacada de las ideas sensibles," "sino como un producto infundado del capricho o de la fantasía" (p. 147). Two separate faculties appear to exist, each capable of participating in the creative act without reference to rational or sensorial activity.

1.7 1789. *Not guided by systematic rules.* Contrary to artists who commendably submit to the continuity of systematic practices, others "sólo se guían sin otras reglas que las que les dicta el capricho." This rebuke comes not for ignoring rules altogether, since "el fuego caprichoso del Bernini" is applauded, but for following them haphazardly without prior determination. The inference may also be that one recognizes the proper rules to follow as those already formulated and ready to be invoked in a coherent fashion, whereas *capricho* has its own set of rules of undetermined and spontaneous character. (Francisco Preciado de la Vega. *Arcadia pictórica en sueño* [Madrid, 1789], p. 104.)

1.8 1792. *A psychological force in the creative mechanism.* Whether by choice or involuntarily, architects arc stirred by a mistaken force into making stylistic errors: "movidos los arquitectos de éste que con toda su razón se puede llamar capricho, han dejado el dentellón sin cortar aun estando talladas las molduras circulares." (Francisco Antonio Valzania, *Instituciones de arquitectura* [Madrid, 1792], p. 100.)

1.9 1794. *A creative source functioning parallel to inventiveness.* "Para ocupar la imaginación mortificada en la consideración de mis males y para resarcir, en parte, los grandes dispendios que me han ocasionado, me dediqué a pintar un juego de cuadros de gabinete en que he logrado hacer observaciones a que regularmente no dan lugar las oras encargadas y en que el capricho y la invención no tienen ensanche." (Francisco de Goya, *Carta* to Bernardo de Iriarte, January 4, 1794. Quoted by Edith Helman, *Jovellanos y Goya* [Madrid: Taurus, 1970], p. 142.)

1.10 (undated). *A faculty in the creative mechanism.* The capability for conceiving and making concrete some mental form or figment is suggested by the title of a work by Francisco López Salcedo, *Despertador a la moda y soñolienta idea de capricho dormido, que entre sueños eseribe la pluma de…*

II. A Concept that Governs Design

II.1 1715. *A concept or motivation prior to the creative act.* One index of terminology in painting lists *capricho* without definition, referring to another term: "véase *Concepto.*" Under *Concepto:* "La idea, o dibujo intencional, que forma el pintor, que inventa, antes de llegarlo a delinear. Y así, llámase *bueno,* o *mal concepto,* segun es el capricho de lo inventado." Elsewhere, a reference speaks of Apeles' compositions done "con ingenioso capricho." (Antonio Palomino, "Índice de los términos privativos del arte de la pintura," *El museo pictórico y escala óptica* [Madrid: Aguilar, 1947], pp. 1149, 1167. Repeated by Francisco Martínez, *Prontuario artístico* [Madrid, 1788], p. 64.)

 II.2 1715. *Exhibiting qualities of conception and design.* An allusion to a Roman palace records approvingly "un follaje, o grutesco de excelente capricho, y gusto." The nature of *grutesco,* with its fantastic and spontaneous whimsicality, determines the meaning of *capricho* here. The grotesque is a fickle or playful floral abstraction embodying an abandoned movement which typifies capriciousness. But beyond this design and how it is conceived, *capricho* enters the aesthetic process itself. It comprises a valuative category on a par with taste. Just as the created work conforms to recognized standards of artistic taste, so does it also achieve excellence in its caprice. (Antonio Palomino, *El museo pictórico y escala óptica* [Madrid: Aguilar, 1947], p. 233.)

 II.3 1737. *An impression or model which gives shape to a work.* Regardless of whether the artist's inventiveness is realistic or highly imaginative, *capricho* must remain within the bounds of verisimilitude: "Y como de la icástica es objeto la verdad; así de la fantástica lo es la ficción; al modo que la pintura, representa algún hombre como es, lo que propiamente se llama retratar, o lo forma de su idea y capricho, según lo verosímil." (Ignacio de Luzán, *La poética,* ed. L. di Filippo, [Barcelona, 1956], I, 67. The text is used by Celedonio N. Arce y Cacho in *Conversaciones sobre la escultura* [Pamplona, 1786], pp. 364-65.)

 II.4 1783. *A factor influencing the norms of a creative act.* The negative influence of *capricho* derives from its inconstancy, an irregularity which contradicts the norms governing beauty. If the beautiful emerges from the imitation of nature, the reason is that the artist adheres to good taste: "ni el capricho, ni el acaso deben influir en este gusto; fúndase en leyes constantes que nos dicta la naturaleza para que conozcamos y gocemos lo bello." When creative elements like good taste have measurable standards of participation, they must not be subverted by unknown variables. (Benito Bails, *Arquitectura civil* [Madrid, 1783], p. 625.)

 II.5 1792. *An impulse void of prior method or plan.* A principal defect of modern building construction is poor or insufficient planning. A well formulated program will bear favorable results, although "bien al contrario sucede, cuando así la colocación como la expresión depende de un capricho sin fundamento, porque privan a la arquitectura de la majestad y elegancia que le es debida." No procedure is justifiable when it substitutes an impromptu vehicle of expression for thoughtful planning. (Francisco Antonio Valzania, *Instituciones de arquitectura* [Madrid, 1792], pp. 118-19.)

II.6 1801. *A haphazard, impulsive urge in the creative act, with its corresponding erratic results in the work.* The artist meets with disapproval when he obeys private impulse to the detriment of imitative norms:

"Porque no debiendo haber en el arte lo que no puede haber en la naturaleza, los volantes y colgantes de los paños, hechos a capricho, son defectuosos, y siéndolo, no se pueden autorizar con el ejemplo de otros pintores, y menos los movimientos y ondulaciones del dibujo en las figuras, cuya simplicidad es siempre preferible, no tanto porque la buscaron los griegos, cuanto por ser más conforme con la razón del arte, y con la naturaleza, que es su tipo." This summarizes the contrast between *capricho* on the one hand, and mimeticism, reason, and nature on the other. (Gaspar Melchor de Jovellanos, *Obras*, II, BAE, Vol. 50 [Madrid, 1952], 158b.)

III. An Aesthetic Quality of Art

III.1 1715. *Conceived oddly. A conception producing a strange or unusual effect.* The technique of *pintura lignaria* uses bits of wood glued to the artifact or drawing, and one such case was "bien singular, de extraña, y bien peregrina arquitectura, y distribución caprichosa; de senos y cajones, con la historia del hijo pródigo, ejecutada en los tableros con embutidos de madera." The manner of distribution could not have been "haphazard" in the twentieth-century sense, since the design had both a concept and a purpose behind it. What is *caprichosa* is the quality of distribution, whose character produces the specifically *peregrina* or bizarre effect. The nature of the design itself shows a peculiar conception. (Antonio Palomino, *El museo pictórico y escala óptica* [Madrid: Aguilar, 1947], p. 82.)

III.2 1715. *Producing wonder regardless of intention.* The adjective *caprichoso* is used in a positive sense during a discussion of natural wonders which, it is suggested, may be of interest to artists:

(a) rocks in the form of fish, one stone among them so detailed that it revealed mouth, eyes, "y otras menudencias, tan puntuales, que admiran; y habilitado con unas aletillas, y cola de oro, parece un delfín, muy caprichoso." (Antonio Palomino, *El museo pictórico y escala óptica* [Madrid: Aguilar, 1947], p. 296.)

(b) "otras piedras, que, dado el pulimento, se ven unas ciudadelas, y edificios, de muy caprichosa, y artificiosa composición." (Palomino, pp. 296-97)

(c) these accidental forms exist without regard to artistic purpose, their charm consisting of the unexpected or fanciful nature of their existence: "Y además de esto, no es de omitir la variedad hermosa de los manchados jaspes, donde se ven muy artificiosos caprichos." (Palomino, p.297)

III.3 1737. *Unexpectedly fantastic but pleasing in effect due to the imagination.* "La fantasía, pues, del poeta, recorriendo allá dentro sus imágenes simples y naturales, y juntando algunas de ellas por la semejanza, relación y proporción que entre ellas descubre, forma una nueva caprichosa imagen, que por ser toda obra de la fantasía del poeta la llamamos imagen fantástica artificial." (Ignacio de Luzán, *La poética*, ed. L. di Filippo [Barcelona, 1956], I, 162-63.)

III.4 1774. *A quality of inventiveness, antic without being ridiculous or absurd.* "La invención, o es propia, como la de Miguel Angel Bonarrota, o loablemente extraña, como la de José de Ledesma, o ridiculamente caprichosa, como la que refiere Claudiano, libro I, contra Eustrapio, o extravagantemente ingeniosa y maravillosa, como la de Gerónimo Bosco, a cuyas pinturas llaman *los disparates de Bosque* [sic], porque se compone de partes en sí perfectas al parecer, amontonadas disparatadamente, pero en realidad inventadas, y con relación al intento de la pintura seriamente ingeniosa, digna de saberse y admirarse." (Gregorio Mayáns y Siscar, *Arte de pintar* [1774] [Valencia, 1854], p. 69.)

III.5 1779. *Of a disordered and agitated character.* For intensely emotional moments in music, the irregularity of spontaneous effects is recommended. Whereas tranquil intervals require conscious uniformity of measure, "no es justo / Observar estudiada simetría / En la turbada agitación del susto. / Bien al contrario, el caprichoso gusto / Contratiempos emplea, y suspensiones, / Haciendo que alternadas se subsigan / Figuras de diversas duraciones, / Que sin orden se sueltan, o se ligan." (Tomás de Iriarte, *La música* [Madrid, 1779], pp. 46-47.)

III.6 1782. *The product of whim or impulse.* "Cierto poeta /... cuyos caprichos / antes que puedan / ponerse en limpio / ya en los teatros / son aplaudidos." (Tomás de Iriarte, "La berruga, el lobanillo y la corcova," *Poesías,* ed. A. Navarro González [Madrid: Espasa-Calpe, 1963], p. 102.)

III.7 1782-92. *A pleasing quality of conception or design.* "La parte de la escultura entre sus delicados adornos es sin duda de un mérito sobresaliente, tanto en las medallas que corren a lo largo del gran zócalo sobre que descansa el primer cuerpo, cuanto en las pilastras que comparten de arriba abajo la fachada con grotescos de graciosa invención y capricho, uno y otro trabajado con el mayor gusto y prolijidad." (Gaspar Melchor de Jovellanos, *Obras,* II, BAE, Vol. 50 [Madrid, 1952], 277a.)

III.8 1788. *Producing disorder.* Style, defined as the particular manner in which artists execute their work, is affected adversely in the works of Churriguera, Herrera, and Donoso: "el desarreglado estilo en los últimos tiempos por los caprichos de los más modernos, especialmente por el Borrumino... y entre nosotros, por los Herrera, Donoso y Churriguera." (Diego Antonio Rejón de Silva, *Diccionario de las nobles artes* [Segovia, 1788], pp. 102-03.)

III.9 1797. *A haphazard, multiform spatial arrangement.* Pleasing effects may stem from uncontrolled factors influencing spatial disposition: "según se condensan y apiñan, o se clarean y entreabren las nubes de mil formas caprichosas, que sirve de diadema o de turbante a sus gigantadas cumbres [de los Pirineos]." (José Mor de Fuentes, *La Serafina,* ed. I. M. Gil [Zaragoza, 1959], p. 89.)

III.10 1797. *A composition of confused variety.* "... por un lado la selva inmediata, y por el otro la vertiente contrapuesta, esmaltada en caprichoso realce, de rocas, arroyuelos, cortijos, y praderías... " (José Mor de Fuentes, *La Serafina,* ed. 1. M. Gil [Zaragoza, 1959], p. 152.)

III.11 1805. *Irregular and odd.* "... así por sus proporciones como por su nueva, extraña y caprichosa forma, es del más gracioso efecto y ennoblece considerablemente el edificio." (Gaspar Melchor de Jovellanos, *Obras,* V, BAE, Vol. 87 [Madrid, 1956], 363a.)

III.12 1805. *A pleasing mixture of conventional and unexpected effects in architecture.* The plan to combine anticipated and unexpected elements in the same structure produces an aesthetic experience of unconventional and capricious character: "Las bóvedas de la galería alta siguen la misma degradación en proporciones más reducidas... y de este modo completo el caprichoso designio de agradar con la hermosura y sorprender con la osadía y aparente ligereza de su obra." (Gaspar Melchor de Jovellanos, *Obras*, I, BAE, Vol. 46 [Madrid, 1963], 394a.)

III.13 1805. *Pleasingly irregular in architectural form.* As a countermeasure to the good and necessary linear symmetry of architectural interiors, a capricious element introduces pleasant spatial variety: "Así es como el artista quiso representar estas bóvedas péndulas en el aire, y es fácil concebir cuán extraña y graciosa será su apariencia, y cuánto gusto y pericia supone la simétrica degradación de estos arcos, que enlazándose por todas partes y en todos sentidos entre tan desiguales muros, producen la más elegante y caprichosa forma." (Gaspar Melchor de Jovellanos, *Obras*, I, BAE, Vol. 46 [Madrid, 1963], 394a.)

III.14 (undated). *A graceful breaking of rules.* "No hablo de la fachada de Santa María... ni de otras obras semejantes, donde todo es capricho, todo superfluidad." (Leandro Fernández de Moratín, *Obras póstumas* [Madrid, 1867], I, 566.) Cited by Morcuende, who gives this definition: "Obra de arte, en que el ingenio rompe, con cierta gracia o buen gusto, la observancia de las reglas." (Federico Ruiz Morcuende, *Vocabulario de* D. *Leandro Fernández de Moratín* [Madrid: Academia Española, 1945, 1.)

IV. A Synonym for General Irrationality and Extravagance

IV.1 1743. *Related to the fantastic and contrary to system.* Capricho is antithetical to both skill and careful method, as in the counterposition of "razón y arte" against "antojo y capricho." In view of these pejorative implications, the designer must be careful to "justificar que no todo el sistema que propusiere es fantástico o de puro capricho." (Martín Sarmiento, *Sistema de los adornos de escultura del nuevo Real Palacio de Madrid* [1743-1747], in F. J. Sánchez Cantón, *Opúsculos gallegos sobre bellas artes de los siglos XVII y XVIII* [Compostela, 1956], pp. 211, 200.)

IV.2 1745. *Foolish and absurd, without basis in experiential reality.* It is proper to disparage nonsense seemingly derived from erudition or philosophical reflection: "Antes bien ostentara un tedioso desprecio de todas ellas [noticias], diciendo que no son otra cosa que sueños o caprichos disparatados, con que los extranjeros quieren engaitar las gentes." The context here is pragmatic skepticism. Taking a moderate position between philosophical rationalism and religious dogmatism, the intellectual refuses to tolerate irrational expression in discourse. He balances dogmatic faith against free scientific inquiry, and rejects both popular and learned superstition. Here the notion of *capricho* involves an irrational creation divorced from experience in the waking world. The nuance of *caprichos* is attenuated, since it requires reinforcement by the adjective *disparatados*. (Benito Jerónimo Feijoo, *Obras escogidas*, I, BAE, Vol. 56 [Madrid, 1952], 545a.)

IV.3 1779. *Lacking weight or substance*. The expressive content or meaning in music is poorly served by caprice, although other effects may be achieved brilliantly: "Hay quien tampoco adorna los finales / Con frívolos caprichos, o fermatas, / En que la voz, preciada de instrumento, / La expresión sacrifica al lucimiento." (Tomás de Iriarte, *La música* [Madrid, 1779], p. 89.)

IV.4 1779. *Aimless divergence in music having patternless yet intricate movement*. The work's structure does not conform to a central principle but meanders with a progressively diminishing coherence of movement and with increasingly more divergent modulations: "Primero del Cretense laberinto / Los rodeos y senos contaría, / Que el progreso distinto / Con que de su principio se extravía / La caprichosa voz, cuando modula, / Y por sonoros trámites circula." (Tomás de Iriarte, *La música* [Madrid, 1779], pp. 11-12.)

IV.5 1783. *The opposite of necessity, an unpredictable, erratic force*. "[Hay] en todo orden de arquitectura las partes esenciales, distinguiéndolas de las que ha introducido la necesidad, o añadido el capricho." (Benito Bails, *Arquitectura civil* [Madrid, 1783], p. 678.)

IV.6 1785. *Empty of purpose or significance*. "La escultura del ornato arabesco era del todo insignificante, pues no permitiendo el Alcorán esculpir ningún viviente, se dieron los árabes a inventar lazos y figuras de puro capricho, sin objeto ni significación alguna." (Gaspar Melchor de Jovellanos, *Obras*, I, BAE, Vol. 46 [Madrid, 1963], 385b.)

IV.7 1787. *Playful and fantastic*. One attribute of the grotesque mode in painting and sculpture is "aquello que trae consigo una especie de fantasía y capricho"; "lo que es extravagante y ridículo." (Esteban Terreros y Pando, *Diccionario castellano con las voces de ciencias y artes y sus correspondientes de las tres lenguas francesa, latina e italiana* [Madrid, 1787], II, 242.)

IV.8 1792. *Private, impulsive wish*. In the political context of the rational, public good: "... este tribunal, que dictaba leyes al universo,

veneró por leyes los más disparatados caprichos de los emperadores."
A reference to the Roman Senate. (León de Arroyal, *Cartas económico-políticas*, ed. J. Caso González [Oviedo: Universidad de Oviedo, 1971], p. 153.)

 IV.9 1797. *Contrasting with sober truth.* Goya's engraving titled "Idioma universal" or "Autor soñando" bears the description: "Su intento sólo es desterrar vulgaridades perjudiciales y perpetuar con esta obra de caprichos el testimonio sólido de la verdad."

 IV.10 1797. *Complicated yet neither serious nor to the point.* "...vas a oír de refresco cierto cuentecillo un si-es-no-es largo de talle, y viene a ser, dejándonos ya de aparatos caprichosos y burlescos, en su legítima y desnuda sencillez, del tenor siguiente... " (José Mor de Fuentes, *La Serafina*, ed. I. M. Gil [Zaragoza, 1959], p. 184.)

 IV.11 1799. *Irrational and extravagant.* The well-known advertisement of Goya's "colección de estampas de asuntos caprichosos, inventadas y grabadas al agua fuerte" offers little direct semantic meaning. The contextual information surrounding this quotation characterizes "asuntos caprichosos" as social "extravagancias y desaciertos." Human confusion, unenlightened deeds, and a mind "acalorada con el desenfreno de las pasiones" all serve as subject matter. Therefore the artist responds with comparable irrationality: the material encourages "la fantasía del artífice" and awakens his sense of "el ridículo." *(Diario de Madrid,* February 6, 1799.)

V. WHIM, FANCY, QUIRK

V.1 1737. *Momentary whim.* Dramatists produce plays, "ya cómicos, o ya mixtos de cómico y trágico, sin razón y sin arte, guiándose los poetas por su capricho, por la costumbre, por la imitación, o por el gusto de los autores de compañias cómicas." (Ignacio de Luzán, *La poética*, ed. L. di Filippo [Barcelona, 1956], II, 319.)

 V.2 1761. *Luck or chance....*" en este ejercicio de los postes tiene más parte el capricho y la ociosidad que la virtud." (Manuel Lanz de Casafonda, *Diálogos de Chindulza*, ed. F. Aguilar Piñal [Oviedo: Universidad de Oviedo, 1972], p. 100.)

 V.3 1761. *A sudden, undiscerning whim.* "... tantas historias inútiles y fabulosas, escritas sin nervio, sin elocuencia, y sin el menor discernimiento y crítica, siguiendo los historiadores su imaginación y capricho." (Manuel Lanz de Casafonda, *Diálogos de Chindulza*, ed. F. Aguilar Pinal [Oviedo:Universidad de Oviedo, 1972], p. 57.)

V.4 1774-78. *Personal whim or product of such whim.* "... figuras que tuve por capricho de algún pintor demente." (José Cadalso, *Cartas marruecas*, ed. L. Dupuis and N. Glendinning [London:Tamesis, 1966], p. 50 *[carta 13].*)

V.5 1774-78. *Sudden whim and changing fancy.*
(a) "... son infinitos los caprichos de la moda." (José Cadalso, *Cartas marruecas*, ed. L. Dupuis and N. Glendinning [London: Tamesis, 1966], p. 167 *[carta 76].*)
(b) "...el poderoso así colocado no puede dispensar los empleos y dignidades según su capricho ni voluntad, sino según su mérito." (Cadalso, p. 121 *[carta 55].*)
(c) "... este comercio siempre será dañoso a España, pues la empobrece y la esclaviza al capricho de la industria extranjera." (Cadalso, p. 96 *[carta 41].*)

V.6 1774-78. *Unexpected changes and quirks in fortune.*
(a) "Hermanos nos hace un superior destino, corrigiendo los caprichos de la suerte... " (José Cadalso, *Noches lúgubres*, ed. N. Glendinning [Madrid: Espasa-Calpe, 1961], p. 64.)
(b) "Aquí me tienes, fortuna, tercera vez expuesto a tus caprichos." (Cadalso, *Noches*, p. 61.)
(c) "Los caprichos de la fortuna le son indiferentes." (José Cadalso, *Cartas marruecas*, ed. L. Dupuis and N. Glendinning [London: Tamesis, 1966], p. 118 *[carta 53].*)
(d) "... voy a exponerme a los caprichos de la fortuna y a los de los hombres, aun más caprichosos que ella." (Cadalso, p. 159 *[carta 70].*)

V.7 1779. *A preference or inclination.* Non-intellective processes like perception, habitual action, or special inclination arc not susceptible to ordinary judgments of meaning: "Si es propiedad interna del sonido, / Si es costumbre, o capricho del oído, / El juicio filosófico lo duda." (Tomás de Iriarte, *La música* [Madrid, 1779], p. 15.)

V.8 1781. *Female whim.* "Anarda la bella / Tenía un amigo / Con quien consultaba / Todos sus caprichos; / Colores de moda, / Más o menos vivos, / Plumas, sombrerete..." (Félix María Samaniego, "La hermosa y el espejo," *Fábulas*, ed. E. Jareño [Madrid: Castalia, 1969], p.205.)

V.9 1782. *Strange or odd phenomenon.* "Salía de su cajón / aquel ridículo bicho; / y el ave, desde el balcón, / le dijo: '¡Raro capricho!' " (Tomas de Iriarte, "El guacamayo y la marmota," *Poesías,* ed. A. Navarro González [Madrid: Espasa-Calpe, 1963], p. 49.)

V.10 1785. *Quirk of fortune.* "... ¿de dónde vino el gusto de este ociosísimo ornato? Es preciso buscarle un origen o en la necesidad o en el capricho; y no teniéndole en la primera, debemos atribuirle al segundo, y rastrear la razón que le inspiró." (Gaspar Melchor de Jovellanos, *Obras,* I, BAE, Vol. 46 [Madrid, 1963], 384a.)

V.11 1785. *Unmotivated change of mind.* Vehement criticism is made of the work of Jose Churriguera, Pedro de Ribera, and other "delirantes" responsible for "esta depravación" consisting of "el arte de soñar a ojos abiertos": "dado todo el mundo a imitar, a inventar, a disparatar, en una palabra; perdida la vergüenza, y puestos en crédito la arbitrariedad y el capricho, ¿cuál es el límite que podían reconocer los ignorantes profesores?" (Gaspar Melchor de Jovellanos, *Obras,* I, BAE, Vol. 46 [Madrid, 1963], 387b.)

V.12 1785. *Ignorant, destructive fancy.* "Privados de conocimientos matemáticos, ignorantes de los principios de su profesión, y entregados a su solo capricho, violaban a porfía todas las máximas de la razón y el gusto." (Gaspar Melchor de Jovellanos, *Obras,* I, BAE, Vol. 46 [Madrid, 1963], 372b.)

V.13 1787. *Inconstant in love.* "Hay Adonis que se inclina / a una Venus caprichosa, / engañosa, desdeñosa, / que si ayer le miró fina, / hoy le envía a pasear." (Tomás de Iriarte, *Poesías,* ed. A. Navarro González [Madrid: Espasa-Calpe, 1963}, pp. 127-28.)

V.14 1787. *Abrupt feeling in love.* The stable and tranquil love of pastoral idyll contrasts with modern love: "Caprichos, celos, sustos, desvelos, / riñas, mudanzas, / desconfianzas, / ficción y enojos, / son el amor de moda / que gozan otros." (Tomás de Iriarte, *Poesías,* ed. A. Navarro González [Madrid:Espasa-Calpe, 1963], p. 123.)

V.15 1789. *Feminine whim.* A woman stirs her lover's feelings, "ya encendiéndole con rabiosos celos... ya acibarándole sus fugitivas y momentáneas dulzuras con las veleidades, caprichos e inconsecuencias tan frecuentes en las hermosas." (Esteban de Arteaga, *La belleza ideal,* ed. M. Batllori [Madrid: Espasa-Calpe, 1955], p. 112.)

V.16 1796. *A faddish desire or vagary among women.* Mutability is one trait of bad taste, and a chief agent of mutability is caprice. This idea may be set in the context of women's fashions, in order to illustrate how objects are distorted by a variety of extravagant devices: "... y como esta alteración se puede hacer de infinitas maneras, las modas de las mujeres son tan mudables como sus caprichos." (Antonio Eximeno, *Del origen y reglas de la música* [Madrid, 1796], p. 193.)

V.17 1797. *Feminine whim.*
(a) "... los caprichos que gobiernan de continuo a todas las mujeres." (José Mor de Fuentes, *La Serafina*, ed. I.M. Gil [Zaragoza, 1959], p. 83.)
(b) "¿Te parece, señora, / Que por tu rostro bello, / En dándote el capricho / Ha de venir corriendo / El numen a servirte?" (Mor, p. 61.)
(c) "... pero al cabo es mujer, y el principio novelesco de mi trato con Serafina le habrá hecho títere, como dicen, y se le puede haber encaprichado de tal modo, que desecharía por lograr este personaje tan adocenado, muchos Apolos." (Mor, p. 54.)

V.18 1805. *Whim or fancy.* Apropos of cultivated fields and their "graciosa simetría": "Sus líneas tiradas en diferentes direcciones, que la situación y calidad de las tierras o el capricho de sus dueños determinan, se encuentran y se cruzan por todas partes y en todos sentidos, y alejan el fastidio de la unformidad." (Gaspar Melchor de Jovellanos, *Obras*, V, BAE, Vol. 87 [Madrid, 1956], 347b-348a.)

V.19 (undated). *Strong wish or fancy.* Morcuende defines the following examples as "antojo, deseo vehemente":
(a) "Este capricho enseña /Que en lances tan urgentes / Excesos imprudentes / Se deben evitar." (Leandro Fernández de Moratín, *Obras póstumas* [Madrid, 1867], I, 102.)
(b) "Hablando en general, me pareció bien todo lo que es adorno... los asuntos de arquitectura, de un género caprichoso y extravagante, sin conexión ni belleza." (Moratín, p. 363.)
(c) "Todo es caprichoso y nuevo, todo compuesto de preciosos mármoles y recargado de adornos." (Moratin, p. 525.)
(d) "Después que se apartaron los artífices de la imitación de lo antiguo, no hicieron otra cosa que extrañezas caprichosas." (Moratín, p. 566.)
(Federico Ruiz Morcuende, *Vocabulario de D. Leandro Fernández de Moratín* [Madrid: Academia Española, 1945], 1.)

VI. Emotional Tonality
VI.1 1779. *A lighthearted feelong, festive and amusing.*

(a) The extremes of psychological tonality in music and dance form the polarity of solemn and carefree emotions: "la marcha grave / la giga caprichosa." (Tomás de Iriarte, *La música*. [Madrid, 1779], p. 110.)

(b) Works rendered with humorous liveliness use playful rhythms and light style: "Los juguetes festivos y graciosos, / Compuestos de pasajes caprichosos / En el estilo cómico, parlante, / Con un compás simétrico y saltante, / Propio de la burlesca pantomima, / Que al buen humor, y aun a la risa anima," (Iriarte, p. 37.)

VI.2 1787. *Lively and gay....*" el diestro ruiseñor / con caprichoso canto / alegra al labrador." (Tomás de Iriarte, *Poesías*, ed. A. Navarro González [Madrid:Espasa-Calpe, 1963], p. 117.)

VI.3 1805. *Having an improbable, illusory character.* In a singularly unrealistic state of mind, Jovellanos tells of an "ilusión" in which he can almost hear imagined sounds and detect unreal effects: "no se puede mirar de parte alguna sin que hiera fuertemente la imaginación y despierte en ella las ideas más caprichosas. Alguna vez, al volver de mis paseos solitarios, mirándole [la tenebrosa caverna], a la dudosa luz del crepúsculo, cortar el altísimo horizonte, se me figura ver un castillo encantado, salido de repente de las entrañas de la tierra, tal como aquellos que la vehemente imaginación de Ariosto hacía salir." (Gaspar Melchor de Jovellanos, *Obras*, I, BAE, Vol. 46 [Madrid, 1963, 398b.)[10]

---

10 This study was first published in *Hispanic Review* 44(1976), 239-255. Reprinted by permission of the University of Pennylvania Press.

6
Larra's Nightmare

THE UNIQUE FEATURE OF Larra's grotesque involves his psychological involvement with the literary form that he practices. He cultivates the satirical essay, a distortive genre by definition, in which personal sentiment additionally distorts the social and political material that provides his subject matter. While Larra's imagination is certainly at work, it contrasts with the more fantastic fictional narratives and poetry discussed elsewhere in this book, a fantasy that lends itself more easily to grotesque images. In Larra, a troubled state of mind governs his articles and sketches, which themselves portray a conflicted society that edges toward its own imbalance. Where the grotesque manifests itself, it originates in the stresses placed upon caricature by an emotionally unstable author. The resulting images are not so blatantly deformed as they are, say, in Gracián or Torres Villarroel. But they are perhaps more subtle in that they reflect the faualt lines of psychobiographical and political realms. This interplay, in order to be verablized, has literary recourse to perceptual devices and psychological metaphors that deform both the events observed and the authorial persona.

My approach to Larra and his grotesquerie should be placed in the contrasting context of traditional scholarship. With increasing exaggeration, Larra became the hero of Leftist scholars from 1900 to the end of the Francoist era in 1975. His reputation reflected growing idealization, particularly in the 1960s and early 1970s, both in the literary world and in some scholarly circles.[1] When writers like Azorín and Baroja marched

---

[1] A "revolutionary" Larra whose suicide is a positive refusal of a political situation rather than a negative political inadaptability is portrayed by C. Alonso in "Larra y Espronceda: Dos liberales impacientes," *Literatura y poder. España 1834-1868* (Madrid: Editor Alberto Corazón, 1971), pp. 15-55. A similar view holds that the suicide was "una profesión final de dignidad," and that

to Larra's graveside and paid homage to his memory in 1901, everyone understood that a group of intense young men were eager to find a hero in their moment of need. But even as they fantasied the impassioned Larra as the supreme symbol of national tragedy, they recognized and spoke of his paradoxes and faults. Then later, during the Civil War, Communist Party member Cernuda wrote a commemorative poem on the anniversary of Larra's death in 1937, speaking only of his virtues and using them to denounce the Fascist effort to suffocate freedom.[2] The outcry against intellectual stiflement continued thereafter among such Leftist writers as Juan Goytisolo, who singled out Larra's position as a "committed" writer. He praised not only Larra's moral honesty in dealing with censorship but also his efforts to "promover una cultura nacional autenticamente popular."[3] Goytisolo did not document his opinion about a popular national culture, and I believe it to be false. But the view did coincide with Seco Serrano's historical positioning of Larra among the precursors of "La toma de conciencia de la clase obrera y los partidos políticos de la era isabelina."[4] Here too the documentation was weak, and it belonged to that segment of Larra scholarship which tends to exalt its subject.

There is also a realistic group of scholars—Tarr, Ullman, Varela, Escobar—who have written on Larra objectively without sacrificing their sympathy for him. But it should be possible to approach Larra from a perspective other than those which seek biographical or political information, stylistic analysis, and literary sources. A contextual study making Larra visible in his aesthetic dimension can provide a focus to correct the exaggerations already mentioned. By examining the grotesque aesthetic in relation to Larra's self-image and his social values, we may raise (if not answer) psychological questions whose thrust can

---

Larra, as a "diabólico perturbador de la paz de espíritu del buen burgués," maintained an "actitud dignísima ante un mundo que se le hunde." Manuel Lloris, "Larra o la dignidad," *Hispanic Review*, XXXVIII (1970), 184, 187, 193.

2 Bearing the title "A Larra con unas violetas," the poem includes these verses: "Escribir en España no es llorar, es morir, Porque muere la inspiración envuelta en humo, Cuando no va su llama libre en pos del aire." Luis Cernuda, *La realidad y el deseo* (1924-1962) (México: Tezontle, 1964), p. 142.

3 *El furgón de cola* (Paris: Ruedo Ibérico, 1967), p. 15.

4 In *La revolución de 1868. Historia, pensamiento, literatura*. Selección de Clara E. Lida e Iris M. Zavala (New York: Las Americas, 1970), pp. 25-48.

drive home the modernity of his writings more convincingly than his alleged revolutionism does. When the psychobiography of this liberal and bourgeois writer one day appears, his life and works will be revealing for their contradictions and for the incompatibility between his unconscious prejudices and his political ideas.

In fact, if Larra's voice is more authentic today than it ever was, the reason is due not to the sincerity mentioned by Goytisolo, but to the modern ring of his ironic hypocrisy. His articles are full of deliberate inhibitions, and behind his humor lie a number of class fears which betray his vulnerability as a committed journalist. He was a progressive who knew how to be extremely moderate. And by holding to his moderation against the *exaltados* he experienced a certain ineffectiveness that many of us are familiar with today, and which in fact is the political impotence of all intellectuals who find themselves in the democratic opposition.[5]

---

5 I follow Pierre Ullman in using the term "progressive," which he contrasts with "moderate." It is of course accurate to identify the two factions of liberalism as *progresista* and *moderno* during the ministry of Martínez de la Rosa, as distinct from *exaltado* and *moderado* during the Triennium. But when the *progresistas* themselves divide into extremists and moderates (i.e., *mendizabalistas* and the Isturiz clique), these distinctions lose their usefulness for the historical problem of liberalism vs. revolutionism. Modern Leftists view Larra as a strong progressive tending toward the masses but restrained by inhibitory scruples. I see Larra as a moderate defined by his inhibitions and falling back upon his middleclass center of gravity. Ullman would doubtless disagree with me, since he compares Larra with Blanco White, who criticized Jovellanos and the moderates in 1812. Yet Ullman introduces two kinds of evidence in his excellent description of the liberal dilemma in Spain from the French Terror and the War of Independence to the Junta Central of 1812, the Triennium, and the 1830's. On the one hand, Larra "perceived the ineluctability" of progressives turning into fanatical *exaltados* while moderates evolved into "advocates of stagnation." In this light, Larra's suicide becomes the only solution. On the other hand, he was prepared for "political compromise" as a member of parliament and had "stanched his satirical vein." Not only had "Fígaro sensed that this leftist rebellion against a Liberal regime had set a terrible precedent," but he published his articles in "ultra-Moderate newspapers." See *Mariano de Larra and Spanish Political Rhetoric* (Madison: The University of Wisconsin Press, 1971), pp. 30-34. The question remains as to the political significance of Larra's suicide (quite apart from its link to his love life). Does it signify his inability to be either an extremist or a moderate? If he could not be an extremist,

Larra did of course believe in reform, but he was far from a devotee of the people's revolution. It can be demonstrated that he literally shrank from the masses, as indeed in general he disliked being touched physically. He complained about the censor, but he managed to survive quite nicely under official censorship, including Mendizábal's. He watched ministers come and go, but confined his criticism to social generalities instead of specific political or economic programs. This is why, until recently, literary historians used to call him a *costumbrista* and, perhaps worse, a man of no true party due to his "esquiva naturaleza."[6] His good social manners as an upper bourgeois led him to avoid dealing *ad hominem* in print, and he often tried to curry favor with his readers. Finally, as a disappointed politician and a desperate lover, he decided that the charade of living was no longer worthwhile.

Larra left a legacy, however, of articles and sketches that demonstrate how conscious he was of his duplicity. After 1833, when Fernando VII died, and especially after the fall of Zea Bermúdez, he lived in a state of compressed rage that he vented in a variety of violent ways: through sarcasm, in savage caricature, in grotesque episodes, by literary self-mutilation, and finally by suicide. These mechanisms turn Larra into a fascinating specimen from the standpoint of liberalism's classic failure in Spain. And when we consider the diminished effectiveness of liberal politics in democratic societies today, we may regard Larra as the most relevant writer of Spain's 19th century.

I. Political Nightmare and the Grotesque Aesthetic

Not only did Larra participate in the social carnival of his age, but he perceived it as a "pesadilla política." This was true as much for the last months of his life as for the first months of the Fígaro period and the regime of Martínez de la Rosa. In November and December of 1836 Larra published three of the four articles termed by Ullman the famous tetralogy of pessimistic essays. These personal texts are well known for their lugubrious and macabre elements, normally taken to prefigure Larra's death as well as the destructive nature of Spanish politics. In "El

---

then his moderation motivated the suicide. And if indeed he was a moderate, the act prevented him from becoming a conservative like Jovellanos.

6 Julio Nombela's opinion in 1908, cited by Ullman and contested in part (p. 66).

día de difuntos de 1836" the spectacle of Madrid as a vast graveyard extracted from Larra a frightened shout: "Fuera, exclamé, la horrible pesadilla, fuera!"[7] One month later, in "Horas de invierno," he used the same metaphor: "Escribir en Madrid es llorar, es buscar voz sin encontrarla, como en una pesadilla abrumadora y violenta" (II, 290-91). The next day the subtitle "Delirio filosófico" served to characterize "La Nochebuena de 1836." During these final months, Larra represented his reality as a bad dream, filled with absurdity and madness. He stratified his perception of reality, superimposing private desperation upon public conflict.

But these were not the first occasions that Larra the *persona* or social critic, and the existential man had responded to crises with the metaphor of nightmare. During his residence in Paris in 1835 he composed the satire "Cuasi" and subtitled it "Pesadilla política." He also composed—in French, no less—a lyrical monologue, later translated, which symptomized his loneliness and alienation, his street wanderings where

> me ardía la cabeza; mis cabellos revueltos descubrían mi frente pálida y agitada; sentía pesar sobre mí una mano de hierro que me oprimía... Era mi patria entera que se apoyaba sobre mí... Era la fiebre, y tras la fiebre la pesadilla (IV, 331).

Still earlier, in 1834, a more objective Larra recalled the recent panic during the cholera epidemic in Madrid: "Fue una pesadilla la que se apoderó de los espíritus" (IV, 335). And so we find with each step backward in Larra's career, that his increasing objectivity and greater emotional stability before 1835 still did not exclude the nightmare metaphor from his consciousness. In 1833 he ridiculed the Carlist position by describing the traveller in "Nadie pase sin hablar al portero" as someone who "creía que soñaba y que luchaba con una de aquellas pesadillas, en que uno se figura haber caído en poder de osos" (I, 294). And again in 1833, "en medio de mi pesadilla" (I, 315) he reviewed the history of Spanish liberalism and wondered "si fue realidad lo del año 20 o pesadilla, si fue obra de sonámbulos lo del 23, o verdadero candilazo de moro encantado" (I, 312). In other words, the intermittently nightmarish final four years of Larra's life deepened their stratification across

---

7   *Obras,* ed. Carlos Seco Serrano (Madrid: Biblioteca de Autores Españoles, 1960), II, 282. All references are to this edition.

the sociopolitical level and, increasingly after 1835, in the substratum of personal experience. Chiefly for this reason he embellished the structure of reality with appropriate images of distortion. The result promoted, as he intended, the vigorous condemnation of social manners. But the imagery indicated as well that Larra sensed the inevitable sham of his own role in the mascarade, although he acted it out with the decency of a sensitive liberal. In this way he exposed not only social absurdity, but also the incongruity of his own divided self through the medium of thin disguises and unconscious slips.

This interpretation of a self-contemplating Larra, of a journalist compromised by his bourgeois inhibitions, will not be popular among scholars, but can be documented only by entering into digression. Let it suffice to point out his snobbishness, his allusions to food and clothes, his changes in pseudonyms which amount to a heteronymic compulsion, his insomnia, his boyish insecurity, his remorse, his self-accusations—all these constitute the psychobiographical problem. Add to it his childhood experiences: changing cities and countries, forgetting Spanish and speaking French from age four to eight, relearning Spanish, lacking an authoritative father-figure, seeing the real father disappear frequently and later feeling betrayed by him as a rival. The evidence would demonstrate that Larra's adult sense of disdain and ridicule was a defensive mechanism as well as a class attitude, and that consequently it contributed to the ambiguity of his liberal position vis-a-vis political authority.

In any event, Larra's distaste for physical contact was symbolized by a monocle, and this emblem provides the key to his grotesque aesthetic: "llevo conmigo un lente, no porque me sirva [para ver], pues veo mejor sin él, sino para poder clavar fijamente mi vista en el objeto que más me choca, que un corto de vista tiene licencia para ser desvergonzado" (I, 290). This attitude was insolent, and only possible when the subject felt a sense of superiority toward the object of his contemplation —a human object, to be sure. But, we might ask, did not wearing glasses when not needed produce a deliberate nearsightedness, and did not this mean a mildly aberrant form of perception? The answer was yes, it did, though the practice conformed to a general definition of the satirical perspective and to this degree was not unusual. But then Larra went further, using another metaphor: "colocado detras de mi lente, que es entonces para mi el vidrio de la linterna mágica, veo pasar el mundo todo delante de mis ojos" (I, 290). Here the perceptual conditions had changed. Instead of a simple eyeglass, Larra held a magic lantern which produced wondrous images. These marvelous scenes differed from normal reality precisely in their ability to amaze or astound. The purpose of Larra's magic lens was to focus on the strange wonders of Spanish society, customs which were ridiculous, comic, foolish, and absurd. To the extent that the lantern projected only spectacular or satirical images, rather than the normal features of daily life, it deformed reality. Therefore even though Larra claimed to be impartial, he reported what he saw with very little objectivity. That is to say, he selected primarily negative elements which he exaggerated in accordance with his critical motives. At certain moments, these deformations extended to the deliberate practice of the grotesque on the principle of selective magnification.

Now here, we must distinguish between the caricature of normal satire and the grotesque aesthetic which sprang from Larra's nightmare. Larra began to publish in 1828, and these articles involved a *duende satírico* who was witty, uncomplicated, and surgically clean in his attacks. Even the *pobrecito hablador* of 1832 appears to be free of the violence and distortion that characterize the later grotesque mode. That is, there is no method of deliberate plastic deformation whereby incongruous images acquire disturbing emotional overtones, or where the distortion derives from absurd or uncanny techniques of representation. This definition does not apply to Larra's early satire. The articles published between 1828 and 1832 display all of the comic distortions that fall short of grotesquerie: caricature, exaggeration, burlesque. If we compare a few examples from this period with those of later years, the differences will become clearer. Notice the early satirical portrait of his nephew, and how pale and abstract the graphic line appears when surrounded by moral sarcasm:

> Este tal sobrino es un mancebo que ha recibido una educación de las más escogidas que en este nuestro siglo se suelen dar… monta a caballo como un centauro, y da gozo ver con que soltura y desembarazo atropella por esas calles de Madrid a sus amigos y conocidos; de ciencias y artes ignora lo suficiente para poder hablar de todo con maestría… Habla un poco de francés y de italiano siempre que había de hablar español, y español no lo habla sino lo maltrata… (I, 86)

In contrast, here is how Larra's lens distorts the image of the laboring masses in 1835, personified by "el *hombre-raíz*, el *hombre-patata*":

> ...sólo el contacto de la tierra puede sostener su vida... su frente achatada se inclina al suelo, su cuerpo está encorvado, su propio pelo le abruma, sus ojos no tienen objeto fijo, ven sin mirar... un caos de fanatismo, de credulidad, de errores... Es la muchedumbre inmensa que llaman pueblo, a quien se fascina, sobre el cual se pisa, se anda, se sube; cava, suda, sufre. Alguna vez se levanta, y es terrible, como se levanta la tierra en un terremoto... (II, 55-56)

In this portrait, the turgid quality of the texture, the earthy darkness, the moral degradation, belong somewhere between Goya's peasants in *Viejos comiendo sopas* and Van Gogh's *Potato Eaters*.

By way of contrast once again, notice the realistic spatial and linear description in 1828 of the writer covered with snuff:

> ...en una mesa bastante inmediata a la mía se hallaba un literato; a lo menos le vendían por tal unos anteojos sumamente brillantes, por encima de cuyos cristales miraba, sin duda porque veía mejor sin ellos, y una caja llena de rapé, de cuyos polvos, que sacaba con bastante frecuencia y que llegaba a las narices con el objeto de descargar la cabeza, que debía tener pesada del mucho discurrir, tenía cubierto el suelo, parte de la mesa y porción no pequeña de su guirindola, chaleco y pantalones... (I, 10)

Here the hyperbole is limited to a few selected symbols —the glasses and the snuffbox— and these do not alter the realism or the placid emotional tone of the scene. On the other hand, "La Nochebuena de 1836" offers a grotesque and perhaps paranoid fantasy which includes a horrible and menacing vision:

> ...figuróseme ver de pronto que se alzaba por entre las montañas de víveres una frente altísima y extenuada; una mana seca y roída llevaba a una boca cardena, y negra de morder cartuchos, un manojo de laurel sangriento. Y aquella boca no hablaba. Pero el rostro entero se dirigía a los bulliciosos liberales de Madrid, que traficaban.

Era horrible el contraste de la fisonomía escuálida y de los rostros alegres. (II, 314)

In all these examples, the optical techniques of imagistic proportion and dimension fall into two separate categories: grotesque deformations or satirical caricature. But there are also differences in the psychological confrontation with reality, and here we must deal with the emotional disposition of Larra's nightmare.

The grotesque portraits just cited embody only one kind of distortion, susceptible to much less subjectivity than some of the other prismatic aberrations such as carnivals, mascarades, dream sequences, and dehumanized visions. If we return to the metaphor of the monocle or lens, we begin to understand the link between aesthetic practice and the tormented personality of Larra as narrator. This time the lens image takes place in the context of satirists and their functions. Larra is rejecting the notion that satirists are carefree writers who delight in tearing their subjects into pieces. And he says that "ese mismo don de la Naturaleza de ver las cosas tales cuales son, y de notar antes en ellas el lado feo que el hermoso, suele ser su tormento. Llámanle la atención en el sol mis sus manchas que su luz, y sus ojos, verdaderos microscopios, le hacen notar la fealdad de los poros exagerados, y las desigualdades de la tez en una Venus… " (II, 164). Thus we find that even at the very moment when Larra was asserting his ability to be objective—"ver las cosas tales cuales son"—he admitted bluntly that he had a microscopic perspective when regarding the external world, and that consequently this microscopic focus was the factor responsible for his deformations. Moreover, his "don de la Naturaleza" was a source of "tormento" because it destroyed his sense of beauty—"Venus"—and this gift urged him to search more zealously for the ugly side of things. No man could be happy with this kind of predisposition. In the case of Larra's sensitive and turbulent spirit, the focus eventually sickened him and acted as a depressant to his already despondent temperament. It was a dangerous visual talent for a journalist to have, particularly when his literary selves were constantly dying and reviving among the ruins of Madrid's city-cemetery—el Pobrecito Hablador, el Bachiller Munguía, Andrés Niporesas, Fígaro—all popping up at one time or another in the *mascaradas políticas* of the city.

II. Behind the Veils of Heteronymy

These pen-names and satirical selves reflect the aesthetic sensibility just described. But they do not explain the man, that is, the man Larra wanted us to see behaving self-consciously. Who was this individual anyway? He was in fact a newspaperman and theater critic with a family to feed, a reputation to make, and a foreign background that never allowed him to feel at home with his countrymen. This should have been enough to drive him into a state of self-consciousness in his public role as writer. But instead of concealing his inadequacies he created a narrative persona willing to describe his idiosyncrasies with ironic and disingenuous humor. His quirks and characteristics are satirized along with the larger social conditions around him. Yet there is a second irony of a more serious kind that Larra might not have been totally aware of, an egotistical self-observation which despite the humor tells much about his personality.

Here Larra's personal remarks took an odd turn, because they revealed more about his self-image than about his true biography. For example his physical body greatly occupied his awareness. He followed an impulse to call attention to his small size, a fact which may have been inconsequential biographically but which suggested a wish to compensate for making so slight a visual impression on people. Such is the value of references like "miréme de alto abajo, sorteando un espejo que a la sazón tenía, no tan grande como mi persona, que es hacer el elogio de su pequeñez" (I, 199-200). Beyond the demands of mere literary descriptiveness came an urge to measure or situate himself materially in the world.

It also amused Larra to depict himself sitting inconspicuously in cafe corners on the pretext of eavesdropping for material to write about. This literary pose is unconvincing, for he could not have relied on so crude a strategy: "seguro ya de que nadie podría echar de ver mi figura, que por fortuna no es de las mas abultadas, pedí un vaso de naranja" (I, 9). What did happen was that while writing his article subsequently he found it important to reestablish his psychological location in the cafe and to retrace his relationship to the people he would describe. He had an outsider sensibility, very much aware of himself and his alienation as he saw and traced the journalist-observer sitting in his mental corner. The cafe nook gave that feeling a tangible form.

What about more subtle allusions to estrangement, to the fact that he had been a Spanish-speaking schoolboy in France, or a French-speaking teenager in Spain? Such references are absent, and we find instead a psychic detachment narrated in terms of physical distantiation from the world. In Larra's worst moments he wandered the streets autistically ("no hay cosa que tenga a mis ojos color… indiferencia y despego a cuanto veo"); a dislocated prowler of places ("sálgome a la calle, éntrome por los cafés, voyme a la Puerta del Sol, a Correos, al Museo de Pinturas, a todas partes, en fin, y en ninguna puedo decir que estoy en realidad" [I, 290]). The exiled boy and repatriated youth return, in this spiritual expatriation, as symbolic recrudescences. Trifling details like insignificant stature and spatial distance from the world reinforced the dislocation experienced by Larra. A figure so unobtrusive in a city so colorless ought to have slipped into place somewhere, but no reality seemed tangible enough to contain his restless nature.

Larra's sense of corporeal self was anchored by moral isolation, and he wrote with an eye toward his body. The alien environment frequently assaulted his person, as when "un grandísimo brazo vino a descargar sobre uno de mis hombros, que, por desgracia no tienen punto alguno de semejanza con los de Atlante" (I, 114). That heavy arm belonged to the famous *castellano viejo*, a middle-class boor. And here the trifling detail begins to acquire some significance. Elsewhere Larra voices thick distaste for the close contact of large families that crowd together in coaches rented for special occasions. The lower classes also grow too familiar and must be kept at arm's length: "mi sastre es hombre que me recibe con sombrero puesto, que me alarga la mano y me la aprieta; me suele dar dos palmaditas o tres… cada vez que me ve" (II, 27). And how does Larra's social life fare? While he enjoyed rubbing elbows with the rich at carnivals and balls, "donde había codeado a la aristocracia," he did indeed detest the mobs at the theater, "donde me habia codeado a mí la democracia" (I, 347). The word-play was irresistible, but sentiment preceded the pun. He left no doubt that he resented the dirty world's invasion of his person and his property when he said, "lleve usted un cigarro encendido. No habrá aguador ni carbonero que no le pida la lumbre, y le detenga en la calle, y le manosee y empuerque su tabaco, y se lo vuelva apagado" (II, 28). These details can be multiplied, and suffice to suggest that Larra was not much of an egalitarian, and that he constructed his basic plane of reality in protective isolation: "—¿Es posible que nadie sepa aquí ocupar su puesto? ¿Hay tal confusión de clases y personas?" (II, 28).

How contemptuous of the masses Larra really was can be debated. Much textual evidence needs to be assembled, but to do so here would be digressive. My point is that details like walking and sitting serve as self-revelations which under certain stresses uncover or at least insinuate still other attitudes. Individual examples of, say, body contact in the context of class feelings may be explained on perfectly innocent grounds. But the confluence of examples as a thematic pattern must also have some significance, and the matter will bear further study in future occasions. In any event, these physical problems bring us to the fact that Larra was unable to sleep very well. He said nothing of how often he awoke during the night, but his difficulty in falling asleep took the customary literary form of passing confessions which, upon examination, produce a cumulative effect that is more disturbing than funny. He projected the image of an insomniac amusing himself with the world's folly, but the elements are too incompatible to be persuasive. Playing the sly cafe-observer, he managed to "meterme en rincones excusados por escuchar caprichos ajenos, que luego me proporcionan materia de diversión para aquellos ratos que paso en mi cuarto y a veces en mi cama sin dormir" (I, 9). Surface and concealed meanings balanced each other. The literary subject was the oft-repeated need to gather material for articles, and so "en mi cama sin dormir" came ostensibly as an afterthought. Yet once the irony of "escuchar caprichos ajenos" fades, we begin to wonder what transpired during "aquellos ratos que paso en mi cuarto... sin dormir." Was the entire sentence intended to be ironic, and if so why should Larra wish to humor us with his insomnia?

One answer is that lack of sleep was a problem which lingered in his consciousness the morning after, disguising itself subsequently as one of several literary allusions to working habits. The reference held a private meaning known only to Larra, who was too subtle to rationalize his problem openly. Thus he dissimulated and wrote pretentiously: "cuando en un día de ésos, en que un insomnio prolongado, o un contratiempo de la víspera preparan al hombre a la meditación, me paro a considerar el destino del mundo... " (II, 38). Such lofty detachment on the morning after would have been admirable if true. The more common reaction might be irritability toward the world due to exhaustion. At best Larra may have been too wrapped in himself to ponder events philosophically; his work did not, in any case, permit direct self-absorption. We can only conjecture what sentiments he felt while sitting at his desk, but we are obliged to note that he could not resist mentioning his sleepless affliction and the aftereffects that weighed physically upon him.

These references were Larra's only concession to the need for subjectivity. His personality kept a visible presence without creating a preoccupation with self as a literary topic. He eschewed details that would have gained credibility among middle-class readers—clothes, living conditions, family—and instead casually selected the aberration of insomnia. This detail went unnoticed by a public either indifferent to his newspaper altogether or concerned only with those paragraphs dealing with manners. But the stratagem helped Larra to escape the burden of loneliness in moments of self-contemplation. Without this extraliterary dimension it is difficult to account for Larra's dual role in the preliminary material of his articles, a duality whereby he becomes the reader's confidant in a perspective outside the topic and yet slips himself into the content as a character.

By means of these insinuations he signaled a code of mute anguish, his otherwise gratuitous remarks carrying undertones of acute self-awareness: "No sé por qué capricho extraordinario, y en oposición con mis hábitos antiguos, el 31 de este diciembre que expira hubo de asaltarme el sueño mucho más pronto de lo que acostumbra… " (II, 50). This easy slumber, however, was followed by an unpleasant dream. Once again Larra seized the opportunity to narrate himself into his article for reasons independent of the prefatory remarks required for the subject. His readers cared little whether he fell quickly asleep, nor would they remember previous references to his nocturnal habits. But for Larra, the rarity of a nightly repose made the topic irresistible, something to celebrate secretly in public.

On the other hand, he left no doubt about his customary torment, at times making light of it but also defining it by the metaphor of civil war: "ya estaba yo agachado esperando el aguacero y sin poder conciliar el sueño. Así pasé las horas de la noche, más largas para el triste desvelado que una guerra civil" (II, 313). However prophetic the metaphor in its social dimensions proved to be for Spain, it was just as symptomatic of Larra's private disorder. If ever two organisms existed which never learned the rhythmic mechanisms of rest and recovery, they were Larra and Spain, both of whom qualified as specimens constantly at war with themselves. Political antagonisms seemed as interminable as sleepless nights.

Here we must remember the convergence of Spanish political conflict during the 1830's with the internal strife that plagued Larra. He was challenged by the duality of the liberal movement. He remained ambivalent about class identifications. And he seemed insecure about siding definitively with political positions, finding it easier to attack satirically than to advocate soberly. The strain drove him to weariness and despair, with neither condition eased by financial certainty. Thus he pursued his newspaper career, arising in fatigue, sitting despondently at his desk (in a modish swivel chair), and composing half-mad dialogues with alter egos in the hope of counteracting, and eventually banishing, his warring emotions. He even invented a servant-valet who could give him the following advice:

> Escucha: tú vienes triste como de costumbre; yo estoy más alegre que suelo... ¿Por qué te vuelves y te revuelves en tu mullido lecho como un criminal, acostado con su remordimiento, en tanto que yo ronco sobre mi tosca tarima? ¿Quién debe tener lástima a quién?" (II, 316).

In this way, Larra afflicted himself with public secrecy. His dialogue in "La Nochebuena de 1836" offered him a form of punishment whose self-lacerating method remained concealed from the reader. Why he allowed his servant to expose him as an alleged "criminal" will never be known, but it is clear that his sense of guilt for something— his ambiguity?—egged him on to make public atonement. He published the Unamunian-style dialogue, or monodialogue, structured on the process of *desdoblamiento*. And then he boldly accused himself through the voice of his fictitious "acquaintance." The technique afforded subtle and contradictory ironies that fulfilled Larra's confessional wish and desire for punishment. By creating an independent prosecutor to hint mysteriously at unspecified crimes, he exposed himself without having to make a direct statement of guilt. He could also objectify the self-torture by assigning the role of his accusatory self to another person who, moreover, belonged to a different social class. Thus Larra was able to see himself condemned by the outside world while being satisfied that his self-incrimination would remain secret.

The key word here was *remordimiento,* an inexplicable allusion in the shifting perspectives of Larra's self-contemplation. These shifts suggest frightful psychological stresses that compounded chronic insomnia with deep-seated concerns surfacing to his consciousness and keeping him awake. The original causes of Larra's failure to sleep, therefore, include several related possibilities: (a) an excessive self-awareness and consequent inability to extricate himself through a falling away from consciousness into its opposite state of sleep; (b) a tight grip on his bodily and emotional sense of self which prevented sleep from exercising its obliterating power over him. It is pointless to review the rich psychoanalytical literature on this subject, for Larra provided the material in his metaphors of fragmentation and in his allusions to both physical size and his spatial relationship to the non-self. Taken together, these references comprise the primary evidence of a sensibility that deformed the world in periodic moods of dejection.

III. The Guilt-Ridden Liberalism of Bourgeois Satire

The psychobiographical profile, therefore, essentially portrays a young bourgeois liberal who wrote under a variety of stresses: pressure from his family, who kept him alert to their censure; pressure from himself as he succumbed to the clowning behind his satire; pressure from his "other" self, the doubting, objective observer in his *desdoblamiento*. This *cogito* pushed him into a state of perpetual self-dissection, including special moments when he contemplated his literary death and wrote his own epitaph. No wonder he appeared distempered and bitterly indifferent. Yet at the same time, beneath his anguish, there swelled a secondary awareness, a knowledge of his semi-fraudulent relationship with the reading public. After all, his readers were solid citizens of the professional, business, and political worlds. He needed their subscriptions and so curried favor, at times, with his middle-class peers by using phrases like "confesemos ingenuamente," as if he didn't realize that his next words would shock and titillate them.

Indeed, Larra tried to draw sympathy from his readership by showing boyish charm or by adopting a false naïveté. Occasionally he apologized to his well-mannered readers in advance of impolite remarks. But in all this he knew exactly which expressions corresponded to what feelings, and he probably despised himself for wearing his poses as naturally as the masks worn by other people at the balls he described with such frequency. In sum, a basic part of his existence ran contrary to his role as social critic. He craved attention, needed compassion, and longed to be accepted by his own kind—the very middle-class individuals whom he criticized so often. The fact is that he seldom acted without taking a side-glance at social opinion, and in this regard let us remember that he did not defy society in the vigorous manner of a Romantic rebel or a bohemian. On the contrary, his sincerity as a satirist faltered when it came under the eroding influence of middle-class preoccupations. In his mind he was truly divided and he wavered accordingly. On one hand, he presented himself as a distracted thinker driven to melancholia by the folly around him, though he seemed to draw solace from this image. On the other hand, he hated that maladjusted condition and yearned for normalcy in the bourgeois way: "mala crianza sera, pero… " (I, 290); or he would say, "la disposición de nuestro ánimo, que no sabemos dominar" (II, 248); or else, "el mal humor, que habitualmente me daba todo el aspecto de un filósofo" (I, 331). Curiously, Larra combatted the mischievous image that he sought to create. While persuading everyone of his malice, he anxiously tried to dispel the image, "la mala interpretación que se da generalmente al carácter y a la condición de los escritores satíricos" (II, 161). As we can see, he could not have it both ways.

For these reasons, Larra's commitments were indecisive. He moderated his reactions in the very midst of his extremes. Even melancholia was a commodity to capitalize on, now as he gaily disguised it and now as he bared his breast for the edification of readers. It should be obvious that his dejection did not end as "la cosa más alegre del mundo," although this was how he defined satire. And plainly his writing a phrase like "la idea de servir yo entero de diversión" (II, 280) must have provoked a certain anguish. Proof of this came in the metaphor describing satirists, offered while disabusing readers of their misconceptions:

> Supone el lector, en quien acaba un párrafo mordaz de provocar la risa, que el escritor satírico es un ser consagrado por la Naturaleza a la alegría y que su corazón es un foco inextinguible de esa misma jovialidad que a manos llenas prodiga a sus lectores. Desgraciadamente… no es así. El escritor satírico es por lo común como la luna, un cuerpo opaco destinado a dar luz, y es acaso el

único de quien con razón se puede decir que da lo que no tiene. Ese mismo don de la Naturaleza de ver las cosas tales cuales son, y de notar antes en ellas el lado feo que el hermoso, suele ser su tormento. (II, 164)

He saw himself living in shadow, like the moon, providing amusement without being able to laugh himself. On the contrary, signs of laughter sprang from his general emotional extremism and suggested a touch of schizoid mania. The metaphor of an opaque moon was especially meaningful in this regard, as one of many images of reflection and transparency which Larra used to convey distorted or absurd facets of reality. Here, the incongruity of the unlit moon giving light, or a sad clown inspiring laughter, expressed the discomfort of the actor whose mask was worn so tightly.

Understanding this, Larra disguised his self-knowledge so subtly that the famous dialogue on Christmas Eve 1836 is barely seen as the shockingly self-lacerating text that in reality it is:

Tu eres literato y escritor, y ¡qué tormentos no te hace pasar tu amor propio, ajado diariamente por la indiferencia de unos, por la envidia de otros, por el rencor de muchos! Preciado de gracioso, harías reír a costa de un amigo, si amigos hubiera, y no quieres tener remordimiento... Ofendes y no quieres tener enemigos... Te llamas liberal y despreocupado, y el día que te apoderes del látigo azotarás como te han azotado... Ente ridículo, bailas sin alegría... Yo estoy ebrio de vino, es verdad; ¡pero tú lo estás de deseos y de impotencia! (II, 316-317)

All the themes discussed thus far were recapitulated here: the vanity and the need for friends or approval, the loneliness and remorse, the naive hope for a double standard, the acknowledgement of hypocrisy, the joyless laughter. A new theme, the sense of impotence, also appeared to dominate all others and to suggest their motivating source. Yet this theme sprang not from psychological problems but from the political etiology of Spanish society. Social conditions propagated the excrescences of impotent malaise. The uneasiness that pervaded Larra's consciousness formed part of his psychic symptomology, and it nourished a more active malevolence—satirical in nature.

Larra's dual career as Fígaro illustrated how the satirist lived at the heart of liberal failure and intellectual impotence. He epitomized the emotional core of this condition by a "cloud" of melancholy on his brow, "pero de aquellas melancolías de que sólo un liberal español en estas circunstancias puede formar una idea aproximada" (II, 279). In Fígaro's first life, he was "regañón y malhumorado," and then he emerged from the political ruins of the cemetery to a second career in a "mundo de dolor y de amargura" where he could write, "(¿qué verdad más triste que un periódico de la oposición?" (II, 304). The blame lay with the hopeless social sphere which thwarted the best-intentioned political efforts and which drove sensitive men to hyper-frustration. The causality was relentless and irrevocable. Here was Larra the writer, whose life's role depended on the social context, taking as the prime subject for his criticism that very social context. The absurdity of this contradiction baffled him, placing many stresses on an already delicate sensibility. Had he been either a revolutionary or a reactionary, his dilemma would have diminished. But as a liberal, Larra depended on moderate thought structures that reinforced rather than alleviated the pressures convening on him from the social dimension. For example, he opposed censorship on ideological grounds and fought it on the day-to-day journalistic level; yet he lived with the censors to the point where he could carve out a career and meet the required deadlines. Other examples of contradictory moderation can be found in his social philosophy, but they would take us far afield.[8] The point is that these paradoxes stretched the framework of his political nightmare. As a bourgeois liberal with a special class upbringing, he harbored prejudices incompatible with his other values, and the effort to reconcile them wasted his emotional energy. His sense of decency and respect for the individual was repeatedly declared. But his good manners tarnished the role of social critic with the film of hypocrisy. The "progressive" liberal—some might say the revolutionary—in Larra was impotent precisely because the bourgeois in him insisted on maintaining good relations with a society that he fundamentally repudiated.

---

8 One such contradiction is visible in a passage on censorship involving a pamphlet by Espronceda, in which Larra declares: "pero el escritor público que una vez echó sobre sus hombros la responsabilidad de ilustrar a sus conciudadanos, debe insistir y remitir a la censura tres artículos nuevos por cada uno que le prohiban... debe protestar... sufrir, en fin, la persecución, la cárcel, el patíbulo si es preciso" (II, 214).

It was impossible to remain intellectually resolute with a mind so quick to see paradoxes, to make inversions, and to draw antithetical conclusions. Yet while he changed his mind often he felt defensive about it. Each new position was sincerely believed, like a fresh beginning offered to an agile thinker who, unfortunately, all too quickly glimpsed the defects of every position. Parallel to this came the changing literary identities and the newly invented pen-names adopted for changing circumstances. Each shift in character brought with it another point of view, yet the cause of liberalism in Larra's generation embraced fixed purposes. When we reach the deathbed scene of the Bachiller Munguía, we find him confessing with his last words that "siempre tuve mis opiniones como mis vestidos, y cada día me puse uno… Arrepiéntome en la hora de la muerte" (I, 154-55). There is deliberate irony here, but it fades before an unconscious irony in which Larra witnesses his own demise. He often killed his literary self, and this fact should suffice to demonstrate his need to purge himself. He allowed part of himself to die with each alter ego, and this too is proof of self-castigation following confession of "sin." But the fact that his resurrection always took the form of a new literary personage calls attention to the ambiguity of his orientation as a social critic. Like the well-dressed bourgeois who wore different clothes every day, the middle-class Larra cast aside one liberal mask for another whenever necessary. There was no hypocrisy in this in the traditionally moral sense, although Marxist critics might find contemptible an apologetic remark like "batuecos hay que no tienen nada que echarme en cara" (I, 154). In the 19th century, no one could ask for more than what Larra freely gave: an admission of guilt and a symbolic suicide.

But what about the psychological effects and their literary form? On the mildest level they consisted of ironic distance and evasion by means of pseudonymic disguise. At times there was a stranger level of turmoil and self-contemplation, which resulted in a numb detachment where he said: "Recibo insensible las impresiones de cuanto pasa a mi alrededor; a todas me dejo amoldar con indiferencia y abandono; en semejantes días no hay hermosas para mí, no hay feas, no hay amor, no hay odio" (I, 290). And at other times his attention turned inwardly to inflict sharp incisions upon his psyche. These occasions were moods of self-accusation phrased in a language that gave insight into the nature of his psychosocial pathology. Larra isolated his allegedly "criminal" character on the one hand, and summoned his bourgeois exterior self to appear as the chief witness for the prosecution. He arraigned his guilty middle-class nature before the tribunal of his divided personality in the form of a monodialogue that went as follows : "Tú acaso eres de esos criminales y hay un acusador dentro de ti, y ese frac elegante, y esa media de seda, y ese chaleco de tisú de oro que yo te he visto son tus armas maldecidas. —Silencio, hombre borracho…" (II, 316).

It is hard to imagine a more callous assault on one's own personality, yet Larra proceeded with a battery of images as pitiless as his moral judgment of himself. He dressed impeccably for the tribunal, and appeared before the sessions of his febrile thought with an elegance that he assumed other people saw him as possessing. Clothes were his weapons, the armour which protected him against the threat of class confusion, and the armament which he would use to cow his opponents. He would face the overfamiliar tailor, the rude water-carrier asking for a match, and the boisterous petty-bourgeois family—and he would keep them in their places by this sartorial strategy.

This is where we reach the essential value of Larra's work as a critique of liberalism in his own age and in ours. He recognized the failure of the liberal position as a political alternative and as a critical methodology. The words of his accuser summed it up perfectly: he was an "hombre de partido, haces la guerra a otro partido; o cada vencimiento es una humillación, o compras la victoria demasiado cara para gozar de ella" (II, 316). On the day that *he*, Larra, would get control of the whip, he would lash out as he had been lashed at earlier. This shattering truth could scarcely be admitted, and only in the most despondent of moods did he face the implications. On days like Día de Santos, or the dying moments of the old year, he conceived the lugubrious thoughts which belong to his most famous articles. But if all Madrid was a cemetery, Larra was the keeper of the graveyard, chronicling the burial of each illusion and poking around the tombstones for signs of life. No one has ever doubted that Larra identified with the moribund aspect of Spanish culture, or that he suffered over it. Yet we must also see that a link existed between that cultural cemetery and the life and death of Larra's alter egos. His perception of liberalism's failure parallelled the death of Fígaro, and each new political regime brought fresh hope or despair which was echoed in articles that were correspondingly hopeful or desperate.

Since Larra's sense of impotence lurked behind even his most hilarious articles, it was inevitable that he resorted to morbid and even grotesque representations of reality during his pessimistic periods: "Heme aquí de nuevo saliendo entre las tumbas, impasible como un muerto; sacando la cabeza por entre las ruinas como un secretario de la Gobernación" (II, 303). Or, "¡Fuera, exclamé, la horrible pesadilla, fuera! ¡Libertad! ¡Constitución!" (II, 281). He was submerged in his emotions, and to gain distance he looked at the world through the lenses of distortive magnification. This method was facilitated for him by the conditions of Spanish history. But his personality encouraged the choice of method even more. It was no accident that his manic-depressive states took their most frequent literary form in the context of masked balls, nightmares, and drunken or macabre grotesqueries. Deformation was the most natural expression of Larra's self-destructive tendencies. And insofar as social reality corresponded to or mirrored his inner incongruities, it produced an integrated political nightmare whose center was an anguished, modern liberal.[9]

---

9 This study was first published in *Revista Hispánica Moderna*, 38 (1974-75), 153-66. Reprinted courtesy of the University of Pennsylvania Press.

7
Espronceda and the Romantic Grotesque

THE EVOLUTION OF THE Romantic grotesque in Spain begins with Goya and ends with Bécquer.[1] Between these two figures stands another contributor to the aesthetics of distortion, José de Espronceda, whose works reflect an intermediary phase which recapitulates earlier trends and prefigures later ones. The grotesquerie of *El diablo mundo* and *El estudiante de Salamanca* is somewhat removed from the twisted caricatures that serve Goyaesque social satire, for it hints at the eerie, incongruous supernaturalism that is to come in Bécquer's *leyendas*. Yet Espronceda's practices continue to be influenced by the ethical concerns of an earlier age. His use of typically Romantic diabolical motifs is reminiscent of the Dantesque tradition, but just as the Christian element begins to impose itself, it is dispelled by a larger psychological atmosphere not too different from the modern sensibility.[2] This vacillation is an interesting literary phenomenon, for its mixture of morality and nightmare draws upon categories as diverse as the macabre, the Bacchic, and the dreamstate.

---

1 On Espronceda's Romanticism, the following are most useful for background: Joaquín Casalduero, *Forma y visión de "El diablo mundo"* (Madrid: Insula, 1951), and *Espronceda* (Madrid: Editorial Gredos, 1961); and Alessandro Martinengo, *Polimorfismo nel "Diablo mundo" d'Espronceda* (Torino: Bottega d'Erasmo, 1962). All quotations refer by page to *Obras completas*, ed. Jorge Campos (Madrid: Ediciones Atlas, 1954); and by verse number to either *El estudiante de Salamanca*, ed. Benito Varela Jacome (Salamanca: Anaya, 1966)-ES; or to *El diablo mundo*, ed. J. Moreno Villa (Madrid: Espasa-Calpe, 1955-DM.

2 Casalduero says of *El estudiante de Salamanca*: "la arquitectura gótica dantesca se ha convertido en un torbellino, No hay el menor contacto entre la racionalización y sistematización de Dante y el sentimiento de ultratumba de Espronceda," *Espronceda*, p. 195.

I. Poetic Theory and the Grotesque

A good summary of Espronceda's theory of the grotesque can be constructed by inference, on the basis of a general statement about Neoclassical poetics at the end of *El diablo mundo:*

> ¡Oh, cómo cansa el
> orden! No hay locura
> igual a la del lógico severo;
> y aquí renegar quiero
> de la literatura
> y de aquellos que buscan proporciones
> en la humana figura
> y miden a compás sus perfecciones (p. 147a; *DM, 5778-84)*

This rejection of Neoclassical order fails to specify what might replace the old aesthetic, but the very concepts repudiated invoke their own antithesis. Several new notes can be heard if we mute such familiar tones as "orden," "proporciones," and "perfecciones." Old words like these are sounds of a pre-Romantic concert, and they must be slurred in order to detect the angular rhythms of Espronceda's infernal symphony.[3] In the new score, the important notes are "compás," "humana figura," and "lógico," which become transported into a new key. The grotesque rendition of "compás" is probably the most striking feature of both *El diablo mundo* and *El estudiante de Salamanca,* where cacophonies and broken cadences mark the violent irregularity of their form. Similarly, it is the "humana figura" which is denaturalized and used as the deformed basis for the macabre beings who haunt the magic world of these poems. As for "lógico," its antithesis in the irrational, sometimes absurd perception of reality is fundamental to the poems as a whole, as well as to their grotesque episodes.

Thus Espronceda conspicuously dismisses the aesthetic principles of previous generations even with respect to how the grotesque will be practiced. He goes beyond emphasizing the heterogeneity of forms and

---

[3] The similarity between "e! aquelarre espectral" of Part IV and the last movement of Berlioz's composition of 1830 has been noticed by Fradejas Lebrero, cited by Varela Jacome. The latter also quotes Berlioz's own description, p. 15.

the blending of genres ("en varias formas, con diverso estilo, /... ora en trivial lenguaje, ora burlando" [p. 97b; *DM*, 1372-77]).

These innovations are conventionally Romantic, but they barely touch upon the problems of the grotesque. By challenging the logician's authority in the councils of artistic law, Espronceda calls attention to his own advocacy of disorder. This is his real point, the intention to follow caprice, whim, and haphazard fancy without regard to rules: "conforme esté mi humor, porque a él me ajusto / y allá van versos donde va mi gusto" (p. 97b; *DM*, 1378-79). If the *capricho* is the operative principle for poetic creation in general, then its specific effect on the grotesque is readily grasped. To repudiate the "lógico severo" is to invoke his adversary, the irrationalist, whose unbridled imagination will breed every kind of excess, including disproportion and madness. Such an alternative allows for near chaotic dementia and liberation, and in the case of one rejuvenated character, release is found "en su agitada fantasía, / volando con locura el pensamiento, / en vaga tropa imágenes sin cuento" (p. 103b; *DM*,1949-51*)*.

These verses also demonstrate how an exacerbated imagination works. In the light of the first quotation, they add nuances to the concepts of "compás," "humana figura," and "lógico." Rhythm ceases to be measured against some predictable regularity, and acquires convulsive, uncontrollable qualities ("agitada," "volando con locura"). The image of the human figure is replaced by "vaga tropa [de] imágenes," a generic imprecision enabling other creatures besides human beings to be included within the circle of grotesquerie. And instead of logic, the operative faculty is "fantasía." The references cited are surprisingly consistent, despite their random occurrence in the poems, and they tend to confirm each other in their theoretical implications. They are also supported in practice by the general atmosphere of frenzy, noise, and violence among the uncontrolled movements of people and scenes—themselves often deformed. While they may be typical of Romantic spontaneity and inspiration, these elements are also peculiar to the grotesque mode as a conscious aesthetic position. It would be useful, therefore, to describe this theory of grotesque creation before presenting examples from the works themselves.

First, however, I should dispose of one possible criticism. Readers may wonder why I do not distinguish between *imaginación* and *fantasía*, as Coleridge did between *imagination* and *fancy*. Two reasons persuade me that such a distinction is both unwarranted and confusing. First, my purpose is not the same as Coleridge's, who intended to establish a value judgment as well as a metaphysical principle by means of the distinction. He was led to devise these separate concepts during his defense of Wordsworth's early poetry, which he noted lacked "turbulence of imagery" and "arbitrary and illogical phrases, at once hackneyed and fantastic." Perhaps this describes the work of Espronceda's "fancy," but I find the axiological basis of the distinction immaterial to my discussion. As for the metaphysical definitions of "primary" and "secondary" imagination, they are hardly suitable for Espronceda's grotesquerie. There is neither "the living power and prime agent of all human perception," nor the struggle "to idealize and to unify." On the other hand, Espronceda exhibits a good deal of "delirium," in which "the fancy brings together images which have no connection natural or moral, but are yoked together by the poet by means of some accidental coincidence." All this would seem to counsel against using the word "imagination" at all, and to suggest that "fancy" is the proper word to be used throughout this essay. But such a course would leave me without a term to embrace the problems of epistemology and the psychology of the senses. It would also wrongly identify as a single creative process two separate processes: the one which the critic observes to be Espronceda's, and the one which Espronceda states or implies in his poems. It would, finally, be arbitrary to select Coleridge's concepts and ignore, say, those of Wordsworth, Nerval, and Lautréamont. It is therefore more sensible to use the general term "imagination" as it is normally employed in philosophy and aesthetics.[4]

The second reason for disregarding the distinction is that to do otherwise is to suggest that Espronceda and his contemporaries carefully distinguished between *imaginación* and *fantasía*. There is little evidence to warrant such a suggestion. During the so-called "pre-Romantic" period, Terreros y Pando gave the primary definition of *fantasía* as "Imaginación, cierta potencia que se atribuye al alma racional y sensitiva… 'Las especies o imágenes de los cuerpos hacen su impresión en

---

4 See further my "¿Luces sin llustración? Las voces «imaginación/fantasía» como testigos léxicos." Francisco La Rubia Prado y Jesús Torrecilla (directores). *Razón, tradición y modernidad: re-visión de la llustración española.* Madrid: Tecnos, 1996: 133-92.

la fantasía.'" He then continued: "Se toma también por cierta determinación del alma a creer, o querer las cosas según la impresión de los sentidos… 'Este juzga según su fantasía. N. ama según su fantasía.' Vanidad, capricho. Cosa arbitraria, sin regIa, ni método. También llaman fantasía a aquello que es harmonioso y bueno, pero fuera de las reglas comunes… sin regIa alguna."[5]

These secondary implications were ignored in the 19th century. An art historian refers to Juan de Juni's "arquitectura licenciosa y recargada con mil adornos grotescos, parto de su fecunda y acalorada imaginación."[6] Larra uses the words interchangeably:

> Columpiándose mi imaginación entre mil ideas opuestas, hijas de la confusión de sensaciones encontradas de un baile de máscaras, me dormí;" "el sueño y el ayuno, prolongado sobre todo, predisponen la imaginación débil y acalorada del hombre a las visiones nocturnas y aéreas, que vienen a tomar en nuestra irritable fantasía formas corpóreas cuando están nuestros párpados aletargados por Morfeo *(El mundo todo es máscaras)*.

The theory of grotesque creation begins with Espronceda's view of imagination. He assumes that poets are endowed with the normal creative faculties associated with fantasy, but that due to their yearnings and restlessness, their capacity is somehow impaired. New stimuli are thus required to reactivate the imaginative process. One recourse is to furnish the means for distortion and enchantment:

> Optico vidrio presenta
> en fantástica ilusión
> y al ojo encantado ostenta
> gratas visiones, que aumenta
> rica la imaginación. (p. 62a; *ES*, 283-287)

---

5 *Diccionario castellano* (Madrid: Impr. de la viuda de Ibarra, hijos y compañía, 1787), II, 325.

6 Eugenio Llaguna y Amirola, *Noticias de los arquitectos y arquitectura de España desde su restauración,* ed. Juan Augustín Ceán-Bermúdez (Madrid: En la Imprenta Real, 1829), II, 69.

The mechanisms normally at work in the imagination are thus newly engaged in two ways. The magical vision of the "ojo encantado" lends its special power, and sense perception is newly focused in order to produce illusionary effects. With this groundwork of sorcery and sensory illusion, a considerable number of grotesque transformations can be effected, as we will see later.

Another aid to the imagination is the dream, which merges its voluntary process with the poet's conscious talents. The dream is not to be considered an internal faculty like the creative imagination, but rather an exterior force whose activity is assimilated by the poet's mind.[7] As depicted by Espronceda, it is a second source of fantastic visions, which is to say, a second imagination. In Adán's dream, for example, the symbolic climb to the mountain peak involves an aspiration beyond the self to increasingly higher flights of fancy. The use of the fiery winged horse characterizes the fulfillment of that goal through an unbridled ascent to the pinnacle of sensory and creative freedom ("siguiendo a mi loca fantasía, / jinete alborozado en mi bridón" [p. 133; *DM*, 4556-57]).

Within the experience of this dream, two psychological events encourage grotesque exploitation. The psychology of the situation is summarized by the couplet "en incesante vértigo y locura, / desvanecida en confusión la mente" (p. 133a; *DM*, 4568-69). The presence of vertigo is one factor in the distorted perception of reality. At the same time, the dizzying state has its source in the poet's drunkenness, a theme whose Dionysian echoes also have implications for the grotesque. The vertiginous aspect is complemented by the allusion to madness, which indicates a second approach to the concept of imagination. If vertigo involves perceptual relationships, especially space, and inner sensations of a kinaesthetic nature, "locura" belongs to a more metaphysical order. It depends on older traditions of inspirational madness on the one hand, and on radical types of derangement on the other. The mental "confusión" that results, therefore, does not refer simply to the endemic emotional instability that ravages much of the Romantic sensibility. It also implies, and leads to, specific forms of disfiguration wrenched from

---

[7] While dreams do not comprise an extensive theme in Espronceda's work, their external quality is fairly clear. Cf. "¿Será que el alma su inmortal esencia / Entre sueños revela... /... a la espantada / mente oscura del hombre?" (p. 92a; *DM* 836.)

the molds of confused sensory and intellectual categories.

II. The Psychology of Deformation

Dreams can thus be understood in a facultative sense, as mechanisms which furnish secondary imaginative constructs. Whether dreams are of internal or external origin is less important than how well their fantasy-making apparatus operates. In any case, the problem was of little interest to Espronceda. The coherence of dreams, on the other hand, concerned him a great deal, and he used types that ranged from mild, chimerical dreams to those which produced "figuras mil en su delirio insano" (p. 92a; *DM*, 846).

But beyond the dream state lie still other means of intensifying the Romantic imagination. Espronceda's poetic frenzy bears vestiges of an inspirational theory running parallel to oneiromancy. The central idea here is that creativity feeds on psychic states marked by turbulence and confusion. If the source of this inspiration is external, either divine or diabolic, Espronceda does not acknowledge it. He does place the creative energy within a dreamlike frame of reference, making subject matter rather than psychological mechanisms the focal point. The turbulent vision itself, and especially its fantastic core, is utterly at variance with the real world. Therefore the dream may be enlisted as a metaphor to explain the unreal, impossible, but vividly convincing images that swarm to the surface of the conscious mind. Yet the substance of this metaphor properly belongs to the domain of inspiration and not dream.

Thus we have principles associated with the activity of poetic imagination: emotional violence and imagistic perception divorced from reality. A third principle, already mentioned, is vertigo. This involves both a physiological experience and a perspective toward the world. It is the dizzying sensation that interferes with normal sensory knowledge, while also recoiling upon the subject's internal sense of his physical and psychological conditions. As an active event in the imaginative process, vertigo helps to shape or misshape the configuration of objects and events perceived in the world. It also affects the subject's kinaesthetic perception of himself, his sense of the body's balance and behavior. All this is tersely stated in an octet summarizing most of the conditions or faculties mentioned thus far:

Y como el polvo en nubes que levanta

> en remolinos rápido el viento,
> formas sin forma, en confusión que espanta,
> alza el sueño en su vértigo violento:
> del vano reino el límite quebranta
> vago escuadrón de imágenes sin cuento
> y otros mundos al viejo aparecían... (p. 92a; *DM*, 852-858)

Every activity derives from the distorted dreamstate and takes place within its elastic framework. "Remolinos" is the metaphor used to embrace several psychological and formal categories. Yet the fact remains that two separate kinds of deformation are taking place. On the one hand there is the mental condition, which is not only confused but is a "confusión que espanta." This means that it is an emotional state compounding severe perceptual inaccuracies with disturbed negative feelings. Moreover, the spasms of fear are quite different from the purely sensory experience of the vision itself, and they convulse the deep-seated emotional core which supplies Espronceda with his material for his mood-building. On the other hand, we have the surface images themselves, with indeterminate shapes that float along regardless of the subject's ability to focus correctly upon them. The independence of these images cannot be overestimated, for they are separate entities in their own right, no matter how unstable or defective the viewer's faculties may also be at the time. Finally, this is a supernatural world, and the poet relies on two different sources or levels of deformation, one stemming from the subject's own condition, and the other from the magic nature of the phenomena. Thus the "vértigo violento"' provides one kind of distortion in the perception of things, while the "vago escuadrón de imagenes sin cuento" bears witness to irregularity and confusion among the things themselves. The subjective category penetrates the phenomenal one, and perhaps even influences the final description of events. But the reference to "formas sin forma" suggests that the contents of the whirlwind-dream are imprecise anyway, even though their psychological framework suffers from its own impairment.

The separation and fusion of these two categories, perception and image, is what makes the atmosphere so fantastic. How do the two processes actually work? If we take an episode consisting of a dual sequence, we can easily distinguish the attributes of each type. In part one, another whirlwind analogy is used, but now it is restricted to the objective representation of the vision:

> Como nubes que en negra tormenta
> precipita violento huracán
> Y en confuso montón apiñadas
> de tropel y siguiéndose van,
> Y visiones y horrendos fantasmas,
> monstruos raros de formas sin fin...
> Así, en turbio veloz remolino
> el diabólico ejército huyó (p. 89b; *DM*, 589-610)

We are obviously meant to be impressed by the linear imprecision of the images, and by the violence of their movement. Pictorial detail is difficult to find in passages like these, and whatever is vivid from a visual standpoint can be traced to the blending of forms, the smudging of outlines, and the swift motion of changing masses. It is this dynamics of amorphism which is intensified by the element of violence. The torrential sweep of moving images eliminates the need for clarity of line. A sense of space replaces the delineation of forms, and whatever plasticity exists is achieved by describing not specific shapes but the location of masses: their direction and how they are grouped *(precipita, montón, apiñadas, tropel, siguiéndose, remolino)*.

When we move past the external account of the scene to its subjective counterpart, we can see how decisive the distinction is between formal and psychological categories. The perspective now assumes the subject's point of view, and the events narrated are the workings of his own faculties as they react to the grotesque phenomena already described.

> Embargada y absorta la mente
> en incierto delirio quedó,
> y abrumada sentí que mi
> frente un torrente de lava quemó.
> Y en mi loca falaz fantasía
> sus clamores y cánticos oí,
> y el tumulto y su inquieta porfía
> encerrado en mi mismo sentí. (p. 89b; *ES*, 617-624)

Side by side, the two passages could not be more dissimilar in sensibility, even though they deal with the same event. The only carryovers from the first account are the noises of the infernal horde. Otherwise, part two reveals a private experience joined to an analysis of the subject's irrational mind. Most striking is the centrifugal frame of reference. Whereas the first passage bursts outward in every direction, the second one turns inward and down toward a hidden center within the self. The imagery is full of encirclement, restriction, shrinking away (*embargada, absorta, abrumada, encerrado*). The vocabulary reflects introspection rather than observation, as if the sources of events were imaginary and not in the external world. In order to make sense of the monstrous vision, the poet attributes incoherence and madness to his faculties. The "incierto delirio" is supposed to account for the imbalanced perception of the already disordered images. And the "loca falaz fantasía" further explains the insensate vision by declaring the imagination to be out of control and susceptible to the errors of illogic and absurdity.

Nevertheless, a prior deformation exists here. Even before the poet contemplates them, the images are already grotesque. What, then, is the purpose of attributing a deformative power to the subjective processes of contemplation? The answer lies in the subjectivity of the Romantic vision. It is inconceivable that the subject not be caught up in the object's field of action, or not participate in its mode of being-in-the-world. This participation can mean communion or alienation, pathetic fallacy or objective antipathy, but in either case the subject must be emotionally involved with the object. In the grotesque aesthetic, the subject-object relationship is usually negative, with parallel disfigurations evident on both sides. The subject is deluded, or he suffers from delirium, or else he is victimized by the superior unnatural forces around him. In any event, he is not responsible for initiating the grotesque, even though his psychic reactions offer grotesque structures that correspond to the external forms. We can see, therefore, that Espronceda's concept of imagination plays a role in the grotesque by way of the subject's inner psychological experience. But the concept must be construed narrowly, excluding artistic creativity and inspiration, and referring only to the kinds of perception that the subject may be prone toward. A "loca falaz fantasía" will interfere with the normal apprehension of things and distort them. This makes the problem epistemological, not aesthetic.

III. The Bacchic Strain

Related to the psychology of deformation is another factor typical of the Romantic movement: Bacchic revelry. If mind submits weakly to the vagaries of imagination, it is just as vulnerable when the senses are intoxicated. Drunkenness is usually exploited for its dramatic interest in episodes of abandon, in carnival scenes, and in witches' sabbaths. However, the Bacchic strain can also be used for grotesque ends. This role is fulfilled intermittently in *El diablo mundo*, beginning with the devils' "tartárea-bacanal" at the start of the work, and ending with the "inmunda orgía" of the macabre tavern near the conclusion. In these cases, intoxication is a theme or a motif. However, it also changes into a technique in *El estudiante de Salamanca*, where the hero's reeling senses magnify the process of disintegration as he sees it in the world around him.[8]

It is the second aspect which requires our attention. While external events are isolated from their impact on the subject, Espronceda allows them to be temporarily replaced by spurious cause-effect relationships, which are suggested as possible explanations for what is happening. For example, Felix sees a sinister figure wavering before him, "tal vez engaño de sus propios ojos, / forma falaz que en su ilusión creó, / o del vino ridículos antojos" (p. 69a; *ES, 733-734*). But then the interpretation is rejected, "que ya mil veces embriagarse en vano / en frenéticas orgías intentara" (p. 69a; *ES, 739-740*). Nevertheless, two possible sources of deformation have been indicated, "ilusión" and "vino." Regardless of their actual participation in the present vision, they are singled out as perception-distorting agents. As a hypothesis, the "forma falaz'" wrought by the imagination is justifiably considered to be a serious sensory problem, and we have already seen proof of this. Not so, however, for wine. It merely stirs up "ridículos antojos," hardly to be taken seriously when one considers the drunkard's preposterous condition. The reference exploits the foolish aspect of drunken contexts, demeaning the horror inherent in the spectre and rendering its ominousness ambivalent. True, the read-

---

8 Circumstances like this one remind Martinengo of the Walpurgisnacht, which he treats in *Polimorfismo...* , p. 43. Despite Casalduero's contention that "el tema de 'Fausto' es un obstáculo para penetrar *El diablo Mundo*" *(Forma...* p. 90*)*, Martinengo has dug deeply into the question of "Espronceda ante la leyenda fáustica," in *Revista de Literatura*, 29 (1966), 35-55. See note 8.

er grasps the implications of the menacing apparition, and his terror is reinforced. But for the moment, the explanation based on drunkenness is pushed to the background, and the scene continues:

> La calle parece se mueve y camina,
> faltarle la tierra sintió bajo el pie;
> sus ojos la muerta mirada fascina
> del Cristo, que intensa clavada está en él.
> Y en medio el delirio que embarga su mente,
> y achaca el al vino que al fin le embriagó,
> la lámpara alcanza .. , (p. 69b; *ES*, 761-767)

Here is a second reference to the influence of wine, and it is not humorous at all. Intoxication can no longer be regarded as a hallucinatory cause, and with this possibility gone, the street-tremors begin their ominous threat.

What actually is happening to Felix? He is in the throes of a "delirio," a concept intended to mark the growing duality of the situation. Independent supernatural forces have been established on one hand, and private confusion on the other, thus complicating the external madness. Moreover, a grotesque note emerges from the confrontation of Dionysiac and Divine principles. It could scarcely be otherwise, since the street is obedient to its own delirium, while the protagonist staggers against the lurching background. The Christ image intrudes upon the scene incongruously with its fixed and presumably sober state. We should note at this point that "delirio" refers to sense perception only, since Felix's mental faculties still permit him to understand events rationally. In fact, his last gesture of self-defense is a rationally conceived stratagem: he will face the weird powers around him with an air of bravado: "Y un báquico cantar tarareando, / cruza aquella quimérica morada / con atrevida indiferencia andando, / mofa en los labios y la vista osada" (p. 74b; *ES*, 1261-64). The levels of grotesquerie now multiply, with the uncanny environment receding before the disparate raucousness of the irreverent student. His levity clashes with the deadly serious challenge thrown out by those beings pitted against him. And there is further incongruity in the gay but hollow song that dances in the atmosphere, the very air that readers perceive to be laden with certain doom.

Throughout the scene, the role of drunkenness assumes a special character, having little to do with the use of wine to exalt the senses for inspirational purposes, and still less with the pleasure-seeking bacchanals of Romantic exoticism. Inebriation has both a psychological and a moral purpose. It produces a dislocation of the senses that erroneously claims responsibility for the chaos glimpsed in the surrounding reality. And it turns the hero's reckless mockery into an absurd moral stance, given the grave religious retribution that awaits him. Drunkenness as a state of mind offers no method for coping with the hostile environment, and as a mode of behavior it is the most grotesque response that can be made to a desperate situation. The drunken state wavers between perspectives, simulating an epistemological problem while exerting an imbalancing effect upon Felix. At the beginning, he thinks, "O Satanás se chancea, / o no debo estar en mí, / o el Málaga que bebí / En mi cabeza aun humea" (p. 72a; *ES*, 1035-38). And by the end, every possibility except the correct one is mentioned to explain the source of the nightmare around him. Indeed, the fact that he can reason clearly is enough to remove this episode from the usual Romantic category of Bacchic themes and place it instead under a grotesque heading.

IV. The Macabre

So much for the psychological predisposition of the grotesque. Turning to its formal execution, we find three different approaches, which will be the subjects of the next sections. The first makes use of macabre elements, a component which is familiar enough in the Romantic repertoire to require little comment were it not for Espronceda's deliberate distortion. It is one thing to parade skeletons, ghosts, or monsters for the purpose of creating pure emotional states like terror and fear, but it is something else again to invent impure mixtures of indefinable moods that combine laughter, fright, and disgust. The macabre in its nongrotesque form is unadulterated and rarely comic. Its frightening aspects are unmistakably frightening, and whatever is ugly or morally repugnant maintains a purity of character. When horror and suspense are to be emphasized, death is imbued with an air of supernaturalism, and when revulsion or shock are intended, we find devices that play on the physical and moral differences between the living and the dead.

Differences between nongrotesque and grotesque macabre usage can be demonstrated easily by tracing the corpse motif in Espronceda's poems. A traditionally macabre scene shows the following stereotype: "y en una estancia solitaria y triste, / entre dos hachas de amarilla cera, / un fúnebre ataúd, y en él tendida / una joven sin vida / que aun en la muerte interesante era" (p. 144a; *DM*, 5430-34). The triteness of this example illustrates the basic techniques of the conventional macabre as they became derivative Romantic formulas. There is also a suggestion of necrophilia, another staple motif. On the other hand, a new macabre accent appears in the description of another feminine figure, who is compared to a corpse: "de vagos contornos confusa figura, / cual bello cadáver, se alzó una mujer" (p. 92a; *DM*, 866-867). The reversal of metaphorical terms transforms the entire basis of comparison. Normally, it is the corpse which is the subject described, with its necrophilic appeal linked to certain preserved human qualities. Thus, the usual comparison is to a human being. In this case, however, the subject itself is human and alive, with the corpse acting as the point of reference. The terms of the metaphor are reversed, although the woman is neither a cadaver nor a figure with cadaver-like traits. Despite this, she is likened to a "bello cadáver," a bizarre qualification by any standard of female beauty except a grotesque one. The deformation of the image depends upon the attribution of beauty to a corpse, a fact then used as a standard by which to measure this woman's beauty. Such a standard, gauged by a necrophiliac's taste, can only be termed a perversion. No matter how we turn the phrase "cual bello cadáver," even while admitting that some female corpses are beautiful, there is no contextual indication that the woman is meant to display mortuary qualities. The description is not only macabre, it is grotesquely so.

Another conventional use of the macabre also hints at a new orientation, the blurring of spheres of reality: "Era más de media noche, / antiguas historias cuentan, / cuando en sueño y en silencio / lóbrego envuelta la tierra, /los vivos muertos parecen, /los muertos la tumba dejan" (p. 59a; *ES*, 1-6). These opening lines of *El estudiante de Salamanca* trail off into commonplace allusions to ghosts and witches, but for a moment they suggest the idea of confused realities where the living and the dead become indistinguishable, at least on the surface. Those who are alive take on the appearance of the dead, and the dead rise up into a state of animation. This macabre reality is then extended to other areas without regard to any descriptive logic. For example, in one simile concerning the earth under the effects of a storm, the macabre image is gratuitous: "Y entre masas espesas de polvo / desaparece la tierra tal vez, / cual gigante cadáver que cubre / vil mortaja de lienzo soez" (p. 89b, *DM*, 597-600). The corpse motif is converted into an abstract configuration having little to do with its original meaning, and it joins a vocabulary of grotesque allusions whose application does not directly involve normal usage. The words "cadáver" and "mortaja" no longer retain their primary reference to authentic funeral scenes. On the other hand, their very transference to a metaphorical plane shows a refinement in the concept of the macabre. From realistic immediacy in scenes such as the one cited earlier describing the girl in the coffin, there evolves a language that is once-removed from macabre reality. This language, when applied to other subjects, imbues them with the same morbid pallor of the original, while the incongruity of such usage renders the image grotesque.

The most vivid of Espronceda's macabre effects occur in the area of animation. Playing on hypersensitive fears of being touched, he uses grimacing skeletons in stiff formation to amass a sense of forward motion:

> y al tremendo tartáreo ruido
> cien espectros alzarse miró:
> de sus ojos los huecos fijaron
> y sus dedos enjutos en él...
> se acercaron despacio y la seca
> calavera, mostrando temor,
> con inmóvil, irónica mueca
> inclinaron, formando enredor. (p. 77a; *ES*, 1488-1501)

The technique is as elementary as the result is frightening. This is why the same elements are often borrowed by later generations, especially by the surrealists, to create atmospheres of terror or paranoia. It is not the physical aspect of the skeletons that is significant but rather the sensibility that emerges: encirclement, irony, relentless stares. In contrast, another scene provides a fairly intricate portrait of a skeleton:

> El cariado, lívido esqueleto,
> los fríos, largos y asquerosos brazos
> le enreda en tanto en apretados lazos

> y ávido le acaricia en su ansiedad.
> Y con su boca cavernosa busca
> la boca a Montemar, y a su mejilla
> la árida, descarnada y amarilla
> junta y refriega repugnante faz. (p. 77b; *ES, 1554-61)*

The episode involves the bizarre marriage of Felix to Elvira's ghost, and the graphic diabolism of the entire scene is reflected in the rich details of this excerpt. Once again a taste of necrophilia can be detected, except that now it is the hero, not a dead woman, who is passive and without desire. This reversal of the standard love-death scene makes the situation eerie, although the effect also owes much to the textural qualities of the description. The amorous duet offers the gruesome spectacle of cadaverous lust and human disgust, of a dead body eager for the warmth of living flesh, and for the touch of a young man's cheek. As the skeleton's mouth approaches to complete the half-formed kiss, the grotesquerie of love is fulfilled. The lover is sexless yet full of aggressive desire. With effort, we remember that this figure was once a woman, and that her partner is now a trapped victim stripped of the masculine resources that used to serve him at appropriate times. As the pursued male, he must play a passive role, acting the part of a corpse in an inverted necrophiliac situation. The lover-skeleton grotesquely assumes the necrophile's role, and this is the final irony in the most incongruous Don Juan scene ever written.

V. Acoustical Distortion

The macabre, then, is one of the approaches undertaken in the formal construction of the grotesque. The second basic method involves devices of a sensorial nature. These techniques are acoustic and visual, as might be expected, with a sea of noise finally obliterating whatever linear coherence that might have been gained by pictorial means.[9] Where sounds and shapes blend almost perfectly, as at the beginning of *El diablo mundo*, the strongly imagistic representation is still covered gradually by a flood of different noises:

---

9 Casalduero speaks of the "confusión auditivo-visual que expresa el dramatismo de la noche de Walpurgis," *(Forma...* , p. 35). See note 3.

Y en medio negra figura / levantada en pie se mece,
de colosal estatura / y de imponente ademán.
Sierpes son su cabellera / que sobre su frente silban,
su boca espantosa y fiera / como el cráter de un volcán.
De duendes y trasgos / muchedumbre vana
se agita y se afana / en pos su señor....
Bullicioso séquito / que vienen y van,
visiones fosfóricas, / ilusión quizá.
Trémulas imágenes / sin marcada faz,
su voz sordo estrépito / que se oye sonar,
cual zumbido unísono / de mosca tenaz. (p. 86a; *DM*, 261-286)

Due to the overwhelming spatial confusion, it is easy to overlook the presence of pure grotesque figures here. So too, the overall cacophony can easily blot out the carefully drawn pictorial imagery. For example, the grotesque "negra figura" is of a "colosal estatura" with a head crowned by "sierpes" and followed by a swarm of goblins and elves. And yet this graphic image is rendered imprecise by movements like "se mece," "se agita," and "vienen y van," as well as by a vague spatial-chromatic blur in which the fluidity of shapes and motions merge into a vibrant illusion of forms: "fiera como el cráter de un volcán," "visiones fosfóricas," "trémulas imágenes / sin marcada faz." At the same time, the cacophonous sound grows in prominence, beginning with the controlled noises associated with the "negra figura" ("silban," "boca... de un volcán"). Added to the din ("bullicioso") are other noises emitted by the "muchedumbre vana" until the last verses impose a uniform veneer of sense data with their "zumbido unísono." The entire episode is a remarkable harmony of dissonant elements, with grotesque shapes receding before dynamic movements of masses, and with the sharp pictorial impact being counterbalanced by the appeals to sound. Despite the excess and exaggeration, the scene is somehow held in check, and what fills our mind is a masterful *symphonie fantastique* in which the grotesque is but one controlled component among several.

Nevertheless, it is the acoustic factor which ultimately dominates the sensorial aspects of Espronceda's works, and when one leaves his major poems, it is with a head aching with sound rather than dulled by a riot of color. The variety of auditory allusions is enormous, a range that in itself might be considered out of proportion. Yet dissonances become distorted enough to warrant special attention, particularly in the description of actual sound-making. That is, sound is interesting not only as a descriptive trait to color an event, but also as a phenomenon in itself, by virtue of the manner in which it is produced. We see this in the way Espronceda seems to be fascinated by the hollowness of resonance, the emptiness within the shell of sound as contrasted to the wall of vibration itself. In the passage "temerosas voces suenan / informes, en que se escuchan / tácitas pisadas huecas" (p. 59a; *ES,* 8-10), the emphasis falls on the tenuous outlines of sound rather than on its substance: tone, pitch, volume, etc. The lack of form, a carry-over from the ghostly shapes of the imprecise setting, has its acoustic counterpart in muffled tones. Like negative space in sculpture, a soft echo is the hollow content of silence. In grotesque usage, this device amplifies the doleful insubstantiality of the phenomenon, and even of its source:

> resonando cual lúgubre eco
> levantóse en su cóncavo hueco
> semejante a un aullido una voz
> pavorosa, monótona, informe,
> que pronuncia sin lengua su boca,
> cual la voz que del áspera roca
> en los senos el viento formó. (pp. 77b-78a; *ES,* 1779-85)

The eerie howl is disembodied and without form, yet it is described variously with emotion-laden qualifications that surround the central physical fact of its hollow concavity. In another instance, the hollow echo of steps caused by a "maldecida bruja / con ronca voz" raises the dead from their tombs. These two cases use empty resonance to deform the voices present, and then give special counterpoint to their terrifying effect by referring to concurrent sounds made by other agents. When a full cacophony is constructed on the basis of many different noises, it is heard against the uncanny background of a world shattering into pieces:

> Y algazara y gritería,
> crujir de afilados huesos,
> rechinamiento de dientes
> y retemblar los cimientos

> y en pavoroso estallido
> las losas de pavimento
> separando sus junturas (p. 76b; *ES,* 1448-54*)*

In short, grotesque sensory perception occurs during the weird or distorted presentation of sounds, either alone or in conjunction with sinister supernatural beings. However, it also depends ultimately on a vision of reality which irrationally decomposes amid the most horrible of shrieks and shapes. The din is terrific, and if most of the auditory references are merely noises heard under amplification, the effect produced in the reader is one of unrelieved dissonance. The act of listening is abolished and everything is reduced to a state of hearing or being heard. It is a condition of the most elementary kind, where sounds assault the ear without any other effort or act of comprehension on the part of the subject. This primitive disjunction is also part of the larger vision of reality, a world which traps human victims in a tangle of unrelated phenomena. Sounds are emitted from unlikely places in response to the general disintegration of the environment, and these emissions are intended to frighten the protagonist and reader, and also to convey the sensory experience most likely to reign during cataclysmic moments.

VI. The Nascent Dream-Grotesque

The third and final approach in the formal construction of the grotesque is the simulation of disturbed dreamstates. What we have just seen represents an inferior form of symphonic fantasia composed with the paraphernalia of stock supernaturalism. In the nascent dream-grotesque, the quality of the components as well as of the technical execution is excellent. The high point of creativity is reached in *El estudiante de Salamanca,* where the hero races madly to his death along avenues subjected by an evil sorcery to constant change. The situation is comparable to a nightmare without the sophisticated symbolism that has come to the conscious surface in the twentieth century. As the narrative turns into a frantic state of mind, the dominant feeling is one of psychological disorientation induced by the contradictory information given to Felix's senses as he tries to find his bearings:

> Y cuando duda si duerme,

si tal vez sueña o está
loco, si es tanto prodigio,
tanto delirio verdad,
otra vez en Salamanca
súbito vuélvese a hallar...
y en su delirante vértigo
al vino vuelve a culpar (p. 72a; *ES*, 1022-31)

With the immediate reality in epistemological doubt, a grotesque representation emerges from the narrative. An ever-changing environment is combined with mental imaginings. Physical and emotional planes transfuse each other with elements flowing freely in both directions. To develop an exegesis of this incongruous phenomenology would be laborious, but there are at least ten factors that affect the grotesque results, and they can be listed as follows:

1. abrupt and antithetical mutations naturally acquired, without recourse to magic explanations ("y desaparece / de súbito la ciudad: / palacios, templos, se cambian / en campos de soledad" [p. 72a; *ES*, 999-1001])
2. the anxiety-laden sense of spatial relationships (throughout)
3. the frightening instability of normally solid masses ("Y ve fantásticas torres / de eterno pedestal / arrancarse, y sus macizas / negras masas caminar" [p. 71b; *ES*, 976-79])
4. the confounding of geometrical principles, and the allusion to invalidated physical laws ("apoyándose en sus ángulos / que en la tierra en desigual, / perezoso tronco fijan" [p. 71b; *ES*, 980-982])
5. the use of arhythmical dances by contorted figures ("en danzas grotescas / y al estruendo funeral / en derredor cien espectros / danzan con torpe compás" [p. 71b-72a; *ES*, 986-989])
6. the precocious air of surreality, and the realistically depicted otherworldliness reminiscent of much modern painting ("en un yermo y silencioso / melancólico arenal, / sin luz, sin aire, sin cielo" [p. 72a; *ES*, 1002-04])
7. the hallucinatory extremism of endless processions of phantoms, etc. ("Y el juicio voy a perder / entre tantas maravillas" [p. 72b; *ES*, 1044-45])
8. the sense of paranoia and the motif of haunting eyes ("Y en la sombra

unos ojos fulgurantes / vio en el aire vagar que espanto inspiran, / siempre sobre él saltándose anhelantes: / ojos de horror que sin cesar le miran" [p. 73b; *ES*, 1173-76])9. the reconstitution of architectural concepts by the presence of chimera and fantasy ("Todo vago, quimérico y sombrío, / edificio sin base ni cimiento / ondula cual fantástico navío" [p. 74a; *ES*, 1221-23])
10. the assassination of Time ("Corre allí el tiempo, en sueño sepultado. / Las muertas horas a las muertas horas / siguen en el reloj de aquella vida, / sombras de horror girando aterradoras, / que allí aparecen en medrosa rueda" [p. 74a; *ES*, 1228-32]).

The finale of this adventure consists of an endless spiral descent which "el juicio pone en loco desatino / A Montemar" (p. 74b; *ES*, 1319-20), and during which the hero is assailed by brutal howls and sarcastic screams, applause, laughter, mockery, all while being buffeted by the maelstrom that drags him down. It is a splendid performance, except that it is real; a drunken fantasy transformed into infernal reality; a nightmare whose end is an awakening into the retribution of insanity and grotesque machination.

To sum up, it is useful to think of Espronceda's grotesque as the means for supplementing the creative imagination. His advocacy of disorder begins with whim, follows haphazard fancy, and ends by breeding excess and disproportion. The process results in an interpenetration of subjective and phenomenal categories. In the external world, violence, blurred outlines, and the dynamics of amorphism prevail. In the subjective world, a centrifugal orientation is coupled to an involuntary vertiginous kinesthesia. A sense of encirclement and of retraction becomes the inner response to the "loca falaz fantasía" and the "incierto delirio." Perception-distorting agents, such as wine, make their contribution to the grotesque too. Yet the physical world is also responsible, as demonstrated by the duality apparent in the dislocation of the senses and the supernatural environment. Conventional themes such as the Bacchic, the macabre, and the Dantesque are transformed or adulterated, while Christian motifs provoke morally ambiguous attitudes. The most unusual contribution to the grotesque is Espronceda's inversion of necrophilia to the point where love-making and cadaverous animation are not far apart. The sensory aspects of grotesquerie emphasize space and sound; in addition to cacophony, uncannily hollow sounds are used as the acoustic counterpart of negative space. Finally, there are premonitions of Surrealist practice in the paranoid, phantasmagoric vision, and especially in the chronological perception of time.[10]

---

[10] This study was first published in *Studies in Romanticism*, 11 (1972), 94-112. Reprinted with permission.

8
Bécquer and the Romantic Grotesque

AS SCHOLARS BEGIN TO pay more attention to the host of literary problems attached to the grotesque, the case for recognizing separate stages in grotesque literature grows increasingly stronger. We may now speak of a "Romantic" grotesque as distinct from Renaissance or twentieth-century manifestations, and although there is still much to learn about these differences, certain identifying traits are clearly distinguishable.[1] For example, we know that the eerie sense of a half-dream, half-nightmarish a.tmosphere, which is often typical of the grotesque in general, takes a unique form in the Romantic "fantasy-piece" or nocturnal story, as cultivated by narrators like Hoffmann, Poe, and Bécquer. We also know that the traditional presence of supernatural elements in much of the grotesque acquires a special configuration in the Gothic fiction of England, and that caricature and destructive wit strike the note of "Satanic" humor with particular emphasis in the Romantic period. The same may be said about madness, terror, Beauty

---

1 In addition to the two general books, Wolfgang Kayser, *Das Groteske: seine Gestaltung in Malerei una Dichtung* (Hamburg, 1958), and Arthur Clayborough, *The Grotesque in English Literature* (Oxford, 1965), see Paul !lie, *The Surrealist Mode in Spanish Literature* (Ann Arbor, Mich., 1968); Lee Byron Jennings, *The Ludicrous Demon: Aspects of the Grotesque in German Post-Romantic Prose* (Berkeley, Calif., 1963); Max Milner, *Le Diable* (Paris, 1960); Eric Newton, *The Romantic Rebellion* (New York, 1962); Mario Praz, *The Romantic Agony* (Oxford, 1933); Patricia M. Spacks, *The Insistence of Horror* (Cambridge, Mass., 1962); Nicholson B. Adams, "The Grotesque in Some Important Spanish Romantic Plays," *Todd Memorial Volumes* (New York: Columbia Univ., 1930), I, 37-46; Edward Bostetter, "The Nightmare World of 'The Ancient Mariner'," *Studies in Romanticism*, I (1962), 241-254; David Sices, "Musset's *Fantasio*: The Paradise of Chance," *Romanic Review*, LVIII (1967), 23-37; and John Van Eerde, "The Imagery in Gautier's Dantesque Nightmare," *Studies in Romanticism*, I (1962), 230-240.

and the Beast, and other familiar landmarks in the realm of grotesquerie: they all have much in common with the universal characteristics of the grotesque, and yet they are found to be most highly developed in what we generally call the age of Romanticism.

These traits do vary from country to country, just as the very concept of Romanticism differs in specific traits according to nationality. But this does not mean that individual studies will not contribute to the overall understanding of the grotesque aesthetic, or to the definition of Romanticism, even where interpretations vary. With this in mind, I have written the present essay. Bécquer's works are not only the most important in Spanish Romantic literature, but they raise questions that are fundamental to European aesthetics in the second half of the nineteenth century. Many of these issues have already been discussed, although few critics have tried to relate the large body of nonfictional prose to the more famous *rimas* and *leyendas*. The purpose of the analysis that follows is to evaluate the role played by the grotesque motifs which appear throughout all of Bécquer's writings, from his tales to the historical narratives and regional sketches.

The significance of this grotesque mode in Bécquer's works is far from minor. To define it is to help dispel the shadow of vagueness that so effectively obscures the technique behind the supernatural atmosphere. And to isolate it as a sensibility is to reveal Bécquer's place in the development of the grotesque aesthetic in Spain, from Quevedo and Goya before him, to Spanish Surrealism afterwards. Moreover, by discussing the grotesque as a Romantic phenomenon we can draw the lines of convergence between fantasy and historical realism, self and society, and nature and the supernatural. With this approach, we will discover that the prosaic works as well as the imaginative ones belong to Bécquer's late Romantic vision. They are all unified by a grotesque presence—an exaggeration or a deformation which produces a reality that is neither tragic nor comic, and neither real nor unreal, but incongruous, absurd, and beyond the normal range of human experience. Sometimes this reality grows out of Bécquer's conscious effort to create a grotesque mood, but at other times he simply observes a grotesque style or event that is already there before him. In every case, however, there are a number of principles which we will find to be operative.

The first of these is the fact that the mechanisms of imagination depend in good measure on distortion and violence. Secondly, this subjective distortion is linked to a larger chaos in the universe, whose tragic force can be glimpsed by poetic fantasy. Third, the manifestations of that universal chaos are found in the grotesque aspects of Nature and art, and particularly architecture. They are also found in a "second" reality, a nether-world of demonic forms. And finally, both realities often fade away in the presence of the commonplace and disillusioning environment that we all live in, which can also be grotesque. In the sections that follow, I will take up each of these principles in detail.

I

If the aesthetic problems associated with the term "grotesque" are complicated, the semantic ones are not, at least as far as Bécquer and his Spanish contemporaries are concerned. For to them the word had simple and fairly precise connotations. According to Pagés, "grotesque" gained currency in Spain during the latter part of the eighteenth century, and by the middle of the nineteenth, had come to mean "ridiculous" as well as contorted or bizarre.[2] Bécquer uses the word frequently, and always in this sense rather than with the original designation of an ornamental design. On the other hand, he seems to restrict the definition to two special levels of meaning, one spatial and the other emotional. As far as this affects the individual's relationship to his surroundings, "grotesque" means ungraceful or out of harmony, due to the incongruous manner in which that individual occupies space. For example, in one of Bécquer's episodes he tells of a witch being pushed off a cliff, with her skirts catching onto the brambles, so that she hangs suspended and shouting in midair: "Los mozos seguían desde lo alto sus grotescas

---

2 "...ridículo y extravagante por la figura o por cua!quiera otra calidad," as in these examples:..." si un pintor se atreviese a introducir esta figura grotesca en un cuadro de aquel asunto, se burlarían de ellos inteligentes... " (L. F. de Moratín); "Vienen, en fin, a acabarla de desentonar las dos figuras grotescas de Don Quijote y Sancho" (M. J. Quintana). Also "irregular, chocante, grosero y de mal gusto," as in these examples: "Bulle el grotesco tumulto/ En algazara infernal: / Ya de la excitante orquesta / Al voluptuoso compás" (Campoamor); "... comparten (las pilastras) de arriba abajo la fachada con grotescos de graciosa invención y capricho" (Jovellanos). Aniceto de Pagés, *Gran diccionario de la lengua castellana (de Autoridades)* (Madrid, 1902).

evoluciones esperando el instante en que se desgarraría el útimo jirón de la saya a la que estaba sujeta y rodaría, dando tumbos de pico en pico, hasta el fondo del barranco..."[3] The choice of "grotesque" was doubtless influenced by the presence of the witch but the quality of the word is not determined by the kind of subject involved but by the type of movement made by her body. The adjective has little in the way of emotional value, whereas the conclusive discord of the witch's limbs is sketched in with a vivid outline.

In contrast, it is the emotional connotation of "grotesque" which is stressed elsewhere, when Bécquer refers to himself as feeling so awkward that he realized that "sentado en una silla estrecha y empinada, se está como vendido y haciendo una figura grotesca" (p. 713). As before, the sentence suggests the same awareness of spatial relationships: a single body standing out incongruously from the background. But the real point is Bécquer's painful self-consciousness, which highlights a feeling about his posture and not the physical posture itself. Thus, the word "grotesque" retains its loosely spatial innuendo while casting a penumbra of feeling as well. This emotional factor is of first importance, as we will see, in the truly grotesque scenes where the word itself is not used but where the result is more profoundly artistic than the usages we are now considering.

It would seem, then, that the rather nontechnical meaning of "grotesque" would have rendered the word ineffective for Bécquer, except as a vague epithet. However, a closer look shows that Bécquer's usage gave the word a well-defined limit in its range of connotations. Basically, he intended "grotesque" to imply anything bizarre and out of proportion, whether its effect was to amuse or to disturb. In one case, he links the grotesque to laughter by describing an attitude "no tan grotesca como la del buen regidor aragonés, que ora dejándose caer la gorra de una cabezada, ora roncando como un órgano o balbuciendo palabras ininteligibles, ofrecía el espectáculo más chistoso que imaginarse puede." (p. 506). Yet for the most part, it was the unpleasant features of the grotesque that were suggested, the least offensive of which can be found in Bécquer's remarks concerning his aversion to large municipal cemeteries:

---

3 *Obras completas* (Madrid: Aguilar, 1973), p. 609. All references are to this edition and hereafter will be cited in the text.

...aquella triste parodia de jardín con flores sin perfume y verdura sin alegría, me oprimen el corazón y me crispan los nervios. El afán de embellecer grotesca y artificialmente la muerte me trae a la memoria a esos niños de los barrios bajos a quienes después de expirar embadurnan la cara con arrebol, de manera que, entre el cerco violado de los ojos, la intense palidez de las sienes y el rabioso carmín de las mejillas, resulta una mueca horrible. (p. 528).

The extent of this repugnant quality acts to suppress all traces of comic undertone, but at the same time, the "mueca horrible" is equally distant from any fearful or horrifying nuance.

The basic definition of "grotesque," then, remains the same—a bizarre distortion that reaches neither tragic nor comic proportions, but induces instead a low-keyed sense of disquietude due to our awareness of the violence done to the principles of harmony and compatibility. We know all of this intuitively rather than by perceiving it on a consciously intellectual level. For this reason, Bécquer's usage in these cases may be called commonplace and popular. My point in quoting them is to show that despite their vague and aesthetically superficial meaning they do fall within a specific range of nuances for Bécquer, and in fact represent his assimilation of an entire concept. It is important to establish this fact from the beginning, for it means that Bécquer's grotesque is a natural phenomenon. The best proof of this is his casual, unstudied employment of the word. The latter does not stand out as a conscious choice, or as the embodiment of a complex idea. It is instead an integral part of Bécquer's vocabulary, spontaneously chosen to represent a natural response within his emotional framework.

Going beyond Bécquer's unaffected vocabulary usage, we find that the first and most important foundation of this grotesque aesthetic depends upon the idea of imagination. Here, of course, much has been said by critics, who have pointed out that there are many components in this central concept. However, we must not fail to note the prominence of distortion in Bécquer's notion of imagination, more from the standpoint of theory than of practice. Many of his remarks about fantasy are dominated by a concern for aberration and abnormality. These are not offered in any neurotic sense, but rather as an expression of how irrational factors can function independently within the creative mechanism. The phenomenon of irrationalism is in itself a complex matter, requiring us to decide which of its operations we think belongs to the grotesque aesthetic. That is, we must consider the following questions. Is irrationalism the rejection of empirical proofs, and with this the acceptance of a fantastic dream world as reality? Does it affirm the primacy of the emotions, and the subjective over the objective? Or again, does it seek to abandon the categories of logical thought and replace them with an uninhibited association of images? And finally, does it propose to destroy the nerve center of the will in order to permit an alien force to gain hold of the creative faculties?

All of these possibilities are, in varying degrees, true of the irrational character of Bécquer's art. But the grotesque partakes of this irrationalism most critically with respect to the last factor, the idea that the creative process has somehow gotten out of control, that it is captured and ruled by a force beyond the poet's will. Textual evidence for this indicates that the process occurs in two stages. First is Bécquer's desire for lyrical fantasy, which, when set in motion, quickly transforms itself into an independent impulse. Bécquer's imagination outstrips his will, and things get out of hand: "una vez aguijoneada la imaginación, es un caballo que se desboca y al que no sirve tirarlo de la rienda" (p. 123). This uncontrollable factor is now more than simple irrationalism, for it will lead the poet beyond the limits of his responsibility. At this point, the second stage begins. The fruits of Bécquer's imagination are his only in part; they have grown at an alarming pace, like hothouse plants spurning the care of the cultivator. Hence the well-known metaphor of fertility and birth in the "Introducción sinfónica." That image seems quite normal at first, and the reference to "los extravagantes hijos de mi fantasía" (p. 40) does not necessarily imply anything grotesque. But then we learn that these offspring are "desnudos y deformes, revueltos y barajados en indescriptible confusión" (p. 40), and later, that they pass in extravagantes procession, pidiéndome con gestos y contorsiones que os saque a la vida" (p 41).

It is clear that these future inhabitants of the Bécquerian universe are remarkable at this point for their deformities and not for their lyrical or magical qualities. Admittedly, they are awaiting the medium of "the word" in order to cross the abyss between idea and form. And granted too that the mature form taken by his rebellious children is predominantly fantastic instead of grotesque. But the fact remains that Bécquer has described the deepest wellspring of his inspiration in terms of a subtle grotesque conceit. Even more, he holds "los rebeldes hijos de la imaginación" responsible for his infirm, feverish state of mind. He is insomniac because of then and his sleeplessness completes the vicious circle of conception and genesis extending beyond his conscious will:

> El insomnio y la fantasía siguen y siguen procreando en monstruoso maridaje. ¡Sus creaciones, apretadas ya como las raquíticas plantas de un vivero pugnan por dilatar su fantástica existencia…! Necesario es abrir paso a las aguas profundas, que acabarán por romper el dique… (p. 40).

One searches the preceding passage for some trace of a constructive attitude on Bécquer's part toward his primal creations, but in vain. True, his imagery stresses both abundance and potency and these are in keeping with the larger metaphor of productivity. Nevertheless, the creative process also contains a grotesque episode, and graver still the aim of that process seems to be to release Bécquer from a painful burden. Evidently, this is the only value which the poet sees, for his stated desire is to find relief, although originally he had hoped for a normal birth of beauty.

From another standpoint, it is possible to regard the whole of Bécquer's introductory statement as an elaborate rhetorical convention, and, indeed, this is true insofar as it continues the age-old metaphor of mental conception and incubation. On the other hand, Bécquer was not obeying an artistic precept here, since he uses its formula to exploit the new elements that he had added: violence and the relief from excess. Proof of this can be found in the significant repetition of the same image in the story "El caudillo de las manos rojas." And by more than just coincidence, it is the tormented and pursued Romantic hero who experiences the event: "Gigantes cataratas de sangre negra y espumosa, que se estrellan bramando sobre las oscuras peñas de un precipicio terrible; imágenes espantosas y confusas de desolación y terror; estos son los fantasmas que engendra su mente durante las horas de reposo" (p. 51). Here too, the problem consists of being rid of the afflicting microcosm that is usually conjured by the minds of Romantic seers. The idea of finding in that mental world some evocation of beauty, even of a demonic kind, is more remote, although the artistic effect is indeed evocative in an aesthetic sense.

This same story also continues the theme of excessive abundance, for the god of Sleep is personified with ninety hands that contain as many goblets filled to the brim with a sleeping potion. More revealing, the train which accompanies Sleep is described as comprising "sus hechuras [que] lo siguen en grupos fantásticos. Estos se agitan y confunden entre sí, dando ser a nuevas y rápidas metamorfosis, locos delirios, embriones de confusas ideas, semejantes a las que produce en mitad de la fiebre una imaginación débil y sobreexcitada" (p. 67). The similarity to Bécquer's own state of mind needs no further elaboration. Let us note, however, that this confused and uncontrolled activity appears in a form resembling a grotesque interlude, and that it enters unbidden, like the visitation of an alien will. We must, of course, take into account the degree to which this is traditional. For example, we might be reminded of Plato's *Ion*, but if so, we cannot also fail to notice how the two are different as well. The Bécquerian soul here is tortured, not ecstatic, and it does not associate its experience with a divine Good. On the other hand, we might also recall the legends concerning the incubus and the nightmare, and in this instance we find Bécquer drawing closer to the grotesque aspects of those literary themes. But once again there is a major change, in that he remains theologically indifferent. Bécquer displays none of the religious feeling or moral conviction that once had forced all forms of demonic grotesquerie into the mold of God-versus-the-devil.

Despite this departure from tradition, we might still validly question why Bécquer's references to "imágenes espantosas," "rápidas metamorfosis," and "locos delirios" constitute anything different from the mild grotesquerie of the Dantesque style. The answer requires a study beyond the scope of this chapter, but it can be safely said that the question has little to do with comparing structures and forms. The issue is, rather, that the Romantic grotesque releases the aesthetics of supernaturalism from the grip of religious doctrine, exploits a secular horror, and cultivates religious themes largely for their artistic value. This sweeping statement will have many exceptions, to be sure, but without such a generalization it is impossible to say anything meaningful about what makes Romanticism different from earlier sensibilities. The divergent orientations in Quevedo's *Sueños* and Goethe's *Walpurgisnacht* scene should confirm the truth of this, at least as far as grotesque usage is concerned.

We come, then, to the wider significance of Bécquer's concept of imagination. Insofar as there exists an abnormal sphere within his powers of creation, the grotesque emerges as the product of an "enferma imaginación" (p. 742) which was acknowledged for more than the usual rhetorical reasons. When Bécquer says that "tengo en la cabeza una multitud de ideas absurdas que siempre me andan dando tormento mezclándose y sobreponiéndose a las pocas negociables en el mercado del sentido común" (p. 798), there is far more than just editorial modesty here. He is introducing a concept of absurdity which, in an incipient form, points to a source of anguish that will grow increasingly prominent with each succeeding generation of artists. The word "absurdas" may very well mean "senseless" or "foolish" in this context. But it is difficult to believe that Bécquer himself regarded his themes in that way. He intended something more than frivolous fantasy, since his reference to "tormento" suggests a more complex emotional involvement with the subject matter. More important, absurdity becomes an artistic device with which to build an entire work. Bécquer speaks of this when pointing out certain themes "sobre que yo hago mil y mil variaciones, en la que pudiéramos llamar absurdas sinfonías de la imaginación" (p. 384). We have, then, one of the earliest examples in Spanish literature of a grotesque element that offers a clue to the post-Romantic crisis in sensibility. That is, the concept of absurdity here points to the two separate directions in which modern literature, from post-Symbolism to early Surrealism, was to follow.

In one of these developments, we have the idea of the "enferma imaginación," with its suggestion of the neurasthenic self that so preoccupied *fin-de-siècle* poets like the *modernistas*. And in the other, there is the absurdity which later acquired a more objective role in movements like Surrealism. Of the two tendencies forecast by Bécquer, the objective aspect of his grotesque seems to be more significant than any possible neurotic interpretation. In other words, where the lyrical as opposed to the descriptive aspect of his aberrant imagination enters the scene, it is the objective side that takes precedence. This is one reason why Bécquer's *leyendas* have a distant and impersonal ring to them despite their charged atmosphere.

A good example of how the objective converges on the subjective and dominates it occurs in "El Miserere," when the wandering composer is overcome by the music of a Maundy Thursday service: "Siguió la ceremonia; el músico, que la presenciaba, absorto y aterrado, creía estar fuera del mundo real, vivir en esa región fantástica del sueño, en que todas las cosas se revisten de formas extrañas y fenomenales " (p. 197). As in so many other places, Bécquer tends to portray the "other reality" rather than give a psychological analysis of the emotions, a preference that we will examine later in detail. What interests him are the "formas extrañas y fenomenales," and these are found already fashioned not only in the dream world but in the very fabric of his inspirational experience. Thus, in the famous third *rima* which counterposes reason against inspiration, the latter is given an objective character that draws on the non-self as well as on the self. Inspiration is the "Sacudimiento extraño / que agita las ideas," and it evokes "deformes siluetas / de seres imposibles." In fact, even the echo of absurdity is brought in, by means of "palabras sin sentido; / cadencias que no tienen / ni ritmo ni compás" (402-03). Subjective aspects are present too, of course—soul, memory, madness—but these are the conventional elements, whereas the only really new one—"actividad nerviosa / que no halla en qué emplearse"— describes an impatient creator more than an introspective psychologist.

Thus, the solid roots of Bécquer's Romantic imagination permit at least one tendril to grow in a new direction. Creative activity includes the cultivation of dissonance as well as harmony, meaninglessness as well as understanding, and deformation as well as verisimilitude. These syncopations in the normal rhythms of life are the beginnings of a new sensibility, which, in modern times, has used distortion to find insight into reality. Of course, inspiration is only half of the creative process, and Bécquer goes on to describe reason as the other agent in this dual partnership. But this is precisely the point: Bécquer is foreshadowing a rational approach to the grotesque potential of man's imagination. From here on, the creation of a complete aesthetics of incongruity and the belief in the logic of the absurd are assured, and they will become the twentieth-century revision of the Romantic grotesque.

There is one final aspect to Bécquer's position regarding imagination. This concerns the linking of history to fantasy, and it is important because in his study of social reality Bécquer finds grotesque elements as well as the usual historical ones. It is interesting, therefore, to discover in the *Historia de los templos de España* the following statement, which enables us to appreciate Bécquer's state of mind while he contemplated not only statuesque heroes, but also gargoyles, and while he thought not only of heroic deeds but also of decadence:

> El poeta, a cuya invocación poderosa, como al acento de un conjuro mágico, palpita en sus olvidadas tumbas el polvo de cien generaciones; cuya imaginación ardiente reconstruye sobre un roto sillar un edificio, y sobre el edificio, con sus creencias y sus costumbres, una edad remota; el poeta, que ama el silencio para escuchar en él a su espíritu, que en voz baja y en un idioma extraño al resto de los hombres le cuenta las historias peregrinas, las consejas maravillosas de sus padres; que ama la soledad para poblarla con los hijos de su mente... puede a su antojo...dar vida a esa era portentosa de valor y de fe... (p. 774-75)

As Bécquer turned his attention from the past to the present, his uses of the imagination became increasingly realistic. Or, to put this another way, Bécquer's Romantic imagination makes use of everyday reality as well as fantasy. He shifts from the dream world to historical reality, and within the latter he distinguishes between the permanent body of past history and the changing kaleidoscope of the social present. What is noteworthy for our purposes is that the grotesque is one of the few constants in this shifting process.

For example in architecture, whose fixed embodiment of history offers Bécquer much for his imagination to dwell upon, the poet comments on certain grotesque details. And he also notices similar features in the passing carnival, whose transient structure is part of the present social scene. In other words, the Romantic sensibility of the *rimas and leyendas* finds its obverse in realism with the prominent components on both sides being the grotesque. This is of decisive importance in the evolution of aesthetic ideas after the Romantic movement, especially from Symbolism to Surrealism.

If we accept the general notion that after *Les fleurs du mal* (1857) aesthetics developed from the subjective to the objective, and from the lyrical to the empirical—in short, toward a greater degree of realism despite certain hermetic recessions—then the extent to which this realism is deformed by modern art becomes a crucial problem. I will discuss Bécquer's practices in this respect in the next sections, but the point now is that he put social reality at the service of his Romantic imagination so that the latter might explore the grotesque possibilities of the former. The consequences may be few, but they are revealing. The main result is that for the first time we can understand the difference between transfiguration and disfiguration in art. Social reality has always been transformed by the artist, but only in modern times has it been systematically disfigured. This is why we must place so much importance on the Spanish grotesque within the European concert of discords. For Spain has produced a grotesque not only by literary convention but by cultural reality. And Bécquer represents a turning point in Spanish literature in that he expresses more than a passing interest in the distortions, as well as the norms, of that reality. Bécquer's interest in his country's Medieval history and architecture, an interest which is typically Romantic, also extended to the Spanish carnival, which is not. There are many carnivals in Romantic literature, and this too is a subject deserving separate treatment. But, as we will see later, the squalid Spanish carnival, with its decidedly un-Romantic qualities as well as its Romantic ones, foreshadows a number of modern grotesque forms, particularly those of Solana and Valle-Inclán. In Bécquer's case, his remarks on history and the imagination are equally pertinent to his contemporary social reality, and regarding this reality, the carnival was a significant detail to have been selected.

II

We see, then, a dual activity on the part of the imagination: the creation of fantasy on the one hand, and the understanding of history on the other. On this basis, we may say that Bécquer's use of the grotesque falls into two associate categories, the first of which I will discuss now. This is the category of fantasy, which consists of trying to represent the "other world" that exists beyond ordinary reality. Bécquer's short stories depict an extra dimension whose laws have little to do with the usual flights of fancy that occur in the "real" world. Although Bécquer's total concept of reality is too intricate to deal with here, it is clearly more than just a problem of the interaction of the dream world with everyday reality. It also involves the notion that another world exists beyond this one, in a dimension that is rarely glimpsed by the poet, and then only with the fortuitous aid of his imagination. Occasionally this second world impinges upon the first and confounds the laws of man. But more often it is man who oversteps the bounds of his reality, and exceeds the limits of his imagination. It is then that the destructive and grotesque features of that other dimension make themselves known, and create the tragic conditions that are depicted in the *leyendas* and *narraciones*.

The most important fact about this other reality is that it coexists with Nature. Indeed, in some irrational way it may be said to be the other side of Nature, much in the same manner that Alice found the reverse of her world when she stepped behind the looking-glass. The difference is, however, that instead of discovering a world in reverse proportion, Bécquer encounters an unfamiliar and distorted realm. His netherworld of magical beings frequently has nothing to do with the known laws of Nature. And yet while it exists independently of Nature, it often functions within Nature, forming a wondrous but bizarre infrastructure all its own. Holding the key to the door of this world-behind-the-world is the gnome, one of Bécquer's most intriguing subjects. According to his account, gnomes live deep within the mountains, and his description of one of their caverns reveals something of the relationship between Nature and the netherworld:

> ...unas galerías subterráneas e inmensas, alumbradas con un resplandor dudoso y fantástico, producido por las fosforescencias de las rocas, semejantes allí a grandes pedazos de cristal cuajados en mil formas caprichosas y extrañas. El suelo, la bóveda y las paredes de aquellos extensos salones, obra de la Naturaleza, parecían jaspeados como los mármoles más ricos..." (p. 219).

The problem in analyzing passages like the foregoing and the ones that follow is a difficulty which must be faced in any Romantic literature that seeks to create a mood. After a while, such passages acquire a uniform texture, and their mysterious tone begins to sound monotonous. The truth is, however, that Bécquer chose his words deliberately, and our task is to sort out the different categories in what appears at first sight to be an undifferentiated piece of Romantic rhetoric. Indeed, the above passage contains such a vivid and richly detailed scene that it is important to recognize how the author sets off the various levels of reality. He does this by means of a central discord, the phrase "mil formas caprichosas y extrañas," which separates the natural domain from the infranatural one. These two adjectives do not belong to the sphere of Nature's influence because they refer to an object which is immune to the force of natural law. By contrast, the other elements in the scene are designated as the "work of Nature." Moreover, the physical sense of space is well-established, while the abstract laws of causality, comparison, and substance are also acknowledged. These traditional elements of reality are supplemented by a number of familiar Romantic building-blocks ("fosforescencias," "bóveda," "jaspeados"). Therefore, what remains independent of these law-obeying landmarks of reality are the " mil formas caprichosas y extrañas." These may not be very striking in their originality, but when seen in their "resplandor dudoso y fantástico" they represent the only elements which directly produce our sense of irreality. Indeed, the phrase "obra de la Naturaleza" would be gratuitous were it not for Bécquer's desire to contrast the two separate domains of Nature and her strange counterpart. And if we read on, we discover that the description amplifies the mood, but does not add any further unreal or extra-logical details to the scene.

Thus, even before we reach the description of the gnomes, the underground cavern is established as part of the Romantic grotesque by virtue of its detachment from the world of Nature. Not only is it foreign to the natural landscapes of Romantic poetry, but it has a touch of uncanniness which cannot be found in ordinary Romantic fantasy. The first difference needs no illustration, but as for the second, we can see the contrast by the following excerpt from the sketch "A la claridad de la luna": "Los objetos toman en su luz un tinte misterioso y fantástico... En esas noches serenas, y a la claridad de la Luna, la imaginación ve aparecer sobre el haz de la Tierra todos los quiméricos seres de la leyenda. Los gnomos... las undinas..." (p. 653-54). Clearly, whatever eerie or mysterious quality pervades the night, it is the result of the poet's imagination. His hallucination, whether an extreme example of the pathetic fallacy or of a more serious delusion, derives from his own psychological disposition. On the other hand, the description of the gnome's cavern is proffered as a matter of fact. The cave's existence depends on no man's imagination, and still less on what man calls the laws of Nature. The objective uncanniness of the "other" reality does not need the psychological support of human sensibility.

For this reason, another strange episode elsewhere crystallizes the difference between the natural and grotesque worlds. In that scene, a sorcerer invokes an animated hurricane of magic spirits, air, and water. Then, two distinct faces of reality can be seen side by side, each autonomous and both acting in accord with their separate laws:

> Nada más extráño y horrible que aquella tempestad circunscrita a un punto, mientras la luna se remontaba tranquila y silenciosa por el cielo y las aéreas lejanas cumbres de la cordillera parecían bañadas de un sereno y luminoso vapor. Las rocas crujían como si sus grietas se dilatasen, e impulsadas de una fuerza oculta e interior, amenazaban volar hechas mil pedazos. Los troncos más corpulentos arrojaban gemidos y chascaban próximos a hendirse, como si un súbito desenvolvimiento de sus fibras fuese a rajar la endurecida corteza. (p. 583)

This coexistence of separate dominions is all the more incongruous because it juxtaposes such divergent moods. Like many grotesque admixtures, this one owes its effect to the combination of incompatible elements: tranquility and violence. All of Nature is in repose except for one sector that is wracked by the tensions of a foreign energy. Although the natural world is following its own harmony, another system has seized part of its domain and broken into its rhythm. Both the "hidden inner force" and the "sudden loosening" are alien processes, harmonic in themselves since they submit to the rules of the magician's incantations. But they interfere with Nature's basic rhythm, with a result that is like a momentary collision with a rotating gyre. For a while, a crack-up seems imminent, but the larger frame regains its equilibrium.

The question will be raised as to why the sorcerer's tempest should be called grotesque instead of merely supernaturaL The answer is that not all supernaturalism is grotesque, nor all grotesquerie supernatural. In addition to the theological connotations of the word "supernatural," its usage tends to obscure the essential incongruity of the grotesque. Examples such as chivalric novels, fairy tales, and episodes in Dante's Inferno all represent types of supernaturalism, and yet they are not all necessarily grotesque. This is because they usually follow a systematic pattern of norms which gives them an inner coherence that is visible once the reader grasps the rules. The grotesque, on the other hand, is capricious and incoherent, devoid of any apparent law from which it might derive congruence. In the passage cited, there is no earthly or supernatural reason for the breakdown of Nature's harmony. The gnomes who hammer at their mountain forges produce a "sinfonía diabólica" (p. 628) that cannot be regarded in either religious terms or as part of a supernatural order that transcends the natural world. Bécquer's idea is to present the problem of concurrent realms which interpenetrate each other, and where phenomena such as metamorphosis make the traditional categories of natural-supernatural irrelevant. He suggests not so much a domination of one realm by another—which occurs in supernaturalism—but rather a coexistence of autonomous worlds, each of which is the perverse of the other. Thus, even the fantastic components of the one are governed by the principle of coherent harmony. On the other hand, even the realistic elements of the other are rendered incongruous.

Nevertheless, the terminology is much less important than the typology. It is not so much a question of whether the world of gnomes should be called supernatural, but whether the forms inhabiting that world display the bizarre distortion which, as I suggested at the beginning, constitutes the minimal definition of the grotesque. The following passage, appearing in a factual narrative tone, reveals what deviations from Nature the grotesque involves:

> Medio escondidos entre aquella húmeda frondosidad discurrían unos seres extraños, en parte hombres, en parte reptiles, o ambas cosas a la vez, pues transformándose continuamente, ora parecían criaturas humanas deformes y pequeñuelas, ora salamandras luminosas o llamas fugaces que danzaban en círculos sobre la cúspide del surtidor. Allí, agitándose en todas direcciones, corriendo por el suelo en forma de enanos repugnantes y contrahechos, encaramándose en las paredes, babeando y retorciéndose en figura de reptiles o bailando con apariencia de fuegos fatuos sobre el haz del agua, andaban los gnomos, señores de aquellos lugares, cantando y removiendo sus fabulosas riquezas. (p. 220)

The two principles in operation here which confirm the grotesque image are the metamorphosis and deliberate misproportion. Both help to bridge the gap between complete implausibility and naturalistic distortion. That is, a grotesque rendition would be an incredible and foolish monstrosity were it not for the recognizable changes of form that link the effort to one's own experience. By the same token, the grotesque is saved from being a mere deformation of naturalistic forms by the technique of transferring proportions. Both of these methods are at work here, and they help to place the grotesque beyond the natural world and into the "other" reality.

When we talk about metamorphosis, we must bear in mind that there are several types, and that Bécquer does not follow either the Ovidian or the evolutionary kind. In other words, his creatures do not undergo a transformation from one pure shape into another, like Narcissus from youth to flower. Nor do his creatures recapitulate various stages of the scale of evolution, like the paintings of Bosch and Dalí. To judge from the passage quoted above, it is the impurity of the figures which stands out. Their ambiguous and hybrid nature is stressed, rather than the form from which or to which they have changed. In other words, whereas Ovidian and evolutionary metamorphoses play up the stages within the process of change, Bécquer emphasizes the dynamic process itself. As a result, we cannot be sure exactly what it is we are watching, except that it is an impure being and that it is caught in a state of flux. As for the misproportion, the technique is self-explanatory. It is worth mentioning, however, that the phrase "enanos repugnantes y contrahechos" is not a redundancy, since " enanos repugnantes " by itself would have been sufficient for a grotesque effect. The "contrahechos," then, along with "babeando y retorciéndose," exaggerate the already distorted attitudes of Bécquer's figures.

At the same time, it is important to observe the emotional tenor of the description. The gnomes are irresistible, not dreadful, and if they destroy unsuspecting victims, it is because their appeal is stronger than the fear they may inspire. One such gnome is described as "un hombrecillo transparente; una especie de enano de luz semejante a un fuego fatuo, que se reía a carcajadas, sin ruido, y saltaba de peña en peña y mareaba con su vertiginosa movilidad" (p. 232). This portrait suggests that the grotesque can be a blend of ugliness and contortion without leaving the sensation of nightmarish uneasiness. Indeed, we may contrast two psychological modes in the aesthetics of distortion: a benign grotesque, in which neutral and sometimes attractive elements contrive to produce an atmosphere of harmless or adventurous fantasy; and a malignant grotesque, which acts to reproduce the dark landscape of malaise. To Bécquer's mind, gnomes represent the more appealing range of emotions—despite the fear they sometimes inspire—since they hold one key to the mysteries of the universe which were so passionately sought after by the Romantic poet. Let us recall in the famous rima "Espíritu sin nombre," where Bécquer catalogs his own poetic traits in a series of stanzas that all begin with "I," that he also includes, "Yo, en las cavernas cóncavas, / do el sol nunca penetra, / mezclándome a los gnomos, / contemplo sus riquezas" (v [62], 408). Thus, any hint of a diabolical power emerging from the story "El gnomo" is colored by the idealism of a yearning Romantic poet. The situation is comparable to the fatal lure of the woman in "Los ojos verdes." If the gnome is a destructive force, the power he represents is viewed as irresistibly fascinating rather than ominous in the eyes of the victim.

Bécquer's thematic portrayal of the gnome does not, quite obviously, mean that Satanism and other forms of supernatural horror are less significant in his work. But it does mean that there are various types of supernaturalism, not all of which are grotesque. For example, in the sketch "A la claridad de la luna" we find the following scene:

> A veces, como una casta matrona cubre su rostro con el velo si hiere su vista el espectáculo de la embriaguez, la Luna se envuelve en su manto de nubes, entre las cuales asoma tal vez un rayo de su luz, que entonces tiene un resplandor siniestro y sombrío. Esas son las noches en que los genios impuros congregan sus asambleas, y las brujas y los vampiros danzan en torno a Luzbel, prestándole homenaje. (p. 654).

Clearly, there is nothing grotesque here despite the implied drunkenness, the sinister light, and the "impure forces" milling about. What is missing is any sign of incongruous deformation intended to be used for aesthetic effect rather than for moral illustration. All the elements are supernatural in the traditional sense of portraying the notion of evil, while the opportunity to focus on the vampires, to describe the dance, or to explain the meaning of those "forces" is ignored.

In contrast, an episode which occurs for moral reasons—villagers preparing to execute an evil witch—turns into a lengthy description of purely formal elements. As the witch conjures,

> Las nieblas oscuras seguían avanzando y envolviendo las peñas en derredor de las cuales fingían mil figuras extrañas, como de monstruos deformes, cocodrilos rojos y negros, bultos colosales de mujeres envueltas en paños blancos y listas largas de vapor, que, heridas por la última luz del crepúsculo, asemejaban inmensas serpientes de colores. (pp. 567).

This is a good example of the kind of Romantic grotesque whose focal point is Satanism. The details all diverge from the theological point of departure and acquire an aesthetic value of their own by virtue of the mood and picture they create. Content is less important than structure, and the formal elements of the scene (color, shape, spatial relationships) hold the greatest interest. As opposed to any of its Dantesque counterparts, this type of grotesque is gratuitous instead of didactic. At its best, it seeks the eternal forms of beauty, which includes the diabolical, and it regards art as the conveyor of that beauty. This is what makes the grotesque so characteristically Romantic, rather than Medieval or Counter-Reformational, and here we must think of Monk Lewis and Poe as well as of Baudelaire. In fact, the idea of beauty, including Satanic beauty, without an accompanying ideology so dominates Bécquer's description that the narrator in the story continues to elaborate the details of the above scene for their own sake, until his listener interrupts him, impatient to hear the outcome. Thus, the world of witches loses its primary significance as the antagonist of universal Good, and becomes instead a component of a universal aestheticism.

III

The examples of metamorphosis, misproportion, and Satanism could be multiplied, but the point remains essentially the same: whatever reality is, it contains a dimension which is unaffected by Nature, human imagination, and the traditional supernatural world. But this is not the only dimension whose grotesque captures Bécquer's attention. He also takes notice of it in architecture, a fact which in itself would not ordinarily be startling, given his interest in all the other aspects of art as well. But his comments on cathedrals, temples, and ruins are much less routine when they consider the role of distortion in relation to the whole. These observations are not analytical or theoretical, but they recognize that the grotesque plays an important role in architecture, and this, as Hugo's use of the gargoyle has shown, is one of Romanticism's special achievements.

The most interesting of these statements appears in the second letter of *Desde mi celda*, and brings together many of the themes that have been, or will be, under discussion here. In this letter, Bécquer identifies the artistic temper of the Middle Ages with his own Romantic sensibility. The common ground between these sensibilities, with their hovering haze of mystery, becomes the site of the historically perennial grotesque edifice. The scene takes place in a "Byzantine" church, and, typically, it occurs "cuando la noche se aproxima y comienza a influir en la imaginación con su alto silencio y sus alucinaciones extrañas" (p. 524). Thus, from the beginning, Bécquer establishes the independence of a distortion-producing agent beyond his own imaginative faculties. But then, in a revealing choice of images, he goes on to characterize the Medieval creative genius in the very terms he had used to depict the grotesque impulse in his private vision:

> ... pueden distinguirse las largas series de ojivas festoneadas de hojas de trébol, por entre las que asoman con una mueca muda y horrible esas mil fantásticas y caprichosas creaciones de la imaginación que el arte misterioso de la Edad Media dejó grabadas en el granito de sus basílicas: aquí, un endriago que se retuerce por una columna y saca su deforme cabeza por entre la hojarasca del capitel; allí, un ángel que lucha con un demonio y entre los dos soportan la recaída de un arco que se apunta al muro; más lejos... las estatuas de los guerreros abades más ilustres... (p. 524-25)

Everything here points to Bécquer's intellectual and perceptual involvement, as well as his emotional rapport: his eye for architectural details, the sense of historical continuity, and the identification he makes between grotesque sculpture and the forms of his inner fantasies. Indeed, this intimacy across the ages is confirmed by the similar structure of the imagery favored by both the architect and the poet, as well as by the single pattern of their thought processes. Not only are the stonework motifs repeated in Bécquer's fiction, as we will see, but they are the same "creaciones fantásticas y caprichosas" that emerge from his imagination without the control and order of conventional inspiration.

At the same time, the structural details of the architecture also indicate the extent of Bécquer's involvement. They represent a fusion of decorative and functional elements that can be perceived immediately by the prose account. According to the latter, the grotesque is not isolated from the principal components of the building's frame, nor even from the rest of the ornamentation. Just as the deformative profiles grow out of the regular lines of the columns and arches, so does the fantastic design blend in with the more naturalistic flair of the garlanded façade. As a concretion, the grotesque figures add strength to the pillars and support to the archways above. And as an abstract fantasy, they rescue the familiar symmetries and floral shapes of the cloister from a tedious representationalism. In effect, then, Bécquer sees in this aspect of architecture two principles which he himself employs in the fictional narratives: formalism and mystification. In relation to cathedral design, perhaps it is more appropriate to phrase this as structural integration and transcendence, but the result is the same in any terminology. That is, on the one hand, the decor interacts with the functional elements until a single architectonic purpose is achieved. In literary terms, this is equivalent to making the formal aspects of the story (images, lyricism, sensory detail) as inherently valuable as the actual subject matter (plot, characters, philosophy). And on the other hand, the psychological impact of the architectural reality transforms the experience of the entire structure into a perception which goes beyond that reality. Again, in terms of Bécquer's narratives, this transcendence or mystification is the elevation of mood so that it becomes an end in itself, reaching beyond the primary effect of the story line and its philosophical tensions. In this way, what Bécquer notices about the grotesque in architecture is very similar to what we may observe about his own *leyendas*. That is, he regards it as the special spring that releases art from the necessities of form and content, and the lever with which to raise the spectator to another plane of reality.

If we turn to some of the short stories, we can confirm this prominent role of architecture, for Bécquer's fiction reveals a deep-seated awareness of that most concrete of arts. It is not simply that he sometimes tended to see natural formations in architectonic terms ("una gruta natural, formada por enormes peñascos que parecen próximos a deformarse" [p. 51]). He also contrived to integrate his architectural setting into the central action of the story. Usually this meant creating an atmosphere with the help of that setting, and making the mood a key to the story. But sometimes it involved implicating the environment directly, as in "La ajorca de oro." Here, the hero is driven insane by the mass of stone figures that seem poised to attack him in the church. It is interesting to watch the progression of verb forms, as well as the gradual crescendo of grotesque notes:

> ...lo miraban con sus ojos sin pupila. Santos, monjes, ángeles, demonios, guerreros, damas, pajes, cenobitas y villanos se rodeaban y confundían en las naves y en el altar... mientras que, arrastrándose por las losas, trepando por los machones, acurrucados en los doseles, suspendidos en las bóvedas, pululaba, como los gusanos de un inmenso cadáver, todo un mundo de reptiles y alimañas de granito, quiméricos, deformes, horrorosos. Ya no pudo resistir más. (p. 135)

This extraordinary scene operates on several different levels, but two of them—the spatial and the metaphorical—are the most relevant here. The sense of space owes its clarity of definition to the past and present participles, each one of which is designed to express a particular kind of spatial activity. Not only do they denote varying modes of occupying space, but they convey different qualities of stasis and movement. The participles represent a wide field of spatial energy, and yet the intensity of each element contributes to a larger architectural effect. Indeed, the entire range of dynamics is intimately related to the architectural force gathered behind the psychological mood. The impact begins on this spatial level, but then extends to the entire configuration of elements that drives the hero mad. That is, the configuration of the central nave, which is a total *Gestalt*, gathers the individual positions in space into a new dynamism that transcends the original line of perception. Instead of presenting a panoramic sweep of the whole, Bécquer provides a climactic fusion of the structural parts, so that the nave acquires a metaphorical power that charges the emotional atmosphere. Thus, the verb "pululaba" in the metaphor "los gusanos de un inmenso cadáver" acts to combine the separate spatial intensities into a single mass of psychological pressure that culminates in the grotesque finale. Far from contradicting the established positions in space ("arrastrándose," "trepando," "acurrucados," "suspendidos"), the word " pululaba" translates them into a figurative and emotion language without sacrificing the spatial dimension.

This type of prose is not the only kind that takes note of the grotesque in architecture. Factual works do so as well, and their link to the *leyendas* consists of the descriptive detail which is common to them all. For example, by way of contrast, the following description of the atrium of a Byzantine church ruin, taken from the story "La rosa de pasión," could just as easily be found in a factual account of a real temple: "... [zarzales] entre los que yacían, medio ocultos, ya el destrozado capitel de una columna, ya un sillar groseramente esculpido con hojas entrelazadas, endriagos horribles, grotescas e informes figuras humanas" (p. 298). Although the purpose of this passage is to create a mood, there is nothing artificial about the details or their arrangement. The description is, in fact, a realistic one, and in view of the gossamer fantasy that holds most of the *leyendas* together, it is good to remember that this coarser texture is also there. Indeed, even some non-grotesque references to architecture bear evidence of a hard-core realism underlying the imaginative framework. To cite one instance that just misses distortion, Bécquer's allusion to the cathedral at Toledo ("La ajorca de oro") tends to depict the vault as a naturalistic structure transformed. That is, it undergoes a metamorphosis that leads to chaos, although not quite to grotesquerie:

"Figuraos un bosque de gigantescas palmeras de granito que al entrelazar sus ramas forman una bóveda colossal y magnífica, bajo la que se guarece y vive, con la vida que le ha prestado el genio, toda una creación de seres imaginarios y reales.... Figuraos un caos incomprensible de sombra y luz... " (p. 118-19).

The techniques involved here stop short of the grotesque stage without dispelling the aura of fantasy. But in the image of petrification, transformation, and harmless chaos, Bécquer uses realistic elements as the basis for his imaginative evocation.

It is no surprise, therefore, that the converse holds true for Bécquer's nonfictional writings. Here, an element of fantasy filters through the prosaic mesh of factual detail. This serves as a second link between the *leyendas* and Bécquer's other prose works, but even more important, it preserves the continuity of the writings as a Romantic whole. The presence of a personal sensibility assures the integrity of lyrical subjectivism even in works that point the way to an age of increasing *costumbrismo* and realism. It is especially important for the aesthetics of the grotesque because it is the best proof of the seriousness with which Bécquer took note of various grotesque manifestations. His acknowledgement of such details underscores the relevance of the grotesque to contexts that were basically realistic instead of imaginative. A case in point is the description of a "Byzantine" temple, where a woman's statue "perfumaba de misterio y poesía aquella selva petrificada y apocalíptica, en cuyo seno, y por entre las guirnaldas del acanto, los tréboles y los cardos puntiagudos, pululaban millares de criaturas deformes: sierpes, trasgos y dragones, reptiles con alas monstruosas e inmensas" (p. 760). Although the poetic evocation is strong, the larger context reveals a detached and aestheticist interest in the history of architecture. Thus, the grotesque elements are no longer governed by the imagination to the same extent that they were in Bécquer's fantasy pieces. Belonging to a historical reality, they provide us with the reminder that distortion is not only one of the "hijos extravagantes" of imagination, but a factor in real life as well. And with this we have the additional perspective of recalling how grotesque motifs in modern times derive more and more frequently from social reality rather than from private nightmare.

The significance of this submergent imagination occurring within a fairly realistic context is prophetic. The presence of a subjective sensibility plants Bécquer's work firmly in the Romantic tradition, and yet its aesthetic historicism foreshadows a greater objectivity in the art movements of the future. The situation is comparable to that of Jovellanos' description of the castle at Bellver. There, the new factor was a personal lyricism that rescued the historical account from a Gallardesque tediousness. And a new Romantic undercurrent could unmistakably be perceived. In Bécquer, it is the realistic tone that stands out against a brooding Romanticism in the prose. And this, in turn, prefigures the emergence of a new sensibility. The following passage reveals the nature of Bécquer's detachment and the degree to which a subject-object awareness replaces the ambiguous dream moods of the fictional narrations:

Largo rato estuve contemplando obra tan magnífica [un templo bizantino], recorriendo con los ojos todos sus delicados accidentes y deteniéndoseme a desentrañar el sentido simbólico de las figurillas monstruosas y los animales fantásticos que se ocultaban o aparecían alternativamente entre los calados festones de las molduras.

Una por una admiré las extrañas creaciones con que el artífice había coronado el muro para dar salida a las aguas por las fauces de un grifo, de una sierpe, de un león alado o de un demonio horrible con cabeza de murciélago y garra de águila; una por una estudié así mismo las severas y magníficas cabezas de las imágenes de tamaño natural que, envueltas en grandes paños, simétricamente plegados. custodiaban inmóviles el santuario, como centinelas de granito… pp. 759)

All of this, remarks Bécquer, belonged to "la mejor época del arte ojival" which was "el modelo perfecto del misterioso amor." What is remarkable about the observation is its sentimentalism in the face of deliberate analysis. The conclusion about love which Bécquer draws from his perusal of the architecture is hopelessly Romantic and almost beside the point after the enumeration of grotesque figures. But the sentimental idea on the heels of a method of rational inspection represents the curious blend of fancy and fact which Bécquer was capable of producing in some passages of his prose. His reference to the symbolic meaning of the monsters is tantalizing, not only because he does not explain it, but because there is little evidence in the *leyendas* that he used such motifs with a symbolistic intention. The minute character of Bécquer's study is constantly brought to our attention by his own words: he pauses with great deliberation at each figure along the wall, noting its position in relation to the others and extracting details even about the symmetrical folds in the stone tunics. Indeed, the grotesque motifs themselves seem unimportant beside the analytic methodology with which they are approached. It is no longer madness but method that prevails, and instead of imagined entities we have the concrete materials of reality. Whereas Jovellanos succumbed to the mood inspired by his architectural studies, Bécquer succumbs, in a sense, to their academic lure.

Some critics will point out that Bécquer's comments on the grotesque in architecture should be regarded as a natural rather than an extraordinary part of any discussion of architectural design. The grotesque aspect must not, of course, be overemphasized for two reasons. First is the fact that we have no way of knowing Bécquer's motives,[4] and second, the grotesque is only one of many items that are treated in his essays on architecture. At the same time, the passages reviewed so far are unusually fruitful in their implications. Both in the narratives and the nonfiction there is a marked tendency toward rational control: in the stories, we found the apparently vague mood to be quite tightly structured; and in the essays, the author was very much aware of being a conscious analyst in the presence of an object-specimen. In taking one last example, we will see that all this adds up to a bold but simple fact. Bécquer not only embodies the Romantic sensibility, but he articulates the hopes of the positivistic society that followed it. While the grotesque may have served him as material for Romantic literature, his observation of that grotesque in a historical reality prompted him to consider man's hopes for social progress and the pursuit of truth. Thus, insofar as Bécquer's references to grotesque motifs are a constant in his work, we come to realize that if his Romanticism is deep-seated, his view of the century's last decades is long-ranged. This is supported by an interesting section in *Caso de ablativo* entitled "Burgos."

This sketch is conceived in a train, with Bécquer's disposition, significantly enough, affected by "uno de esos ensueños ligeros y nerviosos" which, he says, is so typical of train rides (p. 1041). He sees the Burgos skyline at night, and writes:

> ... he visto destacarse, como dos fantasmas negros, las gigantes agujas de su catedral. En este momento me ocurre qué pensarán esos monstruos de piedra, esos patriaracas y esos personajes simbólicos, tallados en el granito, que permanecen día y noche inmóviles y asomados a las góticas balaustradas del templo, al ver pasar entre las sombras la locomotora ligera... Acaso saludarán, con una sonrisa

---

4 There is, however, this fantasy while Bécquer reflects upon his death as a glorious poet: "Una airosa ojiva, rizada de hojas revueltas y puntiagudas, por entre las cuales se enroscaran, asomando su deforme cabeza, por aquí un grifo, por allá uno de esos monstruos alados, engendro de la imaginación del artífice, bañar en oscura sombra m sepulcro" (536).

extraña la realización de un hecho que esperan hace muchos siglos. Acaso esas simbólicas figuras grabadas en la entreojiva de la catedral, jeroglíficos misteriosos del arte cristiano que aún no han podido descifrarse, contienen la vaga predicción de las maravillas que hoy realiza nuestra época. (p. 959)

In effect, this statement upholds the value of formalistic obscurity, showing how it is finally vindicated by the cumulative understanding of succeeding generations. What appears in one age to be an incomprehensible aesthetic is revealed subsequently to embody truths as yet undiscovered by rational means. From fantastic symbolism to capricious distortion, the hidden depths of irrational and evasive art forms contain intuitions beyond the comprehension of other disciplines. In this way, "la Edad Media, tan llena de ideas extrañas, de aspiraciones infinitas, de atrevimientos inauditos," created "el magnífico prólogo lleno de símbolos y misterios de este gigante poema que poco a poco va desarrollando la Humanidad a través de los siglos" (pp. 959-60).

This idea is quite different from the usual observation about works of art stating universal truths or summarizing the wisdom of their epoch. Bécquer's notion involves one cosmic truth whose revelation unfolds progressively with the advance of technological knowledge. However, even though yesterday's alchemists and astrologers are the scientists of today, they are all preceded by the artist-prophet, whose genius is concealed by the obscure, and sometimes mad, formulation of his insight. It is the artist's "hieroglyphic" signs which anticipate their scientific discoveries. From the beginning, he recognizes and transfigures the universal truth into an arcane and mysterious art form. The prime example of this for Bécquer was the early manifestation of Christian fantastic art. Moreover, the indecipherable transfigurations of Gothic architecture were doubly appealing to him since he too, as a narrator, employed his own share of mysterious effects. Bécquer seized upon the unreal aura of the Medieval period, both as he saw it projected against the Burgos skyline, and as he interpreted its role in history. And he glimpsed in the "wondrous masses of stone," among other places, the first attempts to resolve "los más grandes problemas científicos y sociales." This was the age that "quiso arrancar a la Naturaleza el secreto de la transmutación de los metales, a los Astros, el secreto del porvenir, y, por último, en el delirio de su entusiasta locura, a Dios el secreto de la vida" (p. 959). The language here is dramatic, and if it does not reflect our current views of the Middle Ages, it does conform to what we have seen to be Bécquer's own attempts to draw the secrets of reality from both Nature and the "other" dimension. He admits, therefore, that "tal vez por eso encuentro yo como una relación secreta entre esta última palabra de nuestra civilización," meaning the locomotive, and the "vetustas torres" of the cathedral (p. 960). Addressing the latter, he pronounces its grotesque forms to be the aesthetic revelation of an incompletely understood cosmic law:

> Con vuestros antepechos calados como el encaje, vuestras agujas delgadas y esbeltas, vuestros canalones de animales monstruosos y fantásticos, y esos miles de figurines extravagantes que se combinan y confunden con un sin número de detalles a cuál más caprichosos y escondidos; vosotras sois toda una creación inmensa que nunca acaba de revelarse del todo, en que cada una de las partes es un mundo especial, una parábola, una predicción o un enigma no resuelto... (p.960).

This, then, is the cathedral's architectural beauty, and as an unresolved enigma, says Bécquer, it is what men create in imitation of God's wisdom while they search for the unifying principle in all existence.

IV

When Bécquer is optimistic, therefore, he looks upon technology as the pragmatic shape of human creativity, a late form which confirms the intuitions first revealed by art. We must view this attitude, with its hopes for a better future, in the same light as Bécquer's practical interest in history. That is, they both led him away from the Romantic imbroglios of the type entangling the volatile figures who came before him. Like his Victorian counterparts in England, Bécquer was a second or third generation Romantic, with all the optimism and pessimism which this heritage was imposing upon the arts by the new science of the day. But this very contradiction in his writings, if we may call it that, also made him a precursor of generations to follow. A Romantic sensibility, coupled with a realistic social awareness, produced in him many moments of weariness, indifference, and ennui. And this was a far cry from the agony and desperation of the earlier disillusioned Romantics.

A prime example of this burnt-out Romanticism is Bécquer's treatment of the Spanish carnival. Here, he begins to evoke what we might term the spirit of Goethe and Berlioz as he recalls the festive atmosphere of bygone years. His recollection of past carnivals includes sunlight, crowds, and the special festivity in which he saw "agitarse, rico de colores y luz, un océano de cabezas alegres, de trajes brillantes y de máscaras bulliciosas e inquietas. Todo saltaba y reía a nuestro alrededor" (p. 1084). All of this, Bécquer maintains, has disappeared, and a mood of deflation and hollow gaiety has appeared in its stead. As we will see, what had replaced the ebullient Romantic grotesque of the traditional carnival was a muted and off-key grotesque. But before discussing this, the norm itself should first be examined, since it is here that Bécquer fixes the standard of healthy and wholehearted activity in contrast to the destructive and often self-conscious carnivalesque atmosphere of the modern period:

> Las descompuestas voces de la embriaguez, las estridentes carcajadas de la locura, los breves monosílabos de las promesas, las cortesanas frases de los galanes, las rápidas palabras de las citas, los discordantes ecos de las músicas, el incesante son de las chanzonetas, el hervidero confuso de la multitud oscura y apretada, entre la cual surcan, por aquí una figura grotesca, por allá un mamarracho imposible, por acullá una comparsa que culebreando entre el gentío parece una serpiente monstruosa de abigarrados colores.... (p. 1084)

This classic description includes most of the essential components of a carnival. From the lively motion and emotion to the infinite variety of sounds, these elements are not in themselves grotesque, but some of their inner combinations lead to that very effect. Thus, the "figura grotesca" and the "mamarracho imposible" are indispensable parties to the carnival celebration, and their special extravagance comes not only from their dress, but from their parody of human animation. There is also an entire series of noises—shouts, laughter, mumbling, music, rhythmic beats—that are all "descompuestas," "estridentes," and "discordantes." And finally, if drunkenness underlies the general atmosphere of gaiety, a kind of spatial intoxication takes hold of the physical setting and its movements. In other words, just as emotions are at their uninhibited peak, so too has motion ceased to have any restraints ("hervidero confuso," "serpiente monstruosa"). The scene is straining at the seams, and several of its episodes have already burst through the limits of normal experience.

What, then, are we to make of these characteristics, taking them together as the basic model of a standard carnival? First of all, this is Bécquer's version of a typical carnival, which is to say, it is a Romantic conception. It omits the symbolic nature of the celebration and it avoids mentioning either religious motifs or the cause and cultural value of the event. Secondly, the carnival is seen to be the apotheosis of merriment and the evasion of reality. And it is here that the grotesque enters, for the attempt to reach a more intense level of fun-making leads to an excessively pitched hilarity, much like the sound of a too tightly wound stringed instrument. At the same time, the participants' emotional involvement is so complete that none of them is aware of the unreal and discordant situation. They are all attuned to their own score, which seems natural and harmonious to them, and only the spectator outside the scene can bear witness to the general cacophony. This is what we might call a pure grotesque, where there is no self-consciousness within the setting, no room for the malaise, detachment, and destructive irony of, say, the Surrealist grotesque in the twentieth century.

However, this glad and spontaneous carnival is not the kind which Bécquer finds to be celebrated in his own day, and it is here that we reach the crucial issue. Bécquer experiences a deflated moment in which he thinks that "el Carnaval ha muerto," and that each year, like a legendary corpse, "se levanta aún de sus tumba para bailar en un baile mudo, de una mímica grotesca y horrible a un tiempo, en el que solo se oye el crujido de sus choquezuelas descarnadas..." (p. 1086). The circumstances for this remark are that it had been raining during the day, and the evening is still wet, thus discouraging the merrymakers from leaving their houses. And so, reports Bécquer, the unused facilities stand like a skeletal apparatus waiting to be filled by the mass of humanity that will give it life. Despite this journalistic context, it is difficult to believe that Bécquer was engaging in some hour-by-hour coverage of the weather and its threat to the festivities. If he was just being a reporter, then the cheerful ending, when the sun appears and Bécquer exchanges his writer's gloom for a lively carnival mask, is nothing less than an embarrassing bit of bathos. However, the piece is far from being foolish, and it bears the subtitle "A 'Pot Pourri' de pensamientos extraños." Moreover, it is also the first bit of evidence for what we will find to be a strong vein of post-Romantic disillusion, approaching the modern whimper of T. S. Eliot and leaving behind the thunderclaps of Espronceda. Bécquer here pivots between two worlds, looking back at the healthy distortions of the Romantic carnival's liberating escapism, and facing the brink of the disturbed, self-destructive grotesquerie of the Solanas and the Valle-Incláns.

If any further proof is necessary for Bécquer's relegating the carnival to a past era, it can be found in his essay "El Carnaval." The tone of this piece is uneven, but it begins with an unmistakable satirical bite, making clear the author's indifference to this seasonal event. It goes on to explain why the carnival's purpose has ceased to be relevant. In the tyrannical days of the Italian princes, a "periódica explosión de libertad y de locura" was required for the sake of public discipline. Accordingly, "La política y el amor pedían prestado su traje a Arlequín, y el alegre ruido de los cascabeles del cetero del bufón urdían la trama de su novela sangrienta o sentimental" (p. 1097). But in Bécquer's own generation, the carnival no longer has such an identity. What, he asks, can a woman declare behind the protection of a mask that she or someone else has not already uttered under the cover of her fan at the opera? And what would we dare to do with our faces covered "en el bullicio de la orgía" that we have not already dared in the boudoir? The fact is, writes Bécquer categorically, "el Carnaval no tiene razón de ser; y sin embargo existe….sale todos los años de su tumba envuelto en su haraposo sudario, hace media docena de piruetas en Capellanes, en el Prado y el Canal, y desaparece" (p. 1098). And to justify these opinions, he presents us with a sociological analysis of the Madrid celebrations.

What is important for us here is not the details of the analysis itself, but rather the phenomenon as a whole. The very fact that Bécquer's theory exists at all helps us to measure the approximate distance between him and the fading of the great Romantics. And it provides a rough estimate of how much ground remained to be covered before the frontiers of twentieth-century art would be glimpsed. For example, Bécquer's analysis takes no interest in the carnivalesque atmosphere, or its colors and discordant details, but is concerned rather with the pragmatic implications of its social situation. Turning his back on aesthetics, he embraces ethics, and gains an ironic distance on both which foreshadows the eventual amorality of art toward the end of the century. Similarly, Bécquer's intellectualizing discourse contains nothing new in the way of ideas, but it does represent an early stage in the ever-deepening isolation of the artist's ego from the spontaneous life of the senses and emotions around him. We have here one of the instances when Bécquer was unable to immerse himself in the carnival atmosphere: his emotions before the debased spectacle grow detached, critical, and sometimes sardonic. In time, the detachment would for younger artists become alienation, and irony would turn into "black" humor and other self-conscious distortions. In Bécquer's work, this inevitable progression is revealed in its very early stages. His indifference begins with a withdrawal from "la masa inconsciente que forma bulto en todas las grandes fiestas," and it is then sustained by the cheap and insipid" fanfare of the festivities:

> El Rastro... desbordando por las calles vecinas a los portillos de la Ronda, inunda la pradera con un océano de telas mugrientas, trajes haraposos, guiñapos y objetos sin forma, color ni nombre, que aún conservan la señal del gancho del trapero... Los felpudos, las esteras viejas, el lienzo de embalar y el papel son las estelas más a la última en esta grotesca danza, donde en vez de dijes de oro, plumas de color y piochas de brillantes, lucen cacerolas y aventadores, escobas y aceiteras, ristras de ajos y sartas de arenques....El Carnaval de la Pradera es, si no una noche, un verdadero *día de Walpurgis* con sus rondas infernales, sus visiones horribles, sus carcajadas estridentes, su confuso vocear, su abigarrado conjunto y su confusión indecible. (pp. 101-02)

This daylight counterpart of the Goethean Witches' Sabbath is indeed symbolic in its clarity. Bécquer. sees the faded, glamorless charade for what it is: a tattered exercise in tin-pan merriment. That is, he *believes* that the modern carnival is vulgar. Regardless of the true picture, Bécquer's version is painted unromantically because he is too detached to be carried away by the cheap panoply. As he implies, to witness a Walpurgisnacht by day is like watching a dress rehearsal: all the inner workings are exposed, and the magic spell of the evening performance has not yet descended to conceal them. Nor will it ever, for the age has grown too weary to support such emotional anachronisms. If the populace at large chooses to preserve these external forms, there are those in the vanguard of aesthetic awareness who realize that the whole affair should be put to rest:

> Tal es el Carnaval de Madrid. Así, revolcándose entre el légamo de la vanidad, las necedades y el vino, agoniza, en medio de la atmósfera del siglo XIX, por falta de aire que purifique sus pulmones, el Carnaval de la tradición y de la Historia. Derramemos una lágrima a la cabecera de su lecho de muerte, y preparémonos a poner el inútil antifaz y el cetro de cascabeles sobre su tumba (p. 1102).

It is not difficult to guess what Bécquer meant by the cryptic phrase "en medio de la atmósfera del siglo XIX." During his sober and unexalted hours, his prose supports a cautious optimism over the new pragmatism, and "el espíritu propio de la época de transición que alcanzamos" (p. 1127). In view of this, his disillusion with the Spanish carnival may be considered a positive attitude, a sign of health in the Romantic sickness which pitted artist against society. Such a signal, like others we have seen, alerts us to the future course of events in aesthetics, and particularly to the oncoming wave of realism which Bécquer himself met halfway in his *costumbrista* articles.

However, the wide sweep of this realistic wave also opened up several deep eddies. One of these was the stifling hermeticism that distorted the original Romantic subjectivity and often rendered it grotesque. This too was the result of a disillusion with Romanticism and its yearning idealism. Therefore, Bécquer's emotional distance from the carnival may also be seen to reflect the beginning of a post-Romantic malaise that later turned into alienation and artistic schizophrenia. For example, if we examine Bécquer's disenchantment with the legend of Roncesvalles, we discover an unusual image, the use of a mannequin as a symbol of essential truth:

> La crítica histórica, esa incrédula hija del espíritu de nuestra época, nos ha enseñado a sonreírnos de compasión al oír el relato de esas tradiciones, que eran el brillante cimiento de nuestros anales patrios, y desnudando uno por uno a nuestros héroes nacionales de las espléndidas galas con que los vistiera la rica fantasía popular,

empañando con su hálito de duda la brillante aureola que ceñía sus sienes y derribándolos del pedestal en que los colocó la leyenda, nos ha mostrado su descarnada armazón, semejante a un maniquí risible... (971)

This is surely one of the earliest usages in Spanish literature of the mannequin motif, an idea which became so central to Surrealist aesthetics, and whose symbolic metamorphosis can be traced from *I Pagliacci* to Eliot's hollow, stuffed men, and finally to De Chirico's wooden heroes. In Bécquer, the image is quite removed from the Romantic lament for outcasts, misfits, and clowns. On the other hand, its sense of ridicule contains only the first seeds of the cruel dissections which were to be undertaken in the twentieth century. But the image remains an important one because of its analogy of stripping the skeletal figure disguised as a man with the exposure of man's myths and illusions. Given Bécquer's mood, the disillusioning process is not especially tragic, at least not in this moment of prosaic lucidity. In fact, his realistic sense of history affords him several insights into the nature of post-Romantic disillusion, both in terms of what ridiculousness means as a concept, as well as of which images best represent the sad spectacle of ridiculous men.

Bécquer's awareness of imagery and, indeed, his search for modern images to reflect the new emotional deflation acquire their best expression in a long passage discussing the meaning of dolls in modern life. Like the mannequin, the doll's position is fixed in such a way that its commonplace characteristics can be seen in relation to something outside of itself. Rather than using it to show the familiar trivialities of its inanimate existence, Bécquer sets the doll at a human angle, and interprets it symbolically as an abject, pathetic man. His description begins with a little girl "que tenía la mirada alta, serena, dulce y al par dominadora, traía colgado de un brazo, y en una postura descoyuntada, risible y lastimosa a la vez, un muñeco, una especie de polichinela, del que no hacía más caso que el suficiente para no dejarlo escapar de entre sus pequeñas garras de terciopelo rosa" (. 688).

The doll in itself is a modest beginning, but we must remember that Bécquer's doll no longer has the same purpose that was served by the puppets and automatons of Romantic literature, of Hoffmann's or Jean Paul's narratives, for example. This in itself is significant, since the doll, far from inhabiting a fantasy world, falls awkwardly to the lowest plane of ordinary reality: the lifeless object. More important, the doll acquires relevance to the world of men by means of a new kind of incongruity. No longer embodying a fantastic form of humanity, the doll suggests instead that man is an exalted form of marionette. Whereas the Romantics were engrossed by the fantasy world created by their grotesque automatons, modern artists have turned to reality, and to the reduction of human beings to the status of animated dolls. This reversal is a significant event in the transition from the Romantic grotesque to the modern grotesque. And Bécquer manifests it by entering into a discussion of what this implies for man. Although he shifts from the level of imagery to that of speculation, he does not lose sight of the realistic application which doll imagery can have in illuminating the human condition. Thus, while we are bound to be disappointed by Bécquer's failure to create new images with this motif, we must bear in mind that his commentary occurs at the dawn of a new sensibility. And even though he confines his reflections to a single subject—woman's power over man—the very choice of a doll for his analogy, and a Punchinello at that, indicates the wide scope of possibilities sensed by Bécquer:

> ...ese muñeco mismo puede ser tema fecundo, no ya de divagaciones poéticas, sino de las más altas especulaciones filosóficas.... "El hombre es juguete de la mujer," y es verdad: pobres polichinelas, el mundo parece estrecho a nuestras ambiciones: este es un héroe, aquel un genio... todos nos agitamos y luchamos y algunos vencemos, hasta que aparece al fin la mujer... nos agarra por cualquier parte y nos lleva tras sí como esa niña lleva el muñeco, sin que nos quede otro recurso sino pedirle a Dios que la postura no sea del todo ridícula o traiga un descoyuntamiento demasiado grave. (p. 688-89)

Lest we forget, this passage occurs during a good-humored argument about whether a little girl in a portrait embodies, even embryonically, the delights and dangers of a mature woman. Nevertheless, the image of the doll is no afterthought, for the implications of its grotesque pathos fit in with Bécquer's general notion of the ridiculous and the absurd. Here again, the very idea constitutes something new. The accent is on the awareness of a different era, where man's psychological capacities are no longer in accord with the expectations of Romanticism.

Somehow the element of awkwardness has crept into the concept of absurdity, whereas it could not have at an earlier period. The Romantics may have been out of place, histrionic, and even incongruous, but their self-contained world had the structure of an inner harmony. Bécquer, on the other hand, notes that ridiculousness is a new posture in the repertoire of gestures, and one which must be contrasted with grace. "La ridiculez," he writes, "es un accidente moderno en la historia de las costumbres" (p. 661), and with this glimpse of a detached irony in the realm of the ridiculous, we are again set forth on the road to modern absurdity and grotesquerie:

> La ridiculez es una cosa horrible que hace reír.
> Es algo que mata y regocija.
> Es Arlequín que cambia su espada de madera por otra de acero, asesina con ella en broma y dice después a su víctima una bufonada por toda oración fúnebre.
> Es Mefistófeles, con peor intención y menos profundidad, que se burla de todo lo santo.
> Es Falstaff, menos filósofo y más raquítico, que empequeñece todo lo grande.
> El ridículo se encuentra un paso más allá del sublime, porque se encuentra un paso más allá de todo.
> Y, lo que es peor, un poco más acá también.
> Es un monstruo que nos tiene tendida una red inmensa y oculta. (p. 662)

Also interesting to see is which literary figures are chosen to mark the distance between past dignity and present foolishness. Harlequin is a natural selection, and the aesthetic evolution he undergoes from seventeenth-century burlesque to twentieth-century grotesque would require a study in itself, regardless of what has already been published. As for Mephistopheles, it would appear that Bécquer chose him as spontaneously as he did the other Goethean elements previously noted. In the devil's present form, there seems to be some parallel with the daylight Walpurgisnacht of the Spanish carnival: as the original deteriorates under the insensitive treatment of an uncomprehending age, its characteristics become garishly accentuated until they acquire a hideous but banal veneer. And finally Falstaff, "que empequeñece todo lo grande" is the epitome of the post-Romantic deflation. Not only are noble ideals cheapened by his rhetoric, but their sentiment is debased by his vapid emotions.

All three, Harlequin, Mephistopheles, and Falstaff, are definitely infratranscendent figures. They mark the decline of Romantic aspiration, just as the mind that conceived them in this present form marks the rise of an anti-Romantic reaction. This is why Bécquer mentions the idea of sublimity in the very next breath. While Hugo had used this concept in defining the grotesque as the reverse side of the sublime, and whereas Nietzsche will polarize laughter and the sublime, Bécquer stands in a transitional middle ground. When he says that the ridiculous is beyond the sublime and, even worse, on this side of it, he expresses intuitively what the modern grotesque has borne out. That is, the deformation of what is noble in life, society, and ideals (i.e., from man to doll, carnival to cheap masquerade, and Hamlet to Harlequin) occurs in an inverse proportion to the Romantic effort to transcend reality. Bécquer is thus predicting the fall from the sublime to the ridiculous, for he knew that its representation would have to be in terms of banality, not beatitude, and by means of distortion, not transfiguration.

V

Having said this much, we are left with the touchy question of what kind of a Romantic Bécquer was, and where his treatment of the grotesque leaves him in this regard. The case for his Romanticism, of course, is overwhelming in view of his *rimas* and *leyendas*, which are, after all, his most significant creations. Nevertheless, if we carry the study of his grotesque motifs to its conclusion, we are forced to consider the problem of Bécquer's *hastío*, ennui, and post-Romantic disquietude. The fact is that with respect to these feelings, Bécquer is closer to Baudelaire than to Byron, and still closer to Machado after the latter's *modernista* period than to Espronceda before *El estudiante de Salamanca* was written. Admittedly, we are on treacherous ground here, for there are many moods and intellectual attitudes in Bécquer's writings. And yet this may well be the point, for in so short a life-span a variegated pattern of antithetical emotions and themes indicates better than anything else how inconsistent a writer's sensibility can be. Not that Bécquer is any more contradictory than other Romantic writers. He is capable of exaltation or despair, and can evoke both ideal beauty and grotesque horror. But these attitudes are Romantically consistent because they are derived from the same extremism: subjective, impassioned, and idealistic. In contrast, there are other moments of contradiction in Bécquer's sensibility that are revealing for their emotional distance from the Romantic mood. What are we to make, for example, of an altogether uninspired experience—flat, neutral, and devoid of the familiar inner tension? Such is the case in one of the *rimas*:

> Hoy como ayer, mañana como hoy,
> ¡y siempre igual!
> Un cielo gris, un horizonte eterno,
> ¡y andar…, andar!
> Moviéndose a compás, como una estúpida
> máquina, el corazón;
> La torpe inteligencia, del cerebro
> Dormida en un rincón. (LVI[20], 438)

The poem may, of course, be explained by the simple fact that Bécquer was tired, or depressed—a condition which we must allow him as a human being. But could he, as an artist, actually regard this mood as a suitable theme for Romantic poetry? To experience the full range of human emotions is only normal, but to select a given emotion for the main subject of a poem is another matter, and entirely a matter of aesthetics. It is precisely by such selectivity in theme and feeling that we can determine the different trends in artistic sensibility. Therefore, what is important about this poem is its acceptance of a heretofore unpoetic sentiment, the mutation of Romantic despair. If we compare this theme with its more typical counterparts, the difference becomes apparent. Bécquer's tone is far removed, for example, from the tragic brooding of Larra's despair, just as it is equally distant from the feigned cynicism of Espronceda. Although his mood is no pose, it has none of the intensity which we usually associate with Romanticism. Instead, the flatness of feeling borders on insensitivity, and its indifference in the dissection of the self comes close to being destructive.

Furthermore, the poem's methodical process of introspection has a near-mechanical quality that foreshadows the more drastic anatomies of modern grotesque imagery. This brings us to the second important point. Moments like these in late-Romantic literature represent an undermining of pure feeling. Uncertain mixtures of ill-defined sentiments cloud the air, and frustration takes the place of the normal discharge of pent-up emotions. When enough of these moments accumulate, the last vestiges of the Romantic superstructure collapse, and the full symptoms of neurasthenia appear. This is what happens in much of *modernismo*, as Machado's early poetry demonstrates, and from here the gates to the modern sense of absurdity are but a short distance away. Then, finally, a newer and more cruel grotesque emerges, where instead of stupid clock-hearts and doll-men, we have uncannier images of dehumanization.

In view of subsequent developments, therefore, Bécquer's unfeeling interludes must be evaluated in terms of what new grounds they open for exploration. It does not matter that Bécquer traversed very little of that ground himself, for he did something equally important. By detaching himself from the Romantic mood, he underscored the possibilities of an aesthetic based on objective deformation rather than on lyrical distortion. Since he was realistic about Romanticism, he revealed his emotional position with respect to his Romantic predecessors. And that, coupled with the grotesque variations in his traditional *leyendas*, makes him more modern than his *rimas* might indicate. Let us note, for example, how Bécquer's realistic attitude is expressed in his description of Roncesvalles, for it is here that he confesses to the failure of his imagination to recapture the enthusiasm which he believes should be felt at this historical site. He wonders, "¿Por qué me fatigo evocando recuerdos de los tiempos pasados para tratar de sentir una impresión grande y profunda, mientras mis miradas vagan, a pesar mío, de un punto a otro, distraídas e indiferentes? Nada ha cambiado aquí de cuanto nos rodea, es verdad; pero hemos cambiado nosotros... (p. 971).[5]

---

5 The rest of this passage is worth quoting for its biographical interest: "he cambiado yo, que no vengo en alas de la fe, vestido de un tosco sayal y pidiendo de puerta en puerta el pan de la peregrinación, a prosternarme en el umbral del santuario, o a recoger con respeto el polvo de la llanura, testigo de sangriento combate, sino que, guiado por la fama y de la manera más cómoda possible, llego hasta este último confín de la Península a satisfacer una curiosidad de artista o un capricho de desocupado."

This answer is as true as it is honest. Bécquer's awareness of the change in himself is comparable to his sense of historical change: they both free him from the sensibility of his period. Thus, we can understand his impatience with the maudlin and vulgarizing romantic girl Elena—"que comenzó a hablarme del canto de los pajaritos, de las nubecitas color de púrpura, de la poética vaguedad del crepúsculo y otras mil majaderías de este jaez" (pp. 767-768) although a moment later he is enthralled by a Beethoven melody. We are also prepared to find Bécquer so far removed from Romantic feelings that he can contemplate the phenomenon of Romanticism as a whole and reduce it to a formula.[6] And finally, we may regard his sense of realism as offering him an alternative to the lyrical expression by which he manifested his profoundest visions. That is, given the evasive and often ineffable intuitions which Bécquer sought to communicate, it is possible to consider the grotesque mode as a secondary idiom, a minor one, to be sure, that helped to articulate certain attitudes which ran tangentially to the spirit of Romanticism.

As I have indicated, some of these attitudes reflected a psychological deflation, while others sought to bridge the gap between history and subjectivity. But there is yet another type of attitude, and with this I will conclude my discussion. The tragic vein in Bécquer's lyrical vision has a well-known destructive quality, as many of the *leyendas* can testify. These stories often end in death or madness, and their power is such that they can envelop us in their somber and fatalistic mood. However, whereas most of those cases lead to tragedy, there is one notable instance which leads to the grotesque. And since this grotesque is ironically detached instead of emotionally involved, its link to the post-Romantic tendency that I have been describing becomes crucial. The story at issue is "La creación," which depicts man's tragic condition with icy objectivity and,

---

6 "Figuraos una noche serena, un cielo azul oscuro sembrado de puntos de oro, un mar de plata en cuyas olas se quiebra y chispea la claridad de la luna, un esquife ligerísimo que corta las aguas dejando en pos una estela ancha y brillante, el profundo silencio la inmensidad y las notas de una canción que flotan en el aire, donde la melodía se mece impregnada en voluptuosa languidez al cadencioso golpe de remo. No hay poeta romántico, no hay niña novelesca que no haya soñado alguna vez este cuadro del mar, la cancioncilla, el barquito y la luna; cuadro magnífico, situación llena de poesía, de la que se ha abusado tal vez, pero que indudablemente es hermosa" (p. 780).

moreover, with the kind of cruel, indifferent mockery that we normally associate with twentieth-century techniques. The point is, however, that the depiction comes as an alternate approach to the usual sentimental endings that are Bécquer's trademark. This means at least in one instance, that he found distortion and ridicule to be as valid a technique for representing the human condition as his more serious and subjective methods were.

The story reflects the same philosophy that underlies many other narratives, namely, that "el mundo es un absurdo animado que rueda en el vacío para asombro de sus habitantes" (p. 302). But the story soon goes off on a bizarre track of its own, representing the world as the misshapen creation of celestial children who have observed Brahma's laboratory experiments with worlds and lives, and who are bent on imitating him. These children construct Earth amid laughter and monstrous confusion, and then contemplate their work:

> Un mundo deforme, raquítico, oscuro, aplastado por los polos, que volteaba de medio ganchete, con montañas de nieve y arenales encendidos, con fuego en las entrañas y océanos en la superficie, con una humildad frágil y presuntuosa, con aspiraciones de dios y flaquezas de barro. El principio de muerte, destruyendo cuanto existe, y el principio de vida, con conatos de eternidad, reconstruyéndolo con sus mismos despojos: un mundo disparatado, absurdo, inconcebible: nuestro mundo, en fin.
>
> Los chiquillos que lo habían formado, al mirarlo rodar en el vacío de un modo tan grotessco, lo saludaron con una inmensa carcajada, que resonó en los ocho círculos de Edén. (pp. 310)

All of this, including the pessimistic finale which is too long to quote, is a marvelously contrived satire that is not only unfunny but produces a slight tremor of uneasiness. What is more, it is in keeping with Bécquer's tragic vision. But there is something ferocious in the distortion here, a trace of unfeeling deliberation which is not characteristic of the author. It is as if, in a perverse moment, he took special pleasure in portraying the mortal world in such lacerating terms. The image of a toy Earth being tossed about raucously, and the abandonment of humanity to capricious children, are ideas that evoke a certain insensitivity. We can detect a streak of hardness—braced by bitterness and vulnerability, perhaps—that allowed so sentimental a writer as Bécquer this weird display of interest in grotesque manipulation.

Whatever its causes, the narrative turns out to be a familiar statement of Bécquer's pessimism formulated by unfamiliar means. Its use of the grotesque as an alternative to the straightforward, dramatic presentation of life and destiny is an important change. The exalted emotions of the traditional somber mood are exchanged for a deliberate and pitiless exposure of human absurdity. In one sense, this takes us back to the theory of ridiculousness which Bécquer found so pertinent to the condition of his age. And in another sense, we are led to the description of unglamorous carnivals, which Bécquer also presented as a reflection of his disenchantment. And finally, this grotesque points ahead to a progressively more destructive tendency in the history of aesthetic ideas.

It is the latter development which should impress us the most as we conclude our study. The Romantic revolt, despite its excesses and theatricality, was essentially a committed movement—to ideals, to passions, to the self, to Nature. In the measure that the grotesque participated in this Romanticism, it functioned in the service of such commitments. On the other hand, the anti-Romantic reaction appropriated the grotesque for increasingly gratuitous exercises. And this last example of Bécquer's grotesque bears many traces of the aloofness which eventually became the hallmark of modern art. Thus, if Bécquer could not be one of the original Romantic poets for Spain, he was for Europe among the first to anticipate the new perception of absurdity. His grotesque had Romantic characteristics, true, but at critical moments it diverged significantly from tradition and flickered with the pale, uneasy light of another age.[7]

---

7 This study was made possible by a grant from the Guggenheim Foundation. It was first published in *PMLA* 83 (1968): 312-31. Reprinted by permission of the Modern Langauge Association.

9
Antonio Machado and the Grotesque

IT HAS BEEN SAID that Spanish genius is unrivaled in the creation of grotesque art.[1] Works by Cervantes, Quevedo, Goya, Solana, and Lorca testify to the variety of forms the grotesque can take from the comic and pathetic to the pathological. Yet the exact nature of this aesthetic category still eludes us, and we permit genre and media of diverse psychological and philosophical tendencies to be included under the grotesque. This is unavoidable as long as a theoretical treatise is not written, but even without one it should be clear that at least in the twentieth century the grotesque has tended toward homogeneity. Whether we consider Surrealist distortions, Dadaist humor, the Pirandello-Gênet theater, or Freudian literature, whatever is grotesque is also self-conscious, anti-Romantic, and absurd. An ulterior purpose seems to motivate the modern grotesque, whereas in earlier periods it enjoyed a certain abandon and purity of expression. Motifs such as the gargoyle, cyclops, the Satanic, and Beauty and the Beast are no longer cultivated, while traditional puppets and mechanisms have acquired new emotional dimensions.

I believe that the grotesque in our age emerges from the disintegration of Romanticism, and that we have a rare opportunity to observe this process in the poetry of the Spaniard Antonio Machado. I will refer to Romanticism in its most liberal and commonly accepted sense, and will include Symbolism among its last forms insofar as this movement is an exacerbation of Romantic subjectivity. Machado's reputation rests on the fact that he grapples with the fundamental problems of contemporary Europe: time, the existential self, and social realism.[2] His first

---

1 Wolfgang Kayser, *Das Groteske in Malerei und Dichtung* (München, 1960), p. 12.
2 On the subject of time, see J. López-Morillas, "Machado's Temporal Interpretation of Poetry," *JAAC*, VI(1947), 161-171.

period ends with the rejection of the Symbolist aesthetic, whose *fin-de-siècle* form in Spain was called *modernismo* (1907). He also abandons Bergsonian philosophy at this time for a rather objective analysis of Castile's outer and inner landscapes (1907-1917). Toward the end of this second period and throughout the third, Machado comes under the influence of Husserl and Heidegger, although anticipating the latter in writings prior to 1925 (1917-1939). What concerns me in this chapter is a number of critical moments during the first two periods when the mirror reflecting the poet and his environment abruptly cracks, causing certain distortions in image to appear. From the standpoint of Machado's total work these moments are relatively infrequent. But they occur in twenty poems, as well as in his prose writings, and their implications extend to the aesthetic crisis of our century.

Machado's position vis-à-vis Romanticism is best understood by comparing Hugo and Baudelaire with respect to the grotesque. We know from the preface to *Cromwell* that the genre was not alien to Romantic ideology. Hugo categorized the grotesque with the beautiful, arguing that it eliminated monotony from the drama and could be used to inject horror or laughter into tragedy. He justified his enthusiasm for this "reverse side of the sublime" by noting that, in Nature's infinite beauty, darkness and light, evil and good, the unshapely and the graceful existed side by side. From the fruitful union of the grotesque and the sublime issued modern genius. But Hugo's concept suffered the limitation of making the grotesque a technique that served some other effect. Only after Baudelaire, and Goya's black paintings before him, released the grotesque from its instrumentalism did it come to be valued for itself.

This self-sufficiency was possible because Baudelaire, like Machado after him, understood the principles of Goya's art. Both poets saw in Goya an aesthetic of violence, of the uncanny, and of the fantastic that was complete in itself and yet gave rise to a socio-moral vision of man. The purely formal and the purely ethical are in Goya raised to their highest power, both remaining independent and yet linked to each other cryptogenically. Although Baudelaire and Machado replace much of the fantastic with the ugly, the basic rule is unchanged. While one speaks of a hospital "adorned with only one large crucifix, / where tearful prayers reek from excrement,"[3] the other refers to a convent's "¡Amurallada / piedad, erguida en este basurero!," or describes a moribund Castilian village thus: "Allá, en la plaza, mendigos y chicuelos: / una orgía de harapos."[4] The two poets effectively control their sentiments while allowing the external incongruities to represent themselves. This is essentially a Goyesque approach: the eye selects from reality details which are intensified, enlarged, and carried to their logical extreme. Deformation is a selective magnification.

This technique is used sparingly by Machado but with a range that covers the supernatural, the fantastic, insane and criminal types, and impressionistic landscapes.[5] What results is an un-Romantic national portrait whose moral image is in good measure pencilled with naturalistic distortion; a wounded Spain "con sucios oropeles de Carnaval," "pobre escuálida y beoda" with blood, a nation whose citizens once were young and "encinta de lúgubres presagios. / cuando montar quisimos en pelo una quimera" (CXLIV). The carnival, a scene frequent in the grotesque, is used in other contexts by Machado to introduce the mask motif, as we will see. In the quotation cited, the scene is carried away from complete objectivity by a strong undertow of sentiment—Machado's love for Spain. He and Baudelaire differ from Goya in this respect. The poets' discreet emotional presence in their verse heightens the effect of their technique by dignifying the grotesque with pathos. Goya, in contrast, appears to have had no interest or feeling for his deformed subjects, and—as Ortega has pointed out—his lack of sympathy explains Goya's style and the fact that his human beings are really interchangeable dolls with masks for faces. On the other hand, a Goyesque poem by Baudelaire describes several hump-backed crones (*Eves octogénaires*) trotting like marionettes while the poet watches them tenderly at a distance (85). As for Machado's tenderness for *la España negra*, it pervades every poem where the Castilian countryside is depicted somberly.

---

3 *Œuvres complètes* (Paris, 1961), p. 13. Further references will follow texts. All translations are mine.

4 *Poesías completas* (Buenos Aires, 1951), CXXXII. All quotations from Machado refer to the Losada editions, which will be abbreviated as follows: *Los complementarios:* C; *Abel Martin:* AM; *Juan de Mairena* (2 vols.): JM, JM-II.

5 See the following poems: "La tierra de Alvargonzález," "Los asesinos" iv, LIV, XCIV, C, CVI, CVII, CVIII.

The tradition of a deformed Spain has been carried further in this century by a painter whom Machado calls a "Goya necrómano." This is Solana,[6] whose work prompted Machado to record some significant observations. The poet finds three key elements in Solana's aesthetic: the unhealthy voluptuosity of painting what is dead as if it were alive and vice versa; the nightmarish reality of animating manniquins and paralyzing human faces; the feverishness of an ingenuous naturalism (C,19). Machado, who was most conscious of the history of aesthetic ideas, recognized in Solana's work the complementary vision of Spanish genius. What interests us from the standpoint of Machado's poetic is that he found in Spain's grotesque tradition a confirmation of his own belief that "todo poeta tiene dos musas: / Lo ético y lo patológico" (C,19). The fulfillment of this binomial, and especially its first term, came during the poet's middle period, when the Castilian landscape and the tenets of social realism superseded his Romanticism. As for the pathological, its manifestations remain independent of Machado's personal psychology, in a way resembling Dalí's cultivation of "critical paranoia."

The psychological distortions in Machado's work show clearly the poet's sophistication. He distinguishes between the irrationalism of the Romantics, whose idealism and faith in the universality of language affirmed their belief in reason, and the collapse of metaphysical idealism in the post-Romantic era, when the poet confines his world to the boundaries of his psychological awareness and "explora la ciudad más o menos subterránea de sus sueños "(C, 115). Machado credits the French Symbolists, and especially Verlaine's exaltation of music, with the defeat of Cartesianism. Thenceforth artists aspire to the pure expression of the subconscious, calling upon obscure faculties rooted in the subliminal areas of their being (AM,98). Surprisingly, although Machado knew Freud's work, he says nothing about it, and he remained skeptical of psychoanalysis (JM-II,38). Yet elsewhere he declares himself a dedicated self-analyst and interprets a dream about a professor (Machado) accused of corrupting students by training their minds instead of their bodies. The dream is given a political explanation, but two details make it pertinent to the artistic reasons for Machado's grotesque. In the dream the professor is accused by a strange, stentorian-voiced little man

---

6 For an introduction to Jose Gutiérrez Solana, see Anthony Kerrigan, "Black Knight of Spanish Painting," *Arts Magazine* (May-June, 1962), 16-20.

dressed in an ecclesiastical cassock and the three-cornered hat of the Civil Guard, who is a representation of ambiguous masculinity (JM-II,145ff). This disguise has bearing on Machado's constant self-doubt as a poet.

The Civil Guard, the tough embodiment of authority in real life, is a frequent symbol of potency and brutality in Spanish art. The motif reappears in a nightmare where Machado is led away to be hanged for an unspecified crime. Here the tricorn symbol is transformed into a hatter's block set upon a slowly rising scaffold mast on which the poet will be executed. The hangman is a barber who looks like the accuser of the previous dream. There is some discussion in the nightmare, and in a subsequent verse fantasy similar to it, as to whether Machado can be decapitated instead of hanged. The barber image also occurs in an early poem where Machado curses an artificially trimmed garden and the ineffectiveness of his poetic office (LI). In all cases Machado is uncertain of himself and the power of poetry, and in the verse fantasy he even produces a chaotic fanfare of drums and trumpet blasts that contrast with the poet and his weak-winded horn (AM,67ff). Machado's dream symbolism is restricted to these grotesque contexts, and combines the mechanism of displacement with other Surrealist details like wax figures and disquieting streets. The significance of these examples lies in their objective extension of the Goya-Solana pathology to embrace contemporary forms of expression and to link the latter with the erosion of Romantic values. How Machado reveals this erosion is described in the next Section.

The comic mode is the last element in Machado's grotesque, and probably the least. Although the poet is noted for his ironic and humoristic attitudes in the philosophical writings and verse aphorisms, the Spain that he casts in the shadow of Cain is unrelieved by laughter. In this he differs substantially from the theories of Baudelaire and Nietzsche. For Nietzsche there are two possible forms by which the artist represents the true nature of things: the sublime and the comic. Once the artist penetrates the core of reality—the terror and absurdity of existence—he transforms his reflections either by the sublime, which is the artistic conquest of the awful, or the comic. The comic is the artistic release from the nausea of the absurd.[7] In Machado, however, whatever is grotesque in the image of Castile is represented by the horrific rather than the humorous. It is true that with respect to his own existence Machado reacts with mockery to the dilemma of personality, as I will show. But his laughter is real, not artistic, and does not release him from the absurd but is rather the product of it. As for Baudelaire, who defines the grotesque as the "absolute comic," the genesis of laughter is Satanic, and while this concept applies to Goya, it does not to Machado, despite the mark of Cain on the Castilian brow.

In one other area Machado's use of the grotesque departs from Baudelaire's notion of the absolute comic. It is in his diagnosis of Romanticism's demise. Baudelaire distinguishes carefully between the absolute comic art form which is unaware of its nature, and the artist, who is a double man able to be himself and someone else at the same time. Machado eradicates this distinction. He traces the self-awareness of the modern lyric to the poet's doubts about his emotive values. The poet compensates for this loss of esteem by engaging in a "fetichism of objects." But he realizes that external things have also lost their value because they depended upon the very sentiments that are no longer prized. Thus contemporary art cannot take itself seriously. Objects

> Se emancipan del lazo cordial que antes las domeñaba, y ahora parecen invadir y acorralar al poeta, perderle el respeto, reírsele en las barbas. En medio de una imaginería de bazar, el poeta siente su íntimo fracaso, se ríe de sí mismo y, en consecuencia, tampoco prestar a sus creaciones otro valor que el de juguetes mecánicos (C,36-37).

Machado carries this notion to a devastatingly logical conclusion. He invents a character with a "máquina de trovar," a piano-phonograph apparatus that manufactures poetry. Since the individual sentiment of Romanticism is now suspect, the inspirational force behind this machine is a collective muse. That is, the Romantic poet has bared his soul with the ostentation of a bourgeois boasting of his coaches and mistresses. The distance between his feelings and those of the mainstream of humanity has grown wider, and his singing sounds like a falsetto. The

---

7 *The Birth of Tragedy* in *The Philosophy of Nietzsche* (New York, 1954), p. 985.

mainstream begins to call the Romantic lyricist insincere, yet it is not that the latter sings of unfelt emotions, but that the former cannot feel them as well. Hence the troubador machine, which composes songs for the masses about generic feelings. Its poems are about the group, not the individual, and whereas the Romantic wrote "La canción del verdugo," the modern invention will produce a "canción de los aficionados a ejecuciones capitales." As a consolatory note, Machado adds that the machine has only an interim purpose, until a new sensibility arises with new poets to express it (AM,52ff). The factors responsible for this state of suspension can be seen in Machado's own poetic conflict, which we can now begin to examine.

II

From the point of view of subsequent hermetic poetry, it is not unfair to say that Romanticism suffered from an over-exposure to nature. The familiar apostrophes which poets addressed to their natural surroundings would have sounded insincere on the lips of Machado, whose generation found the intimacy between man and nature already broken. Whereas the Romantic enjoyed an informal relationship with his environment, the modern was acquiring the formalities of scientism. The familiarity of one was analogous to a dialogue between independent personalities, while the detachment of the other resembled the confrontation of a knower and an object. This estrangement had two aesthetic expressions: the emotional distance of an Hérédia or a late Cézanne, and the masquerade of a Verlaine. Machado converts the second form into the grotesque by muting a morbid note with a burlesque one, as in one poem where a premonition of death in a damp garden is greeted by a hidden bird's mocking whistle (XXVIII). Both styles represent the same idea: that the physical intimacy between man and nature is incompatible with the affective distance between them. Yet Machado's grotesque is the later and more acute representation, where the intellectual structure of the discord is reinforced aesthetically by an incongruity. Even when the poet is absent from his environs, the latter respond in the same key, as in one poem describing the backdrop for a village scaffold: "El lienzo de Oriente / sangraba tragedias, / pintarrajeadas / con nubes grotescas" (XLVII).

Another change in the post-Romantic awareness of nature was the

Symbolist transformation of reality by *apparences sensibles*. These alleviate the first traces of a self-conscious fear of insincerity and show an irreverence toward nature that permitted the senses to alter it. As Jean Moréas wrote in 1886,

> [An enemy] of teaching, declamation, false sensibility, and objective description, symbolic poetry seeks to dress the Idea in a sensible form.... Symbolic art consists of never going as far as the concentration of the Idea in itself. Thus, in this art, nature's tableaux, human actions, all concrete phenomena... [are] sensible appearances designed to represent their esoteric affinities with primordial Ideas.[8]

This poetic evolved into a hermetic preoccupation with the language of sensibility which made little sense to the linguistically rational side of Machado's temperament. In moments of protest against himself for having employed the modernists' diction he exclaims, "¡Malhaya tu jardín!... Hoy me parece / la obra de un peluquero" (LI), or else he ridicules the style as a cosmetic (XCVII).

The problem of nature's independence awakened Machado's sense of the grotesque in the presence of the Symbolists' rhetoric. This had not troubled either the Romantics, who were too occupied with their experience of reality, or the Symbolists, who were busy analyzing their psychological states before nature. But Machado was incapable of such analysis without feeling the absurdity of half a landscape submitting to the shadows and silences of a mood while the other half swaggered out of reach (*cielo fanfarrón*—XLV). Amiel's observation that "a landscape is a state of the soul"[9] was true only to the extent that a poet was committed to an introspective consciousness of the landscape; as soon as he tried to know it independently of his spirit, he introduced a disruptive attitude that differentiated between subjective and objective reality. This attitude, which is intellectually expressed by antithesis, is formulated poetically by the grotesque. A good example of the progressive dislocation of the poet's awareness is the treatment given to the moon during these periods. Whereas conventional Romantic depictions—Leopardi's,

---

8 Quoted in G. Michaud, *La Doctrine symboliste* (Paris, 1947), p. 25.

9 "Un paysage quelconque est un état de l'âme." Henri-Frédéric Amiel *Journal intime*, 10 Février 1846.

for example—make the moon autonomous, with attributes that coincide with the poet's ideals, the Symbolist-like Baudelaire imprisons the moon within his own subjectivity:

> ...not the white moon of the idylls that resembles a cold bride, but the sinister, intoxicating moon, suspended in the depths of a stormy night and buffeted by the racing clouds; not the peaceful and discreet moon visiting the sleep of pure men, but the moon torn from the sky, vanquished and in revolt, which the Thessalian Sorceresses harshly compel to dance on the terrified grass! (289).

Baudelaire represents a radical shift, for although the Romantics also viewed the moon subjectively, they nevertheless preserved its traditional associations in meaning.

When Machado sees the moon manipulated by the Symbolists' egotistical sensibility, his rational impulse is to restore the objective balance. But he cannot do it without also pointing out the absurdity of the Symbolists' delusion. Thus he sets, on the one hand, a familiar nocturnal scene: the clock striking a melancholy one a.m., while, on the other hand, the moon appears as a gleaming skull against the lowered horizon. Meanwhile, the ill-played music of a mazurka floats by half-innocently and half-mockingly (LVI). Thus Machado accomplishes what Marinetti would propose several years later in the Futurist manifesto *Tuons le clair de lune*. Elsewhere Machado satirizes a "luna de hojalata" (CLVII), a tambourine-playing moon (AM,70), and, in a general travesty of Romantic sentimentalism, a "cándida luna de abril" (LII, LXXI). Here are successive modifications of the ego-phenomenon relationship. In the first period sentiments are genuine, and the poet is content to find their correspondences in the object he contemplates; in the second period these genuine sentiments transfigure the object and make it part of the poet's "soul-state." In Machado, the object is made to contradict his feelings in a mocking reassertion of independence which casts doubt on both the legitimacy of his emotions and the adequacy of their poetic setting. That Machado's dissolution of the Symbolist pathos is a grotesque achievement becomes still more obvious when compared to Verlaine's *Claire de lune*, where nearly-sad bergamasks dance fantastically among ecstatic fountains without becoming incongruous because all elements are touched by the same emotional aura.

Machado's grotesque is more than just the fruit of a mismated rationalism and Symbolism. His own mind is bored with the emotions that his heart takes seriously. The grotesque is the broken image of an existentialist's self-contemplation. The source of this image is derivative—the ennui of Mallarmé's *Brise marine*—but its special deformative character depends upon Machado's ironic observation of his own irony. This is developed in several stages. In the first we find the genuine feelings of Machado the man: the "llama pura" of Romantic love and a "mala tristeza" that attenuates it. Machado the poet must deal with these two emotions, and finding listless love an unworthy hybrid, he responds with a "bostezo." This is the second stage: the poet's emotional response, tinged with irony, to the man. But Machado the man is also aware of Machado the poet. Hence the final stage, the poem itself, which contains not only the poet's yawn but the man's ironic judgment that his poetic attitude is a histrionic declamation. The poet yawns at the man, concealing his irony with an actor's rhetoric, while the man is ironic toward the poet for his fraudulence. The written poem incorporates both ironies and is grotesque because it gives an overlapping image of Machado, who is viewed by the double focus of the two ironies (XVIII, XLIX, LVI). This analysis is new in poetry because it shows the serious man contemplating himself in the act of self-mockery. It is comparable to a man grimacing at himself in a mirror, a situation that has become a recent existentialist theme. The grimaces are not important in themselves; what is significant is that the man wants to see himself making them. This desire to see is quite serious and converts the grimacing man into a clown who bears no resemblance to the contemplator. Meanwhile, the object of the grimaces is the original man, previous to his wish to see and previous to his facial distortions. This original man becomes the mirror image, and although he will physically appear to be grimacing, the contemplator knows that it is "someone else" who is staring back at him grotesquely from the mirror. Thus the image, like the poem, remains a serious reflection, and because it is serious but appears to be mocking, it is also grotesque.

We should also take notice of the distance between Machado and traditional Romantic irony. The Byronic pose is not self-analytical but is directed outward to deal with a social conflict. Byron's self-consciousness and self-ridicule are defense mechanisms designed to make others think that there is another Byron. In reality, there is only one, a Byron of indivisible seriousness whose sensitivity is protected by a burlesque veneer. In contrast to Machado, Byron cultivates his pose seriously.[10] He is aided by an artist's faith in the efficacy of his medium, for only an unruffled confidence in his poetic office can account for Byron's assiduous masking of his real emotions. Machado, however, conceals neither his true feelings, nor his ridicule of them, nor his impatience with the verbal form they both take. He writes, referring to the poet and his audience, "Le tiembla al cantar la voz, / Ya no le silban sus coplas; / que silban su corazón" (CLXI: liv). No one, not even Machado, is interested in the poet's heart, for the readiness of his confessions makes it suspect. Nor can we esteem the poem as did Byron, because it has become a disguise or an evasion. Machado's sense of the grotesque awakens to what appears to be a self-torture but is really the laceration of lifeless poetic tissue.

There is one form of Romantic irony that approaches Machado's transcendence of his own ego. This is the self-parody which Irving Babbitt describes as the Romantic ironist's striving for the Infinite.[11] The poet must stand aloof, then aloof from this aloofness, in an infinite transcending process. But once again, such a poet is not concerned with the psychology of his awareness, and he is serious about his irony because it is a way of affirming the self. Machado's grotesque depends upon the duplicities of his own consciousness.

The consequences of these new mechanisms lead directly to the disquieting aspects of Surrealism. Although Machado was not a Surrealist, we find in him the first elements of the modern nightmare: the ego represented by a shadow on a deserted steppe under a fiery sun, no one knowing whether its tears are its own or those of a *histrión grotesco*. The ego then becomes a spectre wandering in a nebulous labyrinth of mirrors, while moans echo from deep grottoes (XXXVII). Here the themes of alienation, loss of identity, and dehumanized reality are treated more coherently than in their fully disfigured Surrealist forms. Machado is disturbed by the symptoms of personality distintegration that have been hastened by his solitude. He thinks of his memory as a network of galleries that store recollections in pictorial guise. But the further he

---

10 See Harriet MacKenzie, *Byron's Laughter* (Los Angeles, 1939).
11 *Rousseau and Romanticism* (New York, 1955), pp. 241-242, 263-266.

explores, the more intricate the maze becomes. Not only do the galleries descend to darker levels of awareness, but the depiction of some remembrances seems more vivid than present reality. When faced with portraits of himself, Machado is confounded by the spectacle of his personality objectified. He becomes a spectator to his own drama, seeing it through temporal mirrors whose sharp images alternate with blurred reflections. When Machado writes his poem, he is like the man who, having awakened from a nightmare, scarcely recognizes who it was in it that wept.

These intuitions, which prior to their artistic expression are a matter for human psychology, are in poetry exorcised, so to speak, and manipulated at will like pliable shapes. Their total effect is grotesque because as erstwhile serious elements they are now arranged in vaguely distorted, sometimes absurd, attitudes. The poet commandeers his memories, visions, and fears like a puppeteer mounting his show with complicated figurines, a theme which later becomes one of Surrealism's most grotesque features (XXX). Or, he summons up past hopes on a marionette stage in the form of smiling little figures that are an old man's melancholy toys (XXII). Or, again, he merges a reverie of rose-tinted chimeras and flowered walks with a dream of twisted paths through a bitter land, shifting scenes from sunken crypts to ladders above the stars (XXII). The entire structure of the grotesque, from the symbols of depth psychology and escapism to the poet's voluntary self-transfiguration, is based on Machado's ambivalent feelings toward his own performance. We must bear in mind that he is about to enter a phase of social realism. It is difficult to find comparable examples in literature of this grotesque limbo between the comic innocence of earlier puppets and harlequins, whose artificiality was never in doubt, and the subsequent eerie absurdity of Surrealist mannequins. Machado's aesthetic crisis occurs where the planes of reality and emotional abstraction intersect.

The problem of death also lurks beneath Machado's distorted surfaces, a theme that persists throughout his literary activity. In the majority of poems death is treated with utter gravity or with an unmistakable stoic irony. But occasionally it erupts as a bizarre protest against temporality: "y quiero, sobre todo, emborracharme, / ya lo sabéis… ¡Grotesco! /Pura fe en el morir, pobre alegría / y macabre danzar antes de tiempo" (LXXV). This last gesture of gladness, born of desperation and perhaps defiance, is made at the edge of nothingness, but instead of a sober existentialist affirmation which Machado finds empty, he chooses the most perfect kind of absurdity: one where the very method of mocking death—drunkenness—is inadequate, pathetic, and grotesque. Elsewhere the poet refers to himself as a visionary, a melancholy drunkard, and a lunatic guitarist (LXXVII), and this Dionysian strain recalls more conventional grotesque patterns where morbidness is counteracted by frenzied affirmations through song and excess. Inebriation has always played an important role in saturnalian distortions, but missing from this tradition is the philosophical awareness of death that Machado uses for an additional aesthetic dimension. As for the dance, although only a detail in Machado, it is useful to recall its broader significance. The *danza de la muerte* does not belong to the grotesque category since its performance is didactic and compulsive: Death is the master whom doomed men must obey. But the *danse macabre* is grotesque, for it represents Death's temporary renunciation of his office to participate in the merriment of the living. The incongruity arises from Death's inappropriate conduct and from the nonchalance with which the revellers accept his presence. But the latter are still within the realm of mortality, and Death has crossed over to join their celebration. This type of grotesque is less severe than Machado's, which recognizes the futility of a dance that joylessly fills in time before Death's arrival.

Having analyzed the relationships of personal experience, mortality, and the aesthetic expression of both, Machado has no choice but to denounce his artistic posture as inauthentic. He sees his poetic sentiments as a façade concealing a circus performer who is Machado in disguise. Reflecting upon his own death, he observes, "Mirando mi calavera / un Nuevo Hamlet dirá: / He aquí un lindo fósil de una / careta de carnaval" (CXXXVI:xlviii). These words tell us an awful truth: Machado could not overcome his self-awareness, even when contemplating his own death. As Sartre has said of Baudelaire, his fundamental attitude was that of a man bending over himself, watching himself see. By transcending the self that is to die (the skull-mask in another man's hand), Machado also transcends the horror of death's inevitability, something that neither the drunkard nor the dancer could accomplish. At this point he understands that his death will be nothing more than a carnivalesque image of his life, that his *life* was in fact an emotional pastiche. Machado spares himself nothing as he portrays a buffoon laughing at his tragedy.

The buffoon is ruthlessly deformed, a hump-backed little dervish, big-bellied, jovial, and picaresque, engaged in a twisted dance (CXXXVIII). The distinction is still finer elsewhere, as the buffoon himself is derided by a malformed wall-shadow (CL VII). The poem, then, disparages the artist's psychological conflict while making of it and its philosophical consequences the very subject matter of poetic deformation. And by this route Machado leads us to a fundamental aesthetic principle of our time, that no aspect of existence is absolved from the absurd or from the artistic derision which absurdity encourages.

Machado's contribution to the grotesque is best understood in terms of the shift from a moral-aesthetic to an existentialist preoccupation. The deterioration of Romantic values was but temporarily checked by the Symbolists. Once Machado ceased to be distracted by the problems of style and image, he developed a self-awareness that placed the entire Symbolist aesthetic in doubt. The grotesque expresses the poet's transcendence of his ego and the equivocal nature of his feelings. Whereas its more objective, Goyesque form is linked to the distortions of external reality, its subjective form foreshadows the psychological practices of Surrealism. In all cases Machado reveals in the grotesque the loss of Romanticism's absolute frame of reference. It is from the incompatibility of emotional and expressive planes that the sense of absurdity and the grotesque emerges.[12]

---

12 This study was first published in the *Journal of Aesthetics and Art Criticism*, 22 (1963), 209-16. Reprinted by permission of Blackwell Publishing.

10

Paranoid Grotesquerie in Solana

THE STUDIES OF CAMILO José Cela and J. Rof Carballo[1] have shows how the painter José Gutiérrez Solana's aesthetic can be clarified by an analysis of his prose sketches and by a psychological interepretation. One aspect of that aesthetic, the literary grotesque, will be examined in the following pages. The incongruity established by the coexistence of a recognizable reality and its partial deformation will be seen in (a) the representations of reality, and (b) the perception of those representations. Since the grotesque passages in Solana's writings occur in relation to the quasi-real world of mannequins and automatons, they have the added importance of approaching the reality of the plastic arts.

I. THE CONFUSION OF REALITIES
Solana arouses his *realidad inquietante* by means of focusing on the horrific aspects of a theme to the exclusion of all else, so that his own concentration produces an aberrant vision of the whole. For example, a description of old women on a pilgrimage observes "... otras llevan en brazos niños enfermos y tullidos, con la cara de cera y con ojos que parecen de vidrio..."[2] The realism is unequivocal, but so excessive that it produces uneasiness because of the absence of compensatory elements. The picture becomes too real because it isolates a single plane of reality. This technique of distortion by omission is not enough to create

---

1 See, respectively, *La obra literaria del pintor Solana* (Madrid, 1957) and "Máscara de la muier en la pintura de Solana," in *Entre el silencio y la palabra* (Madrid, 1960), pp. 298-330.
2 *La España negra* (Madrid, 1920), p, 81, abbreviated henceforth as EN. Other abbreviations: MC—*Madrid callejero* (Madrid, 1923); I—*Madrid: Escenas y costumbres, primera serie* (Madrid, 1913); II—*Madrid: Escenas y costumbres, segunda serie* (Madrid, 1918).

207

the grotesque; on the other hand it does achieve dehumanization, as in the scene about "... una mujer tuerta, con una venda en los ojos, como los caballos de los toros, con la boca desdentada, negra como una fosa; una mujer zamba y manca que toca las castañuelas con movimientos de muñeco al alzar los pies con alpargatas como si bailase... " (I, pp. 107-108). The image of a woman who moves not like a human being but with the awkwardness of a doll suggests a shaky distinction between the living and the animate. Human activity here is given in terms of doll-like animation. Clearly the preceding references to "la cara de cera" and "ojos que parecen de vidrio" are neither conventional nor accidental. The fusion—or confusion— by Solana of human figures and mannequins is the chief power of his grotesque prose.

Mannequins, dolls, and wax or mechanical figures prompt multiple descriptions in the painter's prose. For Solana, the canvas's two dimensions are inadequate supports for the qualities of a four-dimensional being. The mannequins are as close to human reality as an artifice can be, both spatially and in the temporality attained by movement. Such representations surpass pictorial limitations, and at the same time they compromise the distinction between imitative representations and reality. Such is the psychological foundation of Solana's prose. The imagination establishes unconscious rules of convention allowing it to judge the measure by which a work of art transforms reality. In this way the mind can gauge the margin of deviation between verisimilitude and reality. Since mannequins are too real, they confuse the real and the imitative. The mind forgets momentarily their artificiality, and upon remembering it clashes with the original impression of "reality," thus producing the grotesque. Solana was absorbed by his encounter with painting, a plastic medium that, distinct from painting, bordered ambiguously on the real.

> Al calor de la lumbre una aldeana con pañuelo a la cabeza y pclo de persona tapado por un pañuelo, corpiño azul de estameña y refajo amarillo de bayeta. En la mano tiene la cana y el copo: está hilando. De vez en cuando se incorpora con un movimiento de muñeco y mueve la cuna de un niño que llora entre panales. En otro compartimiento vemos dos muñecos que representan dos niños negritos lujosamente vestidos, con el cuerpo de trapo. Uno colgado de las anillas y otro del. trapecio, dan vueltas y hacen piruetas. Sus padres,

viejos negros, sentados en sillas, con las cabezas de cartón, los ven trabajar. (I. p. 158),

One scene is as human as the other is mechanical, but the deliberate juxtaposition becomes disconcerting. In the first, its duplicity arises from the human clothes, the sound, and the actions; in the second, allusions to rags, cardboard, and trapeze are unequivocal. The reappearance of the expression "movimiento de muñeco" increases the ambiguity by its gratuitous nature, while in the former, it was needed to describe the woman. Once the threshold of feigned reality is crossed, there is no doubt about where the frontiers are between the human and the animate, but there is a fleeting hesitation in which the scene becomes grotesque.

Solana extends his vision of life as a pathetic tragedy to the world of automatons. By adding to their behavior a new emotional facet, he introduces the incongruity of patent artificiality conceived with sentimental values usually reserved for human situations.

> El viejo se incorpora entre el chirrido de resortes que mueven todas estas figuras mecánicas, se sienta en la cama de golpe, como si pidiese agua y se sintiese por la fiebre morir, con el rostro espantado y angustioso, porque nadie acude a socorrerle, nadie se sienta en la silla que tiene a su cabecera a su mano diestra, (I, p. 159).

Solana shifts from mechanical action to the sphere of pathos, entering into emotional relations with automatons and appealing to the reader's intimate feelings. To harbor such feelings here is absurd, because mutually exclusive zones are confused in this call for compassion. But Solana's aesthetic is based on the need to reproduce his gloomy conception of the world. He measures out the link between what is real and what is pretense; he suggests the relationship between meaningless mechanics and tragic vitality. In a wax-figure exhibit of medical operations he comments: "Parece, en este momento, que somos personajes también de cera y que nos podremos deshacer o romper" (MC, p. 33). And he infuses humanity into the reversed situation:

> [Unas figuras de madera] representan un baile de aldeanos flamencos, como los de los cuadros de Teniers. Se retuercen bailando el

compás de la música. De pronto, el reloj no funciona, se siente un ruido de ruedas dentro de la caja, como si fuera a romper, cesa la música, y las figuras, como si las hubiese detenido en sus movimientos más graciosos, se paran bruscamente. (I, pp. 159-160).

Through subtle connections between the real world and the mannequins ("una música... como la voz de un viejo cantante," "nuestro guía ha dado cuerda a los relojes de sonería"), the idea of death becomes grotesque. The humanization of the mechanism is parallel to the dehumanizing technique applied to the living beings, with the same disquieting effect. But, regardless of the ambiguity in these scenes, Solana realizes that a ridiculous disharmony accompanies the proximity to life:

> El que está vestido de negro resulta el más trágico cuando asoma por la obscuridad de la puerta y se ve el blanco de su camisa y la cara muy amarilla, con la barba crecida y el sombrero echado por la frente... Las pelotas rebotan alrededor de estos muñecos, que tienen algunos rota la nariz o una oreja de los golpes, y cuando les dan en la cabeza y les tiran el sombrero resultan más ridículos, pues enseñan el cogote negro y barnizado... (EN, p. 46).

Solana is highly sensitive to the tragic aspects involved in droll situations, and he notices that physical deformation exists even in animated games.

I have suggested that one of the causes of the grotesque is the tenuous frontier between pretense and reality. Solana tends to step over this line and represent one for the other; or else he assumes that it is difficult to perceive that distinction in the tetradimensional world of mannequins. This type of plastic representation is not so far removed from life as a painting; it lacks the dimensional restrictions that can calm the cautious reader. The more the boundary between reality and its representation grows blurred, the more mysterious the experience in each of them. Both can be grotesque if one of them contains elements of the other. A carnival, for example, becomes suddenly unreal when the imagination fixes upon details that do not seem natural to the scene. Conversely, the failure of a plastic art work to maintain its independence of the reality it represents will lead to incongruity. This was a pressing idea for Solana, who understood how human and modeled figured can interchange characteristics:

> Una pareja de novios se quedan inmóviles· apoyados en la barandilla de un balcón, haciendo de figuras de cera. El público que los mira desde abajo los señala y los examina fijamente; éstos se ríen, hablan fuerte, y la gente ingenua queda chasqueada.[3]

Solana intends in this passage to pose several alarming questions. What is the difference between people and statues? To what extent are we like automatons in our movements and bearing? Solana undermines our confidence even more regarding what is human by exchanging the technique of describing mannequins through personal concepts for the description of persons in mannequin-like terms:

> Entonces, aquel hombre jovial, que habla con inmovilidad de autómata, rígido y sin mover un pliegue de su ropa, empieza, ante la estupefacción de la gente, a quitarse la levita, el chaleco, quedando en mangas de camisa; luego, se quita los pantalones, que dándose con unos peleles de punto, sentado en la silla; entonces se ve que tiene unas correas por el pecho; se levanta y separa una pierna, quedándose con ella en la mano, enseñándola al público… (II, p. 28).

This vendor of artificial limbs later declares that, once he is dressed, nobody can tell which of his legs is the artificial one. The method of *realidad inquietante* here promotes doubt with respect to where are the limits of artificiality: in mannequins it is acceptable; in people, unfortunately frequent; and describing one in terms of the other grotesque and unnerving.

The most perfect example of confused realities occurs in a puppet show where Tío Remigio goes furiously crazy:

> Luego coge a doña Micaela por el cuello y la tira cuan larga es, violentamente contra el suelo, con las faldas por encima de la cabeza, viéndosela el corsé, debajo del que tiene unos pechos artificiales y las almohadillas de unas caderas postizas…

---

3   M. Sánchez Camargo, *Solana* (Madrid, 1945), p. 254.

> A don Hilario le deja clavado un cuchillo de cocina en la tripa, y el ventrílocuo, señor León, huye, asustado, con las manos en la cabeza, y se mete por la primera puerta que encuentra, perseguido por el loco.
> Al bajar el telón la gente no sabe si es un muñeco o un hombre disfrazado de autómata.
> Tal vez sea un viejo que hemos visto a la puerta dar las entradas con gran inmovilidad ; parecía una figura de cera, con su traje negro, zapatos blancos, de playa, con puntas charoladas, pelo gris y dos colmillos en su boca desdentada, que brillaban a la luz más que los cristales de sus lentes . (II, p. 133).

Before the show, Solana had noticed in the doorman certain similarities between the statuesque and the human; the ingenuous audience needed a violent spectacle in order to be wondrous. But the effect is identical: to throw into suspicion the traits that traditionally distinguish life from automatism. This suspicion becomes extreme in a scene that is the reverse of the preceding one:

> … no me choca que el portero, que está sentado en una silla, dormido con la cabeza inclinada en un hombro y las manos cruzadas en el vientre, no se haya despertado al oir mis pisadas. "Este guardián de la sala debe de tener un sueño muy pesado," nos decimos, sin apenas haber reparado más que en un bulto humano.
> Pero al observarlo en un análisis detenido, nos choca su rostro y sus manos demasiadamente pálidas y su inmovilidad inquietante, como si estuviera durmiendo un sueño de siglos y que el tiempo se hubiera detenido, sin empañar de polvo el hule de la visera de su gorra y el brillo de sus botas. Entonces notamos una impresión molesta, que el portero, por su rigidez continua y que habíamos tomado por ser vivo, es un muñeco de cera.[4]

Just as animation is not necessarily a human activity, absolute immobility is no guarantee of the absence of life, for here the form seemed live. Nor does the initial encounter with form, bearing, and human clothing prove that a figure is alive. The suspension of these commonly

---

4 *Solana* p. 252.

accepted criteria renders indeterminable the nature of the contemplated figure. From this cognitive perplexity arises the grotesque experience, which increases as the observer realizes that the figure is not what it seemed to be.

The essential motivation for Solana's literary preferences is a matter for the psychopathologist. Yet it should not be forgotten that as a painter, Solana's mind functioned in a dual capacity. First, it perceived visual objects that, when alive and human, were recognized in their normal condition. And second, those very objects were apprehended not as real and living but in function of their plastic qualities. The figure is reduced to a series of textural, chromatic, and dimensional qualities without regard to their human element. Both realities are valid, but the second mental process is generally overlooked because it can be invoked by the representation itself. But in Solana's literary descriptions there are unexpected presences of his pictorial mind, his "dehumanizing spirit." Due to the unusual character of such intrusions, they provoke a strong sense of the grotesque.

II. The Paranoid Reaction

It is odd that in his detailed descriptions of people, Solana only takes routine note of the faces, whereas he speaks carefully of the physiognomies of mannequins, for which he reveals so decided a propension. It is also extraordinary that he attributes to the latter human qualities when their postures are of the most innocent passivity. On one occasion, the figures in a store display window attracts the writer, but when he pauses to look at them a transformation takes place in his relationship to them. Solana ceases to be an observer of objects incapable of response and imagines the mannequins as possessing live faculties that enter into human association with him: "Estos muñecos son un anuncio muy llamativo, y nos miran con sus ojos de cristal y nos invitan a pararnos y ver sus trajes de marino" (EN, p. 34). Solana no longer is the single actor in the scene, for he endows the mannequins with motor and even volitional responses. In this respect, they assume active intentions in his mind, which is equivalent to saying aggressive intentions; they take the initative and behave with motivation after he has engaged them passively. This imagined aggression indicates Solana's susceptibility to perceiving atttidues, both genuine and imagined, directed expressly toward him. The same passage refers to some hanging clothes:

Hoy el viento las agita sin cesar; parece que quisiera llevárselas; otras veces las infla como si fueran globos, y al hincharse estas camisas y blusas parece que las da forma humana: las mangas parece que se mueven y nos amenazan... (EN, p. 34).

This example is even more removed from human semblances. In the first case, the figures had definite physical correspondences with the human form, but here the clothes are formless. And of the many conceivable movements that the inflated clothes might suggest, Solana sees them in threatening guises.

Another favorite theme in the Solanesque prose is the wax museum, where he creates a fantastic atmosphere through a mixture of morbid and lively traits in the figures:

...nunca podemos disimular la impresión de misterio que nos produce estas vitrinas de gente que parece muerta y que seguirán usando los mismos trajes que llevaron puestos en vida, y que nos contemplan con sus ojos crueles, impasibles y fijos . (EN, p. 47).

The grotesque operates as an autonomous quality of the object. The figures do not fill a roll of maintaining an appearance in the manner of mannequins that model clothing. On the contrary, they simulate reality. The presence of clothes results in incongruity because they are as live or real as the figures are inanimate. In this first mode of the grotesque Solana superimposes a special interpretation that does not lack paranoid suggestiveness. Although he is objective in describing the eyes as "impasibles y fijos," his irrational faculties divine hostility in the figures ("crueles"). It is difficult to reconcile this simultaneity of neutral and hostile facial expressions. The position of "crueles" placed before "impasibles y fijos" demonstrates that Solana's contemplation is above all psychological and only later literary, intellectual, and painterly. Even if "crueles" were not a subjective judgment, Solana's belief that the figures are observing him transfers the adjective to an emotional status. The passage reveals a mental progression in four stages: allusion to a sensation of mystery; entry into a personal relationship with the observed figures; perception of a cruelty born of his imagination; and recognition of eyes in a neutral state.

The most outstanding example of paranoid vision is a bipartite dream that takes place in the "belicosa" city of Oropesa. The first part refers to the city's attack on Solana:

> De pronto, como cuando se levanta el telón en el teatro, vi como una decoración algo borrosa que salía de las paredes como si no cupiese en el estrecho cuartucho. Sobre un cielo de color de plomo vi la silueta férrea de este pueblo que se iba acercando a mí; sus peñascos parecían que me iban a aplastar. El pueblo estaba como pegado, sin aire ni distancia, en una sábana; parecía pintado y que se iba acercando cada vez más a mí, que descansaba todo en mi pecho. (EN, p. 153).

The dream incorporates while deforming the details of the writer's physical circumstances. The small room becomes oppressive, and for that reason the apparition overwhelms it; the lack of space is transferred to a two-dimensional representation of the city; the bedsheet converts its sense of enclosure into the sense of the threatening city being located on his chest. What has been created is a psychological confusion in which part of Solana's reality is projected into the vision, and the dreamed bedsheet is fused with the real one on feeling and seeing a weight on his chest.

The second part of the dream refers to a Goyesque procession that is converted into a nightmare:

> …vi unas botas enormes que andaban por el suelo, y como por arte de magia salir unos correajes de un amarillo duro y asesino y los tricornios charolados desagradables de dos guardias civiles, las barbas largas y pegadas a los rostros lívidos; estas figuras se iban articulando por piezas, aparecían las orejas y no tenían ojos, después les brotaban las narices, los dedos sueltos andaban por la pared, hasta que se completaron estos fantasmones ridículos y espantables; vi los ojos duros y fieros clavados en mí y el brillo de los cañones de los fusiles; me apuntaban para disparar y no dejarme escapar, como si yo fuera un terrible criminal. (EN, p. 154).

The phrase "fantasmones ridículos y espantables" may be reassuring, but the fact that Solana awakens screaming infuses gravity into the event. The nightmare should not be taken lightly. The motif of freedom comes from the first part of the dream, where it adopted the form of oppression. It is expressed here by the marching boots, the detached body members, and, antithetically, by Solana's inability to escape. The "correajes de un amarillo duro y asesino" and the rifles are symbols of authority within the same theme.

The sensation of incongruity is due to the arrest of a real person by imagined phantoms. Solana sees himself in the dream as fully real. In the oneiric mechanism, the rational self is situated apart from the dream content and can observe on occasion its image in action But the rational self lacks the power to influence the behavior of that dreamed image, a fact that explains the grotesque experience. Another incongruous factor is the manner in which the spectres take shape, reminiscent of the clothes swelled out by the wind, cited earlier. The eyes again stand out in the paranoid reaction; their counterpart are the round rifle barrels that aim at him so fixedly, flashing a metallic shine, just like "los ojos duros y fieros." The latter is the most intimate approximation to the persecution manifested in Solana's writings. And at this point the nightmare loses its grotesque nature and borders on more serious regions of the unknown.[5]

---

5 This study was first published in *Papeles de Son Armadans*. 65 (Agosto 1961), 165-80. Reprinted by permission of the Fundación Camilo José Cela.

11
The Grotesque in Valle-Inclán

IT IS DIFFICULT TO avoid using the word "grotesque" in connection with Valle-Inclán's works, especially when his aesthetics are involved. The reason for this is not simply that he perfected the *esperpento* form, or that he wrote scripts for so-called marionette shows. These tendencies are, along with his stylistic idiosyncrasies, manifestations of a more fundamental attitude, a deep-seated principle which fixes both historical and psychological ideas into a framework of deliberate distortion.

No doubt this principle is better understood by intuition than by analysis, and it is probably best appreciated by Spaniards rather than by foreign devotees of Spanish culture. However, something of its quality can be felt in the undertone of a conversation that takes place toward the beginning of the novel *Viva mi dueño*, which runs, in part: "—¡Aquí todo es bufo! —¡Bufo y trágico! —¡Pobre España! Dolora de Campoamor." (II, 1082). What the speakers are suggesting is that behind the histrionics of Spanish life, a genuinely tragic situation can be found, but that this tragedy can never rise artistically above the maudlin expression given to it by the *vox populi*. And yet Valle-Inclán, whose aesthetic requirements were more demanding than Campoamor's, found himself determined to portray that tragedy on his own terms. As a result, he adopted what he felt was the only alternative left to the modem writer: a bufo-tragic perspective that experimented with the categories of literary deformation. Instead of the cheap sentimentality of the *dolora*, he would use a harsh mockery that played havoc with popular motifs, national history, and the standard responses of the Romantic tradition.

Valle-Inclán's new orientation also exploited the many elements clustered around the concepts of "pueblo," "España," and "dolora." This is why the above conversation is such an interesting summary of his grotesque techniques. It associates three quite different sensibilities—

tragedy, absurdity, and sentimentalism—with a single entity: Spanish society. And since these areas include most of the themes developed by Valle-Inclán, they also affect the entire range of his experimental practices. For example, the popular element in his work produces an extreme realism whose ugly features border on horrible deformation. Then too, the presence of folk culture gives rise to the literary use of superstition and the inclusion of episodes like the carnival, both of which inevitably lead back to certain facets of the Romantic grotesque. On the other hand, the historical aspect of Valle-Inclán's works makes room for a description of the aristocratic element in Spanish society and its role in determining Spain's cultural destiny. This, in turn, permits the appearance of a certain self-consciousness and mannered elegance, both of which are rendered ridiculous by means of stylizations, harlequinades, and Versaillesque parodies. At the same time, the idealism of the aristocracy is vulgarized, and this forges the link with the *pueblo* motif and the decline of Romantic values. And finally, the concept of tragic absurdity enables Valle-Inclán to maintain an implacable scrutiny of personality and behavior in all of his creatures, an activity which he converts into puppetry and pretentious theatricalness.

These are some of the components of the grotesque in Valle-Inclán's works as they are related to the basic vision of a bufotragic Spain. This vision has, of course, been commented on by other critics—most recently by Guillermo Díaz-Plaja in *Las estéticas de Valle-Inclán*—but for the most part their attention has been limited to *Luces de bohemia* and *Tirano Banderas*, or else has not placed much emphasis on aesthetic problems. What I propose to do in this essay is to gather together the grotesque manifestations in all of the other works, and discuss them independently of the two masterpieces. Since we already know a good deal about deformation in the latter, thanks to Pedro Salinas, Anthony Zahareas, and Antonio Risco, there is no need to examine those works again. On the other hand, we must begin to weigh the implications of the grotesquerie that appears in so many forms throughout Valle-Inclán's writings. For example, and by way of introduction once more, we must ask what the intention was in the semi-realistic scene of the *Retablo de la avaricia, la lujuria y la muerte*, which also summarizes so much of the typically grotesque, although in a way that is different from the earlier quotation:

El retablo de vecinos guarda silencio. La difunta, en el féretro de esterillas doradas, tiene una desolación de figura de cera, un acento popular y dramático. La pañoleta floreada ceñida al busto, las tejas atirantadas por el peinado, las manos con la rosa de papel saliendo de los vuelillos blancos, el terrible charol de las botas, promueven un desacorde cruel y patético, acaso una inaccesible categoría estética (I, 820).

I cite this passage now as an excellent synthesis of the aesthetic ideas that I propose to analyze separately in the sections that follow. It is, in effect, a literary representation of bufo-tragic theory. If Campoamor's *dolora* is the normal expression of Spanish sentimentality, then this scene is its aesthetic counterpart as conceived from the dislocated perspective of tragic absurdity. The spectre of death assures the *retablo* of its sobriety and pathos, and yet the setting indicates the author's ironic detachment. Feeling is balanced against cruelty, humanity against wax dolls, and *costumbrismo* against aestheticism. On the whole, moreover, an air of artifice reduces the scene to a level of irreality that is comparable to similar reductions imposed upon the privileged classes in other works.

Such is the pattern of "inaccessible" techniques that will be found throughout this study. The evidence will, in general, fall into several different categories. One of these involves the use of the Romantic grotesque, and the process by which Romanticism degenerates into the schizophrenic sensibility that marks so much of contemporary art. A second group includes those techniques which portray clowns, marionettes, and masks, all part of a compulsive stylization which results from a nostalgia for the Rococo. Still another type of grotesque emerges from literary realism and Spanish history, and leads to the absurd dramatization of popular and aristocratic social strata. And finally, there is the handling of aesthetic violence both for its own sake and for what Valle-Inclán called the "fatalismo geomántico de dolor y de indiferencia." In all of this, we will learn how relatively unimportant chronology is in the works, insofar as the grotesque is concerned. The latter operates as an aesthetic mode throughout Valle-Inclán's career, although in general, of course, the esperpentic grotesque gains the ascendancy over the Romantic grotesque as the years pass.

I. The Revaluation of Romantic Motifs

The best way to approach the modern grotesque is to determine what antecedents, especially in the Romantic tradition, are still reflected in a viable form. The use of the term "Romantic grotesque" should not, by now, require much explanation, especially after the studies of Kayser and Clayborough. In broad outline, it stands for a characteristically Romantic fusion of the subjective and the supernatural, the idealistic and the absurd, and the sensible and the horrific. In Valle-Inclán, this fusion tends to reveal a basic polarization between two kinds of experiences: events which belong to the individual's subjectivity and those that verifiably have occurred outside the subject. In other words, there is a recognizable difference between external phenomena and psychological ones, a distinction which tends to disappear in the later works. The most extreme example in the psychological grouping is the dream-state which overflows into the real world. The well-known description of Benicarlés' hallucination in *Tirano Banderas* is the best instance of this, but the earlier experience of Bradomín in the *Sonata de otoño* is more interesting in view of its date. There, the Marqués tells how "el moscardón verdoso de la pesadilla daba vueltas sin cesar, como el huso de las brujas hilanderas." The peculiar coloration, along with the reference to popular superstition, tends to objectify the nightmare, but then the dreamer falls back within himself in the manner of Bécquer: "La terraza quedó desierta. En medio del sopor que me impedía de una manera dolorosa toda voluntad, yo columbraba que mi pensamiento iba extraviándose por laberintos oscuros, y sentía el sordo avíspero de que nacen los malos ensueños, las ideas torturantes, caprichosas y deformes, prendidas en un ritmo funambulesco" (II, 165).

This type of episode is a pivotal one in the transition between pure Romanticism and the post-Romantic sensibility. The allusions to the tortured soul and psychological inertia hark back to the 19th century, whereas the accent on the inner labyrinths of imagination as the source of deformed images is more modern in its possibilities. Oddly enough, this second path is not followed for long by Valle-Inclán. Instead, he modernizes the opposite pole of the Romantic grotesque: external activity. This change of interest shows up clearly in the treatment of popular superstition and the supernatural. In the story "Rosarito," for example, we read of a huge shadow, perhaps that of a giant bird, running along the wall just prior to the heroine's death: "Se la ve posarse en el techo y deformarse en los ángulos, arrastrarse por el suelo y esconderse bajo las sillas. De improviso, presa de un vértigo funambulesco, otra vez salta al muro, y galopa por él como una araña" (I, 1313). What was an inner "ritmo funambulesco" in Bradomín's dream is here exteriorized, and this change provides the most probable explanation for Valle-Inclán's shift in preference. He was writing narratives and plays, not static poems. Therefore, he needed the kind of spatial freedom which the plasticity of dream images, hanging in mental galleries, could not provide. His own imagery, of course, is quite plastic, but as we will observe again later, it is energized by the sort of movement which ordinary dream images lack. In order to appreciate this, we might compare, say, Dalí's hypnagogic states with the *embrujo* of Goya. The difference between the two in terms of plasticity and sense of energy is quite evident. Valle-Inclán, then, is much closer to Goya and his dynamism than to any other type of plastic dream-state.

The frequent appearance of supernatural motifs, especially witches, would seem to date Valle-Inclán, and reveal his traditionalism. This is true to a certain extent, although the most noteworthy examples of superstition occur not during his modernist period but in his first *esperpentos*. Aside from the instances already noted, the only other early example is a reference in the *Sonata de invierno* to a murmur of sounds and voices "que guardaban un ritmo quimérico y grotesco, aprendido en el clavicordio de alguna bruja melómana" (II, 190). And here, it is evident that the folkloric element is used not directly, but in a contrived role as a kind of literary allusion. In contrast, such works as *Las galas del difunto* and the *Romance de lobos* incorporate supernaturalism directly into the narrative. This does not mean that the self-conscious artifice for which Valle-Inclán is so famous does not apply to superstition, for it does ("una chimenea de piedra, que recuerda esos cuentos campesinos y grotescos de las brujas que se escurren por la gramallera abajo, y de los trasgos patizambos..." *Aguila de blasón* [I, 591]). But the aforementioned works create an atmosphere that is similar to that of Maeterlinck's, with a strong measure of violence added to compound impressionism with expressionism. There are also several effective witches' scenes in the *Romance de lobos* that promote the narrative action instead of forming part of the descriptive background.

But it is in *Las galas del difunto* that action and plastic imagery combine successfully to create a new grotesque effect. Here, a witch disguised as an owl watches as the druggist changes his clothing:

> Se reviste gorro, bata, pantuflas: Reaparece bajo la cortinilla con los ojos parados de través, y toda la cara sobre el mismo lado, torcida con una mueca. La coruja, con esquinado revuelto, ha vuelto a posarse en el iris mágico que abre sus círculos en la acera. El estafermo, gorro y pantuflas, con una espantada, se despega de la cortinilla. El desconcierto de la gambeta y el visaje que le sacude la cara, revierten la vida a una sensación de espejo convexo" (I, 970).

There is still more, but the point is clear. The mixture of painting and shadow-box theater has its peculiar effect as the methods of each interact. What is normally a technique of synthetic cubism, the full-faced profile, is rendered grotesque by movement, by the magic light, and by the preposterous mirror which destroys the geometricity of the scene. Since the face had been twisted into a grimace from the beginning, its portraiture can hardly be viewed as a serious Cubist endeavor. Nevertheless, the plastic quality remains, along with the ample sense of space. And at the same time, the scene takes a step forward in its theatrical experiment, adapting the traditional supernaturalism to an ambiguous flat screen whose figures are convertible into three dimensions.

The grimacing face is one of Valle-Inclán's characteristic motifs, and its presence among the more traditional Romantic elements is one factor in the latter's evolution. In this connection, it is interesting to observe how he even departs from Romanticism in his *modernista* period, although to a lesser degree. One portrait in the *Sonata de estío* depicts some ragged Indian women as "arrugadas y caducas, con esa fealdad quimérica de los ídolos," adding that "parecían sibilas de algún antiguo culto lúbrico y sangriento" (II, 106). The conservative element here is the fact that Valle-Inclán wishes to invoke an aura of exoticism and Romantic mythology about his Indians. He does the same for the striking youth who is devoured earlier by sharks: "Los labios hidrópicos del negro esbozaron una sonrisa de ogro avaro y sensual" (II, 74). This attempt to construct legend out of history, and myth out of reality, is constantly repeated in Bradomín's memoirs, and is part of his Romanticizing. On the other hand, the more exotic his comparisons are, the closer they approach contemporary stylizations, reminiscent of Picasso's African motifs much more than Gauguin's mystic realism. And of course, twenty years after the *sonatas*, the grotesque "ídolo tibetano," with its variations, will be repeated endlessly in *Tirano Banderas* and the last novels.

The entire question of portraiture is an issue which we will return to later when we discuss masks. But insofar as the transformation of Romanticism is concerned, it is noteworthy that the latter's traditional materials are used to forge a new image, even while preserving some of the old Romantic emotionalism. For example, Bradomín complains in the *Sonata de otoño* that "¡El destino tiene burlas crueles! Cuando a mí me sonríe, lo hace siempre como entonces, con la mueca macabra de esos enanos patizambos que a la luz de la luna hacen cabriolas sobre las chimeneas de los viejos castillos" (II, 174). The feelings that have occasioned this analogy are, granted, in the vein of Byronic heroics. Similarly, the stereotype of dancing elves and moonlit castles is too familiar to be effective as an ordinary play of grotesque fantasy. Nevertheless, the image is not trite because it converts tangible data into the abstract figure of Fortune's smile. Moreover, some of the deformation carries over into Bradomín's life, for his intention is that his readers transfer the overtones of "mueca macabra" and "enanos patizambos" to his own biography.

Valle-Inclán's reliance on Romanticism for his distorted effects also includes the use of macabre elements. Traditionally, the most common of these conventions were scenes of horror, violence, and even necrophilia. This last receives a strange twist in the hands of Valle-Inclán when, again in the *Sonata de otoño*, his alter ego resists the powerful temptation to kiss his dead mistress (although he does worse elsewhere). What is grotesque is the mystic explanation offered to justify an obvious depraved impulse. Bradomín compares his feeling of tortured voluptuosity to the way in which the mystics also saw "los más extraños diabolismos" in the holiest of contemplated objects. Thus, his dead beloved is like an inviolate saint whom the devil transfigures for the purpose of tempting him:

> Todavía hoy el recuerdo de la muerta es para mí de una tristeza depravada y sutil. Me araña el corazón como un gato tísico de ojos lucientes. El corazón sangra y se retuerce, y dentro de mí ríe el Diablo que sabe convertir todos los dolores en placer. Mis recuerdos, glorias

del alma perdidas, son como una música lívida y ardiente, triste y cruel, a cuyo extraño son danza el fantasma lloroso de mis amores. ¡Pobre y blanco fantasma, los gusanos le han comido los ojos, y las lágrimas ruedan de las cuencas! Danza en medio del corro juvenil de los recuerdos... (II, 176).

This passage may sound ludicrous to a younger generation today because of its exalted passion, but this is not what makes it aesthetically grotesque. The latter emerges as a result of a serious intent to relate hopelessly disparate elements. The hero's perverse desire may well be likened to a tubercular cat, but not the idealistic feelings of his heart, at least not without provoking some incongruence. Even the author recognizes this as he applies the tag "extraño son" to the cadence of memories that rise and fall with such contradictory traits. Still more of a disparity is the vision of the dancing spectre, which, although rooted in tradition, bears scarce resemblance to the perfumed body which first moved the ardent lover. In all, the confession appears contrived despite its utter sincerity, and its self-conscious analysis leads it still further away from the dramatic exaltation which was originally intended.

A similar episode occurs in *La rosa de papel*, which is part of the *Retablo de la avaricia, la lujuria y la muerte*. It is subtitled "melodrama para marionetas," but it exhibits the same mixture of serious and artificial elements that were just observed. It involves the actions of a drunken widower who is angrily searching for lost money while a group of women mourns over his wife's corpse. He happily finds the money and with "sentimentalismo alemán" and a "tremo afectado y patético" in his voice, he insanely embraces his dead wife. In doing so, however, he knocks over a candle and the body catches fire. The macabre quality of this event, admittedly, is complicated by the overlapping of both ridiculous and sobering emotions, a mixture that will be treated in a later section. But the Romantic residue permeates the scene with the kind of self-awareness that is also found in the Marqués' remembrance. That is, a conventional grotesque element is relocated, so to speak, and given an additional disparity by its new context. We can observe this difference best by taking a very traditional example from the story "El rey de la máscara," and noting the abruptness of mood. Here, a troupe of actors and clowns disguise a dead man as king, "grotesco en su inmóvil gravedad, con su corona de papel, su cetro de caña, el blanco manto de estopa, la bufonesca faz de cartón." He is left behind in a seated position, and when the unsuspecting villagers approach him, "la careta se corrió hacia abajo, descubriendo una frente amarilla, unos ojos vidriados, pavorosos, horribles" (I, 1269). This description needs no comment, for it consists of a device used frequently in film-making today. But what is effective visually in the modern cinema was, after the Romantic period, a literary commonplace in narrative fiction.

The first principle of Valle-Inclán's grotesque, Romantic therefore, is that historical distance, with the critical perspective that this implies, does not eliminate Romantic elements but rather endows them with a self-conscious or ironic context which reinforces the original grotesque image. The second principle involves the metamorphosis of the moon and the allusions associated with it. The role of the moon in Romantic literature both as a symbol and as an image is so diffuse that it would require an essay of its own to do it justice. But the moon does represent the sensibility of Romanticism more than any other single image, in spite of the attention it has received in other centuries as well. The proof of this is the fact that the title of Marinetti's manifesto, *Tuons le clair de lune*, singles out the lunar phenomenon as an object of special attack, identifying it with the essence of Romantic art. We are not unjustified, therefore, in isolating this motif in Valle-Inclán's works, especially when he also makes it assume a variety of forms that illustrate a number of different problems.

One such problem is linked to the macabre element menioned just a moment ago. That is, to what extent is the Romantic moon an agent for evoking a particular atmosphere of mystery and foreboding? In part, of course, the natural condition of the moon is conducive to inspired thoughts along the line of melancholy, solitude, and the unknown. On the other hand, our contemporary stereotype of a nocturnal scene cannot escape the Gothic influence in Romanticism. This is indicated very clearly by Valle-Inclán in one moonlit episode in *Aguila de blasón* where witches and superstitious stories are alluded to for the sake of creating a mood. Similarly, we read in *La corte de los milagros* that the countryside, "a la luz muerta de la luna, tenía la vastedad desolada y vacía de un mar petrificado," and that "bajo la luna muerta, el convoy [tren] perfilaba una línea de ataúdes negros" (II, 895). Examples like these display an interaction of several elements, in which the moon is not more, nor less, important, but where it somehow enhances whatever object or idea it is related to.

In this same way, the religious theme in *Flor de santidad* is presented with a variation, referring to the moonlight at one point with the phrase "bañaba el jardín, consoladora y blanca como un don eucarístico" (I, 1225), and with comparable similes elsewhere in the novel. Although this type of sensibility is rare, its sanctification of the moon parallels the technique used for adapting conventionally Romantic motifs to unRomantic contexts. This means several things with respect to structure and to sensibility. To begin with, the element of lyricism gradually becomes objectified. That is, whereas the older descriptions of the moon involve a personal expression of sympathetic feeling—in Keats, Carducci, and Leopardi—in Valle-Inclán the tendency is to move away from lyricism. The reason for this is partly structural: an interest in narrative and theatrical forms rather than poetry. Thus, even in a lyrical work like *Flor de santidad*, the references to the moon emphasize impersonal characteristics, so that there is a genuine aesthetic distance between the contents of the novel and both the artist and the reader. In a word, the Romantic moon falls under the spell of the pathetic fallacy, and Valle-Inclán's moon functions as a manageable literary component.

This brings us to the second aspect of adapting conventional motifs to unRomantic contexts. The moon image is not only a gauge for measuring the subject-object relationship in Romanticism, but it is an excellent indicator of how much self-consciousness and downright manipulation occurs in a work of art. Since the moon has come to symbolize the epitome of Romantic feeling (again, remembering Marinetti), it never loses its aura of Romanticism even in anti-Romantic contexts. Thus, writers can always make us aware of how differently the moon—and by extension, every structural component—behaves in modern literature. It is more deliberately selected and therefore more obvious in the way it harmoniously fits into the rest of the setting. Such is the case, for example, in the description of a barber's bedroom in *Los cuernos de Don Friolera:*

> Tras de la puerta, la capa y la gorra, colgadas con la guitarra, fingen un bulto viviente. Por el ventano abierto penetra, con el claro de luna, el ventalle silencioso y nocturno de un huerto de luceros. Y la

brisa y la luna parecen conducir un diálogo entre el vestigio de la puerta y el pelele que abre la cruz de los brazos sobre la copa negra de una higuera, en la redoma azul del huerto. Entra el galán con la raptada, encendida, pomposa y con suspiros de soponcio. La luna infla los carrillos en la ventana (I, 1010-1011).

If we proceed sentence by sentence, which is to say, effect by effect, the last line comes as an almost unfair deflation of an interesting nocturnal event. Nevertheless, we have had in the first line some advanced notice of the approaching artifice, and by the time we reach the word "pelele," the underlying manipulation becomes apparent. This does not mean that Valle-Inclán is being playful, although he can be in other instances. What is interesting about the passage is precisely the combination of serious elements and conscious selectivity.

Ostensibly, the scene is written for the theater, so that the setting lacks the contrivance which typifies the marionette pieces. Valle- Inclán is narrating to the reader absorbed in the dialog exactly how the events would appear if they were acted out. And he is demonstrating to the reader, insofar as the latter is aware of aesthetics, how different his usage of the old Romantic devices really is. The traditional forms are still visible, namely, the division of background and foreground, with the nocturnal elements making up the first category; and the separation between nature and the world of men and objects. But those forms suffer the kind of changes already mentioned, and, in addition, they play up the new factor of dehumanization. Perhaps this term is not the best one to employ here, but I do so in order to show exactly how the genesis of the technique comes about. Details such as "fingen un bulto viviente" and the contrast between "pelele" and the whisperings of the moon and breeze represent the first stages in a revaluation of human and nonhuman roles. What is interesting from the standpoint of Romanticism is the reduction of emotional interest there, and also in the sentence "el galán con la raptada, encendida, pomposa y con suspiros de soponcio." This lessened human appeal in the dramatic figures is the reason that nature swings slightly out of rapport. The human value of the characters is less significant than their aesthetic usefulness, so that their sympathetic relationship with nature dissolves as the demands of artifice grow. As a result, the role of nature is also very much reduced, a situation that becomes quite important from *Tirano Banderas* onward. Consequently, "la luna infla los carrillos en la ventana" constitutes a gesture on the part of Valle-Inclán to indicate the irrelevance of Romantic sentiments in this kind of a work. And what he does here by means of moon imagery, he does elsewhere with direct and unfeeling dehumanization.

The vision of a round-cheeked moon evidently appealed to Valle-Inclán, for he repeats it in the *Farsa y licencia de la reina castiza*, with an overtly jocular intent. But now, there is the added note of exhibitionism, as the author demonstrates his orchestrative powers in handling the familiar notes:

> Infla la luna los carrillos, / y su carota de pepona, / bermeja de risa, detona / en la cima de los negrillos… / Suena la orquesta de los grillos / y hace la luna un volatín / en la cima de los negrillos / que le sirven de trampolín. (I, 440-441)

The atmosphere of the context from which these excerpts are taken does, of course, differ from the previous instances. But what remains the same is Valle-Inclán's recognition of what moon imagery has meant to poets in the past. Its Romantic characteristics are shown off with cheek, and rendered grotesque by the very attention called to them. The role of the moon is made whimsical, and the mock-Romantic effect is completed by the language. Although physically the moon has simply become distorted, functionally it has been deliberately misplaced, obliged to appear out of character in a farce. Nevertheless, this is not a burlesque of Romantic sentiment. What is at stake here are not feelings but methods. The important fact is that a technique has been turned against itself in such a way that a stylized extreme is reached which draws attention to itself. The result is a kind of insider's parody intended for playful aestheticians who know the mechanisms that make Romanticism work, and who therefore appreciate the effects of a little tinkering. For those within the dramatic framework, therefore, everything is serious, but the spectator is made aware of how Romantic artifacts have been applied to the wrong situation. That the artifacts are caricatured is also a matter of aesthetic contemplation, for they serve the context in a completely functional way.

What we are faced with, in effect, is establishing the difference between burlesque and stylization. Valle-Inclán is not trying to make fun of Romantic psychology, although this may well be the ultimate effect. Rather, he is attempting to grasp the essential form of a literary convention and stylize it without touching the content. Thus, the traditional Romantic imagery, psychology, and subject matter may remain intact, but their expressive form becomes disfigured. This is what happens in *La Marquesa Rosalinda*, the best example of the distinction in question. The work's subtitle, "farsa sentimental y grotesca," clearly indicates that sentiment and deformation are meant to be compatible partners and not mutually hostile forces. Consequently, the case for explaining the grotesque on the basis of a "visión degradadora" of Spain—to use a phrase most recently and excellently elaborated by Díaz-Plaja— is an oversimplification. Valle-Inclán's social ridicule is not always a factor, and we must be careful to see that his grotesquerie has several varieties, including this formalistic reappraisal of Romantic motifs.

In this area, let us consider one of the first of many references to the moon in *La Marquesa Rosalinda*, where first a human figure, and then a swan are described by moonlight:

Envuelta en el halo quimérico / que da la luna metafórica, / arrastra un prestigio esotérico / como una figura alegórica ... / Interroga el cuello de plata / en los rieles de la luna, / mientras vuela la serenata / sobre el cristal de la laguna (I, 215-216).

Although the versification alone is enough to give away Valle-Inclán's role as the master-contriver of this artifice, his grotesque effect lies elsewhere. It consists of his manner of revising the procedure for evoking atmosphere and emotion, and for initiating the spectator-object relationship. Instead of a direct appeal to the spectator's feelings, we find an aesthetic distance established without regard to the amount of sympathy that can be inspired by what goes on inside the work. In other words, there is no suppression of sentimentalism within the work, for the latter's mood-evoking apparatus is redesigned. It is no longer the perennial swan that sets the tone, but its proverbial neck, which means in effect that the swan has been restyled. Consequently, the spectator delights in the technical revaluation, while the characters and action continue to obey an inner system of unassailable sentimentality.

The grotesque nature of this dramatic farce consists of setting the very human relationships among the characters against the backdrop of pastiche Romanticism. The Marquesa and her entourage belong to one emotional world and Arlequín and his troupe to another. This second world, however, is really a façade, behind which stands a world whose emotions are just as human as the Marquesa's. Here, then, is the first grotesque level, where ostensibly different psychologies interact in a single situation: a heartstruck marquesa in love, a clown acting in a lover's role, and the same clown really in love. When we picture this situation against the unambiguous cardboard backdrop of Romanticism, we reach a second area of grotesque stagework, where genuine emotions cannot be supported by artificial psychological props. And in a final area, while we once were moved by 19th century works whose prose descriptions indicated the scenography to us, we now find stage directions improvised in light verse, and sometimes even in *esdrújula*.

We may conclude, therefore, that the grotesque mode arises directly from the stylization of Romantic motifs that emerge from an obviously self-conscious, exhibitionist background. This extends beyond scenography to the players' speeches themselves, and we will take one last example as an illustration. In a long and important peroration, Arlequín addresses himself to the moon in what must be, from his point of view, a seriously delivered outburst:

¡Oh, luna de poetas y de orates, / por tu estela argentina / mi alma peregrina / con una ansia ideal de disparates! /... ¡Luna que das ensueño a los jardines, / que pones alas en los corazones / y en las cimas azules, oraciones / y en las ondas azules, violines! / ¿Quién el poder a descubir acierta / de tu cara de plata, / de tus ojos de muerta / y de tu nariz chata? /... ¡Hilandera divina de sonetas! / El barro de mi alma se aureola icon tu luz enigmática, / y te saluda con la cabriola / de una bruja sabática: / Luna que de sonar guardas las huellas, / cabalística luna de marfil / tu escribes en lo azul moviendo estrellas: / ¡Nihil! (I, 245-246).

For Arlequín, the key words are *ansia ideal, ensueño, cabalística luna*. For us however, they are *disparates, barro de mi alma, nariz chata*. The first grouping poeticizes the sincerity of a suffering clown, while the second group debases it, and the question of which is meant to have the greater effect depends upon which set of words one is attuned to. Obviously, everything is quite serious to Arlequín, who delivers his speech with a straight face. Even the reference to his own foolishness is made with a matter-of-fact self-acceptance. What is absurd in his soliloquy can only be seen from the standpoint of the spectator, who is amused that someone with a heart of clay should have such exalted emotions. On the other hand, what is grotesque about the scene is that such pretensions are inspired by an over-Romanticized Nature, as represented by the elaborate physiognomy of the moon. Arlequín's summary of the moon's standard features betrays the fact that the old pathetic fallacy is no longer operative. There is no correspondence between his feelings and the moon's appearance, which is rendered both silly and *recherché* by the words "chata" and "marfil." It might be argued that the grotesque element is Arlequín himself, along with his soul that greets the moon with a "cabriola / de una bruja sabática," and that the moon is simply a flippant stereotype of the Romantic view of Nature. Even if we grant this interpretation, however, the important point is what happens to the pathetic fallacy. It is destroyed, but it is not substituted for either by realism or by hermetic symbolism, two alternatives which were the regular choices of writers in the post-Romantic period. Instead, Valle-Inclán produces a dislocation which preserves sentimentalism while introducing a grotesque note. Æsthetic manipulation succeeds stylization and creates the emotional disparity that will produce sharper deformations elsewhere.

II. Harlequin and the Psychology of Masks

Any discussion of the moon is bound to bring up the name of Pierrot, just as any discussion of Harlequin inevitably raises the problem of what the clown motif signifies in the modern period. These, too, are complex issues, involving diverse media and recalling works by Verlaine, Rouault, Picasso, and Schonberg. In Valle-Inclán, the issues are of the utmost importance, because they crystallize the early psychological disturbances that ultimately require expression by means of masks, marionettes, and buffon-like personages. Thus, what Valle-Inclán reveals about Pierrot, Colombina, and Arlequín in *La Marquesa Rosalinda* can be regarded as prototypical of the more drastic disfigurements of humanity that occur in his other works. Not that there is any progression of forms from early to late works, but in this troupe of clowns we find the common denominator of psychological incongruity that affects their counterparts in other writings. Basically, these characters participate in a grotesque situation which is humorous rather than horrific, but their role as travelling comedians acquires a tragic tone as they become involved with the world that they are supposed to entertain.

The conflict arises out of a confusion over where the stage-ground is supposed to be located. On one side are the Marquesa and her circle, presumably meant to be the human audience for whom the *commedia* will be performed. And on the other side are Colombina and her two lovers, the farcical entertainers who are seen off-stage living the parts they act out in the theater. This is one factor in the grotesque situation: the transposition of absurdity to a human dimension, where stilted and ridiculous people who are perfectly acceptable as stage figures appear bizarre when they start to mingle with human beings. Then there is a second factor: the overflow of theatrical farce into real life, and the infusion of human frailty into the behavior-styles of the comedians. This happens as the members of each world interact with the other, in this case, Rosalinda and Arlequín.

From the situation just described we may infer a concept that has bearing on the validity of dehumanization in modern art. No artistic representation of humanity can be totally divorced from the human problems that it depicts. That is, for Valle-Inclán, an art-for-art's-sake rendition of life in the manner of a Punch-and-Judy show is an unacceptable form of expression. This is an important idea in the light of the *esperpentos* and late novels, where the peculiar blend of dehumanized aesthetics and social awareness bears witness to the fact that Valle-Inclán never fully embraced the abstractionism or the uncommitted fantasies of his period. In *La Marquesa Rosalinda*, the poet-director commands that "mezcle sus risas Colombina / a los sollozos de Pierrot, / en una farsa peregrina." But the author never allows us to see the play in isolation, and he foils the intention of the director. The latter's purpose is the purely aesthetic one of diverting attention away from emotionalism of any sort by neutralizing every emotion with its opposite: "Soy el poeta que el tablado / puebla de trucos y babeles: / Para el amor desesperado / tengo rimas de cascabeles." He intends by means of frivolity to trivialize feeling among his audience, who is in search of a diversion from life's problems. Accordingly, his theory of farce is that the lyrical impulse should be pulled away from its human roots and replanted in the sawdust of the drama workshop. He declares, therefore, "y sollocen otros poetas / sobre los cuernos de la lira, / con el ritmo de las piruetas / yo rimo mi bella mentira" (I, 213). And to a great extent, the poet is successful. At one point Colombina lurches forward "como una muñeca, / toda vana y hueca, / pintada de harina" (I, 240), and later, "se va Pierrot bamboleante, / y bajo la luna espectral, / toma un relieve alucinante / su cara cubierta de cal" (I, 244). These incidents all confirm the "bella mentira" which is presented in opposition to the lyrical "truth" of the tragic poets. So that, in effect, there is no way for the audience to identify its own condition with that of the players.

On the other hand, Valle-Inclán reminds us that his farce is "sentimental" as well as "grotesca," and it is here that the aesthetic barrier begins to falter. If Pierrot scratches his head in the moonlight with bewilderment, he is more than just a fool: "Trágico, a fuer de ser grotesco, / sale Pierrot hacienda zumba. / En su rostro carnavalesco / hay una mueca de ultratumba" (I, 243). Even though there can be no possible identification between this situation and our own, there is, nevertheless, a sympathetic chord that is faintly perceptible. Any reminder of death has a sobering influence, and there is little difference between the reference here and the dark, violent ones made in the later works. Thus, at this point, the grotesque effect hardens. The aesthetic distance achieved through ridicule disappears when this ridicule expresses a philosophical position. Such is the case when Polichinela enters prancing, beating his hump as if it were a drum: "Entre mis dos jorobas vuela la humanidad: / La del pecho es locura, la de atrás necedad" (I, 249).

In this appearance, the combination of intellectual accuracy and physical deformity awakens our sense of incongruence, but at the same time, we unconsciously draw the clown into our own orbit of experience. The same proximity is suggested later on when Arlequín utters a wealth of Romantic platitudes to Colombina, thus displaying his sensitivity in one banal but human moment. Still more meaningful to us is his anti-Romantic attitude in the face of all his sentiments. Speaking of lovers, he remarks that

"el misterio de la cita, / un bostezo será después," and of life, he says that "¡todo es uno y lo mismo! / Y si se vuelve del revés, / una montaña es un abismo. /... ¡Yo soy el único sensible!" (I, 275).

This grain of post-Romantic truth becomes the justification for the new farce or *comedieta* which Valle-Inclán is attempting to write. The intent to portray serious emotions, or at least to express a fundamental vision of life, is present, but it is no longer possible to do so with the old 19th century methods. In fact, this vision is so far removed from the traditional idealism that its most effective form is an anti-Romantic one. And what better irony than to work a few Romantic conventions into an atmosphere of clowns and hunchbacks. Thus, love becomes ennui, heroic escapades become Harlequinades, and serious philosophy emerges from the garble of foolish commonplaces.

The underlying principle of all this is stated by Arlequín: "La moral de la vida es ésa: /¡Una armonía de contrarios!" (I, 275). Once this idea is grasped, the entire pattern of anti-Romanticism can be understood. The notion is not at all like Hugo's concept of the grotesque as being the reverse side of the sublime—an idea which also reveals a harmony of contrasts. Nor is this grotesque concept an antithesis from which a new synthesis is born. Rather, the grotesque is itself the synthesis, a product of Romantic sentiment (thesis) destroyed by the antics of a few strolling clowns (antithesis). Thus, the distortions of the latter are relatively unimportant in establishing the kind of grotesque which Valle-Inclán is seeking in this work. To present deformity for its own sake is also a type of grotesque, but the clowns do not fall into this category. To deform what is normally human is to render the subject grotesque, but in the case of Polichinela and Arlequín, the original norm is already to some extent a distortion. Therefore, the real grotesque impact comes as a result of what these distorted semblances of humanity do with the sentiments and values of that humanity.

At the same time, the mannerisms of the clowns are worth noting for their relationship to comparable stylizations in the later novels. After Arlequín is warned by hired swordsmen to leave town, his response is to "saluda burlando, / con una pirueta grotesca" (A, 273). Elsewhere, he does his pirouette "saludando al modo de Francia, / y evoca un ritmo de opereta / con el ritmo de su elegancia" (I, 302). And both Polichinela and Colombina are described with the words "funambulesca," "marioneta," and "grotesco." What did Valle-Inclán mean by all this? Did he intend the work to be performed by puppets? If so, then why does one of the characters greet Arlequín with the hope that "tu tablado de farsas y babeles / ahuyentará las cortesanas penas" (I, 220). Clearly, some personages, at least among the nobility, are supposed to be human regardless of whether they are represented by puppets, actors, or verbal images in the mind of the reader. And by this token, the clowns also gain their measure of humanity. The real question, then, is why Valle-Inclán felt the need to reduce all of these characters to less-than-human beings. And the answer goes straight to the causes of the modern psychological predicament: the quest for identity, the sense of alienation, the multiplication of selves in a multiple reality. For, if existence is believed to be absurd, then what better figure to enact this absurdity than the clown? And once this character becomes stylized, how far away is he from, a marionette? Similarly, if social values are doubted, then the roles which carry them out must also be suspect, a suspicion which eventually leads to a preoccupation with masks and theatrical experiments.

These problems find an interesting focus in one of the poems in *La pipa de kif*, "El circo de lona." There, after a description of some circus acts, we are taken backstage to see what life is like behind the glossy bravura:

> El payaso ante el espejo / se despinta con cerote, / y se arranca el entrecejo / de pelote. / A su lado una mozuela, / luciendo el roto zancajo, / recose la lentejuela / de un pingajo. /... Riñas, sordas libaciones, ¡lamen los platos los perros, / se desperezan los leones / tras los hierros! /... ¡Circos! ¡Cantos olvidados / de fabulosas edades! / ¡Heroicos versos dorados / de Alcibíades! (I, 1151).

What first strikes the eye in this passage is the drab discoloring of the rainbow-like illusions of Romanticism. But extending beyond this is the image of the clown unmasking himself before the mirror. If we ask ourselves what he sees, the answer comes echoing back from the speech by Arlequín, quoted earlier, where he concludes with the word "¡Nihil!," for the fact is that he sees a nonentity staring back at him from the mirror. The implication is that the spectator is not the only one to be enveloped by the gloom of disenchantment, for the very components of the illusion are themselves subject to a reversal. In this case, the clown himself cannot play his own role with conviction. The absurdity that he faces in the mirror originates not from the droll visage painted so gaudily, but from the meaningless mask behind the mask: his own face peering out abjectly from the make-up. Like Arlequín's self-knowledge, this confrontation is effected in a mood of deflated realism, after the disparity between external and internal attitudes has finally been perceived.

This basic perception into the self and its role exists in several other forms in addition to that of the clown. Indeed, we might even speak of a morphology of facial representations, beginning with the influence of the late Romantic grotesque. For instance, as we have already seen, masks were used during Valle-Inclán's modernist period to cast a veneer of myth and idealism over certain exotic figures. But during the same period a more severe example of deformation occurs in the story "Mi hermana Antonia," where the narrator declares of one character: "En verdad que parecía una gárgola. No podía [yo] saber si perro, si gato, si lobo. Pero tenía un extraño parecido con aquellas figuras de piedra, asomadas o tendidas sobre el atrio, en la cornisa de la Catedral" (I, 1277). The characterization offers no insight into the man's personality, but this was exactly Valle-Inclán's intention. Human value in this case was to be indicated by surface textures, by the loss of personal traits, and indeed, by animalization. In the later works, the same externalities are again emphasized, with the identical purpose of minimizing the suggestion of inner character. And so, in the puppet-show *La cabeza del dragón,* the extreme is reached with "el heroico General Fierabrás," where "la punta de la nariz le gotea sin consideración, como una gárgola" (I, 409).

The rationale behind Valle-Inclán's attitude toward his creatures is stated only once in his works, but so unmistakably that it is clearly relevant to all the cases we have been discussing. In *La lámpara maravillosa,* he develops the idea that the authentic self is disguised and often becomes suppressed by the imposition of roles that are thrust upon it throughout life. Even when we try to know ourselves, the variety of character traits and contradictory behavior patterns make it seem as if we have been engaging in one fictitious charade after another. Hence, the image of the mask acquires a special significance in expressing the lack of trascendence which mars our evasive personalities. This is how Valle-Inclán puts it:

> ¡Cuántas veces en el rictus de la muerte se desvela todo el secreto de una vida! Hay un gesto que es el mío, uno solo, pero en la sucesión humilde de los días, en el vano volar de las horas, se ha diluido hasta

borrarse como el perfil de una medalla. Llevo sobre mi rostro cien máscaras de ficción que se suceden bajo el imperio mezquino de una fatalidad sin trascendencia. Acaso mi verdadero gesto no se ha revelado todavía, acaso no pueda revelarse nunca bajo tantos velos acumulados día a día y tejidos por todas mis horas. Yo mismo me desconozco y quizá estoy condenado a desconocerme siempre.... las máscaras del vicio... han dejado una huella en mi rostro carnal y en mi rostro espiritual, pero yo sé que todas han de borrarse en su día, y que sólo una quedará inmóvil sobre mis facciones cuando llegue la muerte (II, 608-609).

The statement then goes on to describe the details of the dead man's grotesque features, but the point about ego ambiguity is evident. It is interesting that this central idea of character confusion is illustrated in religious terms. The reason is due partly to the devotional nature of the book *La lámpara maravillosa*. Although the place of religion in Valle-Inclán's thinking is irrelevant here, it is useful to weigh the possibility that the moral symbolism of animals might help to explain why there are animalizations in his later grotesque sequences. If this is so, then the desire to ridicule humanity by means of animalistic deformations is only one reason behind the dehumanized treatment of certain characters. Religious motifs, or semi-moralistic vestiges of them, would be another. Instances such as the description of the disguised *comadreja* in *La corte de los milagros:* "el cuerpo magro, ambiguo, de una elasticidad viciosa, en el sayo varonil, acentuaba su esencia de monstruo" [II, 979]; or, in the same novel: "El Doctor abismaba la carátula de perro canelo en un gran gesto" (II, 1022); or, finally, one of Don Friolera's moods: "los ojos de perro, vidriados y mortecinos, se alelan mirando a la niña" (I, 1027) —all of these techniques may also be echoes of a defunct religious vocabulary of allegorical animals now used for an aesthetic effect.

At any rate, what is important is that we recognize a definite concept of the self and its ambiguity behind the creation of Valle-Inclán's personages. There is a metamorphosis of personality-masks among the grotesque portraits, and of these portraits the animalizations are the most plastic in quality while the clown like representations are the most psychological. And yet there is little psychological analysis in the works as a whole. What we find instead is that the clown's self-confrontation is repeated with different effects that are no longer Romantic. For example, in *Aguila de blasón* we read:

> *Don Galán* se arrodilla y hace la señal de la cruz con esa torpeza indecisa y somnámbula que tienen los movimientos de los borrachos. La imagen del bufón aparece en el fondo de un espejo, y *El Caballero* la contempla en aquella lejanía nebulosa y verdeante como en la quimera de un sueño. Lentamente el cristal de sus ojos se empaña como el nebuloso cristal del espejo (I, 634).

This subtle "stage direction" takes one or two steps away from the realistic narrative found both in the circus poem and in the short story quoted a moment ago. There is a near-Surrealist quality about it, reminiscent of Benicarlés' hallucination in *Tirano Banderas* and perhaps even of Lorca. We may speak now of a depersonalization, stemming from the play of mirror images as well as from the dream-like element. Nevertheless, the "quimera de un sueño" does not belong to the Romantic tradition as much as it does to the plastic experiments of the modern period. Indeed, this is where the paradox of personality emerges, for the *bufón* appearing in the mirror seems unreal because of the reflections and blurs that prevent a close correspondence of images. Thus, whereas El Caballero should be seeing himself in the mirror, he watches instead the inverted parody of his caste, a clowning figure who, by the visual sleight of hand, is kept in deliberate confusion by Valle-Inclán.

So much, then, for what we may call the psychology of masks as it is applied to clowns, jesters, and semi-serious evasions of reality. In these cases, Harlequin can be seen as a transitional figure between the 19th century sensibility and the modern aesthetic of distortion. There are, however, more drastic experiments in this area, and we turn to these next.

III. Types of Dehumanization

Once the alienation of personality was understood by Valle-Inclán, he shifted his attention to the methods by which it might be expressed plastically. Not that he was ever interested in depth psychology as such, but the soul-searching of Arlequín gives us a clue as to why Valle-Inclán's characters look or behave like puppets. There is no rigorous chronology here, nor do I mean to suggest that there is one given moment after which only visual representations prevail at the expense of "psychological" ones. Nevertheless, wherever personages are grotesque, they are characterized by externalities, the implication being that their personalities are not worth exploring. Thus, the mirror becomes a very useful technique for rendering portraits and distortions, as we have seen. A different use of the mirror has similar results in *Gerifaltes de antaño*, where three separate dimensions are juggled in the same scene:

> Por un salón reflejado en el fondo de un espejo, viene una vieja muy encorvada. Agila sonríe pensando que aquella vieja tan menuda, presa en el cristal, quiere salir para bailar sobre la consola dorada, entre los daguerrotipos. Pero de pronto, la vieja huye del espejo y entra por una puerta... La sombra de la vieja es muy grotesca en la pared, y la alcuza marca el garabato de una nariz bajo el borde pringado del manto (II, 512).

Actually, there are two steps involved here, only one of which is grotesque. The reflected image is merely a representational form, although it is framed in the mirror much like the smaller console photographs are, so that in this position it gains a new perspective. The mirror portrait, which is a step removed from reality, is followed by a harsher representation in the shape of a deformed wall shadow. Both images of the real figure indicate Valle-Inclán's preference for a physical rather than a psychological sketch of his characters.

This technique of fixed forms in a reduced human setting can be traced back to Valle-Inclán's ideas concerning Romantic conventions. Daguerrotypes and two-penny novel illustrations had the same mannered charm for him as *art nouveau* and the styles of the '20's have for us today. But they also served as the material for ironic or distorted revisions, again very much like our current experiments with pop, kitsch, and camp. For example, in *Gerifaltes de antaño* we find the following scene: "Quedaron los dos silenciosos y conmovidos. En aquel gran salón de la abuela evocaban el aspecto amoroso y Romántico de los héroes novelescos que en las litográficas del año treinta se dicen sus ansias bajo una cornucopia, enlazados por las manos en el regazo del sofá, que tiene caído al pie un ramo de flores" (II, 509). And in *Viva mi dueño* we visualize how "el Heroe de los Castillejos escorzóse en el sillón con saludo de litografía" (II, 1319). This air of striking a pose that is reconstructed from the Romantic period is really more a product of historical distance on the narrator's part than the result of a deliberate exaggeration of the original subjects themselves. It was this kind of ironic detachment which Valle-Inclán capitalized on during his efforts to caricature the literary personages just seen. They are not distorted in any real way, but they appear extravagant because certain details which are alien to the new sensibility seem to stand out in a bizarre fashion.

Frequently, the devaluation of psychological material led Valle-Inclán back again to a few variations of his mirror effects. A good example of how different motifs are integrated on this basis into a single vignette occurs in one esperpentic episode that is described scenographically:

> *Don Friolera*, sentado ante el velador con tapete de malla, sostiene un album de retratos: Se percibe el pueril y cristalino punteado de su ceja de música. *Don Friolera* en el reflejo amarillo del quinque, es un fantoche trágico. La beata se acerca, y pega a la reja su perfil de lechuza" (I, 1006).

If we compare this representation with the lithograph analogies, we notice how cleverly the elements have been shifted around. The trite convention is no longer found in the human pose, but in the inanimate music box, which functions in a manneristic fashion that we will see more of later. On the other hand, the epithet "fantoche trágico" indicates the author's value judgment concerning the lives of his personages. In its grotesque combination of traits, the phrase expresses the quality of their condition as well as the form. On the other hand, if we compare this passage with a related one in *La corte de los milagros,* we can see at once when Valle-Inclán intended merely to ridicule:

> Adolfito abría los ojos con falsa sorpresa, como si presintiese y no alcanzase veladas intenciones. Para fijarlas ponía el gesto clásico y bobalicón del comediante que representa El *Vergonzoso en Palacio.* Una mariposa volaba en el círculo del quinqué. A intervalos, la péndula del reloj proyectaba en la oscuridad una risa momentánea y dorada, redonda y jocunda como el vientre de un dios tibetano. El

Ministro, la cara en la convulsión de la luz verde, transponía a un claroscuro inverosímil su mueca gitana (II, 1009).

Despite the fact that we see Valle-Inclán continuing to repeat himself with unusual consistency over the years, the truth is that his motifs vary a great deal in function, if not in kind. In this case, we find no hint of tragedy, not even in a degraded form. Instead, there are several traces of humor, at the beginning and end of the passage, which are offset by two grotesque effects. One of these is the comparison of the pendulum's sound to human laughter, a simile that exchanges inanimate and animate categories, and reduces the value of the latter. The other humorous touch is the inverisimilitude of the grimace, which is linked to the Tibetan idol and to the theatrical pose, and is the last in a series of dehumanizing references that make it impossible for the word "tragic" to be applied.

What we have just seen is the essential structure of the distortions in facial description that mark the later works. They all culminate in the novel *La corte de los milagros*, whose narrative depicts the mummification of living characters as a natural matter of course. Phrases such as "su mueca de difunto humorístico" or "un gesto perplejo en los craqueles de la careta" become the norms for indicating to the reader how these people are supposed to look. Thus, what was an alternate mode in the esperpentic realism of *Tirano Banderas* becomes an integrated grotesque style in this novel. Common to all such episodes, regardless of when they were written, is the central doubt concerning personality which Valle-Inclán reveals in *La lámpara maravillosa:*

Otro día, sobre la máscara de mi rostro, al mirarme en un espejo, vi modelarse cien máscaras en una sucesión precisa, hasta la edad remota en que aparecía el rostro seco, barbudo y casi negro de un hombre que se ceñía los riñones con la piel de un rebeco (II, 560).

Probing more deeply than Arlequín ever could, Valle-Inclán discovers the Unamunian sham of the social mask, and he feels a gnawing doubt about which self is the true one. But, not content to stop there, he searches back to the prehistory of man's character-role, suggesting the primitive and perhaps even animalistic metamorphoses of the human face.

This search has still other implications which relate to the masks and puppets that appear so frequently. The insecurity of each role, the lack of permanence in retaining each face, removes the concept of stability from the structure of human existence. Life, when seen through the perspectives of mirror and memory, produces the kind of sensation that is described in *La corte de los milagros* during a train-tunnel scene: "En la oscuridad de los túneles el tiempo se alarga, se desdobla, multiplica las locuras acrobáticas del pensamiento" (II, 990). And yet the novelist must demand some kind of permanence if he is to portray his characters as something more than chameleon-like or Protean figures. The problem, in effect, is one of temporality. If time had a stop, the temporary quality of each role would be corrected. Or, conversely, if one could freeze the gestures and actions of these roles, then time would no longer be very important. Quite obviously, these two possibilities have visible aesthetic counterparts in Valle-Inclán's literary practice.

Insofar as putting a stop to time is concerned, it happens by assembling a group of personages who are immune to the march of hours, and incapable of developing psychologically during a progression of narrative events. In short, he gathers together an assemblage of human puppets who remain essentially the same throughout the work. The concept of time, therefore, depends little on action sequences and a great deal on the fact that the characters are unchanged in spite of the events that occur. Indeed, even where narrative structure is experimented with, as in *Tirano Banderas,* the resulting fragmentation is not overly important from the standpoint of time sequence. What is important is the series of static *tableaux* that offer theatrical and plastic effects without calling attention to the temporal qualities of the characters' lives. In such novels, as in the dialogs for marionettes, the immobile faces before us do not reflect the passage of time or the effects of experience. Indeed, they must not, lest they manifest the dynamics of psychological growth, which Valle-Inclán opposes. Therefore, their gestures are predictable, and their poses determined in advance, fixed according to the immutable laws of a style that borrows heavily from the cliches of literary history.

The grotesque in Valle-Inclán, consequently, depends on time sequence much less than on the full visual impact of the moment. This makes it almost as dependent upon space, especially where *retablo* scenes, shadow plays, and other distillations of human activity are shown within a visibly artificial framework. It is through such spatial contrivances that some of the deformation becomes possible. We might even say that Valle-Inclán's perception of the world at such times is like that of the prisoner in *La corte de los milagros*:

> Asustado, miraba en la pared el tumulto de sombras, el guirigay de brazos aspados, ruedos de catite, mantas flotantes, retacos dispuestos. Intuía el sentido de una gesticulación expresiva y siniestra por aquel anguloso y tumultuoso barajar de siluetas recortadas" (II, 930)

This, certainly, is the way he represents reality in most of his works. The question remains, of course, as to why he does so, aside from the reasons that derive from his social philosophy. And one answer is that he conceives of life as an unchanging farce, where time's passage has no influence on the human condition, and where the externalities of a situation—its plastic and spatial values—provide the most interest.

This concept of the immutable absurdity of existence is best represented by puppets and automatons, as we will see in a moment. But it is also well expressed by being unexpressed, which is to say, by a lack of intellectualism and introspection on the part of the characters. The truth of this is given in a rare moment of "psychologizing" when the prisoner referred to above reacts to the wall shadows:

> Batallaban sensaciones y pensamientos, en combate alucinante, eon funambulescas mudanzas, y un trasponerse del ánimo sobre la angustia de aquel instante al pueril recuerdo de caminos y rostros olvidados: Sentíase vivir sobre el borde de la hora que pasó, asombrado, en la pavorosa y última realidad de trasponer las unidades métricas de lugar y de tiempo, a una coexistencia plural, nítida, diversa, de contrapuestos tiempos y lugares (II, 930).

This intricate passage has bearing on the grotesque insofar as the overlapping of time layers is concerned. There is no difference between the past and the present, for both contain elements of confusion. What seems, therefore, to be an aberration in the arrangement of thoughts and sensations ("combate alucinante") is really an accurate composite of impressions that have to do with the "funambulescas mudanzas" of life. It is this mental montage, free of time, that Valle-Inclán perceives and attempts to depict in his writings. Like the facial masks, some of which were isomorphs of the primitive faces of prehistory, these events repeat the memories of other years, in form if not in substance. There is an overflow of temporal awarenesses, emptying into an arena of multiple coordinates. This does not mean, however, that there is any genuine order or meaning in those impressions. What is referred to as "unidades métricas de lugar y de tiempo" is a mathematical formalism that gives shape to absurdity. We find no inner coherence here, merely an organized delineation of meaningless silhouettes glimpsed visually and in the mind's eye. This, of course, is what is so uncanny about Valle-Inclán's grotesque technique. His tableaux, his figures, and his episodic deformations all obey a rigorous system—whether we call it the distorted optics of the concave mirror or the calculus of the absurd. But fundamentally, they all elude the grasp of rational understanding.

The result, consequently, is a method of characterization that emphasizes three kinds of dehumanization. The first is the use that is made of masks and clowns, a method which we have already discussed in relation to other factors. The second is the use of wax and porcelain dolls: still-form figures designed to accentuate a pose or to highlight an isolated moment in space. The third type of characterization consists of marionettes and automatons, both of which emphasize the animated features of the human body without conceding to the latter any human dignity. What is significant about all three methods is not that they comprise separate categories, but that collectively they eliminate the distinction between the *retablos* for marionettes, the *esperpentos*, and the novels. In other words, the method of characterization used throughout is indiscriminately dehumanized regardless of whether Valle-Inclán is engaged in obvious puppetry or in writing dramas and narratives about people. Indeed, some of his most serious themes are done in the trio that constitutes the *Retablo de la avaricia, la lujuria y la muerte*, two items of which are classified as "auto para siluetas," and the third as a "melodrama para marionetas." And, in contrast, such phrases as "fue un gesto cómico y exquisito de polichinela aristocrático" (*Corte de amor*, II, 251), or "el Rey, menudo y rosado, tenía un lindo empaque de bailarín de porcelana" (*La corte de los milagros*, II, 841), are found in episodes where real people are supposedly conducting their affairs.

There is little need to list many examples of these dehumanizing techniques since they are familiar to Valle-Inclán's readers. It bears repeating, however, that *La corte de los milagros* marks the culmination of these methods, and remains a storehouse of many varieties of grotesque snapshots cleverly assimilated into a historical novel form. To borrow a term from photography in this context is quite appropriate, since neither the sweeping effect of a movie camera nor the motionless solidity of sculpture offers the vocabulary that can describe the isolation of a single moment of action within a time interval of fluid motion. Sometimes this activity is graceful, in which case the photograph acquires a statuesque quality ("una actitud de maniquí elegante"). More often, however, it is the awkward and jerky movement of the characters, corresponding to their absurd natures, that must be recorded, in which case they are glimpsed "con un desgarbo aéreo de marioneta," or "con levitación de marioneta."

Although such narrative interpolations are frequent and familiar, they are by no means uniform in structure. Indeed, it would seem that Valle-Inclán used a specific gradation of puppeteering effects that began with shadow plays, progressed to three-dimensional marionettes, and ended with the mechanization of human dolls. For example, in the first group of effects, the human factor prevails even while casting a shadowy unreality over the scene: "La molinera, con quiebro y sandunga, levantaba en la punta del pie la venda del cautivo. El farol aprisionaba en su círculo bailón las figuras, y correteaban por el muro, con intriga de marionetas, las tres sombras" (II, 921). The basic realism of the episode prevails, while an aesthetic penumbra hovers above it as a kind of extra dimension included for its mood-creating power. In the next stage, however, the reverse takes place, and the realistic element becomes stylized while the mechanical action of the puppetry receives a sharper focus than the mere awkwardness it displayed before: "Se saludaron con una genuflexión, como pastores de villancico, y tomaron asiento, sonrientes para el concurso, con gracia amanerada de danzantes que miman su dúo sobre un reloj de consola" (II, 846). In this passage, two separate tendencies begin to emerge that will require our attention very soon. On the one hand is the idealization of the pastoral mode, a falsification of nature that recalls the mannerism of the 18th century. And on the other hand is the metamorphosis of the marionette into an automaton; that is, there is a change from a hidden manipulator who uses strings to a concealed mechanical coil. Together, these developments produce a bold new grotesque.

The role of automatism originated during the Romantic period as a purely formalistic device. Its droll figurines in clockworks, its whimsical and absurd mimes of human activity on a reduced scale, and its uncanny and often bizarre verisimilitude all contributed to the grotesque aesthetic without reflecting any profound philosophical ideas. With the ambiguity of tragic clowns and mimes that arose during the breakdown of Romanticism, a new role for automatons became possible on the basis of the psychological conflicts which resulted from that ambiguity. This is what Valle-Inclán exploits in his descriptions of people who behave like mechanical dolls. For example, again in *La corte de los milagros*, the following passage states openly what usually remains unspoken in most of the works:

> La Marquesa volvió a su enajenado silencio, abismándose en la aridez de una contemplación interior. Miraba ceñuda el pasado, y sólo descubría la continuidad de un dolor largo y mezquino. Este afán marchito, desilusionado, era la vida, pasaba a través de todos los instantes, articulándolos de un modo arbitrario, y no valía más que el resorte de alambre que un muñeco esconde en el buche de serrín:— ¡Qué asco de vida! (II, 877-878).

What we have here is the genesis of a modern psychology, conceived in post-Romantic disillusion and dedicated to the search for new images that express the hollowness of man's personality. Whether the introspection referred to is sterile because it begets confusion instead of clarity, or because the individual is an empty vessel to begin with, is immaterial. The first possibility led certain writers—Unamuno, for instance—to despair over finding the true and permanent self, while the second prompted other writers—like Valle-Inclán—to create the external form of ambiguity by means of these automatic figures. In both instances, the Romantic anguish and its subsequent let-down were supplanted by a psychological and aesthetic distance, a detached ironic stance that permitted, either existentially or esperpentically, a reconstitution of the hollow core of man's inner life.

In Valle-Inclán, this revaluation consists of stuffing his creatures with sawdust, and allowing them to conduct their external lives in harmony with their essence, "como a impulsos de resorte." This is the extent of his psychological probings, although it would have been fatal to improvise further on the basis of so little. On the other hand, he was left with the rich possibility of formal expression, which he developed in an unusual direction. Instead of attempting to describe his human dolls by detailing their appearance, he concentrated on their position at one instant in a given series of movements, and froze it. Thus, what we find is the petrification of a moment in space, the solidification of a tiny area in what is normally a fluid succession of gestures and activities. For example, "la Duquesa petrificaba su gesto magro y curvo de pajarraco" (II, 840). Once again we are reminded of the significance of time in Valle-Inclán's reality. If the moment is frozen, the reason is not to preserve it from the transience of time, but to retain the peculiarly expressive position in space configured by the personage. It is, therefore, the immobilization of spatial fluidity rather than the arrest of temporal flow that creates the distortion. To this extent it is a plastic endeavor, as the following scene indicates: "Y otra vez el relámpago de la casa en susto, con las figuras lívidas, paralizadas en una acción, como figuras de cera" (II, 880). Similarly, the formal occupation of space is more important than the reasons why it is occupied. The desire to petrify the stance is served at the expense of motivation, so that the human value diminishes as the statuesque qualities increase. Nevertheless, the result is grotesque because it is unnatural, a reduction in the context surrounding the particular situation that is thus transfixed. Ultimately, of course, these characters all appear to be absurd, but this is the result of the aesthetic structure that we have been observing.

We may say, consequently, that one reason behind the grotesque use of the marionette-wax doll complex of motifs can be explained by the history of ideas: the dissolution of the Romantic mystiques of personality and the heroic self. A second explanation, however, is a formalistic one. It will be noted that the passages cited do not evoke the sense of uneasiness and incongruity that can be perceived while reading authors like Solana. There is nothing sinister in Valle-Inclán because his techniques derive ultimately from the pleasant frivolity of the French Rococo. His idea was to adopt the manners of 18th century court life to his Spanish subject and then to exaggerate them exponentially. This idea is stated explicitly in *La marquesa Rosalinda* when the poet declares: "Olor de rosa y de manzana / tendrán mis versos a la vez, / como una farsa cortesana / de Versalles o de Aranjuez" (I, 215). The immediate source, however, is the more recent 19th century literary scene mixed with the comic entertainments of the day: "Enlazaré las rosas frescas / con que se viste el vaudeville / y las rimas funambulescas / a la manera de Banville."

But in general, this influence merely crystallized the familiar aesthetic principle that Valle-Inclán had been developing for years, namely, that Spanish literature should be written with the premise that Spain is a cultural deformation of Europe. As a result, French manneristic poses acquire a doubly artificial air when his mind repeatedly imagines them as patterns that can be fitted into stylistic formulas. And with a sly dig at Spain's national rival, Valle-Inclán sets the tone for his farce: "Con las espumas del champaña / y la malicia de sus crónicas, / Francia proyecta sobre España / las grandes narices borbónicas. / Versalles pone sus empaques, / Aranjuez, sus albas rientes, / y un grotesco de miriñaques, / Don Francisco Goya y Lucientes" (I, 215). Thus, the background of the drama between Rosalinda and Arlequín is decorated with a few light grotesque flutters that enliven the symmetries of the Classical European garden.

In a very real sense, the Versaillesque motif here and elsewhere represents a nostalgia for the Rococo. If this sentiment is made to pass through an ironic filter, the reason is not simply a will to distort. The epitome of grace and reason reached during the 18th century could never have been reproduced after the Romantic revolt and its philosophical and psychological impact. Those qualities had been transformed, and it was inevitable that Valle-Inclán should view French classicism through the lens of the Generation of 98, which is to say, across the landscape of barren Castile and over the "marasma actual" of Spanish society. But beyond this, the attraction of Versailles was like the charm of a miniature *object d'art*: the delicacy of its balanced structure made it seem almost unreal. As in so many cases, the steps between charm, quaintness and oddity are short and barely perceptible, especially when the object has an aura of remoteness about it. This made the Rococo charmingly grotesque, a little too *précieux* to be real. Moreover, with a little imagination, the proximity of a symmetrical environment like Versailles to a Goyesque atmosphere like Spain's rendered the former as grotesque as the latter. In this way, the temptation arose on Valle-Inclán's part to have the principle of order imitated in a culture where disorder was the rule.

This application of order is a basic stratagem of Valle-Inclán's grotesque. It operates in mechanical figures and puppets by regimenting natural movements into organized, staccato patterns. It also operates in the imitation of French pastoral settings. As the puppeteer in the *Farsa italiana de la enamorada del rey* explains, a shepherd's dance for the ladies of the court will make use of castanets and the parading of *majos*, all done "a la española usanza." The combination will demonstrate, therefore, that although "son otras marionetas que nunca vió Versalles," they can compete very well with their French counterparts (I, 340). Indeed, this is so much the case that although the work is an Italian farce, it uses Spanish styles, an about-face from the traditional *commedia dell'arte* influence, whose genre Valle-Inclán attempted to rework, and which of course had a wide exposure in France for several centuries. These episodes are not grotesque in themselves, but they do provide the clues for tracing the evolution of the grotesque from its Rococo origins. Thus, when we reach *Gerifaltes de antaño*, the musical discord of two pastoral scenes gains added significance when the rhythms are said to combine with "fantasía grotesca." It is unusual for Valle-Inclán to be this interested in music, but he is looking for effects drawn from a popular source: "Fuera tocaba un aire el tamboril y otro el gaitero. Se trenzaban grotescos, como los zuecos de esos vejetes ladinos que en las fiestas de aldea rompen bailando en el corro de las mozas" (II, 495, 498). Obviously, there is a good deal more realism here than in the Gallicized idylls, and the context is an entirely different one. Nevertheless, the grotesque effect arises from the tacit comparison of this irregular music with the neat, ordered melodies of the 18th century pastoral mode.

Finally, the symmetries of Versailles are also used for grotesque purposes in the technique of petrification mentioned previously. It is here that the divergence between the two sensibilities of mannered elegance and post-Romantic deflation becomes irremediable:

Ei vaho azulado de los olivos se dilataba en onduladas líneas, colmadas de silencio y galvana. Las barcinas esguevas, can matorros de carrascal, resecas y erémicas, pedían agua al cielo. Los rebaños se inmovilizaban sobre los alcores. El rumor de la vida, en el silencio del campo, tenía un compás de eternidad, un fatalismo geomántico de dolor y de indiferencia *(La corte de los milagros*, II, 912).

The timelessness and paralysis of movement in this scene are much less impressive than the instances examined earlier because they involve livestock and not people. On the other hand, the passage not only belongs to the pastoral category under study, but it synthesizes a number of concepts from the 18th, 19th, and 20th centuries. First of all, it places Valle-Inclán squarely in line with the preoccupations of the Generation of 98, if ever there was any doubt about this. Secondly, the passage indicates why there should be a nostalgia for the Rococo: the listless feeling imagined by the narrator (which is, after all, a projection) comes as the logical extreme of effete court life, while that same listlessness cradles a longing for the idyllic joys of the past. And third, the paradox of sorrow and indifference represents the philosophical source of the grotesque.

Because of that *dolor*, Valle-Inclán must acknowledge the Romantic nature of his complaint about society and existence. And because of the *indiferencia*, he must devise new methods for expressing the sorrow and pain. The result is the use of traditional elements in a destructive or derisive atmosphere. Ultimately, this constitutes an anti-Romantic position, for traditional sentiments become submerged in a flood of new techniques and structures whose disparate forms belie the original attitude of the artist. Similarly, conventional themes lose their earlier connotations and become the instruments of a more disfiguring sensibility. The grotesque, therefore, is affected by the trauma of its birth, emerging with "fatalismo geomántico" from the matrix of sorrow, with the mantle of indifferent violence already upon it.

IV. MANIPULATING SPANISH REALITY:
FROM DEFORMATION TO DIGNITY

Perhaps the most original contribution made by Valle-Inclán to the aesthetics of the grotesque in his transformation of popular themes. What we find in his grotesque mode is the reverse side of pastoral idealism, which is to say, realism in the manner of *la España negra*. The latter is a literary theme which still awaits scholarly attention, but in Valle-Inclán it belongs to the type of heroic inversion that began with the picaresque novel, was transformed in the *Quijote*, and was finally recast into various kinds of infrarealism of which *Luces de Bohemia* is the best example.

As we will see, the grotesque in this area depends in part upon intensely naturalistic and even ugly glimpses of reality, a focus which Spanish literature has consistently maintained. This includes scenes of poverty, portraits of beggars, and drab depictions of carnivals. On the other hand, it also proceeds from the debasement of Classical heroism and courtly values, both of which involve a process of vulgarization too. For example, in *La corte de los milagros* we have the following scene:

> Un alarido de antruejo rijoso revoloteaba en el vagón. El convoy perfilaba su línea negra por el petrificado mar del llano manchego. Trotaba detrás, enristrada la lanza, todo ilusión en la noche de luna, el yelmo, la sombra de Don Quijote: Llevaba a la grupa, desmadejado de brazos y piernas, un pelele con dos agujeros al socaire de las orejas (II, 897).

The passage is intended to provide a mood from which the reader will sense a kind of Quixotic permeation of the landscape, a rural mock-heroic atmosphere in which the old knight continues to exist by means of a provincial atavism. This represents a movement away from Versailles, even though other passages in the same novel preserve the Rococo effect by means of their absurd puppetry. In fact, the courtly manner is even undermined by popular elements in the *Farsa y licencia de la reina castiza*, when the entourage of Queen Isabel is described with a vulgar rhetoric: "Farsa de muñecos, / maliciosos ecos / de los semanarios / revolucionarios / 'La Gorda,' 'La Flaca' y 'Gil Blas.' / Mi musa moderna / enarca la pierna, / se cimbra, se ondula, / se comba, se achula / con el ringorrango / rítmico del tango / y recoge la falda detrás" (I, 419). Both the versification and the choice of vocabulary indicate a cheapening of aristocratic tastes, and at the same time they forcast the infiltration of popular styles which will eventually achieve their own artistic status. The point is that the vulgarization of pastoral idealism takes several forms, rural and urban, but in either case the gradual penetration by Spanish reality produces grotesque results.

In addition to this slow division between rarified and popular social strata, we have Valle-Inclán's awareness of how grotesque aesthetics have been evolving in his own work and in the contemporary world. That is, he makes certain allusions to real life which indicate that he was conscious of himself as a grotesque innovator, and a writer who was still catering to the tastes of a minority. For example, in *La pipa de kif* he repeats the farcical situation just quoted, and he fits it into an even more realistic framework: "Yo anuncio la era argentina / de socialismo y cocaína. / De cocotas con convulsiones / y de vastas Revoluciones" (I, 1135). And at the same time, admitting that "me ha venido la ventolera / de hacer versos funambulescos / —un purista diría grotescos—" he awakens in us the suspicion that his words are simply echoes of the *fin-de-siècle* game of shocking the middle class: "para las gentes respetables / son cabriolas espantables." Nevertheless, we cannot be concerned with the writer's sincerity, since the survey of grotesque aesthetics involves the forms and ideas that appear in the works themselves. Consequently, this artistic revolution from below, which mirrors the revolt of the popular classes, can only be viewed as a self-conscious experiment which recapitulates some of the motifs that we have been examining:

> ¿Y cuál será mi grano incierto? / ¿Acaso la flor del alma de un payaso? / ¡Pálida flor de la locura / con normas de literatura! / ¿Acaso esta musa grotesca / —ya no digo funambulesca—, / que con sus gritos espasmódicos, / irrita a los viejos retóricos, / y salta luciendo la pierna, / ¿no será la musa moderna? / Apuro el vaso de bon vino / y hago cantando mi camino" (I, 1136-1137).

This curious bit of vulgarizing has a special aestheticist appeal, and more so to patrons of pop art with a knowledge of art history. Despite their everyday language and allusions, the verses could never appeal to popular taste in the way that Campoamor's did, because they rely for their effect on an appreciation of the history of aesthetic ideas. Moreover, they dispense with all emotionalism, save that type of detached humor which is both playful and destructive at the same time, and which is a pre-condition for Valle-Inclán's brand of grotesque. At the same time, the popular element on which the verses are based is essential to their flavor and eccentricity. Probably the social distance between the reader's background and the material used in the poem gives that material an artistic attractiveness of the kind that tourists find in picturesque fishing villages and "quaint" mountain communities, which in reality are scenes of hardship and misery. The result is that the popular element becomes transformed into a commodity for sophisticates. It is not surprising, therefore, that when the artist reaches the limit of his endurance in bohemian life—having smoked too much from "la pipa de kif"—he ends up in a sanatorium contemplating his experience in the light of aesthetic movements:

> Bajo la sensación del cloroformo—me hacen temblar con alarido interno / la luz del acuario de un jardín moderno / y el amarillo olor del yodoformo. / Cubista, futurista y estridente, / por el caos febril de la modorra / vuela la sensación, que al fin se borra, / verde mosca, zumbándome en la frente (I, 1173-1174).

If we recall how strongly these lines evoke comparable images in Lorca's highly intellectual *Oda a Salvador Dalí*, we need look no further for proof of this idea of aestheticizing low-life. Moreover, Valle-Inclán's transformation of that low-life differs radically from the traditional literary realisms: the picaresque inversions, for example, or *la vie de bohème* depicted in the art of the last decades of the 19th century. To Valle-Inclán, such a life is valuable for its strong experiences, which can be assimilated into the repertoire of distortions devised by modern art. Low life is grotesque not because this is its real quality in fact, but because it has acquired an aura of artistic glamour. We can also view this perception from another angle: the purpose of art itself. What is ugly and disfigured in reality becomes grotesque in art when the artist does not intend his work to be realistic. In Valle-Inclán's case, his purpose is not representational, so that neither his style nor the associations made with Cubism and Futurism can escape the stigma of deformation.

Another reason behind the grotesque in popular contexts is the failure of a work to fall into either of the two categories established by Valle-Inclán as being characteristic of every artistic endeavor. In a statement which deserves to be better known than it is, he defines these two groups:

> En arte hay dos caminos: uno es arquitectura
> y alusion, logaritmos de la literatura;
> el otro, realidades como el mundo las muestra,
> dicen que así Velázquez pintó su obra maestra.
> Sólo ama realidades esta gente española;
> Sancho Panza medita tumbado a la bartola.

Aquí, si alguno sueña, consulta la baraja,
tienta la lotería, espera y no trabaja.
Al indígena ibero, cada vez más hirsuto,
es mentarle la madre, mentarle lo Absoluto (I, 341).

What is ironic about this credo is that it appears in the *Farsa italiana de la enamorada del rey*, a work which is scarcely designed to be either formalistic or realistic. It belongs, along with most of Valle-Inclán's other works, in a third, grotesque category, whether this includes *comedias bárbaras, esperpentos,* or *tablados de marionetas.* This third alternative aims at being one of the "logaritmos de la literatura," but it uses material taken from the "realidades" of Spanish culture. The latter attracts interest because of its qualities of absurdity, disillusion, and decay, thus supplementing the post-Romantic let-down and, at the same time, offering a way out of the poet's subjective dead-end. The result is that what we earlier saw to be a portrayal of clowns for the purpose of resolving the problem of Romantic psychology, has its parallel in the use of popular carnivals for a similar resolution in reality.

If we examine the details of this resolution, we find them carrying out a naturalistic role in technique, while suggesting in effect a kind of popular anti-Romanticism. That is, the subject matter is drawn from the folkloric customs of the masses, but ultimately, the effect is to deny any meaning to the popular rituals which serve the majority in much the same illusory way that Romanticism did for the elite. For example, the poem "Fin del carnaval" describes the aftermath of the "entierro de la sardina" and the accompanying soberness of Ash Wednesday. It allows us to see the instruments of gaiety from the inside, and the sight is a depressing one. The comic figures of Colombina and Pierrot are stripped of their antic charm: the one exuding an "olor de pacholí y sobaquina" in her cheap clothes, the other removing the rouge and powder from his face. Then too, the gay grotesquerie of the "curdela narigudo" with his cardboard nose and old broom becomes lost in a "ciclón" of household items like tin cans, kettles, and frying pans. With confetti decorating the mud in the streets, and dogs that "se lamentan de los yerros de la Humanidad," the pitiful drabness of reality betrays the feeble effort made by men to masquerade their misery. It is an "absurda tarde. Macabra / mueca de dolor" (I, 1139).

All of this means that Valle-Inclán is turning the Roman carnival of Romanticism inside out, denying the color and joy that fantasy once brought to artistic spirits, and, still worse, denying the people as a group their tiny measure of escapism too. His poem presents an inverted *costumbrista* scene, where the narrator stands aloof from the populace instead of sharing their activities sympathetically, and where the emptiness of their folk ways is implied, instead of fulfillment. Trivia replace lively detail and make-believe falls apart into its make-do materials. The Romantic grotesque, therefore, succumbs to Valle-Inclán's realistic eye, and, in a sense, it would appear that he is following the second path of artistic creativity mentioned before, that of Velázquez. However, his poem is not a form of realism, in the way that a documentary piece of literature might be. It is just as unfaithful to the original as the Romantic carnivals were, except that now the carnival is debased instead of exalted. Still less is the poem a naturalistic piece, because first it leaves an impression which is contrary to the emotions felt by the masses during the carnival; and second, its social character does not provide Valle-Inclán with the alternative that he is seeking, now that Romanticism is defunct. In other words, assuming that Valle-Inclán and the Generation of 98 were looking for new literary forms to replace *Modernismo* and the Campoamor-Echegaray post-Romanticism, and assuming the Generation of 98 found that alternative in its social realism, then Valle-Inclán's poem does not even come close to the spirit of this realism. On the contrary, it is neither critical nor constructive nor analytical. It represents, rather, the frustration of an aesthete who cannot find satisfaction by creating realist literature, and who in despair denigrates popular-class reality because its own myths and illusions have failed to give him that satisfaction. And so he debunks the carnival by focusing realistically on the latter's grotesque elements.

Valle-Inclán uses a different kind of realism in works like *Divinas palabras*, where the grotesque is carefully built up out of natural ugliness and is then repeated with thematic frequency. In this work, and in short stories like "Mi hermana Antonia," the popular elements used are the beggar, the village idiot, and the abnormal child. For example, the regular appearance of Miguelín, the hydrocephalic dwarf who moves epileptically through the "tragicomedia de aldea" *Divinas palabras*, seems just as unreal as the mannequins discussed earlier: "El Idiota, los ojos vueltos y la lengua muerta entre los labios negruzcos, respiraba con ahogado ronquido. La enorme cabeza, lívida, greñuda, viscosa, rodaba en el hoyo como una cabeza cortada" (I, 763). The difference is that here the distortion is not artistic, but it has the same impact because other elements of reality are screened out.

The technique is one that we have come to recognize as part of the Goyesque deformation coupled with the pathological instinct of Solana. That is, the eye focuses like a close-up camera lens, systematically eliminating the normal elements in a given context and leaving the abnormal ones naked in all their horror. As Machado once said, every poet has two muses, the ethical and the pathological. Valle-Inclán's muse in this case is clearly the second, and the standards of her photographic selectivity are the aberrations of natural phenomena. These monsters belong to *la España negra*, and they are inspired not by fantasy but by society and nature. Their artistic form produces, to use Solana's term, a *realidad inquietante*, which is to say, a pre-Surrealist horror in broad daylight that is too real to be a nightmare. This type of technique is not dominant in Valle-Inclán, but it is there, and its grotesque features are obviously involved in the general development of his dehumanizations. For example:

> El Idiota agita las manos con temblor de epilepsia, y pone los ojos en blanco. La niña deja sobre el dornajo guindas y roscos, y vuelve a sentarse en medio de los padres, abstraída y extática. Con su hábito morado y sus manos de cera, parece una virgen mártir entre dos viejas figuras de retablo" (I, 762-763).

Here, then, is the more conventional naturalist deformation along side of Valle-Inclán's special *retablo* creation, a *retablo* which, by the way, is strongly reminiscent of the prose writings of Solana.

It is important to remember that this type of grotesque is one of the few unifying forces in the complete works of Valle-Inclán. It can be found early in his career, as in the *Sonata de estío*, toward the middle, as in the *Romance de lobos*, and near the end, as in *La corte de los milagros*. Let us note by way of comparison two passages from the first two works mentioned, and then try to determine what Valle-Inclán had in mind:

> ...[una] monstruosa turba de lisiados nos cercó clamorante.

Ciegos y tullidos, enanos y lazarados nos acosaban, nos perseguían, rodando bajo las patas de los caballos, corriendo a rastras por el camino, entre aullidos y oraciones, con las llagas llenas de polvo, con las canillas echadas a la espalda, secas, desmedradas, horribles (II, 103).

...una hueste de mendigos que han buscado cobijo en tal paraje. Tienen la vaguedad de un sueño aquellas figuras entrevistadas a la luz del relámpago: Patriarcas haraposos, mujeres escuálidas, mozos lisiados hablan en las tinieblas, y sus voces, contrahechas por el viento, son de una oscuridad embrujada y grotesca, saliendo de aquel roquedo que finge ruinas de quimera, donde hubiese por carcelero un alado dragón (I, 669).

What is immediately evident is the great similarity between the two quotations, despite the intervening years and the differing contexts: the first occurs in a modernist novelette, the second in a *comedia bárbara*. Both employ concrete vocabularies, create graphic scenes, and allude to the social status as well as to the physical appearance of the figures. This social allusion is significant, for it is related to the concave mirror theory and the claim that Spanish society is in fact deformed. In a way, the scenes are the confirmation of those esperpentic principles, as well as the expression of them. On the other hand, the two passages are different from each other in that the second has a vague aura of mystery about it. It lacks the sharp clarity of first, and it adds a brooding, supernatural element to the realistic framework. Nevertheless, these less rational elements are also rooted in Spain's popular culture, and they are not alien to the examples of folk superstition which were examined earlier in the chapter. There, however, the supernatural was often an aid to other Romantic grotesques in creating mood. Here, it transfigures Spanish reality in accordance with esperpentic theory. It is interesting therefore, to see how closely these different grotesque components are related to each other even while they operate in contrasting contexts.

Behind these diverse usages of the grotesque, there is a consistent mode of thinking which Valle-Inclán stated rather incompletely in *Luces de bohemia*. It consists of two general attitudes, one toward people, and the other toward historical reality. Valle-Inclán's attitude toward people is like a medical examiner's in a clinic: he is on the lookout for unhealthy types only. He consistently singles out the physical oddities among men, and in order to do this he must maintain the equanimity of a Maese Lotario. He may be neither emotionally involved with these people nor distracted by the norms from which they deviate. Thus, even in so simple a detail as a servant's entrance, it is the aberration which is noted: "Entra otra criada, una moza negra y casi enana, con busto de giganta. Tiene la fealdad de un ídolo y parece que anda sobre las rodillas" (I, 681). The technique here merits a word of comment because the use of *ídolo* is a carryover from the exoticism of the *Sonatas*, discussed earlier. In this case, the sculptural form survives although the effect no longer is to idealize the subject. The important question, however, is what kind of psychological accord, if any exists between the narrator and his subject. Aside from the aesthetic rapport, there is none, and this is what is so remarkable. From the sweet, heavy sentimentalism of Bradomín, Valle-Inclán's temperament has changed completely. There is no bond of sympathy or feeling of revulsion in these later portraits, and what is more, there is nothing of the sociologist's interest either. Thus, having outdistanced the affective responses of the Romanticists, Valle-Inclán also evades the direct intellectual commitments of the realists. It is this factor which makes him different from the other members of the Generation of 98, despite the fact that his work eventually provides a social picture of Spain too. Psychologically speaking, he is a puppet-master in the most profound emotional sense: a manipulator of human objects without regard to sentiments.

The next question is, why? The answer is found in the philosophy expounded by Don Estrafalario, whose theory of the dignity of manipulation is set forth in *Los cuernos de Don Friolera*. In this *esperpento*, the puppet-master urges the principle puppet to kill his innocent wife, and Don Estrafalario, who is watching the show, finds this type of attitude to be superior to the honor play of the national *comedia*. He considers the latter's fierce seriousness an unreasonable outlook when compared to the good-humored spoofs of the cuckold-plays that originated in Italy. The implacable morality advocated by the "Afro-Castilian" theater ("honor teatral y africano de Castilla") fails to suggest the flexibility of life, or, indeed, any of the indifference that people display in their encounters with life. But the gravest drawback is that the Spanish *comedia* gets the playwright involved with its laughter and tears, and this is the biggest mistake. For Valle-Inclán, life must be contemplated for the spectacle that it is, and its artistic reflection cannot indicate any emotional interest in what the characters do or say. As Don Estrafalario remarks, "mi estética es una superación del dolor y de la risa" (I, 992-993), which means not that these elements are banished from art, but that they should confront the viewer without demanding of him any corresponding response.

If we reflect upon this aesthetic, we begin to realize how utterly irresponsible it is in a human sense. Not in an artistic one, of course, as I will point out in a moment, but insofar as it neither requires the viewer to evaluate the work in terms of human experience, nor expects the artist to have anything more than imagination and talent to create his work. Which is quite enough, one might say. Yet this is exactly the point. Up until now, aesthetics has supposed some bond of humanity to exist between author and work, such as that which is found in Cervantes and Shakespeare. But this is precisely what Valle-Inclán wishes to avoid. The perspective he seeks would release him from all intellectual and emotional responsibility to his creatures, leaving him free to contrive, manipulate, distort, or even leave alone the human factors in his works. Thus, the grotesque emerges not only in the first three cases, but even in the fourth, because artistic verisimilitude has traditionally consisted, in part, of the sympathetic treatment of characters, which is to say, an intuitive understanding of their human qualities regardless of how odious they might be. It is grotesque to see that understanding absent in Valle-Inclán, and so, quite apart from how exaggerated his personages are, the mere fact that the affective bond is missing is itself a deformation. This explains the unreal feeling one receives while reading the *comedias bárbaras* and the last novels, even when there is no concrete technique or device to point out as being grotesque. Valle-Inclán has accomplished dehumanization by withdrawing his personality from the scene.

This withdrawal has nothing to do with the personal stamp left on Valle-Inclán's works, which is a matter of style and formal technique. The withdrawal, and the dehumanization that results from it, is based on two related concepts of detachment. One of these is what Don Estrafalario calls the "dignidad demiúrgica" of the puppet-master. It consists of the latter's ability to destroy his personages without compunction. For example, when he urges Don Friolera to kill his wife, he demonstrates his superiority to someone like Iago, another manipulator, in Shakespeare's play. That is, Iago also seems to be a Devil, urging his tragic pawn to commit a horror, but

> Yago, cuando desata aquel conflicto de celos, quiere vengarse, mientras que ese otro tuno [el bululú], espíritu mucho más cultivado, solo trata de divertirse a costa de Don Friolera. Shakespeare rima con el latido de su corazón el corazón de Otelo. Se desdobla en los celos del Moro. Creador y criatura son del mismo barro humano. En tanto ese Bululú ni un sólo momento deja de considerarse superior por naturaleza a los muñecos de su tabanque. Tiene una dignidad demiúrgica (I, 996-997).

In other words, the puppet-master does not attempt to project his own humanity, however indirectly, into his play. This, to be sure, requires an extraordinary psychological frame of mind, and if we think of some of the cold surrealist dissociations—Chirico's mannequins, *Le chien andalou*, automatic writing—we can understand what utter indifference is required. To have a magician's disposition is to paralyze every feeling except for the desire to control. Moreover, it is to place oneself beyond any ethical concern for the results of one's dexterity. The demiurge has something of the Devil as well as the Divine in him, and the will to power is the only impulse he displays in an otherwise emotionless personality. Valle-Inclán may call it dignity, but it is death to feeling.

This leads to the second concept in the theory of detachment. If the artist must not permit himself any human sentiments, he may allow himself the superhuman one of Satanic laughter. The Devil's laugh, of course, is one of the classic forms of the grotesque, because it is a mockery of everything that man is supposed to represent in a universe of reason and moral order. Traditionally, Satan laughs at virtue, sensitivity, and most profoundly, death. Gleeful laughter in the presence of death is probably the most primal expression of both hope and fear in man: an attempt to exorcise the fatal moment by an act of orgiastic liberation. Its appearance in carnivals and in popular mask motifs demonstrates the depth of its penetration into man's unconscious, and for this reason it is too difficult a subject to explore here. Nevertheless, Valle-Inclán was aware at least superficially of how Satanic mirth was the only permissible emotion that the artist might have, and indeed, a necessary one for his success. And so, in a reference to a painting in which the Devil is mocking an unfortunate mortal, Don Estrafalario observes that "me ha preocupado la carantoña del Diablo frente al Pecador. La verdad es que tenía otra idea de las risas infernales; había pensado siempre que fuesen de desprecio, de un supremo desprecio, y no... los pobres humanos le hacemos mucha gracia al Cornudo Monarca" (I, 992).

What this passage suggests is in effect an amplification of the "grotesque Spain" theory presented in *Luces de bohemia*. Why should Don Estrafalario have previously thought that the Devil's mockery was scornful, and what difference does it make if that mockery is really the product of amusement, not scorn? Or rather, what is so significant about this discovery? The answer lies in man's image of himself, which is made with more self-admiration than is warranted. by fact. Scorn is a reaction to something serious, however trivial, whereas laughter is a reaction to something foolish. If the Devil were to act disdainfully, this would imply a modicum of value in the human condition, a shred of dignity which could at least be respected for the air of gravity that it bestows upon that condition. But since the Devil laughs outright, he must see the human endeavor as utter nonsense. It is this realization which has dawned upon Don Estrafalario. Man does not even merit the courtesy of a sneer. He is so ridiculous that his life is a laughing matter. Valle-Inclán's theory is, in effect, a supplement to the ideas of Max Estrella about Spanish culture. The institutions of Spanish life—religious as well as political—are senseless, and only the Devil is clever enough to realize it. For this reason, the Satanic perspective must be adopted by the artist. It is the only means by which he can grasp the essential character of his subject. And, by remaining superior, not "del mismo barro," he can preserve the perfect aesthetic distance.

This, then, is the psychological attitude toward people which supports Valle-Inclán' s grotesque. The other general attitude is the one which he adopts toward historical reality. Here too, the confirmation of a deformed Spain is made quite explicitly, and by a technique which is in closer accord with the Generation of 98 than the practices noted so far. If Spain is a grotesque deformation of Europe, the proof can be found in both political and geographical terms. First of all, the body politic is headed by a decadent aristocracy whose entourage is bizarre and virtually inane. One very vivid scene from *Corte de amor* is sufficient to suggest Valle-Inclán's testimonial method:

> Desde la orilla lejana, un largo cortejo de bufones y de azafatas, de chambelanes patizambos y princesas locas parecía saludar a Rosita agitando las hachas de viento que se reflejaban en el agua. Era un séquito real. Cuatro enanos cabezudos conducían en andas a un viejo de luengas barbas, que reía con la risa hueca de los payasos y agitaba en el aire las manos ungidas de albayalde para las bofetadas chabacanas. Princesas, bufones, azafatas, chambelanes se arremolinaban saltando en torno de las andas ebrias y bamboleantes. Todo el séquito cantaba a cora, un coro burlesco de voces roncas (II, 253-254).

This technique is ostensibly both realistic and documentary, for it evokes a scene which reflects, with the usual novelistic license, an atmosphere having some basis in historical fact. Nevertheless, the stylistic repetitions and stresses carefully allow the grotesque features to dominate and to reduce the situation to a nonsensical hubub.

The second proof of Spain's cultural deformity is just as realistic as the political demonstration. It involves the description of a landscape on the outskirts of Madrid, adding the imaginative effect of delineating the conflict of *las dos Españas*:

> Sobre la Pradera de San Isidro, gladiaban amarillos y rojos goyescos, en contraste con la límpida quietud velazqueña que depuraba los límites azulinos del Pardo y la Moncloa. La luz de la tarde madrileña definía los dos ámbitos en que se combate eternamente la dualidad del alma española. La Corte de Isabel Segunda con sus frailes, sus togados, sus validos, sus héroes bufos, y sus payasos trágicos, obsesa por la engañosa unidad nacional, fanáticamente incomprensiva, era sorda y ciega para este antagonismo geomántico, que todas las tardes, como un mensaje, lleva el sol a los miradores del Real Palacio (II, 1299).

The dualities involved here can be linked to the «grotesque Spain" theory for several reasons. The first is that the opposition of Goya and Velázquez seems to be made not on the basis of differing themes (they both painted the aristocracy without distortion) but on formalistic grounds. Valle-Inclán saw a chromatic violence in Goya which he contrasted to the subdued color tones of Velázquez, and that caused him to associate other antagonisms with this one later on in the passage: populace against royalty, meadow against mountain, Africa against Iberia. Implicit in these, of course, are the convulsions which periodically gripped the nation and threw her national values out of proportion. The other link between the "antagonismo geomántico" and "grotesque Spain" involves what Valle-Inclán had called "el fatalismo geomántico de dolor y de indiferencia." This idea holds that the Spanish mentality is determined by landscape as a function of history, the result being an ambiguity of pain and indifference which is reflected aesthetically in the unfeeling dramatization of tragic marionettes. Thus, geographical determinism, its impact on political history, its reflection in traditional painting, and the way all three are revaluated by Valle-Inclán's "dignidad demiúrgica," give testimony to the cultural antagonisms that lead to distortion.

There is no better conclusion to this analysis of Valle-Inclán's grotesque than to incorporate some of his own aesthetic terminology. In *La lámpara maravillosa*, he draws a distinction between Hellenic and Byzantine forms of beauty which is useful in characterizing his own literary achievement. Although his purpose in this work was to advocate a "quietismo estético" based on Gnostic beliefs, he gives, in effect, a brilliant definition of grotesque art. All aesthetic positions, he suggests, seek an eternal, immutable Beauty, but there are two fundamental methods of arriving at it. One way is by using an external criterion, by looking for Beauty in the pure forms of Platonic ideals, or in the images which reflect those forms. The second method of encountering the Beautiful is more irrational and less objective: by means of Byzantine Gnosticism. Instead of positing a generic concept of Beauty, or allowing archetypes of several kinds of Beauty, the Byzantine vision perceives the individual shape and captures the specific beauty that is inherent in it. This vision is revealed most significantly in the grotesque, because its creation of monsters and incongruities depends on what is aberrant, and hence unique, in a given form. Each disfigurement is different, and deformation is the individual evasion of an ideal generic form. As Valle-Inclán expresses it, "gárgolas, canecillos, endriagos, vestiglos, traían esta nueva intuición entrañada en sus formas perversas, y el carácter, rebusca de lo singular, fue contrapuesto al arquetipo tras el cual había peregrinado el mundo antiguo" (II, 588).

What Valle-Inclán meant by "formas perversas" strikes at the very heart of grotesque aesthetics: the concept of absurdity. He felt that in "los monstruos del arte bizantino... las formas originarias degeneran hasta el absurdo." The reason for this is not very clear, but presumably it is because the nature of monstrosity consists of a deformation of particular traits, a degeneration of individual attributes into distorted forms that are too aberrant, and hence too absurd, to fit into the generic scheme of Platonic forms. In any case, "el espíritu de los gnósticos descubre una emoción estética en el absurdo de las formas, en la creación de monstruos, en el acabamiento de la vida." Since this aesthetic feeling grows out of an intuition of impending death or destruction, the sense of Beauty cannot be derived from the static condition of the images themselves. Instead, "la belleza de las imágenes no está en ellas, sino en el acto creador, del cual no se desprenden jamás" (II, 589).

Unintentionally, then, Valle-Inclán has summarized his own aesthetic of the grotesque on the basis of the polarity between Byzantine and Hellenic concepts of Beauty. It is doubtless more esoteric than is desirable in a critical analysis, and perhaps it is not directly descriptive of his literary practices. Nevertheless, all the elements are there: the perception of absurdity in the face of death, the expression of this absurdity by means of deformation, and the triumph over death by an act of artistic creation. That Valle-Inclán called this aesthetic mode Byzantine instead of using some other name is unimportant. But the fact that he counterpoised it to Classical art is indeed essential. For if nothing else, his grotesque vision is the very antithesis of Classicism, including the ideals of Romanticism. And in the context of modern European literature, his negation of both versimilitude and tragic sentiment is a form of anti-Classicism of the very highest order.[1]

---

[1] This study was first published in *Ramón del Valle-Inclán*. Ed. A. Zahareas. New York: Las Américas, 1968, 493-539.

12
Synthesis

THE VARIETY OF GROTESQUES examined in this book confirms the opinion of one scholar that theories of the grotesque are bound to fall short of its aesthetic totality. Whether the grotesque, as Clayborough suggests, expresses conflict between the natural and the distorted, or, as Kayser suggests, it expresses the estrangement and confusion of realms, these theories are reductive, argues Donald Ross, and they exclude the larger artistic mode that makes the grotesque co-equal to tragedy and comedy owing to its fusion of irony, parody, and enigma. Ross would prefer a *sui generis* approach the grotesque, one that eschews such dualisms as natural/unnatural, or ridiculous/sublime, an approach that instead would encompass more than the shock of amalgams, hybrids, and other forms that foster uneasiness.

No such ambitious approach motivates the following synthesis of the Spanish grotesque. Theory is precluded by the heterogeneity found in the preceding chapters (dating from 1961 to 1976) but also by subsequent studies on Galdós, Quevedo, modern theater, and the Golden Age, among other testimonies to Spain's cultural penchant for unorthodox artistic modes.[1] Collectively they suggest that comparisons or contrasts, parallels or divergences, and uniqueness or pattern are preferable to theorizing as approaches to the Spanish grotesque.

The generalized characteristics and patterns that follow, I believe, are limited to the specific studies in this book.

I Periodization of the Grotesque
The history of the Spanish grotesque properly begins with a few scattered Medieval texts that remain to be assembled and studied. The present book began with a solid block of literary evidence in the Renaissance,

---

1 Studied by, respectively, John Kronik, James Iffland, Peter Podol, Raquel García Pascual, and Henryk Ziomek.

but also with the recognition that a previous grotesque tradition exists in what pastoral novelist Corral called the "ficción gallarda de los antiguos." By this allusion he evoked sundry chivalric references to the giants and Classical monsters that were later assimilated by architects and sculptors into ornamental designs that served to inspire literary images.

The "pastoral grotesque" described in Chapter 1 is probably just one aspect of the Renaissance grotesque. In Spain it appears to be the dominant one, as there is no equivalent to Rabelais or to Elizabethan fiction and burlesque comedy. There is not what Bakhtin calls the "festive madness" that denies terror by means of laughable monsters. Nevertheless, the preeminent Renaissance aesthetic value everywhere is arguably the principle of mimesis, which is premised upon natural harmony. This ideal is exactly what Spain's pastoral exemplifies. When the plane mirror of mimesis cracks, the grotesque appears, but always as a Classically based insertion that jars gently rather than disrupts. Although the novelist sets the grotesque motif in antithesis to Nature, he is not permitted to subvert Nature's ideal order. But viewed in retrospect from 20th-century Modernism, the pastoral grotesque is the ancestor of a deviant deformation of reality. And viewed retrospectively from the Romantic period, the "hombre bestial" of the pastoral grotesque is a prototype of the fierce primitive in the Beauty and the Beast myth, which the Romantics domesticated through pathos.

During the Baroque period the dominant principle is discordant concord. The absolutist world-view continues to hold sway in Gracián (Chapter 2) and in areas studied by other scholars such as Quevedo's works and burlesque theater. But in the Baroque the Renaissance aesthetic idealism succumbs to a liberating energy that permits mimetic extensions and excrescences that range from realism and satire to the scatological and the grotesque. One sees the shift in the transformation of the pastoral brutish *salvaje* into the bestialized men created by Gracián. The latter technique produces a "moral grotesque" in that his excessive corporeal deformations allegorize the corruption of Christian values. The technique's didactic role also reaches back to assimilate Classical monsters into its animal symbolism and to transform the Ovidian stratagem of metamorphosis. At the same time, the convulsive physical plane of the Baroque yields to its ethical cosmos, which tensely controls those disintegrating forces.

The Baroque moralism of Gracián is not the mark of *El criticón*'s originality. This rests rather in its grotesque plastic qualities. Its amalgamation of hybrid forms, human animalizations, and other wrenching disfigurements are the imagistic counterparts of Baroque disproportion and stylistic excess. In fact Gracián's ornate tapestry of stylistic motifs exemplifies the Baroque overgrown framework. In addition, Gracián's work stands at the frontier of two aesthetic sensibilities. Facing backward, Dante's grotesquerie consists of elements that are real when taken singly but when combined produce the standard mixed feelings that define the grotesque, namely, the unnatural, the bizarre, the ridiculous, the sinister, etc.[2] Facing forward, Gracián's puppet-like figures are new to Spain's Golden Age and are harbingers of the automatons conceived by eighteenth-century Romanticists like Hoffmann. Furthermore, images such as "ojos de papel" and "coraçones... de corcho" are impure forms that no longer are metamorphic but presage Modernist inventions like the cardboard or wooden figures and other hybrids depicted by Solana and some Surrealists.

Gracián's bizarre plasticity is not an isolated event in his period. Although he evokes the *capricho* of the painter Bosch, who was active a century earlier, the same concept was executed contemporaneously in the *capricci* of Jacques Callot. His decision to evoke this term is significant in two respects. The deforming technique gains respect by renewing conventional allegory. And as an aesthetic preference the technique sustains a tradition that goes forward through the eighteenth century to Goya, and beyond.

The eighteenth century is the first that abounds in references to the grotesque, both as a theoretical issue and as a literary practice. Here can be found most of the traits that characterize grotesque literary art in general: metamorphosis, zoomorphism, dehumanization, "black" humor, absurdity. The most notable practitioner is Torres Villarroel, whose portraits evoke puppet theater as well as Golden Age *figurón* types and burlesque theater. His kinship to Gracián is visible in his visual power, and yet his art is closer to the *retablo* than to canvas painting.

It is difficult to give this period a defining adjective that is applicable

---

2 See "Grotesque Images in Dante's Inferno: the Problem of the Grotesque Overcome," by Ülar Ploom at website http://www.ameritalia.id.usb.ve/Amerialia.ooo.Ploom.htm

to the grotesque. The term "Rococo" is often used, as are "Neoclassical" and "Enlightenment." None of these is all-encompassing from the standpoint of literary periodization. In Spain, Goya's *capricho* approaches the grotesque without becoming commensurate with it. The inspiration behind Torres Villarroel's grotesque portraits is is not the *capricho* but the dream, which admittedly Goya also exploits. Torres does have Gracián as a precursor, but the latter admires the *capricho* and not the dream. Therefore the best approach to the eighteenth century is, first, to recognize that *capricho* has a diverse meaning and usage throughout, as the Glossary of Chapter 5 shows. Second, we should note that the term *grotesco* also has a broad and diverse conceptualization (Chapter 4). Finally, as an aesthetic practice, the grotesque advances in subtlety by its express link by Torres to the dream and the faculty of imagination (Chapter 3).

The *capricho* and the grotesque, strictly speaking, are independent categories, although the latter may result from the former. They converge in two respects, producing an aesthetic experience as well as involving the creative process. In regard to the aesthetic experience, if a composition causes surprise or unexpected wonder due to its disordered, ridiculous, haphazard, or chimerical features, it is called a *capricho* in eighteenth-century Spanish usage. Regarding the creative process, the term *grutesco* becomes associated by mid-century with the creative act. The reason is in part the eroding authority of Neoclassical treatise writers. So too *el capricho* (with the definite article) signifies a psychological mechanism associated with the imagination, and one that operates unsystematically, thereby producing a defective or grotesque result, depending on how this is judged.

This psychological definition of *el capricho* can be related to the role of imagination in Torres' grotesques. His uncontrolled *fantasía*, working within the dream-process, generates structures at odds with grace, logic, and proportion. The process itself is more relevant to the Romantic grotesque, discussed below, but the structures or images themselves confirm the century-long awareness of a new role for the grotesque. Spanish theorists like Mengs and Arteaga recognize a counter-principle to Beauty that accompanies conventional decorative grotesques. That is, any disconformity to the ideal of Beauty (with all this entails regarding perfection and harmony) risks slipping from ugliness and disproportion into incongruity (Chapter 4). The dictionaries of that period attest to this slippage. Thus *capricho* defined either as a creative power or as a product parallels the lexicographical evolution of the term *grotesco*, where semantic emphasis shifts from animalesque forms that are mimetic to constructions that are fantastic (capricious) or monstrous.

From the eighteenth to the nineteenth centuries there seems not to be any marked transition with respect to the grotesque. It is true that Cadalso's sharp satire seems to foreshadow Larra's sharper bite, but only the latter resorts to nightmarish perceptions. The function of dreams in Torres differs from that in Espronceda, as shown in a later section here. Other original techniques or inclinations, such as a Bacchic strain in Espronceda and a historicized distancing in Bécquer have no precedent.

The Spanish grotesque in the nineteenth century comes under the broad rubric of Romanticism.[3] What gives the grotesque its unique character is a seemingly uncontrolled creative process that governs a medley of themes. The frenzy, horror, hyperbole, and supernaturalism—to mention but a few fantastic elements—are released from the conventional restraints of lyricism and religion. In their place are disssonance, inverisimilitude, and other syncopations that show an irrational source or motive for the grotesque, one that precedes the deliberately rational aesthetic of the absurd in the twentieth century. The grotesque sensibility in nineteenth-century Spain represents a break with its Baroque predecessor and it is also a dead end that requires a new start for later writers.

The Romantic grotesque also adds a dark side to the traditions that precede it. The chapter on Bécquer brings this distinction into perhaps too radical a focus by the antithesis "benign-malignant" grotesque. Even so, the non-threatening details that inform a witch's bizarre posture or the contorted images of "delirios locos" represent Bécquer's harmless grotesquerie peopled by his "hijos extravagantes de mi imaginación." In contrast, the drunken terror of Espronceda's *estudiante* belongs to the same sinister mood of Goethe's Walpurgisnacht (Part One) and related Bacchic scenes.

Despite fantasy's preeminence, Spain's Romantic grotesque does

---

3 In the period of realism, several details in Clarín and a few more examples in Galdós comprise a minor key when compared to the three chapters in this book.

not abandon reality. Not only does Larra dwell chiefly on political and social problems, but Bécquer manifests a keen eye for everyday life, not to mention Spain's history and architecture. At play is the role of imagination, and here the divergent faculties of Bécquer and Espronceda are pertinent. In Bécquer, aesthetic historicism attenuates his subjective sensibility, while in Espronceda it is psychological experience that inspires his lyric. Bécquer's creative mechanism regarding the grotesque is the observation of the historical past, while in Espronceda it is purely epistemological. For the one, a nearly prosaic aesthetic history drives his perception of the grotesque; for the other, a "loca falaz fantasía" distorts his perception. The distinct orientations are combined in Larra, whose fragile psychology subverts his grounding in social reality.

The preceding account indicates that the characteristic grotesque for this period resists an encompassing uniformity, despite important opinions. According to Bakhtin's theory, the most prominent part of the Romantic grotesque is the carnival; the idea of "le grotesque au revers du sublime" is Hugo's major emphasis; and for Baudelaire the "comique grotesque absolu" and Goya's *caprichos* are the dominant features. None of these is commensurate with the Romantic grotesque, nor collectively do they apply substantially to Spain.

The fullest embodiment of Romanticism is arguably Larra, a suicide at age 27. Politically engaged and Byronically mordant, certain of his satirical narratives veer off into a presciently Modernist grotesque. It is equally arguable, on the other hand, that Espronceda is the most complete example of the Romantic grotesque because he incorporates major components of broader European literature. Themes such as Bacchic revelry, macabre inversion, bizarre necrophilia, oneiric mutation, and terrifying hallucinatory cacophony run the gamut of a dark grotesque (Chaper 7). And yet Bécquer cannot be excluded as a Romantic prototype despite his late arrival. Not only does the carnival capture his attention (while not exemplifying the malevolent world cited by Bakhtin), but the "monstrous marriage" of insomnia to imagination triggers his inspiration of the texts examined in Chapter 8. In the end, however, Bécquer's detachment from motifs like Harlequin and dolls anticipates the post-Romantic disillusion. Straddling the transition between Romantic and Modernist grotesques, his mixed moods are a tenuous anchor to the liberating fantasy of pure Romantic grotesquerie.

In the twentieth century, Spain's Modernist grotesque embraces both an earlier post-Romantic sensibility and the Surrealism that emerges from it. This means that an altered subjectivism has combined with a new artistic iconoclasm. Backward-facing examples among the Modernists include Machado's self-ridiculing alienation, which evokes the milder soul-state of Bécquer's *hastío* and disquietude; Solana's uncanny mannequins, which reflect a pathology meriting the sobriquet "necromaniac Goya"; and Valle-Inclán's penchant for the supernatural and the dream format, which are significant vestiges of Romanticism. Forward-facing examples are Valle-Inclán's chimerical rhythms that foreshadow Surrealist dissociations like automatic writing; Solana's mannequins that approach the more contrived figures of Chirico; and Machado's ambivalence toward Romantic sentiment that becomes the soul-less Surrealist methods of critical paranoia and bizarre landscaping.

The three chapters about these authors hinge on one common pivot, that of dehumanization. The complex nature of dehumanization as a grotesque is described in a separate section below. The immediate point is that it comes to gestate within a spiritual or other subjective malaise. Whether it is Machado's ridicule of his mirror image, or Solana's strange pathos for lifeless figures, or Valle-Inclán's farcical sentimentalism, the unifying result is a break with previous norms governing the extreme limits of credible human perception and feeling. Spanish Modernism, as represented by these authors, stylizes with irony not only Romanticism's tortured lyricism but its oneiric and fantasy worlds as well.

And yet this shared technique of dehumanization is not the key to the Modernist grotesque in Spain. Rather, it is logic of the absurd. The themes and methods of these authors again may not be identical, but the same bizarre coherence exists throughout, an objectively undeniable incongruity that makes artistic sense because the component parts are rationally and not chaotically assembled. Absurdity is a concept that belongs to a larger group of philosophical issues in the grotesque that is discussed in a separate section below. What is relevant here is how the methods of dehumanization—zoomorphism, *esperpento*, puppeteering, character burlesque—obey the imperative to represent the world absurdly. It is because the lyrical self is in crisis that Machado projects himself as an "histrión grotesco." It is because the real and the unreal often blur their boundaries that Solana juxtaposes automatons and living persons. And it is because Spain is a deformed version of Europe in the eyes of Valle-Inclán that he resorts to reductive, parodic portrayals. In sum, Spain's Modernist grotesque tends toward a certain homogeneity insofar as its key principle is deliberate absurdity and its technical strategies are self-conscious, anti-Romantic, and distortive.

II *Aesthetics of the Grotesque*

The concept of a "grotesque aesthetics" in this book has meant a technique of conscious distortion aimed at creating incongruity. This definition does not reject implications that are nontextual, such as reader psychology. However the "aesthetic experience" has not been investigated per se because it entails, as implicated by Kayser and Clayborough, reader-response questions about what is uncanny or ridiculous or strange or bizarre. These subjective and relativist terms involve viewer feelings as much as textual phenomena. Insofar as a phenomenology of distortion is demonstrable textually, this book has used those terms when dealing with incongruity, deformation, ambiguity, and unnatural contradiction. These conditions and techniques are discussed in the sections that follow. Of course, much depends on reader perception in some sense but, as far as possible, this book uses "uncanny" and the like with only slight reference to the reader's sense of discomfort or discrepancy.

The aesthetics of the Spanish grotesque are not limited to the text's internal referentiality. They also include a realistic indicator that points to an external context. This indicator is a sociopolitical referent, usually accompanied by an authorial voice. Here the plastic aspect of an incongruous image does not function for its own sake within the literary framework. Instead, it depicts a real aspect of Spanish society, however transformed by artistic illusion. Similarly, stylistic or rhetorical flourishes represent Spain as a historically identifiable reality. These social and historicist contexts are represented either as objectively grotesque or as products of a subjective narrative voice. They depend on distortive literary devices and raise philosophical questions that underpin the genesis of the grotesque. All these characteristics are analyzed in the sections that follow.

II.a Incongruity

The most consensually agreed on feature of the grotesque is its strangeness or incongruity. Yet this feature becomes too vague when its components are separated. One component is the reader's sense of uncanniness. This is a psychological reaction, but it is superfluous when textual narrators themselves assert the experience in their own terms. When Larra describes his insomnia or nightmare, this suffices for the reader passively to grasp the disjointed state of Spanish society. So too in other instances: Espronceda's unbridled imagination that deranges perceived reality, Machado's disoriented sense of selfhood, and Valle-Inclán's dehumanizing revision of cultural categories—all are expressions of an uneasy, misfitted awareness quite independent of the reader. This uncanniness, moreover, need not be textually subjective in order to reflect incongruity. As seen in the pastoral grotesque, the novelist impersonally disrupts harmonious Nature by a discordant design or a supernatural being. Similarly, Gracián and Torres Villarroel bestialize their personages as tokens of moral discord, while Solana automatizes human life in a gratuitous (or stylized) gesture of rendering reality disquieting. The uncanniness in all instances resides in the unexpected reordering of formerly stable categories.

A second component of incongruity is the sense of alienation. Again, while the reader's experience is important, objective analysis should focus on textual evidence. Some representative examples are: Espronceda's assault on structured normalcy places him, among many devices, within a maelstrom and a dizzying delirium; Larra's metaphorical nightmare expresses his own misplaced orientation; Machado uses the labyrinth as a metaphor of his brief identity crisis; and Solana mounts a mannequin exhibit to project his paranoid fears.

A third component of incongruity is the distortion imposed upon the image. The techniques are many. The mildest one occurs in the pastoral grotesque, where the Renaissance harmonious whole sustains a monstrous element without penalty. More weighty are the Baroque caricatures of moral deviance by which Gracián achieves a twice-removed perversion. A hyperbolic version of Gracián's warped *personetes* are Torres Villarroel's portraits, where language itself is violated in pursuit of his zoomorphic purpose. Later, the magic lantern and distancing lens of Larra disfigure his social environment, just as the force of the *estudiante*'s deranged imagination in Espronceda and the aberrant form of Spain's carnival described by Bécquer expose their respective distended realities.

Distortion is itself a nuanced feature of the grotesque. The reason that the Spanish grotesque is so important within Europe's concert of discords is that it clarifies the distinction between transfiguration and disfiguration. Whereas writers routinely transform reality using degrees of transfiguring tropes, they have disfigured it in the Modernist age with deliberate consistency, as the Surrealist movement suggests. Before that, the Romanticists from Hoffmann to Espronceda created occasional illusionist and bizarre situations just off the edge of normalcy. However Bécquer, a Romantic as well, turned the carnival motif back to reality by noting its uniquely Spanish aspect of squalor, an aspect that foreshadowed the Modernist grotesque forms apparent in Solana and Valle-Inclán.

In sum, incongruity is a multistrand factor in the grotesque that privileges the uncanny by means of deformation and alienation. This effect can be enhanced by the supernatural, as shown in Espronceda. However, not everything supernatural is grotesque, the fairy tale being an example. Abnormal forms and situations escape the grotesque category, especially when metamorphosis is involved. The metamorphic process has an inner coherence in writers like Ovid, whose personages move from one pure form to another like Narcissus. The grotesque entails a deliberate misproportion. But here again a difference arises between, say, Valle-Inclán's deformations that are implausible, and the distortions of a Naturalist like Zola, whose "grotesques" tend more toward realism because the reader can follow a coherent set of rules.[4] In contrast, the deformation that Bécquer describes can at times exhibit an impurity of form marked by ambiguous or hybrid shapes.

II.b DEHUMANIZATION AND DEFORMATION

Despite the emphasis on dehumanization when discussing the Modernist grotesque, it is a constant throughout Spain's literary history. Even the pastoral convention of a sculpted savage on a fountain promotes the grotesque because, perversely, its sentimental message is humanizing. More richly dehumanizing is the role played by the *persona-títere* characters in the Baroque grotesque. From Gracián to Torres Villarroel, the procession of sub-human citizens earns ridicule for debasing the reigning value system. Their unresolved nature, neither en-

---

4 See D. Baguley, "Le réalisme grotesque et mythique de " La Terre " in Pour le centenaire de 'La Terre'. *Les Cahiers naturalistes*, 33 (1987), num. 61, 5-14

tirely normal nor fully inhuman, prompts images of contradictory parts reconciled by an unnatural harmony, what Gracián called an "estraña contrariedad." In its extreme form, dehumanization appears through mechanization, as when Solana and Valle-Inclán reduce their subjects to mannequins and puppet-like postures. These Modernist images have a plastic quality that distinguishes them from their more verbally abstract Baroque counterparts.

The techniques employed to dehumanize are both imagistic and stylistic. Bestial images are the most direct tactic, where a person's physical attribute suffers a metamorphic exchange. I give this method the general term "zoomorphism." For example, the coinage "serpihombre" allows Gracián an immediately graphic transformation. Similarly, a torso with "la sangre agua, sin color ni calor, el pecho de cera, no ya de azero" offers sensory allusions that shift feeling away from the living person. The technique extends to spatial disfiguring, such as a twist or a lurch, allowing the idea of monstrosity to animate the grotesque image. The monstrous and the bestial are combined by Valle-Inclán in one character whose gargoyle-like face is indeterminately a dog, a cat, and a wolf. In his later work, facial animalizations are commonplace. Most of the foregoing images are sensorial without depending on color.

A colorist approach appears in the Romantic and Modernist dehumanzations. Bécquer's masquerade, which twists its way alongside a "figura grotesca," seems like " una serpiente monstruosa de abigarrados colores." Although Espronceda is more noted for his acoustical distortions and dynamic spatial turbulence, his achromatic fantasmagoria are pointedly called "visiones fosfóricas." Machado's palette deforms his all-too-human heartache by using metonymic evocations that range from "quimeras rosadas" and "luna de hojalata" to "El lienzo de Oriente / sangraba tragedias, / pintarrajeadas / con nubes grotescas" (XLVII). Since Solana is a painter, his writings unsurprising also use chromatic detail. His dehumanizing vision is linked to paranoid fantasy, as in the nightmare in which yellow- and black-clad civil guards menace him in an impersonal city where "[s]obre un cielo de color de plomo vi la silueta férrea de este pueblo."

Dehumanization of course relies on deformation. However deformation is the larger category. Deformation is best defined as a selective magnification or diminution. This concept rests on a philosophy and a device, both to be discussed in separate sections. The device is some instrument of perception that distorts the human condition, like Larra's magic lantern. The philosophy is the philosophy of art, whereby reality's reflection no longer appears in the flat mirror of mimesis, but rather in a curved mirror. That is, a grotesque made by selectively violating verisimilitude.

The role of style for its own sake can also generate grotesque effects. The foundations of Torres Villarroel's grotesque are convoluted popular speech and metaphors that expand monstrously. Valle-Inclán's static characters are mummified by repetitive epithets like "careta" and "mueca." Other stylistic tactics include the Baroque use of nominalist catalogs that compile animal attributes. Such verbal excess lends the grotesque an abstract power. Carried to an absurd extreme by Torres Villarroel, a gigantic head loses its human trait when seen as "a pleonasm of a head." Such observations deviate from humanistic observation and focus attention on the verbal art itself. Thus, whether an inanimate object is named and grafted onto a human body as in Gracián, or an automaton stands as a metaphor for a person as in Solana, the mechanics of style in these grotesques occupy the foreground. In less harsh dehumanizations, Machado uses symbols like a bufoon or a disoriented spectre in order to dramatize his imagined loss of personality. These instances, while also imagistic, rely on narratorial style and situational distortion.

Another deformative kind of linguistic influence is the way the word *grotesco* evolves semantically over the centuries. Changes in nuance increase allusive power, so that the word no longer is limited to invoking misshapen figures but also modifies temporal rhythms and space itself.[5] Finally, the association of *grotesco* with *capricho* and *fantasía* after the eighteenth century broadens the concept of subverted representation. In other words, new erratic and fantastic tactics deform the object in addition to the traditional mimetic distortions.

The Cultural Substratum of the Grotesque

Underlying the Spanish grotesque is an exaggerated vision of the culture's social, historical, or political condition. The Baroque's view of morally wayward Spaniards diminishes their humanity beyond conven-

---

5 Valle-Inclán uses the word *grotesco* more than any other writer, as in "ritmo quimérico y grotesco." But note also Espronceda's "danzas grotescas," Bécquer's "evoluciones grotescas," and Machado's "nubes grotescas."

tional satire. Gracián's observation that "las bestias hazen del hombre y los hombres hazen la bestia" is the principle that justifies the zoomorphism that carries social criticism into the grotesque realm. Similarly, when Torres Villarroel identifies a citizen as "[un] hombre con raza de mico" he reveals his premise of a degenerate subculture that justifies his barrage of imagistic aberrations. His portraits seldom offer social insight in themselves, but their referential range—disease, gluttony, intemperance, bodily functions—when treated grotesquely implies a dysfunctional body politic. Whereas Gracián's misguided populace is generalized in terms of class structure, that of Torres appears limited to the banal proletariat whose fetid vitality bodes ill for the "rational republic" above it.

The Romantic grotesque as represented by Larra differs from its Baroque predecessor insofar as his framework is the middle class. Whether he magnifies the ill-bred manners of his countrymen or warps their political conflicts into a macabre nightmare, the verdict is that their bourgeois liberalism is a grotesque failure. Beyond the social sphere, Larra's self-laceration, changes of pseudonym, and symbolic suicide together implicate him in the same grotesque. His satire steps beyond caricature by revealing psychobiographical fault lines: his heteronymic compulsions, his incongruous, role-playing disguises, and his insomnia. These conditions underlie his creative power, so that his images are not as blatantly deformed as in the Baroque or Modernist grotesques, only moderated by his vaunted monocle. As Thomas Mann said, "the grotesque is the genuine anti-bourgeois style"[6]

A different aspect of the Romantic grotesque appears in Bécquer's use of imagination in the service of social history. His realistic writings, like his *leyendas*, show interest in the grotesque, a fact that bears upon its later evolution to Modernism. That is, Modernist artists and writers like Solana and Valle-Inclán take realism as the material for grotesquerie, unlike the Romantics. Except for Bécquer, who recognizes that Spain's cultural reality—its Medieval architecture, it carnival traditions—displays grotesque forms that forecast those of the Modernists. Bécquer is a bifrontal Romantic who can indulge in "those faint and nervous reveries" while also pondering the hopes for social progress in

---

6 Thomas Mann, *Past Masters and Other Papers*, trans. H. T. Lowe-Porter (Freeport, N.Y.: Books for Libraries Press, 1968), pp. 240-41.]

a positivistic Spain. In these writings he does not create grotesque images; he contemplates them in the capricious and fantastic forms of aged cathedrals. In their extravagant forms he sees a symbolic language, created by human imagination, that holds cosmic communion with modern artifacts like the locomotive, created by comparable genius. The "secret relationship" between them is the key to history's unifying force. Bécquer's grotesque mingles Romantic and realist orientations that anticipates the Modernist's rational manipulation of the grotesque. After the recognition that the imagination has a grotesque potential, the next phase is a belief in an aesthetics of incongruity, complete with a logic of the absurd.

This aesthetics and logic are fulfilled by Solana and Valle-Inclán. But a transitional phase intervenes: the post-Romantic grotesque of Machado. Here are Larra's scenes of civil conflict re-imaged metaphorically by Spain's reenactment of the Cain-Abel myth. But instead of Larra's sardonic laughter, Machado remains sober before the nation's socio-moral failure.[7] He casts bleak shades over the Castilian plains that recall Goya's black paintings, a landscape at times marred by stunted figures from *la España negra*, a favorite theme of Solana.

In the purely Modernist grotesque represented by Solana and Valle-Inclán, Spain's social reality undergoes considerable deformation. The purpose in Solana's case is primarily aesthetic, whereas it is mainly historical for Valle-Inclán. The beggars, sick children, and old people whom Solana dehumanizes lose any social-class significance that they might otherwise embody; it is rather their stark plasticity as verbal icons that causes their aesthetic appeal to dominate. Nevertheless, their decrepitude is the subject matter, its very existence made palpable to the reader despite the writer's emotional distance. Without didactic commentary, Solana intensifies his somber conception of Spain by undermining its human pathos with mechanical or artificial attributes. Surpassing the ridiculous disharmony of mannequins portrayed as living persons, he describes a one-legged vendor of artificial limbs who

---

7 Where Machado does laugh, he reacts in self-mockery to his personal anxiety as a poet. His laughter differs from Romantic theorists like Nietzsche, for whom the comic mode liberates the artist from the nausea induced by the absurdity that defines reality's essence. It also differs from Baudelaire's Satanic laughter, belonging to the "absolute comic" that defines the grotesque.

speaks like an automaton to his unnerved audience. This conversion of economic misery into spectacle, or the cheap amusements like the wax museum and the tawdry carnival, require a grotesque treatment in order to avoid social realism while preserving social consciousness. Similarly, the dingy clothes shop window displaying a lifeless model speaks for itself as the icon of implicit commercialism. All such instances exploit *la realidad inquietante*, a concept anchored in subjective perceptions but dependent for its material on Spain's historically obective history of popular class hardship.

The cultural insight brought by Valle-Inclán is summarized by his maxim that Spain is a deformation of Europe. Her historical defect is expressed in the verses "Francia proyecta sobre España / las grandes narices borbónicas." As a member of the Generation of 1898, which agonized over the nation's backwardness with respect to nations like France, Valle-Inclán cultivates an aesthetic of the concave mirror. This instrument permits him to reflect both the irrational masses and the decadent aristocracy, the poles between which the middle class fails to harmonize Spain with Europe. Thus the "pueblo" submits to an extreme realism whose ugly portrait borders on deformation. And aristocratic personages are stylized by harlequinades and Versaillesque parodies, thus vulgarizing the ideal of elegance. The repertoire of grotesque techniques is called the *esperpento*, a histrionic fusion of dark comedy, dehumanized portraiture, and bufo-tragic incongruity. Far from Romantic sensibilities, Valle-Inclán's grotesque lacks Larra's personal anguish and Bécquer's sanguine composure. From the "ritmo quimérico y grotesco" of his early work to *Tirano Banderas* and the *comedias bárbaras*, his puppeteering dramatization of Spain's social strata reveals a versatile logician of the absurd.

Epistemology of the Grotesque

Behind the defining features of the Spanish grotesque—its cultural vision, devices, and unique traits—there is the perceptual activity that generates them all. This perceptual process can be the writer's overt psychological condition. It can also be the mechanisms of perception itself, or the metaphors that enable the perceived results. Any of these processes is epistemological in the original sense of offering a vision of reality that is accounted for by a subject-object relationship. Such an epistemology of the grotesque does not appear meaningfully until the Romantic period. Prior to that, Golden Age and Neoclassical grotesques are limited to stylistic, axiological, and preceptist approaches. Gracián has little interest in commenting on the nature of reality, only on its moral dimension, although ultimately his grotesque depends on a cosmology of discord within concord. Similarly, the grotesque portraits of Torres Villarroel are elaborately rhetorical social portraits, with the one exception mentioned below. Nor are the eighteenth-century semantics of the grotesque and the *capricho* anything more than a conceptual effort to define their nuances.

In contrast, the nature of reality, or more precisely the nature of grotesque reality, emerges clearly in Larra's nightmare and in Espronceda's mad imagination. So too in the Modernist period, Machado's fragmented persona, Solana's contrived paranoia, and Valle-Inclán's impersonal concave mirror each produce grotesque realities whose origins are clearly perceptual as distinct from causes like style, situation, or intentional incongruity. Generally speaking, the subject-object relationship is a binomial in which the causal component is as deviant as its grotesque product. The subject may be deluded (Espronceda's *estudiante*), or may suffer from delirium (Valle-Inclán's Bencarlés), or may be victimized by supernatural forces (Torres Villarroel), or may suffer from nightmare (Larra), and so forth. The perceptual process is distorted, and so is the result. The same grotesque results issue from the instruments of perception such as the magic lantern, the monocle, and the curved mirror.

In sum, the perceptual process is of two kinds. In psychological mediation, the subject is not necessarily responsible for initiating the grotesque. In grotesque optics, the subject takes a surrogate by selecting a deforming instrument. The first case includes Larra, who is constitutionally prone to nightmare, and Machado, whose psychic makeup creates his self-image as a *histrión grotesco*. The second case includes Larra's monocle, chosen to distort a politics that he judges to be deformed, and Valle-Inclán's concave mirror, chosen for his belief in Spain's warped version of Europe.

Another perceptual category seems to be psychic but actually is mediative. The dream experienced by Torres Villarroel occurs through an incubus that mates with his imagination. Similarly, the imagination of Espronceda's *estudiante* perceives reality as a delirious series of mutations. Finally, there is Solana's paranoid dream, which this book has treated as psychologically authentic. However, it may also be interpreted as a contrived device to produce the same *realidad inquietante* that he creates in the waking scenes by means of stylistic strategies. Regardless of the type of dream, it exposes a fundamental ambiguity in the grotesque aesthetic. The subject-object dynamic provides no single authority that entirely governs the literary material. Often the interaction between the human source of creativity and its subversive instruments is a discordant one.

All representations made through overt perceptual references offer an abnormal apprehension of the world. At work is a calculus of the absurd intended to eliminate congruence with increasing rationality, beginning with the Romantic nascent dream-grotesque. Here, Espronceda's *estudiante* finds his surroundings to be epistemologically uncertain because his bewitchment gives him contradictory information. In the next generation, Bécquer declares that " El insomnio y la fantasía siguen y siguen procreando en monstruoso maridaje. ¡Sus creaciones… pugnan por dilatar su fantástica existencia…!" Still later, the post-Romantic Machado systematically removes normal elements in certain social scenes, leaving aberration stripped of context. His eye focuses like a close-up camera lens, which betrays the preference in his famous remark that every poet has two muses, the ethical and the pathological. Machado's handful of crisis poems illustrate a crucial transition in turn-of-century sensibilities as they tend toward Surrealist modes of representation. He stages his memories and fears like a puppet-master whose figurines presage Surrealism's fully contorted features. His dehumanized reality is less reductive, and he projects the ego first as a shadow on a barren plain, then as a spectre lost in a labyrinth of mirrors. These visions are precursors of the Modernist nightmare; they are at the same time rooted in post-Romantic and Symbolist introspection.

In producing the grotesque, Modernism's method of deliberate absurdity differs from Romanticism's random perceptions of incongruity. The difference lies in how the subject-object relationship functions. Valle-Inclán renders the object (i.e., tableaux and narrations) grotesque by replacing the subject with a style that depends on photographic selectivity. Even Bradomín's oneiric "ritmo funambulesco" is replaced in subsequent works by external actions, as in Benicarlés' hallucination. In contrast, Espronceda's dizzying representation is entirely subjective. The subject does not perform willful deformations in the manner of Larra's monocle. Instead, the subject is enmeshed in the object's field of events. Romantic subjectivity, by definition, is caught up with the object—for instance, in the pathetic fallacy. Such engagement projects a grotesque product when the subject itself is perceptually distortive, as in a delirium. The reality is in epistemological doubt, whereas the Modernist reality is objectively grotesque by virtue of an "absent" subject.

Philosophy of the Grotesque

Can we speak of a philosophy of the grotesque? The answer is, yes if we can also speak, as we do, of a philosophy of an epoch or of a period. It is certainly accurate to identify the reigning system of the Spanish Baroque as Christian Idealism, whether this involves religiously grounded ethical principles or faith in the Divine concordance of "la sabia naturaleza." The Baroque grotesque reflects these ideas in reverse. Gracián's characters violate the standards of a thought system based upon harmony. Their actions contradict religious morality, just as their faces and bodies contradict the harmony of ideal Beauty. But this contradiction is not made gratuitously for the sake of grotesque artistic techniques. The Baroque grotesque illustrates a philosophy that must be understood didactically. Where perverse conduct is depicted, it signifies a transvaluation of Christian values. Where physical monstrosity is an allegory for moral vice, it signifies the rectitude of absolutist virtue. Deceit and vanity require disfigured human shapes in confirmation of the judgment that ideal Beauty is unblemished.

Romantic philosophy also exhibits absolutist values by its fatalism and supernaturalism, although its subjectivism gives it more lattitude. Espronceda depicts a world held captive by fantastic powers; he is bereft of the historical insight that tempers Bécquer's often "imaginación ardiente." Larra shares both Espronceda's impotence and Bécquer's occacional reasoned understanding. Reality offers all three authors different but entirely Romantic principles for living and writing. Removed from the Baroque's universals, they engage with their social contexts either by succumbing to their irrational faculties or by understanding those contexts satirically and historically. Their grotesques consequently do not signify the converse of the Ideal, as in the Baroque, but rather the negation of a reality that they believe has betrayed its philosophical idealism (e.g., social harmony, truth, beauty). Their grotesques are philosophical rages against loss or unfulfillment.

The philosophy of the Modernist age emerges in a series of linked reactions that follow in quasi cause-and-effect fashion. It originates in the individual's disaffection from society's prevailing values. This alienation unanchors the self from reality, fostering a psychological disorientation that casts doubt on the subject's own identity. Concurrently, the subject's critical detachment enables a strangely impersonal assessment of reality's underpinnings: time, space, matter, and consciousness extending to the human element. In short, a circumstance of perceived absurdity demands new forms of action and representation. The solution appears with the Modernist philosophy par excellence, Existentialism, which engages purposefully in the world under the maxim that if reality is absurd one must live that absurdity with dignity. The aesthetic solution to the problem is just the opposite, at least in the Dadaist and Surrealist movements, and of course in the Spanish texts studied in this book.

The above-mentioned linked reactions may be identified with particular Modernists. The psychological crisis is reflected in Machado. The question of what reality entails is reflected in Solana. And the problem of time and representation is reflected in Valle-Inclán. Together, their grotesques reveal a cohesive relationship. And together, they set up the philosophical framework of Modernism.

Machado reflects upon his own death and calls his skull a carnival mask. His self-alienating act does two things: it mocks death as absurd, and its dehumanizing image foreshadows the bufo-tragic masks of Valle-Inclán. Solana instills motor and volitional responses into his rigid mannequins. His pathos-filled vision of life seems closer to Machado than to Valle-Inclán. However he also projects that pathos upon wax figures and automatons, thereby inviting absurdity like Valle-Inclán. Both Solana and Valle-Inclán petrify motion, resulting in a statuesque pose that devitalizes the living moment. Their humanized mechanisms and dehumanized people declare the meaninglessness of existence.

All three Modernists betray a similar cultural philosophy in their grotesque texts. Machado's distortion of the Spanish popular class draws upon Goya's "black Spain." The stunted underclass living in economic squalor becomes a theme of Solana's sketchbook *La España negra*. Valle-Inclán invents the *esperpento*, an aesthetic form depicting the nation's alleged deformity, but only after discarding an earlier nostalgia for Spain's decadent traditionalism. The aesthetic progression among these authors parallels the philosophical underpinnings. Machado's existentialist realism, tinged with grotesquerie, signals a lost identity thrown upon an autonomous cultural landscape. Solana's paranoid hyper-realism signals a hermetic separation between the subject's feelings and its objectified social context.

As Modernist representations broaden their range of incongruity and dehumanization, the idea of Spain as a living entity appears proportionally diminished. The relation between philosophy and aesthetics becomes increasingly interdependent. Because Spanish reality is believed to be beyond the efforts of the existentialist subject, the aesthetic response is a grotesque rendered with rational, disfiguring absurdity. This, of course, is a counter-rational strategy.

Conclusion

Is there an overarching philosophical idea that characterizes the Spanish grotesque in general? Perhaps it is the idea that metamorphosis is a metaphor for rational disintegration. There is a gradual change in thinking as to the natural and moral worlds: from their objective equilibrium to their subjective disorientation to, finally, their relativist rational absurdity. Parallel changes affect the grotesque after its Spanish practitioners react to their milieu. The boundless human capacity for *capricho* amazes Gracián, spurring him to a more eccentric creative censure. Larra is depressed into macabre and nightmarish musings by the destructive fissures in civic life. And the impersonal artifacts of late industrial society free Solana from logically distinguishing between human life and its simulacra.

This philosophical sequence transforms the grotesque from its original Classical "innocence"—in which its monsters and fantastic arabesques signify nothing beyond their decorative role—into successive forms of allegorical or conceptual meaning. The grotesque of the Baroque protests against the threat of moral subversion; that of Romanticism responds to the loss of historical and personal stability; that of Modernism moves from self-destructive imagery to objectified, calculated deformation. Incongruity and dehumanization are constants from beginning to end, but each new stage finds them further intensified by images that are increasingly unreal, arbitrary, ironic, and harsh.

This transformation by stages is indeed a metamorphosis. It is also a metaphor for rational disintegration because the phases of Idealism's eclipse are clear. The eclipse begins with the Baroque dichotomy of concord (Gracián's moral reason) and discord (his grotesque). The Neoclassical norm that follows upholds rational Beauty, while deviant judgments like *extravagancia* and *monstruo* are discuss by eighteenth-century preceptists. Romanticism as represented by Bécquer is a transition: it faces forward to early Modernist irrationality while embracing traditional grotesques and carnivals. The transition is completed with Machado's alienation, which also anticipates Solana's paranoid detachment. The final breakdown of reason's traditional role is visible in the depersonalized imagery of Valle-Inclán. In all these phases, the grotesque is the vehicle that concretizes Spain's changing status of rationality. Seen as an evolving constant through the centuries, the grotesque's ongoing metamorphosis is a fitting mirror of the philosophical changes that it accompanies.

Bibliography

(El) Censor (1781-1787), ed. E. García Pandavenes. Barcelona: Labor, 1972.
Diccionario castellano. Madrid: Impr. de la viuda de Ibarra, hijos y compañía, 1787.
Diccionario de de la lengua castellana (Autoridades). Madrid, 1734.
Diccionario de la lengua castellana. Madrid, 1791.
Adams, Nicholson B. "The Grotesque in Some Important Spanish Romantic Plays," *Todd Memorial Volumes.* New York: Columbia Univ., 1930, I, 37-46.
Aguilera, Emiliano M. *José Gutiérrez Solana: Aspectos de su vida, su obra y su arte.* Barcelona, 1947.
Albornoz, Aurora de. "Bibliografía de Antonio Machado." *La Torre*, XII (January-June 1964), 505-53.
Alonso, C. "Larra y Espronceda: Dos liberales impacientes." *Literatura y poder. España 1834-1868.* Madrid: Editor Alberto Corazón, 1971, pp. 15-55.
Amiel, Henri-Frédéric. *Journal intime* - 10 Février 1846.
Aranaz y Vives, Pedro. *Reglas generales para que una composición de música sea perfecta.* 1780.
Arce y Cacho, Celedonio N. *Conversaciones sobre la escultura.* Pamplona, 1786.
Arce Solórzano, Juan. *Tragedias de amor* [1604]. Madrid, 1607.
Arroyal, León de. *Cartas economicopolitícas*, ed. J. Caso González. Oviedo: Universidad de Oviedo, 1971.
Arteaga, Esteban de. *La belleza ideal*, ed. A. Batllori. Madrid: Espasa-Calpe, 1955.
Avalle-Arce, Juan Bautista. *La novela pastoril española.* Madrid, 1959.
Baguley, D. "Le réalisme grotesque et mythique de " La Terre " in Pour le centenaire de 'La Terre'. *Les Cahiers naturalistes*, 3(1987), num. 61, 5-14.
Bails, Benito. *Arquitectura civil.* Madrid, 1783.
Bakhtin, Mikhail. *Rabelais and His World.* Bloomington, IN: Indiana Univ. Press, 1984.
Balbuena, Bernardo de. *Siglo de oro en las selvas de Erifile* [1608]. Madrid, 1821.
Barasch, Frances K. "Definitions: Renaissance and Baroque, Grotesque Construction and Deconstruction." *Modern Language Studies*, Vol. 13, No. 2 (Spring, 1983), pp. 60-67.
―――― . *The Grotesque: A Study of Meanings.* The Hague: Mouton, 1971.
Baudelaire, Charles. "De l'essence du rire." *Œuvres complètes*, ed. Y-G Le Dantec et Claude Pichois. Tours: Bibliotheque de la Pléiade, 1961.
Bécquer, Gustavo Adolfo. *Obras completas.* Madrid: Aguilar, 1954.

Bosarte, Isidro. *Observaciones sobre las bellas artes.* Madrid, 1790.
Bostetter, Edward. "The Nightmare World of 'The Ancient Mariner'." *Studies in Romanticism,* I (1962), 241-254.
Botello, Francisco. *Historia de las cuevas de Salamanca.* Salamanca: A. Villargordo, 1741.
Cadalso, José. *Noches lúgubres,* ed. N. Glendinning. Madrid: Espasa-Calpe, 1961.
——— . *Cartas marruecas,* ed. L. Dupuis and N. Glendinning. London: Tamesis, 1966.
Calderón Altamirano, *Opúsculos de oro, virtudes morales cristianas.* Madrid, 1707.
Camón Aznar, José. "El monstruo en Gracián y en Goya." *Homenaje a Gracián.* Zaragoza, 1958, pp. 57-63.
Cano, José Luis. "Machado y la generación poética del '25." *La Torre,* XII (January-June 1964), 483-504.
Capmany, Antonio de. *Filosofía de la elocuencia.* Madrid, 1777.
Casalduero, Joaquín. *Forma y visión de "El diablo mundo."* Madrid: Insula, 1951.
——— . *Espronceda.* Madrid: Editorial Gredos, 1961.
Castro, Francisco de. *Alegría cómica.* 3 vols. Zaragoza, 1702.
Cela, Camilo José. *La obra literaria del pintor* Solana. Madrid, 1957.
Cernuda, Luis. "A Larra con unas violetas." *La realidad y el deseo* (1924-1962). México: Tezontle, 1964, p. 142.
Cervantes, Miguel de. *La Galatea* [1585], ed. Schevill y Bonilla. Madrid, 1914.
Clark, John R. *The Modern Satiric Grotesque and Its Traditions.* Lexington: Univ. Kentucky Press, 1991.
Clayborough, Arthur. *The Grotesque in English Literature.* Oxford: Clarendon Press, 1965.
Corral, Gabriel de. *La Cintia de Aranjuez* [1629], ed. J. de Entrambasaguas. Madrid, 1945.
Correa Calderón, Gustavo. *Baltasar Gracián: Su vida y su obra.* Madrid, 1961.
Covarrubias Orozco, Sebastián de. *Tesoro de la lengua castellana.* Madrid: Luis Sánchez, 1611.
Espina, Antonio. "Solana." *España,* no. 288 (November 6, 1920), 8-9; "S., La Gaceta Literaria (November 15, 1927), p, 5; "J. G. S.: Dos pueblos de Castilla," *Revista de Occidente,* X (October-December 1925), 261-63; "Cuadros de S.," *Revista de Occidente,* XVIII (October-December 1927), 269-72.
Espronceda, José. *Obras completas,* ed. Jorge Campos. Madrid: Ediciones Atlas, 1954.
——— . *El estudiante de Salamanca,* ed. Benito Varela Jacome. Salamanca: Anaya, 1966.
——— . *El diablo mundo,* ed. J. Moreno Villa. Madrid: Espasa-Calpe, 1955.
Eximeno, Antonio. *Del origen y reglas de la música.* Madrid, 1796.
Feijoo, Benito Jerónimo. *Obras escogidas,* I. Madrid (BAE, Vol. 56), 1952.

Fernández de Moratín, Leandro. *Obras póstumas*. Madrid, 1867.
Flint, W. "Wax Figures and Mannequins in Solana." *Hispania*, XLVI *(1963)*, 740-47.
Forner, Juan Pablo. *Los gramáticos*, ed. J. Jurado. Madrid, 1970.
Foster, Ludmila. 1966 "The Grotesque: A Method of Analysis." *Zagadnienia rodzajow literackich* IX (1)1966, 75-81.
——. "A Configuration of the Non-Absolute: The Structure and the Nature of the Grotesque." *Zagadnienia rodzajow literackich* IX(2) 1967, 38-45.
Friedrich, Hugo. *Die Struktur der Modern Lyric*. Hamburg, 1956.
García Pascual, Raquel. *Formas e imágenes grotescas en el teatro español contemporáneo*. Madrid: Fundación Universitaria Española, 2006.
Gómez de la Serna, Ramón. *José Gutiérrez Solana*. Buenos Aires, 1944.
González de Bobadilla, Bernardo. *Ninfas y pastores de Henares*. Alcalá de Henares, 1587.
Goytisolo, Juan. *El furgón de cola*. Paris: Ruedo Ibérico, 1967.
Gracián, Baltasar. *El Criticón*, ed. Miguel. Homera-Navarro. Philadelphia, 1938-40.
Green, Otis. "Cosmic strife-Cosmic harmony." *Spain and the Western Tradition* (Madison, 1963-66), II, 54-63.
Gullón, Ricardo. "Simbolismo y modernismo en Antonio Machado." *Direcciones del modernismo*. Madrid, 1963, pp. 128-53.
Gutiérrez Solana, José. *Obra literaria*. Ed. C.J. Cela, Madrid, 1961.
——. *La España negra*. Madrid, 1920.
——. *Madrid callejero*. Madrid, 1923.
——. *Madrid: Escenas y costumbres, primera serie*. Madrid, 1913.
——. *Madrid: Escenas y costumbres, segunda serie*. Madrid, 1918.
Harpham, Geoffry Galt. On the Grotesque: Strategies of Contradiction in Art and Literature. Princeton: Princeton Univ. Press, 1982.
Heger, Klaus. *Baltasar Gracián: Estilo lingüístico y doctrina de valores*. Zaragoza, 1960.
Helman, Edith. *Jovellanos y Goya*. Madrid, 1970.
——. *Trasmundo de Goya*. Madrid, 1963.
Iffland, James. *Quevedo and the Grotesque*. 2 vols. London: Tamesis, 1978, 1983.
Ilie, Paul. *The Surrealist Mode in Spanish Literature*. Ann Arbor: Univ. Michigan Press, 1968.
——. "¿Luces sin llustración? Las voces «imaginación/fantasía» como testigos léxicos." Francisco La Rubia Prado y Jesús Torrecilla (directores). *Razón, tradición y modernidad: re-visión de la llustración española*. Madrid: Tecnos, 1996: 133-92.
Iriarte, Tomás de. *La música*. Madrid, 1779.
——. *Poesías*, ed. A. Navarro González. Madrid: Espasa-Calpe, 1963.

Isla, José Francisco de. *Fray Gerundio de Campazas,* ed. Russell P. Sebold. Madrid: Espasa-Calpe, 1960.
Jennings, Lee Byron. *The Ludicrous Demon. Aspects of the Grotesque in German Post-Romantic Prose.* Berkeley: Univ. of California Press, 1963.
Jovellanos, Gaspar Melchor de. *Obras,* I. Madrid (BAE, Vol. 46), 1963.
―――. *Obras,* II. Madrid (BAE, Vol. 50), 1952.
―――. *Obras,* V. Madrid (BAE, Vol. 87), 1956.
Kayser, Wolfgang. *The Grotesque in Art and Literature,* trans. Ulrich Weisstein. New York: McGraw-Hill, 1966.
Kerrigan, Anthony. "Black Knight of Spanish Painting," *Arts Magazine* (May-June 1962*),* pp. 16-20.
Krauss, Werner. *Graciáns Lebenslehre.* Frankfurt, 1947.
Kronik, John. "Galdós and the Grotesque." *Anales Galdosianos.* Anejo 1976, pp. 39-52.
Lanz de Casafonda, Manuel. *Diálogos de Chindulza,* ed. F. Aguilar Piñal. Oviedo: Universidad de Oviedo, 1972.
Larra, Mariano José. *Obras,* vol. *2,* ed. Carlos Seco Serrano. Madrid: Biblioteca de Autores Españoles, 1960.
Lavery, David. "A Grotesque Bibliography." http://davidlavery.net/Grotesque/Pages/grotesquebibliography.html
Lida, Clara e Iris M. Zavala. *La revolución de 1868. Historia, pensamiento, literatura.* New York: Las Americas, 1970.
Lofrasso, Antonio de. *La fortuna de amor* [1573]. London. 1740.
Lope de Vega, Félix. *La Arcadia* [1599], ed. C. Rosell, *B.A.E.:* XXXVIII. Madrid, 1950.
López Ibor, J.J. "Solana, existencialista carpetovetónico." *Papeles de Son Armadans,* III, No. 33 bis, 1958.
López-Morillas, Juan. "Machado's Temporal Interpretation of Poetry," *JAAC,* VI(1947), 161-171.
López Salcedo, Francisco. *Despertador a la moda y soñolienta idea de capricho dormido, que entre sueños eseribe la pluma de...* (s.f., s.l.)
Lovejoy, A.O. *Rousseau and Romanticism.* New York, 1955.
Lucio Espinosa, Félix de. *Ocios morales* [1691], 2a ed. Zaragoza 1693.
Luzán, Ignacio de. *La poética,* ed. L. di Filippo. Barcelona: Selecciones Bibliófilas, 1956.
Llaguna y Amirola, Eugenio. *Noticias de los arquitectos y arquitectura de España desde su restauración,* ed. Juan Augustín Ceán-Bermúdez. Madrid: En la Imprenta Real, 1829.
Lloris, Manuel. "Larra o la dignidad." *Hispanic Review,* XXXVIII (1970), 184, 187, 193.
Machado, Antonio. *Poesias completas.* Buenos Aires, 1951.

MacKenzie, Harriet M. *Byron's Laughter*. Los Angeles: Lymanhouse, 1939.
Mann, Thomas. *Past Masters and Other Papers*, trans. H. T. Lowe-Porter Freeport, N.Y.: Books for Libraries Press, 1968.
Martinengo, Alessandro. *Polimorfismo nel "Diablo mundo" d'Espronceda*. Torino: Bottega d'Erasmo, 1962.
———. "Espronceda ante la leyenda fáustica." *Revista de Literatura*, 29 (1966), 35-55.
Martínez, Francisco. *Prontuario artístico*. Madrid, 1788.
Mayans y Siscar, Gregorio. *Arte de pintar* [1774]. Valencia, 1854.
Mazur, Oleh. "Various Folkloric Impacts upon the *Salvaje* in the Spanish *Comedia*." *Hispanic Revue*. 36 (1968), 207-235.
McElroy, Bernard. *Fiction of the Modern Grotesque*. New York: St Martin's, 1989.
Mengs, Antonio Rafael. *Obras de Don...*, ed. J. N. de Azara. Madrid, 1780.
Mercader, Gaspar. *El prado de Valencia*. Valencia, 1600.
Michaud, G. *La Doctrine symboliste*. Paris, 1947.
Milner, Max. *Le Diable*. (Paris, 1960).
Montemayor, Jorge de. *La Diana* [1559], ed. F. López Estrada. Madrid, 1946.
Montestruich Fernández de Ronderos, Pablo de. *Viaje real del rey... Phelipe Quinto*. Madrid, 1712.
Mor de Fuentes, José. *La Serafina*, ed. I. M. Gil. Zaragoza, 1959.
Moreri, Louis. *Gran diccionario histórico*, translated by Joseph de Miravel. Paris, 1753.
Morris, C. B. "Parallel Imagery in Quevedo and Alberti," *Bulletin of Hispanic Studies*, XXXVI (1959), 135-145.
Newton, Eric. *The Romantic Rebellion*. New York, 1962.
Ortega y Gasset, José. *Goya* (Madrid: Revista de Occidente, 1958)
Pagés, Aniceto de. *Gran diccionario de la lengua castellana (de Autoridades.)* Madrid, 1902.
Palomino, Antonio. *Indice de los términos privativos del arte de la pintura, y sus definiciones*. Madrid, 1724.
———. *El museo pictórico y escala óptica*. Madrid: Aguilar, 1947.
——— y Francisco de los Santos. *Las ciudades, iglesias y conventos en España*. Londres, 1746.
Pérez, Alonso. *Segunda parte de La Diana* [1564]. Venice. 1585.
Ploom, Ülar. "Grotesque Images in Dante's *Inferno*: the Problem of the Grotesque Overcome." Website: http://www.ameritalia.id.usb.ve/merialia.000.Ploom.htm
Podol, Peter L. "The Grotesque Mode in Contemporary Spanish Theater and Film." *Modern Language Studies*, Vol. 15, No. 4, Fifteenth Anniversary Issue (Autumn, 1985), pp. 194-207.
Polo, Gil. *La Diana enamorada* [1564], ed. R. Ferreres. Madrid, 1953.

Praz, Mario. *The Romantic Agony.* Oxford, 1933.
Preciado de la Vega, Francisco, A*rcadia pictórica en sueño: Alegoría o poema prosaico.* Madrid: Antonio de Sancha, 1789.
Quevedo, Francisco de. *Obras completas,* ed. Luis Astrana Marín. Madrid, 1932.
Rejón de Silva, Diego Antonio. *Diccionario de las nobles artes.* Segovia, 1788.
Ribbans, Geoffrey. "La influencia de Verlaine en Antonio Machado," *Cuadernos Hispanoamericanos,* nos. 91-92 (1957), 180-201.
Ríos-Font, Wadda C. *From Romantic Irony to Romantic Grotesque: Mariano José de Larra's and Rosalía de Castro's Self-Conscious Novels.* Philadelphia: Univ. Pennsylvania Press, 1997.
Rof Carballo, J. "Máscara de la mujer en la pintura de Solana." *Entre el silencio y la palabra.* Madrid, 1960, pp. 298-330.
Romera Navarro, Miguel. *Estudios sobre Gracián.* Austin: Univ. Texas Press, 1950.
Ross, Donald H. "The Grotesque: A Speculation." *Poe Studies,* vol. IV, no. 1, June 1971, pp. 10-11.
Ruiz Morcuende, Federico. *Vocabulario de D. Leandro Fernández de Moratín.* Madrid: Academia Española, 1945.
Salas, Xavier de. "La pintura de S." *Leonardo,* VI-VII (1945), 305-11.
Salas, Xavier de. *El Bosco en la literatura española.* Barcelona: J. Sabater, 1943.
Salazar y Castro, Luis. *Palacio de Momo.* León de Francia [Madrid], 1714.
Samaniego, Félix María. "La hermosa y el espejo," *Fábulas,* ed. E. Jareño. Madrid: Castalia, 1969.
Sánchez Barbudo, Antonio. *Estudios sobre Unamuno y Machado.* Madrid, 1959.
Sánchez Camargo, Manuel. *Solana.* Madrid, 1945.
———. *Solana. Pintura y dibujos.* Madrid, 1953.
Sánchez Cantón, F. J. *Opúsculos gallegos sobre bellas artes de los siglos XVII y XVIII.* Compostela, 1956.
Sarmiento, Martín. *Sistema de los adornos de escultura del nuevo Real Palacio de Madrid.* Madrid, 1743-1747.
Schröder, Gerhart. *Baltasar Graciáns "Criticón."* Munchen, 1966.
Sebold, Russell. "Torres Villorrel, Quevedo y el Bosco," *Insula,* XV, clix, 1960, pp. 3, 12.
———. "Torres Villarroel y las vanidades del mundo." *Archivum* (Oviedo), VII, i-ii-iii (1957-58), 115-146.
Serrano Poncela, Segundo. *Antonio Machado. Su mundo y su obra.* Buenos Aires, 1954.
———. "Borrosos laberintos." *La Torre,* XII (January-June 1964), 265-84.
Sices, David. "Musset's *Fantasio*: The Paradise of Chance." *Romanic Review,* LVIII (1967), 23-37.
Sobrino, Francisco. *Diccionario nuevo de las lenguas española y francesa.* Quinta

ed. Brusselas, 1751.
Solana. *See* Gutiérrez Solana.
Soriano Fuertes, Mariano. *Historia de la música española*. Madrid: Martin y Salazar, 1856.
Spacks, Patricia M. *The Insistence of Horror*. Cambridge, Mass., 1962.
Steig, Michael. "Defining the Grotesque: An Attempt at Synthesis." *Journal of Aesthetics and Art Criticism*, 29 (1970), 253-60.
Suárez de Figueroa, Cristóbal. *La constante Amarilis* [1609]. Madrid, 1781.
Swift, Jonathan. *Works*. London, 1766.
Tejeda, Jerónimo de. *La Diana de Monte-Mayor*. Paris, 1627.
Terreros y Pando, Esteban de. *Diccionario castellano... de ciencias y artes*. Madrid: Vda. de Ibarra, 1787.
Thomson, Philip J. *The Grotesque*. London: Methuen, 1972.
Torre, Guillermo de. "Solana escritor." *Minorías y masas en la cultura y arte contemporáneas*. Barcelona, 1963, 213-18.
———. "Realismo y superrealismo." *El Sol*, March 8, 1936.
———. "Solana escritor." *Minorías y masas en la cultura y arte contemporáneos*. Barcelona, 1963, 213-18.
———. "Realismo y superrealismo." *El Sol*, March 8, 1936.
Torres Villarroel, Diego de. *Visiones y visitas de...* ed. Russell Sebold. Madrid: Espasa-Calpe, 1966.
———. *Sueños morales*. Madrid: Artes Gráficas Ibarra, 1960.
Ullman, Pierre. *Mariano de Larra and Spanish Political Rhetoric*. Madison: The University of Wisconsin Press, 1971.
Valverde, José María. *Estudios sobre la palabra poética*. Madrid, 1952.
Valzania, Francisco Antonio. *Instituciones de arquitectura*. Madrid, 1792.
Valle-Inclán, Ramón del. *Obras completas*. 2 vols. Madrid: Editorial Plenitud, 1954.
Van Eerde, John. "The Imagery in Gautier's Dantesque Nightmare." *Studies in Romanticism*, I (1962), 230-240.
Van O'Connor, William. *The Grotesque: An American Genre and Other Essays*. Carbondale: Southern Illinois Univ. Press, 1962
Vossler, Karl. *Einführung in die Spanische Dichtung des Goldenen Zeitalters*. Hamburg, 1929.
Wright, Thomas. *A History of Caricature and Grotesque in Literature and Art*. London: Virtue Brothers, 1865.
Zardoya, Concha. "E1 cristal y el espejo en la poesía de M.," *Poesía española contemporánea* (Madrid, 1961), pp.181-215.
Ziomek, Henryk. *Lo grotesco en la literatura española del Siglo de Oro*. Madrid: Ediciones Alcalá, 1983.
Zubiría, R. de. *La poesía de Antonio Machado*. Madrid, 1955.

Thematic Index

Absurdity. 8, 45, 56, 69, 72, 91, 98, 100, 111, 112, 113, 124, 130, 138, 141, 152, 159, 160, 185, 186, 189-92, 193, 197, 198, 200, 201, 204-06, 209, 218, 219, 220, 231, 232, 235, 243, 244, 245, 247, 251, 254, 263, 264, 269, 271, 272, 278, 279, 281, 283, 284
Alienation. 111, 116, 138, 182-83, 203, 235, 271, 273, 283, 285. See also Identity, Masks
Allegory. See Symbolism
Animalization. See Zoomorphism
Architecture. 9, 12, 14, 16, 29, 30, 84, 92, 169-72ff, 178, 253
Automatons. See Puppets
Bacchic. See Drunkenness
Baroque. 8, 18, 30-41, 66, 68, 266-67. 269, 273, 275, 277, 282, 284, 285
Beauty. 8, 12, 14, 16, 26, 29, 30, 48, 76, 78, 81-84, 94, 96, 142, 169, 178, 263-64, 268, 282, 285
Beauty and the Beast. 19-20, 151, 193
Bufoon. See Harlequin
Camera lens. See Optics
Capricho. 8, 32, 80-84, 87-106, 118-19, 131, 267, 268, 284
Caricature. See Satire.
Carnival. 9, 38-39, 161-62, 179-83, 195, 254-55, 274
Classicism. 8, 9, 14, 17, 36, 41, 250, 264, 266, 284
Clown. See Harlequin
Comic, Comedia. See Humor and Laughter.

Consciousness. See Identity
Dadaism. 193, 283
Death. 121, 125, 128, 141-44, 147, 176, 190, 199, 204, 205, 210, 219, 221, 233, 260, 264, 283
Deformation. 18, 24, 31, 33, 35, 43-70 passim, 72-75, 77, 84, 113-14, 130, 135-38, 156-57, 167, 191, 274-76, 280
Dehumanization. 37, 39, 45, 47, 52, 64-67, 208-16, 237-50, 259, 271, 274-76
Delirium. 51, 56, 73, 90, 104, 111, 132, 135, 137, 138, 140, 148, 149, 158, 177, 269, 273, 280-81, 282
Devil, Diabolism. See Satan
Divine. 26, 49, 57, 63, 135, 140, 158, 260, 282
Dolls. See Puppets
Dream. 21, 54, 57-58, 80, 111, 134, 135, 147-49, 196-97, 214-17, 268, 280-81
Drunkenness. 48, 50-51, 74, 127, 134, 139-41, 149, 168, 179, 204-05, 224, 269-70
Eighteenth Century. 45, 67, 280
Epistemology. 9, 28, 74, 112, 135-38, 148-49, 163-65, 199-200, 207-13, 279-82
España negra. 250, 278, 283
Esperpento. 8, 217, 221, 232, 240, 244, 257-58, 271, 279, 283-844
Existentialism. 283, 284
Fantasy. See Imagination
Generation of '98. 250, 255, 258, 261,

295

262, 279. See also Spain
Golden Age. 8, 44, 48, 56, 265, 280
Grotesque aesthetics. 7, 272
Grotesque defined. 8, 16, 24, 29-30,
  45, 72, 73, 78-79, 153, 193, 216,
  250, 253, 259,
263, 267-72 passim
Grotesque philosophy. 282-84
Harlequin. 9, 181, 186, 204, 230-38,
  270
History. See Spain
Humor. 9, 33, 45, 151, 197-98, 232
Hybrid. See Zoomorphism

Identity. 112, 116-121, 125-26, 138,
  199, 201-04, 235-37, 271, 284.
  See also Alienation, Masks
Imagination. 50, 58, 64, 76, 80, 83,
  131-34, 137-38, 149, 152, 155-
  62, 208, 268, 281
Incongruity. 13, 77, 140, 165-66, 185,
  269, 214ff, 271-74
Irony. 61, 33, 109, 116, 118, 125,
  143-44, 180-82, 186, 190, 197,
  202-04, 219, 225, 234, 239-40,
  246, 248, 265
Laughter. 9, 71, 73, 123, 141, 143,
  154, 179, 187, 191, 197-98, 241,
  260-61, 278
Macabre. 75, 110, 127, 129, 130, 139,
  141-44, 149, 204, 205, 223-25,
  270, 277, 284
Madness. 9, 57, 89, 111, 131, 134,
  138, 140, 151, 160, 172, 175,
  190, 266
Mannequins, Marionettes. See
  Puppets
Masks. 28, 37, 195, 236, 238, 241,
  243, 283. See also Alienation,
  Identity
Metamorphosis. 16, 36-37, 41, 45,
  46, 53, 166, 266, 274, 284, 285
Middle Ages. 9, 170-77 passim, 265
Mirrors. 13, 163, 202, 222, 238, 244,
  276, 279, 280, 281
Modernism. 8, 10, 189, 271, 275,
  277, 278, 280, 283-85 passim
Monsters. 9, 12, 13, 18-21, 23, 25-27,
  31, 32, 33-37, 45, 59, 62, 63, 73,
  75, 80-84 passim, 89, 137, 141,
  157, 167, 169, 174-79 passim,
  186, 237, 256, 263-70 passim,
  275, 281, 282, 284, 285,
Moon. 123, 200-01, 223, 225-31,
  233, 275
Music. 19, 82, 83, 84, 91, 92, 98, 99,
  101, 106, 130, 145, 169, 166,
  179, 196, 198, 201, 209, 210,
  223, 240, 249. See Sound
Nature. 11-21, 25-27, 31-32, 48-49,
  55, 163-66, 199-200, 231, 266,
  273, 282
Neoclassicism. 8, 9, 73, 75, 82, 130,
  268, 280. 284
Optics. 112-13, 115, 134, 244, 255,
  273, 280, 281
Painting. 13, 32, 46, 64, 66, 82-85,
  87, 92, 253, 255, 262, 267, 271
Pastoral. 11-21, 245, 249, 250-51,
  273
Perception. See Epistemology
Personality. See Identity
Politics. See Spain
Puppets. 28, 37-40 passim, 65, 184-
  85, 195, 204, 208-14, 234-36,
  242, 244-47, 251, 275, 279, 281,
  283
Realism. 41, 60, 62, 173-75, 254-55,
  278-79, 284
Reality. See Epistemology
Reason. 45, 69, 76, 82, 155-56, 281,
  284, 285

Renaissance. 8, 9, 27, 29, 30, 41, 265, 266, 273
Rococo. 69, 219, 247-50, 251, 268
Romanticism. 8, 9, 19, 25, 31-32, 40, 48, 64, 151ff, 176, 178, 183, 187-94 passim, 198-203, 219-31, 254-55, 68, 266, 269-70, 277, 282-85 passim
Satan. 58, 63, 129, 135, 137, 139, 141, 151,158, 166, 168, 169, 186, 193, 198, 259, 260, 261, 278
Satire. 9, 23, 43, 44, 56, 71, 73, 74, 107-16 passim, 121-23, 129, 181, 191, 266, 269, 270, 277
Self-Non-Self. See Identity
Sexuality. 53-55, 63, 77, 144
Society. See Spain
Sound. 30, 130, 138, 144-47, 149, 150, 179, 196, 221, 241. See also Music
Space. 134, 137, 153, 164, 172, 215, 222, 242, 247

Spain. 45, 50-51, 55, 68, 69, 81, 108-11, 119-24, 127, 272, 195-96, 248, 260-62, 277-79. See also Generation of 98
Style. 59, 61, 66-67, 276, 281
Subjectivism. 280
Sublime. 13, 78, 186-187, 194, 197, 234, 265, 270
Supernaturalism. 25, 165, 168, 274, 280
Surrealism. 8, 148, 152, 1161, 93, 197, 203, 260, 267, 271, 281, 283
Symbolism. 25, 28, 34-35, 55, 69, 114, 134, 161, 175, 177, 189, 193-94, 196, 200-01, 206
Time. 142, 150, 193, 242-43, 245, 247, 283
Uncanny. 140, 164-65, 244, 272, 273
Zoomorphism. 14, 20, 28, 32, 34, 37, 45-50, 52, 79-80, 237, 273, 275, 277

Name Index

Aguilar Piñal. 102-03
Alcázar. 93
Alonso. 107
Amiel. 200
Arce Solórzano. 14, 16, 21
Arce y Cacho. 96
Arcimboldo. 74
Aristotle. 14, 27 A
rteaga. 77, 78, 90, 94, 104, 268
Astrana Marín. 45
Avalle-Arce. 11
Azara. 83
Azorín. 107

Babbitt. 203
Baguley. 274
Bails. 93, 96, 101
Bakhtin. 9, 266, 270
Baroja. 107
Batllori. 77, 104

Baudelaire. 71, 72, 161, 187, 194, 197, 198, 201, 205, 270, 278
Bécquer. 8, 9, 10, 129, 151-92, 220, 269, 270, 271-85 passim
Bergson. 194
Berlioz. 178
Blanco White. 109

Bonarrota. 98
Bosch. 8, 23, 32, 36, 53, 81, 82, 85, 87, 98, 167, 267 Botello. 73, 75
Byron. 187, 202-03, 270
Byzantine. 263

Cadalso. 71, 75, 103
Calderón Altamirano. 74
Callot. 88, 267

Camón Aznar. 23, 34
Campoamor. 153, 217, 219, 252, 255
Campos. 129
Capmany. 83
Carducci. 226
Casalduero. 129, 139
Caso González. 102
Castro. 83

Ceán Bermúdez. 133
Cela, 207
Cernuda. 108
Cervantes. 41, 72. 193, 251, 259
Cézannne. 199
Chirico. 37, 184, 260, 271
Churriguera. 99, 104
Clarín. 269
Clayborough. 45, 72, 265, 272
Coleridge. 131-32.
Collantes. 93
Corral. 20, 266
Covarrubias. 8, 16, 32, 78, 79, 87

Dalí. 37, 53, 167, 196, 221, 253, 260

Dante. 9, 21, 28, 31, 32, 48, 129, 149, 158, 165, 267
Delacroix. 71
Díaz-Plaja. 218, 229
Dionysus. See Drunkenness
Donoso. 99

Dupuis. 103

Echegaray. 255
Eliot. 180, 184

Espronceda. 8, 10, 107, 124, 129-50, 180, 187, 188, 269, 270, 273-85 passim Estrada Nava. 75
Eximeno. 82, 105
Feijoo. 45, 68, 69, 101

Fernández de Moratín. 100, 105-06, 153
Fielding. 74
Filippo. 98, 102
Forner. 75, 79, 82

Galdós. 265, 269
García Lorca. 253
García Pandavenes. 75
Gauguin. 222 Gautier. 71 Gil. 99, 102, 105
Glendinning. 103
Goethe. 139, 158, 178, 182, 186, 269
Góngora. 18

Goya. 24, 44, 53, 71, 72, 73, 78, 88-89, 102, 129, 152-55, 193-98 passim, 221, 255, 262, 267, 268, 272, 278, 283
Goytisolo. 108, 109
Gracián. 8, 23-42, 71, 87, 107, 266-67, 273-85 passim
Green. 27
Gutiérrez Solana. See Solana
Heger. 40

Heidegger. 194
Helman. 44, 88-90
Hérédia. 199
Herrera. 99

Hoffmann. 184, 267, 274
Horace. 14, 77, 27, 80
Hugo. 187, 194, 270
Husserl. 194
Iriarte, Bernardo. 89

Iriarte, Tomás de. 82, 99, 101, 103, 104, 106 Isla. 59, 71, 74

Jareño. 104
Jean Paul. 184

Jovellanos. 80, 81, 93, 94, 97, 99, 100, 101, 104, 105, 106, 153, 174
Juni. 133

Kayser. 7, 45, 72, 272
Keats. 226
Krauss. 23, 34

Lanz de Casafonda. 102-03
Laocoon. 77

Larra. 9, 107-128, 188, 269, 270, 273-85 passim
La Rubia. 132
Lautréamont. 132 Le Dantec. 71
Ledesma. 98
León de Arroyal. 102
Leopardi. 200
Lida. 108
Llaguna y Amairola. 133
Lloris. 108
Lobo. 73
Lofrasso. 17

Lope de Vega. 16, 41
Lucio Espinosa. 87
Luzán. 9, 75-78 passim, 82, 96, 98, 102

Machado. 8, 10, 187, 189, 193-206, 256, 271-85 passim
Maeterlinck. 221
Mallarmé. 202
Mann. 277
Marinetti. 201, 225, 226
Martinengo. 129, 139
Martínez. 96
Martínez de la Rosa. 109, 110
Mayans. 82, 85, 98
Mazur. 14
Meléndez Valdés. 75
Mendizábal. 110
Mengs. 9, 76, 77, 83, 268
Mercadier. 43
Mirabel. 79
Montemayor. 18
Montestruich. 81
Mor de Fuentes. 99, 102, 105
Moréas. 200
Moreno Villa. 129
Moreri. 79
Morris. 38

Navarro González. 99, 104, 106
Nerval. 132
Nietzsche. 187, 197
Nombela. 110
Ovid. See Metamorphosis
Pagés. 153

Palomino. 81, 83, 85, 93, 96, 97, 98
Picasso. 222, 231
Pichois. 71
Plato. 27, 158, 263
Ploom. 267
Polo. 14
Preciado de la Vega. 83

Quevedo. 24, 41, 43-44, 45, 53, 56, 68, 71, 81, 152, 158, 193, 265

Quintana. 153
Rabelais. 9, 266

Rejón de Silva. 77, 79, 99
Ribera. 104
Risco. 218
Rof Carballo. 207
Romera-Navarro. 23
Rouault. 231
Ross. 265
Ruiz Morcuende. 100, 106
Salas. 23

Salazar y Castro. 73
Salinas. 218
Samaniego. 103
Sánchez Cantón. 100 Santos. 81, 82
Sarmiento. 100
Sartre. 205
Schönberg. 231
Schröder. 23, 24, 32 Seco Serrano. 108
Sebold. 43, 56, 59, 66, 68
Shakespeare. 187, 205, 259 Sobrino. 8, 78
Solana. 10, 24, 193, 196, 197, 207-16, 247, 255, 256, 267, 271-85 passim
Solís. 75

Swift. 73
Tarr. 108
Tejeda. 14, 19, 21

Terreros y Pando. 79, 101, 132
Tiepolo. 88
Torrecilla. 132
Torres Villarroel. 8, 9, 24, 43-71, 74, 80, 107, 267, 268, 273-85 passim

Ullman. 108, 109
Unamuno. 246

Valle-Inclán. 8, 10, 24, 217-64, 271-85 passim
Valzania. 80, 97
Varela. 108, 129
Velázquez. 253, 255, 262
Verlaine. 196, 199, 201, 231
Virgil. 9, 21, 75, 77
Vossler. 23
Wordsworth. 132

Zahareas. 218
Zavala. 108
Zea Bermúdez. 110
Zola. 274